SUMMARY OF CHANGES—Change 1 (July 2010)

SECTION	CHANGES
1.1.2.5	Changed wording to say "…and certify non-military pilot weather briefers and tower visibility observers."
1.3.1	Changed wording from "specialist" to "NWS certified pilot weather briefer"
2.1.1	Changed wording from "are considered" to "pertain to"
2.3	Changed wording from "defined in paragraph 2.3" to "defined in paragraph 2.2"
2.3.2	Changed wording from "defined in paragraph 2.2.1" to "defined in paragraph 2.1.1"
2.3.3	Change wording from…"(see paragraph 2.4.2, above)" to "(see previous section)"
3.1.3.9	Changed example wording from "cumulonimbus at 7,500" to "…cumulonimbus at 3,200"
3.1.3.13.19.4	Changed order of clouds to list by height (i.e., CCSL, ACSL, SCSL, rotor)
3.2.1	Change wording from "(Figure 3-7)" to "(Figure 3-10)"
3.2.2.1.1	Corrected section numbering typo
3.2.1.7	Changed coding from "/WV" to "/WX"
3.2.1.10	Changed wording to prevent confusion
3.2.1.12.8	Changed wording from "flight level 310" to "flight level 370"
3.3.1	Changed wording from "(see figure 3-12)" to (see Figure 3-15). Also, changed wording from "Figure 3-8" to "Figure 3-11"
3.3.1.3	Changed wording from "Figure 3-9" to "Figure 3-12"
3.3.1.11	Changed wording from "Figure 3-11" to "Figure 3-14"
4.1.4.1.3.6	Corrected spelling error in Figure 4-11; from "propogation" to "propagation"
4.1.4.2	Deleted long-range Composite Reflectivity since the NWS no longer provides it through ADDS or the (NWS Ridge Radar site).
5.4	Removed this section since the Lifted Index (LI) Analysis DIFAX Chart is no longer produced.
6.2.5	Corrected numbering error on Figure 6-11.
6.3	Inserted G-AIRMET as new primary product. This changed the numbering in the remainder of section 6.
7.1.10	Removed mention of Alaska SIGMETs since they are no longer embedded in the Alaska Area Forecasts (FAs)
9.5	Updated from GTG to the new GTG-2.

SUMMARY OF CHANGES—Change 2 (October 2014)

Section	Changes
1.1.2.1.1	Changed location of NCEP's CO from Camp Springs, MD to College Park, MD.
1.1.2.1.2	Added "through the Aviation Digital Data Service (ADDS);" "and "Forecast Icing Product (FIP), Graphical Turbulence Guidance (GTG), and Ceiling and Visibility Product (CVA)."
1.1.2.1.3	Changed name of Hydrometeorological Prediction Center (HPC) to Weather Prediction Center (WPC). Changed location of WPC from Camp Springs, MD to College Park, MD.
1.1.2.1.5	Changed name of Storm Prediction Center (SPC) to National Hurricane Center (NHC)
1.1.2.4	Changed wording from, "WFO Honolulu serves as the Central Pacific Hurricane Center (CPHC)" to "WFO Honolulu is co-located with the Central Pacific Hurricane Center (CPHC)."
1.1.2.5	Deleted.
1..2.1	Changed the location of the Air Traffic Control System Command Center (ATCSCC) from Herndon, VA to Vint Hill, VA. Changed wording to say "Because weather is the most common reason for air traffic delays and re routings, NWS Meteorologists support the ATCSCC. These meteorologists, called National Aviation Meteorologists (NAMs) orchestrate NWS operations in support of traffic flow management within the NAS."
1.2.2	Added "… and may solicit PIREPs from pilots."
1.2.3	Added "… and may solicit PIREPs from pilots."
1.2.4	Deleted "Automated Flight Service Station (AFSS)"
1.3.1	Changed wording to say "obtained by the pilot from an approved weather source via the Internet (see 1.3.2) and/or from a FSS specialist." Changed wording from "helpful" to "necessary." Added wording "If the briefing updates previously received information, the time of the last briefing is also important. This allows the briefer to provide only pertinent data." Changed wording to say "The briefer enters this information into the FAA's flight plan system. The briefer also notes the type of weather briefing provided. If necessary, the information can be referenced later to file or amend a flight plan. It is also used when an aircraft is overdue or is reported missing. Internet data is time stamped and archived for 15 days. Voice recordings are retained for 45 days."
1.3.1.1.1	Changed and added wording to say "…mountain obscuration, areas of current and forecasted IFR conditions, and other important items such as airport/runway closings, air traffic delays and TFRs."
1.3.1.1.9	Added "Prohibited and Special Flight Rules Areas"
1.3.1.3	Deleted "AFSS"
1.3.2	Added "Pilot Briefing via the Internet."

Section	Changes
1.3.2.1	Added "…NWS…" Deleted "To access the weather information and file a flight plan by this method, pilots use a toll free telephone number to connect the user's computer directly to the DUATS computer."
1.3.2.2	Added "1.3.2.2 Lockheed Martin Flight Services Web Portal Lockheed Martin Flight Services provides a Web portal for flight planning service at https://www.lmfsweb.afss.com/Website/. Pilots must register and create a user account to access the pilot briefing and flight planning functions. VFR Search and rescue services are also provided to registered users who file and activate a VFR flight plan and are equipped with certain GPS location devices."
1.3.3	Text is changed to say "The Aviation Digital Data Service (ADDS) site is a joint effort of NOAA Forecast Systems Laboratory (FSL), NCAR Research Applications Laboratory (RAL), the FAA, and the AWC. ADDS provides the aviation community with textual, digital, and graphical forecasts, analyses, and observations of aviation related weather variables. Additionally, the ADDS contains a flight path tool that allows the user to view data along a specific route of flight. The user can view icing, turbulence, temperature, winds, humidity, AIRMETs, METARs, TAFs, etc. both horizontally and vertically. This site also allows many overlay options including ARTCC boundaries, counties, highways and rivers. Product animation is also possible on the AWC JavaScript image."
1.3.4	Deleted "Automated."
1.3.5	Deleted "AFSS."
1.3.5.4	Deleted "AFSS."
1.3.7.1	Changed wording to say "FIS-B is a ground-based broadcast service provided through the FAA's ADS-B Services UAT network. The service provides users with a 978 MHz data link capability when operating within range and line-of-sight of a transmitting ground station. FIS-B enables users of properly equipped aircraft to receive and display a suite of broadcast weather and aeronautical information products. The following list represents the initial suite of textual and graphical products available through FIS-B and provided free-of-charge. This advisory circular (AC) and the current edition of AC 00 63, Use of Cockpit Displays of Digital Weather and Aeronautical Information, contain detailed information concerning FIS B meteorological products. Chapters 3, 4 and 5 of the AIM contain information on Special Use Airspace (SUA), TFR, and NOTAM products. Text: Aviation Routine Weather Report (METAR) and Special Aviation Report (SPECI); Text: Pilot Weather Report (PIREP); Text: Winds and Temperatures Aloft; Text: Terminal Aerodrome Forecast (TAF) and amendments; Text: Notice to Airmen (NOTAM) Distant and Flight Data Center; Text/Graphic: Airmen's Meteorological Conditions (AIRMET); Text/Graphic: Significant Meteorological Conditions (SIGMET); Text/Graphic: Convective SIGMET; Text/Graphic: Special Use Airspace (SUA); Text/Graphic: Temporary Flight Restriction (TFR) NOTAM; and Graphic: NEXRAD Composite Reflectivity Products (Regional and National).

Section	Changes
	Users of FIS-B should familiarize themselves with the operational characteristics and limitations of the system, including: system architecture; service environment; product lifecycles; modes of operation; and indications of system failure. FIS-B products are updated and transmitted at specific intervals based primarily on product issuance criteria. Update intervals are defined as the rate at which the product data is available from the source for transmission. Transmission intervals are defined as the amount of time within which a new or updated product transmission must be completed and/or the rate or repetition interval at which the product is rebroadcast. Table 1-1 provides update and transmission intervals for each product. Where applicable, FIS-B products include a look-ahead range expressed in nautical miles (NM) for three service domains: Airport Surface; Terminal Airspace; and En-route/Gulf-of-Mexico (GOMEX). Table 1-1 provides service domain availability and look-ahead ranging for each FIS-B product. Prior to using this capability, users should familiarize themselves with the operation of FIS-B avionics by referencing the applicable User's Guides. Users should obtain guidance concerning the interpretation of information displayed from the appropriate avionics manufacturer. Users should report FIS B malfunctions not attributed to aircraft system failures or covered by active NOTAM to the nearest FSS facility by radio or telephone. Users may also report malfunctions by submitting FAA Form 8740 5, Safety Improvement Report, via mail, fax, or email to your local Flight District Standards Office (FSDO) Safety Program Manager. Added Table 1-1. FIS-B Over UAT Product Update and Transmission Intervals, and Table 1-2, Product Parameters for Low/Medium/High Altitude Tier Radios.
1.3.7.2	Deleted second and third subparagraphs.
2	Changed title to say "Aviation Weather Product Policy"
2	Changed first bullet to say "policy guidance for using aviation weather products,"
2.3.1 Second subparagraph	Added wording "…Lockheed Martin, Direct Use Access Terminal Service (DUAT/DUATS
2.3.2 and 2.3.3	Paragraph order was swapped.
2.3.2	Last two sentences deleted.
2.3.3 First paragraph	Content changed to say "An EWINS is a system for gathering, evaluating, and disseminating aviation weather information, and for issuing weather reports and forecasts prepared by properly trained and qualified aviation meteorologists or aircraft dispatchers. Air carriers use EWINS, which are proprietary to each carrier. In order to use an EWINS, each air carrier requires FAA approval.
2.3.3 Second paragraph	First sentence changed to say "…each carrier's EWINS…" FSIMS section corrected to Section 4 Text changed to include part 91K operators.

Section	Changes
	Last sentence changed to say "These approved operators may conduct flight operations using the weather analyses and forecasts produced by their approved EWINS."
Section 7	Added cautionary use note for Area Forecasts (FA).
Section 9	Title changed to "New Generation Weather Products"
9.1	Text changed to say "…4-, 6 -, and 8-hours…"
9.1.3.2	Changed reference to Figure 9-3 to Figure 9-2. Deleted Figure 9-3. Renumbered figures, updated figure references..
9.1.3.4.3	Changed text to read "Confidence depicted on the chart…"
9.1.3.4.4	Changed text to read "Coverage is used to depict the forecast…"
9.1.5 First subparagraph	Text changed to say "The CCFP is a strategic planning tool for air traffic flow management in the 4- to 8-hour forecast period.
9.1.5 Second subparagraph	Text added "…l; however CCFP is available to pilots and aircraft dispatchers as an additional tool for strategic planning.'
9.2 Extended Convective Forecast Product (ECFP)	New section The ECFP Planning Tool (Figure 9 2) is a graphical representation of the forecast probability of thunderstorms. The product identifies graphically where in the United States thunderstorms are likely over the next 72 hours. It is intended to enhance the CCFP. The CCFP is only valid out to 8 hours. This graphical product will use CCFP-style graphics, to facilitate ease of interpretation and use by those already familiar with the CCFP. The product is not a CCFP forecast (it is not forecasting the exact CCFP criteria), but intended to support the long range planning for CCFP type of constraints in the National Airspace System (NAS).
9.2.1 Issuance	The development of the ECFP planning tool was a response to Federal Aviation Administration (FAA) and Industry needs in planning for weather hazards, specifically convection, 1 to 2 days in advance. To meet these planning needs, and to support CCFP planning beyond 8 hours, the ECFP intends to provide traffic planners and collaborators a quick-look forecast of the greatest probability of convection/thunderstorms. By utilizing CCFP-style graphics, users familiar with CCFP can easily determine where traffic constraints are most likely to occur over the next 3 days.
9.2.1	Figure 9.7, ECFP Example added.
9.2.2 Content	This automated graphical forecast is created from the Short Range Ensemble Forecast (SREF) Calibrated Thunderstorm guidance. Probability of Thunderstorm contours are depicted at 40, 60, and 80 percent probabilities, using CCFP-like shading. Hashed areas represent 40–59 percent probability, solid lined areas represent 60–79 percent probability, and solid blue filled areas represent greater than 80 percent probability.
9.2.3 Use	The ECFP is intended for FAA Traffic Managers at Air Route Traffic Control Centers (ARTCC), FAA Air Traffic Control System Command Center (ATCSCC), airline and

Section	Changes
	aviation industry dispatch and flight planners, and commercial weather information providers supporting airline/FAA.
9.2.3	Deleted "The ADDS and AWC JAVA display" entire paragraph
9.2.4 Frequency	The ECFP is available 24/7 with updates issued at 01:00, 07:00, 13:00, and 19:00 UTC each day.
9.3	All paragraph numbers updated due to added section 9.2.
9.3	Changed wording to say "…may be used in conjunction to…" Changed last line from "airline" to "aircraft"
9.3.2	Changed reference in text from Figure 9-7 to Figure 9-8 because of added figure.
	Changed Figure 9-7 to Figure 9-8.
9.3.2.1	Last subparagraph changed reference in text from Figure 9-8 to Figure 9-9.
	Changed Figure 9-8 to Figure 9-9
9.3.2.1.1 First subparagraph	Changed reference in text from. Figure 9-9 to Figure 9-10
9.3.2.1.1 Last subparagraph	Changed reference in text from Figure 9-9 to Figure 9-10
	Changed Figure 9-9 to Figure 9-10
9.3.2.2	Changed reference in text from Figure 9-10 to Figure 9-11
9.3.2.3 First subparagraph	Changed reference in text from Figure 9-10 to Figure 9-11
9.3.2.3 Last subparagraph	Changed reference in text from Figure 9-10 to Figure 9-11
9.3.2.4	Changed reference in text from Figure 9-10 to Figure 9-11 (2 places)
	Changed Figure 9-10 to Figure 9-11
9.3.2.5 Second subparagraph	Changed reference in text from Figure 9-11 to Figure 9-12
	Changed Figure 9-11 to Figure 9-12
9.3.3.1	Added subparagraph Strengths.
9.3.3.2	Added subparagraph Limitations.

Section	Changes
9.3.4	Deleted "The NCWF is a supplement to, but does not substitute for, the report and forecast information contained in Convective SIGMETs."
9.4	Renumbered paragraphs due to added information.
9.4	Changed title to read "Current and Forecast Icing Products (CIP/FIP)"
9.4 First subparagraph	Added "The Forecast Icing Product (FIP) provides the same suite of products describing the icing environment in the future and is solely NWP model-based."
9.4 Second subparagraph	Added "The CIP/FIP product suites are automatically produced with no human modifications. Information on the graphics is determined from NWP model output, observational data including WSR-88D radar, satellite, pilot weather reports, surface weather reports, and lightning network data."
9.4.1	Changed wording to say "The CIP and FIP product suites are issued hourly ~15 minutes after the hour by the Aviation Weather Center (AWC). The products are available through the Aviation Digital Data Service (ADDS) web site at: http://www.aviationweather.gov/adds/icing/"
9.4.2	Added "…/FIP …"
9.4.2	Changed to say "The CIP/FIP products are generated for individual altitudes from 1,000 feet MSL to Flight Level (FL) 300 at intervals of 1,000 feet. Horizontal resolution is 20 km. FIP products are available at 1, 2, 3, 6, 9, and 12- h forecast lead times. By March 2014 these are planned to change to 500 ft. MSL horizontal and 13 km vertical resolution, and forecasts will be extended to 18 h with 1-h granularity."
9.4.2 Last subparagraph	Added "…/FIP…"
9.4.2.1	Changed paragraph reference from Figure 9-12 to Figure 9-13.
	Changed Figure number from 9-12 to 9-13.
9.4.2.2	Changed paragraph reference from Figure 9-13 to Figure 9-14.
	Changed Figure number from 9-13 to 9-14.
9.4.4 First subparagraph	Changed wording to say "The CIP/FIP Icing Probability product can be used to identify the current and forecast three-dimensional probability of icing. The CIP/FIP should be used in conjunction with the report and forecast information contained in an AIRMET and SIGMET.
9.5	Changed wording to say" The Graphical Turbulence Guidance (GTG) product suite provides a three-dimensional diagnosis and forecast of Clear Air Turbulence (CAT) potential. The GTG is created using a combination of computer model output and turbulence observations. The GTG product suite, which consists of the GTG analysis and forecast and Composite analysis and forecast, is automatically generated with no human modifications. It should be used in conjunction with the report and forecast information contained in an AIRMET and SIGMET. The GTG is

Section	Changes
	available for the 48-contiguous states, much of Canada and Mexico and their respective coastal waters.
9.5.1	Changed wording to say "Issuance The GTG analysis is issued hourly. The 3-, 6-, 9-, and 12-hour forecasts are issued every three hours beginning at 00Z. For example, a forecast suite issued at 0600Z would have valid times at 0900Z, 1200Z, 1500Z, and 1800Z respectively. The GTG Analysis and Forecasts, along with the Composite products, are issued by the Aviation Weather Center (AWC) and are available through the Aviation Digital Data Service (ADDS) web site at: http://adds.aviationweather.noaa.gov/turbulence/turb_nav.php.
9.5.2.1	Changed wording to say "The GTG output is available for 1,000 foot vertical intervals between 10,000 feet MSL and FL450. ADDS turbulence page displays every second level starting at 10,000 feet MSL level, while the ADDS Flight Path Tool provides access to all levels.
9.5.2.2	Changed wording to say "GTG Composite Analysis and Forecast The GTG Composite products display the maximum intensity of potential turbulence between FL200 and FL450 (Figure 9-23).
	Deleted Figure 9-23, GTG Example. Renumbered Figure 9-24. GTG Composite Example to Figure 9-23
9.5.3	Changed wording to say "The GTG provides an hourly, high resolution analysis and forecast of clear-air turbulence potential at and above10,000 feet MSL. However, the product is only for turbulence associated with upper level fronts and jet stream while other known causes of turbulence are not forecasted. Strengths 1. The product is issued hourly 2. Turbulence is plotted to a high resolution. Limitations 1. The accuracy of the analysis is dependent on the number of PIREPs available. Typically at night fewer pilot reports are received, so the accuracy decreases. 2. For the GTG forecast, the product is only as accurate the computer model output used to create them. 3. The product only displays clear-air turbulence (CAT) for upper-level fronts and the jet stream. Other known causes of turbulence are not included in the product. 4. Data and forecast are only available for 11,000 feet MSL and above."
Pages 36-40 9.7	New section added "Ceiling and Visibility Analysis (CVA)"

FOREWORD

Aviation Weather Services, Advisory Circular 00-45G, is published jointly by the National Weather Service (NWS) and the Federal Aviation Administration (FAA). This publication supplements its companion manual Aviation Weather, Advisory Circular 00-6A, which documents weather theory and its application to the aviation community.

This advisory circular, AC 00-45G, explains U.S. aviation weather products and services. It details the interpretation and application of advisories, coded weather reports, forecasts, observed and prognostic weather charts, and radar and satellite imagery. Product examples and explanations are taken primarily from the Aviation Weather Center's Aviation Digital Data Service website (http://adds.aviationweather.noaa.gov/).

An online version of this document (including digital images) can be found at http://rgl.faa.gov/

Aviation Weather Services, Advisory Circular, AC 00-45G Change 2, supersedes AC 00-45G, change 1, published July 29, 2010.

Deputy Director, Flight Standards Service

5   GRAPHICAL OBSERVATIONS AND DERIVED PRODUCTS 5-1

1 AVIATION WEATHER SERVICE PROGRAM

The aviation weather service program is a joint effort of the National Weather Service (NWS), the Federal Aviation Administration (FAA), the Department of Defense (DOD), and other aviation-oriented groups and individuals. This section discusses the civilian agencies of the U.S. Government and their observation, communication, and forecast services to the aviation community.

1.1 National Oceanic and Atmospheric Administration (NOAA)

NOAA is an agency of the Department of Commerce (DOC). NOAA conducts research and gathers data about the global oceans, atmosphere, space, and sun, and applies this knowledge to science and service which touches the lives of all Americans. Among its six major divisions are the National Environmental Satellite Data and Information Service (NESDIS) and the NWS.

1.1.1 National Environmental Satellite Data and Information Service (NESDIS)
The NESDIS manages the U.S. civil operational remote-sensing satellite systems, as well as other global information for meteorology, oceanography, solid-earth geophysics, and solar-terrestrial sciences. NESDIS provides this data to NWS meteorologists and a wide range of other users for operational weather forecasting.

1.1.1.1 Satellite Analysis Branch (SAB)
NESDIS' SAB serves as the operational focal point for real-time imagery products and multi-disciplinary environmental analyses. The SAB's primary mission is to support disaster mitigation and warning services for U.S. Federal agencies and the international community. Routine environmental analyses are provided to forecasters and other environmental users and used in the numerical models of the NWS. The SAB schedules and distributes real-time satellite imagery products from global geostationary and polar-orbiting satellites to environmental users. The SAB coordinates the satellite and other information for the NOAA Volcanic Hazards Alert program under an agreement with the FAA and works with the NWS as part of the Washington, D.C. Volcanic Ash Advisory Center (VAAC)

1.1.2 National Weather Service (NWS)
NWS provides weather data, forecasts and warnings for the United States, its territories, adjacent waters and ocean areas for the protection of life and property and the enhancement of the national economy. NWS data and products form a national information database and infrastructure that can be used by other government agencies, the private sector, the public and the global community. The following is a description of NWS offices associated with aviation weather.

1.1.2.1 National Centers for Environmental Prediction (NCEP)
NCEP is where virtually all global meteorological data is collected and analyzed. NCEP then provides a wide variety of national and international weather guidance products to NWS field offices, government agencies, emergency managers, private sector meteorologists, and meteorological organizations and societies throughout the world. NCEP is a critical resource in national and global weather prediction and is the starting point for nearly all weather forecasts in the United States.

NCEP is comprised of nine distinct centers and the Office of the Director. Each center has its own specific mission. The following NCEP centers provide aviation weather products and services:

1.1.2.1.1 NCEP Central Operations (NCO)
The NCO in College Park, Maryland, sustains and executes the operational suite of the numerical analysis and forecast models and prepares NCEP products for dissemination. It also links all nine of the national centers together via computer and communications-related services.

1.1.2.1.2 Aviation Weather Center (AWC)
The AWC, a Meteorological Watch Office (MWO) for the International Civil Aviation Organization (ICAO), is located in Kansas City, Missouri. The AWC issues the following products through the Aviation Digital Data Service (ADDS) in support of FAA air traffic controllers and the National Airspace System (NAS): Airman's Meteorological Information (AIRMETs), Significant Meteorological Information (SIGMETs), Convective SIGMETs, Area Forecasts (FAs), Significant Weather Prognostic Charts (low, middle, and high), Collaborative Convective Forecast Product (CCFP), National Convective Weather Forecast (NCWF), Current Icing Product (CIP), Forecast Icing Product (FIP), Graphical Turbulence Guidance (GTG), and Ceiling and Visibility Product (CVA).

1.1.2.1.3 Weather Prediction Center (WPC)
The WPC in College Park, Maryland, provides analysis and forecast products specializing in quantitative precipitation forecasts to five days, weather forecast guidance to seven days, real-time weather model diagnostics discussions and surface pressure and frontal analyses.

1.1.2.1.4 Storm Prediction Center (SPC)
The SPC in Norman, Oklahoma, provides tornado and severe weather watches for the contiguous U. S. along with a suite of hazardous weather forecasts, including the Alert Severe Weather Watch Bulletins and mesoscale guidance products

1.1.2.1.5 National Hurricane Center (NHC)
The NHC in Miami, Florida, provides official NWS forecasts of the movement and strength of tropical weather systems and issues the appropriate watches and warnings for the contiguous U.S. and surrounding areas. It also issues a suite of marine products covering the tropical Atlantic, Caribbean, Gulf of Mexico, and tropical eastern Pacific.

1.1.2.2 Alaskan Aviation Weather Unit (AAWU)
The AAWU, located in Anchorage, Alaska, is a MWO for the ICAO. The AAWU is responsible for the entire Anchorage flight information region (FIR). They issue the following products for the airspace over Alaska and adjacent coastal waters: AIRMETs, SIGMETs, FAs, Graphic Area Forecasts, and Significant Weather Prognostic Charts (Low- and Mid-level – below flight level (FL) 250).

The AAWU is also designated as the Anchorage Volcanic Ash Advisory Center (VAAC). The VAAC area of responsibility includes the Anchorage FIR and Far Eastern Russia and is responsible for the issuance of Volcanic Ash Advisories (FVs).

1.1.2.3 Center Weather Service Unit (CWSU)

CWSUs are units of NWS meteorologists under contract with the FAA that are stationed at and support the FAA's air route traffic control centers (ARTCC).

CWSUs provide timely weather consultation, forecasts, and advice to managers within ARTCCs and to other supported FAA facilities. This information is based on monitoring, analysis, and interpretation of real-time weather data at the ARTCC through the use of all available data sources including radar, satellite, Pilot Weather Reports (PIREPs), and various NWS products such as Terminal Aerodrome Forecasts (TAFs), FAs, and inflight advisories.

Special emphasis is given to those weather conditions hazardous to aviation or which would impede the flow of air traffic within the NAS. Rerouting of aircraft around hazardous weather is based largely on forecasts provided by the CWSU meteorologist. They issue the following products in support of their respective ARTCC: Center Weather Advisories (CWA) and Meteorological Impact Statements (MIS).

1.1.2.4 Weather Forecast Office (WFO)

A NWS WFO is a multi-purpose, local weather forecast center that produces, among its suite of services, aviation-related products. In support of aviation, WFOs issue TAFs with some offices issuing Airport Weather Warnings, and Soaring Forecasts.

WFO Honolulu is also designated as an MWO for ICAO. As a result of this unique designation, WFO Honolulu is the only WFO to issue the following text products: AIRMETs, SIGMETs, FAs, and Route Forecasts (ROFOR). WFO Honolulu is co-located with the Central Pacific Hurricane Center (CPHC). CPHC provides official NWS forecast of the movement and strength of tropical weather systems and issues the appropriate watches and warnings for the central Pacific, including the State of Hawaii. WFO Honolulu also issues a suite of marine products covering a large portion of the Pacific Ocean.

1.2 Federal Aviation Administration (FAA)

The FAA, a part of the Department of Transportation (DOT), provides a safe, secure, and efficient aerospace system that contributes to national security and the promotion of U.S. aerospace safety. As the leading authority in the international aerospace community, the FAA is responsive to the dynamic nature of user needs, economic conditions, and environmental concerns.

The FAA provides a wide range of services to the aviation community. The following is a description of those FAA facilities which are involved with aviation weather and pilot services.

1.2.1 Air Traffic Control System Command Center (ATCSCC)

The ATCSCC is located in Vint Hill, Virginia. The ATCSCC has the mission of balancing air traffic demand with system capacity. This ensures maximum safety and efficiency for the NAS while minimizing delays. The ATCSCC utilizes the Traffic Management System, aircraft situation display, monitor alert, the follow-on functions, and direct contact with ARTCC and terminal radar approach control facility (TRACON) traffic management units to manage flow on a national level.

Because weather is the most common reason for air traffic delays and re-routings, NWS Meteorologists support the ATCSCC. These meteorologists, called National Aviation Meteorologists (NAMs), orchestrate NWS operations in support of traffic flow management within the NAS.

1.2.2 Air Route Traffic Control Center (ARTCC)

An ARTCC is a facility established to provide air traffic control service to aircraft operating on instrument flight rules (IFR) flight plans within controlled airspace and principally during the en route phase of flight. When equipment capabilities and controller workload permit, certain advisory/assistance services may be provided to visual flight rules (VFR) aircraft.

En route controllers become familiar with pertinent weather information and stay aware of current weather information needed to perform air traffic control duties. En route controllers advise pilots of hazardous weather that may impact operations within 150 nautical miles (NM) of the controller's assigned sector(s) and may solicit PIREPs from pilots.

1.2.3 Air Traffic Control Tower (ATCT) and Terminal Radar Approach Control (TRACON)

An ATCT is a terminal facility that uses air/ground communications, visual signaling, and other devices to provide air traffic control (ATC) services to aircraft operating in the vicinity of an airport or on the movement area. It authorizes aircraft to land or take off at the airport controlled by the tower or to transit the Class D airspace area regardless of flight plan or weather conditions (IFR or VFR). A tower may also provide approach control services.

TRACONs manage the airspace from 10 to 40 miles outside of selected airports and below 13,000 feet. They also coordinate aircraft spacing as they approach and depart these airports.

Terminal controllers become familiar with pertinent weather information and stay aware of current weather information needed to perform air traffic control duties. Terminal controllers advise pilots of hazardous weather that may impact operations within 150 NM of the controller's assigned sector or area of jurisdiction and may solicit PIREPs from pilots. ATCTs and

TRACONs may opt to broadcast hazardous weather information alerts only when any part of the area described is within 50 NM of the airspace under the ATCT's jurisdiction.

The tower controllers are also properly certified and act as official weather observers as required.

An Automatic Terminal Information Service (ATIS) is a continuous broadcast of recorded information in selected terminal areas. Its purpose is to improve controller effectiveness and to relieve frequency congestion by automating the repetitive transmission of non-controlled airport/terminal area and meteorological information.

1.2.4 Flight Service Station (FSS)
FSSs provide pilot weather briefings, en route weather, receive and process IFR and VFR flight plans, solicit and disseminate pilot reports, relay ATC clearances, and issue Notices to Airmen (NOTAMs). They also provide assistance to lost aircraft and aircraft in emergency situations, and conduct VFR search and rescue services.

1.3 Dissemination of Aviation Weather Products

The ultimate users of aviation weather services are pilots and aircraft dispatchers. Maintenance personnel may use the service to keep informed of weather that could cause possible damage to unprotected aircraft.

Pilots contribute to aviation weather services as well as use them. PIREPs help other pilots, dispatchers, briefers and forecasters as an observation of current conditions.

In the interest of safety and in compliance with Title 14 of the Code of Federal Regulations, all pilots should get a complete weather briefing before each flight. The pilot is responsible for ensuring he/she has all the information needed to make a safe flight.

1.3.1 Weather Briefings

Prior to every flight, pilots should gather all information vital to the nature of the flight. This includes a weather briefing obtained by the pilot from an approved weather source via the Internet (see paragraph 1.3.2) and/or from a FSS specialist.

To provide an appropriate weather briefing, specialists need to know which of the three types of briefings is needed—standard, abbreviated or outlook. Other necessary information is whether the flight will be conducted VFR or IFR, aircraft identification and type, departure point, estimated time of departure (ETD), flight altitude, route of flight, destination, and estimated time en route (ETE). If the briefing updates previously received information, the time of the last briefing is also important. This allows the briefer to provide only pertinent data.

The briefer enters this information into the FAA's flight plan system. The briefer also notes the type of weather briefing provided. If necessary, the information can be referenced later to file or amend a flight plan. It is also used when an aircraft is overdue or is reported missing. Internet data is time-stamped and archived for 15 days. Voice recordings are retained for 45 days.

1.3.1.1 Standard Briefing

A standard briefing provides a complete weather picture and is the most detailed of all briefings. This type of briefing should be obtained prior to the departure of any flight and should be used during flight planning. A standard briefing provides the following information in sequential order if it is applicable to the route of flight.

- Adverse Conditions. This includes information about adverse conditions that may influence a decision to cancel or alter the route of flight. Adverse conditions include significant weather such as thunderstorms, aircraft icing, turbulence, wind shear, mountain obscuration, areas of current and forecasted IFR conditions, and other important items such as airport/runway closings, air traffic delays, and Temporary Flight Restrictions (TFRs).

- VFR Flight NOT RECOMMENDED (VNR). If the weather for the route of flight is below VFR minimums, or if it is doubtful the flight could be made under VFR conditions due to the forecast weather, the briefer may state that VFR is not recommended. The pilot can then decide whether or not to continue the flight under VFR, but this advisory should be weighed carefully.

- Synopsis. The synopsis is an overview of the larger weather picture. Fronts and major weather systems along or near the route of flight and weather which may affect the flight are provided.

- Current Conditions. This portion of the briefing contains the current surface weather observations, PIREPs, satellite, and radar data along the route of flight. If the departure time is more than 2 hours away, current conditions will not be included in the briefing.

- En Route Forecast. The en route forecast is a summary of the weather forecast for the proposed route of flight.

- Destination Forecast. The destination forecast is a summary of the expected weather for the destination airport at the estimated time of arrival (ETA).

- Winds and Temperatures Aloft. Winds and temperatures aloft is a forecast of the winds at specific altitudes along the route of flight. However, the temperature information is provided only on request.

- NOTAMs. This portion supplies NOTAM information pertinent to the route of flight which has not been published in the NOTAM publication. Published NOTAM information is provided during the briefing only when requested.

- Prohibited and Special Flight Rules Areas

- ATC Delays. This is an advisory of any known ATC delays that may affect the flight.

- Other Information. At the end of the standard briefing, the specialist will provide the radio frequencies needed to open a flight plan and to contact En Route Flight Advisory Service (EFAS). Any additional information requested is also provided at this time.

1.3.1.2 Abbreviated Briefing

An abbreviated briefing is a shortened version of the standard briefing. It should be requested when a departure has been delayed or when specific weather information is needed to update a previous standard briefing. When this is the case, the weather specialist needs to know the time and source of the previous briefing so the necessary weather information will not be omitted inadvertently.

1.3.1.3 Outlook Briefing

An outlook briefing should be requested when a planned departure is 6 or more hours away. It provides initial forecast information that is limited in scope due to the timeframe of the planned flight. This type of briefing is a good source of flight planning information that can influence decisions regarding route of flight, altitude, and ultimately the "go, no-go" decision. A follow-up standard briefing prior to departure is advisable since an outlook briefing generally only contains information based on weather trends and existing weather in geographical areas at or near the departure airport.

The FSS' purpose is to serve the aviation community. Pilots should not hesitate to ask questions and discuss factors they do not fully understand. The briefing should be considered complete only when the pilot has a clear picture of what weather to expect. Pilots should also make a final weather check immediately before departure if at all possible.

1.3.2 Pilot Briefing via the Internet

1.3.2.1 Direct Use Access Terminal Service (DUATS/DUAT)
DUATS/DUAT which is funded by the FAA, allows any pilot with a current medical certificate to access NWS weather information and file a flight plan via computer. Two methods of access are available to connect with DUATS/DUAT. The first is on the Internet through Computer Sciences Corporation (CSC) at http://www.duats.com or Data Transformation Corporation at http://www.duat.com. The current vendors of DUATS/DUAT service and the associated phone numbers are listed in Chapter 7 of the *Aeronautical Information Manual (AIM)*.

1.3.2.2 Lockheed Martin Flight Services Web Portal
Lockheed Martin Flight Services provides a Web portal for flight planning service at https://www.lmfsweb.afss.com/Website/. Pilots must register and create a user account to access the pilot briefing and flight planning functions. VFR search and rescue services are also provided to registered users who file and activate a VFR flight plan and are equipped with certain GPS location devices.

1.3.3 Aviation Digital Data Service (ADDS)
The ADDS site is a joint effort of NOAA Forecast Systems Laboratory (FSL), NCAR Research Applications Laboratory (RAL), the FAA, and the AWC. ADDS provides the aviation community with textual, digital and graphical forecasts, analyses, and observations of aviation-related weather variables. Additionally, the ADDS contains a flight path tool that allows the user to view data along a specific route of flight. The user can view icing, turbulence, temperature, winds, humidity, AIRMETs, Aviation Routine Weather Reports (METARs), TAFs, etc. both horizontally and vertically. This site also allows many overlay options including ARTCC boundaries, counties, highways, and rivers. Product animation is also possible on the AWC JavaScript image.

1.3.4 Telephone Information Briefing Service (TIBS)
TIBS is a service prepared and disseminated by selected FSSs. It provides continuous telephone recordings of meteorological and aeronautical information. Specifically, TIBS provides area and route briefings, as well as airspace procedures and special announcements, if applicable. It is designed to be a preliminary briefing tool and is not intended to replace a standard briefing from a flight service specialist. The TIBS service is available 24 hours a day and is updated when conditions change, but it can only be accessed by a *touch-tone* phone. The phone numbers for the TIBS service are listed in the Airport/Facility Directory (A/FD).

TIBS should also contain, but is not limited to: surface observations, TAFs, and winds/temperatures aloft forecasts.

Each FSS provides at least 4 route and/or area briefings. As a minimum, area briefings encompass a 50 NM radius. Pilots have access to NOTAM data through area or route briefings on separate channels designated specifically for NOTAMs, or by access to a briefer.

Separate channels are designated for each route, area, local meteorological/aeronautical information, special event, airspace procedures, etc.

The order and content of the TIBS recording is as follows:

- Introduction. Includes the preparation time and the route and/or the area of coverage. The service area may be configured to meet the individual facility's needs.

- Adverse Conditions. A summary of Convective SIGMETs, SIGMETs, AIRMETs, Center Weather Advisories, Alert Severe Weather Watch Bulletins, and any other available information that may adversely affect flight in the route/area.

- VNR Statement. Included when current or forecast conditions, surface or aloft, would make the flight under VFR doubtful.

- Synopsis. A brief statement describing the type, location, and movement of weather systems and/or air masses that might affect the route or the area. This element may be combined with adverse conditions and/or the VNR element, in any order, when it will help to more clearly describe conditions.

- Current Conditions. A summary of current weather conditions over the route/area. PIREPs are included on conditions reported aloft and a summary of observed radar echoes. Specific departure/destination observation may also be included.

- Density Altitude. The statement "check density altitude" will be included for any weather reporting point with a field elevation of 2,000 feet mean sea level (MSL) or above that meets certain temperature criteria.

- En Route Forecast. A summary of appropriate forecast data provided in logical order, i.e., climb out, en route, and descent.

- Winds Aloft. A summary of winds aloft forecast for the route/area as interpolated from forecast data for the local and/or the adjacent reporting locations for levels through 12,000 feet. The broadcast should include the levels from 3,000 to 12,000 feet, but usually includes at least 2 forecast levels above the surface.

- Request for PIREPs. When weather conditions within the area or along the route meet requirements for soliciting PIREPs, a request will be included in the recording.

- NOTAM information that affects the route/area may be included as part of the briefing, on a separate channel, or obtained by direct contact with a pilot weather briefer.

- Military Training Activity. A statement is included in the closing announcement to contact a briefer for information on military training activity.

- Closing Announcement.

TIBS services may be reduced during the hours of 1800–0600 local time only. Resumption of full broadcast service is adjusted seasonally to coincide with daylight hours. During the period of reduced broadcast, a recorded statement may indicate when the broadcast will be resumed and to contact Flight Service for weather briefing and other services.

For those pilots already in flight and needing weather information and assistance, the following services are provided by FSSs. They can be accessed over the proper radio frequencies printed in flight information publications.

1.3.5 Hazardous Inflight Weather Advisory Service (HIWAS)

HIWAS is a national program for broadcasting hazardous weather information continuously over selected navigational aids (NAVAIDs). The broadcasts include advisories such as AIRMETs, SIGMETS, Convective SIGMETs, and urgent PIREPs. These broadcasts are only a summary of the information, and pilots should contact an FSS or EFAS for detailed information.

The HIWAS broadcast area is defined as the area within 150 NM of HIWAS outlets.

HIWAS broadcasts are not interrupted or delayed except for emergency situations, when an aircraft requires immediate attention, or for reasonable use of the voice override capability on specific HIWAS outlets in order to use the limited Remote Communications Outlet (RCO) to maintain en route communications. The service is provided 24 hours a day. An announcement is made for no hazardous weather advisories.

Hazardous weather information is recorded if it is occurring within the HIWAS broadcast area. The broadcast includes the following elements:

- A statement of introduction including the appropriate area(s) and a recording time.

- A summary of Convective SIGMETs, SIGMETs, AIRMETs, Urgent PIREPs, Aviation Watch Notification Messages, Center Weather Advisories, and any other weather such as isolated thunderstorms that are rapidly developing and increasing in intensity, or low ceilings and visibilities that are becoming widespread which are considered significant and are not included in a current hazardous weather advisory.

- A request for PIREPs, if applicable.

- A recommendation to contact FSS/FLIGHT WATCH for additional details concerning hazardous weather.

Once the HIWAS broadcast is updated, an announcement will be made once on all communications/NAVAID frequencies except emergency, EFAS, and navigational frequencies already dedicated to continuous broadcast services. In the event a HIWAS broadcast area is out of service, an announcement is made on all communications/NAVAID frequencies except on emergency, EFAS, and navigational frequencies already dedicated to continuous broadcast services.

1.3.6 En Route Flight Advisory Service (EFAS)

The purpose of EFAS, radio call "FLIGHT WATCH" (FW), is to provide en route aircraft with timely and pertinent weather data tailored to a specific altitude and route using the most current available sources of aviation meteorological information.

EFAS specialists tailor en route flight advisories to the phase of flight that begins after climb out and ends with descent to land. Current weather and terminal forecast at the airport of first intended landing and/or the alternate airport is provided on request. When conditions dictate, EFAS specialists provide information on weather for alternate routes and/or altitudes to assist the pilot in the avoidance of hazardous flight conditions. The pilot is advised to contact the adjacent flight watch facility when adverse weather conditions along the intended route extend beyond the Flight Watch Area (FWA).

EFAS is *not* used for routine in-flight services; e.g., flight plan filing, position reporting, or full route (pre-flight) briefings. If a request for information is received that is not within the scope of EFAS, the pilot is advised of the appropriate FSS to contact.

EFAS specialists suggest route or destination changes to avoid areas of weather that in the judgment of the specialists constitutes a threat to safe flight.

EFAS is provided on 122.0 MHz to aircraft below FL180. An assigned discrete frequency is used to provide EFAS to aircraft at FL180 and above. This frequency can also be used for communications with aircraft below FL180 when communication coverage permits. Aircraft operating at FL180 or above that contact FW on frequency 122.0 MHz are advised to change to the discrete frequency for EFAS.

1.3.7 Automatic Dependent Surveillance – Broadcast (ADS-B)

ADS-B is a surveillance system combining the advanced technologies of satellite positioning, aircraft avionics, and ground-based transceivers. ADS-B equipped aircraft automatically broadcast their identification, current position, altitude, and velocity information approximately once per second. This continuous broadcast of flight data improves aircraft position accuracy beyond the capabilities of current NAS radar/transponder-based surveillance systems.

In the United States, two different data links have been adopted for use with ADS-B: 1090 MHz Extended Squitter (1090ES) and the 978 MHz, Universal Access Transceiver (UAT). The 1090ES link is intended for aircraft that primarily operate at FL240 and above, whereas the UAT link is intended for use by aircraft that primarily operate at lower altitudes. From a pilot's standpoint, the two links operate similarly and support ADS-B and Traffic Information Services-Broadcast (TIS-B). The UAT link will provide additional weather and other aeronautical information through the Flight Information Service - Broadcast (FIS-B).

1.3.7.1 Flight Information Service – Broadcast (FIS-B)

FIS-B is a ground-based broadcast service provided through the FAA's ADS-B Services UAT network. The service provides users with a 978 MHz data link capability when operating within range and line-of-sight of a transmitting ground station. FIS-B enables users of properly equipped aircraft to receive and display a suite of broadcast weather and aeronautical information products.

The following list represents the initial suite of textual and graphical products available through FIS-B and provided free-of-charge. This advisory circular (AC) and the current edition of AC 00-63, Use of Cockpit Displays of Digital Weather and Aeronautical Information, contain detailed information concerning FIS-B meteorological products. Chapters 3, 4 and 5 of the AIM contain information on Special Use Airspace (SUA), TFR, and NOTAM products.

- Text: METAR and Aviation Selected Special Weather Report (SPECI);

- Text: PIREP;

- Text: Winds and Temperatures Aloft;

- Text: Terminal Aerodrome Forecast (TAF) and amendments;

- Text: NOTAM Distant and Flight Data Center;

- Text/Graphic: AIRMET;

- Text/Graphic: SIGMET;

- Text/Graphic: Convective SIGMET;

- Text/Graphic: Special Use Airspace

- Text/Graphic: TFR NOTAM; and

- Graphic: Next generation weather radar (NEXRAD) Composite Reflectivity Products (Regional and National).

Users of FIS-B should familiarize themselves with the operational characteristics and limitations of the system, including: system architecture; service environment; product lifecycles; modes of operation; and indications of system failure.

Update intervals are defined as the rate at which the product data is available from the source for transmission. Transmission intervals are defined as the amount of time within which a new or updated product transmission must be completed and/or the rate or repetition interval at which the product is rebroadcast. Table 1-1 provides update and transmission intervals for each product.

Where applicable, FIS-B products include a look-ahead range expressed in nautical miles (NM) for three service domains: Airport Surface; Terminal Airspace; and En-route/Gulf-of-Mexico (GOMEX). Table 1-1 provides service domain availability and look-ahead ranging for each FIS-B product.

Prior to using this capability, users should familiarize themselves with the operation of FIS-B avionics by referencing the applicable User's Guides. Users should obtain guidance concerning the interpretation of information displayed from the appropriate avionics manufacturer.

Users should report FIS-B malfunctions not attributed to aircraft system failures or covered by active NOTAM to the nearest FSS facility by radio or telephone. Users may also report malfunctions by submitting FAA Form 8740-5, Safety Improvement Report, via mail, fax, or email to your local Flight District Standards Office (FSDO) Safety Program Manager.

Table 1-1. FIS-B Over UAT Product Update and Transmission Intervals

Product	FIS-B Over UAT Service Update Intervals[1]	FIS-B Service Transmission Intervals[2]
AIRMET	As available	5 minutes
Convective SIGMET	As available	5 minutes
METARs / SPECIs	1 minute / as available	5 minutes
NEXRAD Composite Reflectivity (CONUS)	15 minutes	15 minutes
NEXRAD Composite Reflectivity (Regional)	5 minutes	2.5 minutes
NOTAMs-D/FDC/TFR	As available	10 minutes
PIREP	As available	10 minutes
SIGMET	As available	5 minutes
Special Use Airspace Status	As available	10 minutes
TAF/AMEND	8 hours/as available	10 minutes
Temperature Aloft	12 hours	10 minutes
Winds Aloft	12 hours	10 minutes

1 The Update Interval is the rate at which the product data is available from the source.

2 The Transmission Interval is the amount of time within which a new or updated product transmission must be completed and the rate or repetition interval at which the product is rebroadcast.

Table 1-2. Product Parameters for Low/Medium/High Altitude Tier Radios

Product	Surface Radios	Low Altitude Tier	Medium Altitude Tier	High Altitude Tier
CONUS NEXRAD	N/A	CONUS NEXRAD not provided	CONUS NEXRAD imagery	CONUS NEXRAD imagery
Winds & Temps Aloft	500 NM look-ahead range	500 NM look-ahead range	750 NM look-ahead range	1,000 NM look-ahead range
METAR	100 NM look-ahead range	250 NM look-ahead range	375 NM look-ahead range	CONUS: CONUS Class B & C airport METARs and 500 NM look-ahead range Outside of CONUS: 500 NM look-ahead range
TAF	100 NM look-ahead range	250 NM look-ahead range	375 NM look-ahead range	CONUS: CONUS Class B & C airport TAFs and 500 NM look-ahead range Outside of CONUS: 500 NM look-ahead range
AIRMET, SIGMET, PIREP, and Special Use Airspace / SAA	100 NM look-ahead range. PIREP/SUA is N/A	250 NM look-ahead Range	375 NM look-ahead range	500 NM look-ahead range
Regional NEXRAD	150 NM look-ahead range	150 NM look-ahead range	200 NM look-ahead range	250 NM look-ahead range
NOTAMs D, FDC, TFR	100 NM look-ahead range	100 NM look-ahead range	100 NM look-ahead range	100 NM look-ahead range

Users should obtain guidance concerning the content, format, and symbology of individual FIS B products from the manufacturer of the avionics equipment used to receive and display them.

1.3.7.2 Operational Use of FIS-B Products

FIS-B products are intended to enhance the user's situational awareness and enable more efficient use of ATC/FSS/AOCC services. The information provided by FIS-B is advisory in nature and should not be used in lieu of individual pre-flight, in-flight, weather, or flight planning briefings provided by ATC/FSS/AOCC services.

2 AVIATION WEATHER PRODUCT POLICY

The demand for new and improved aviation weather products continues to grow and, with new products introduced to meet the demand, some confusion has resulted in the aviation community regarding the relationship between regulatory requirements and the new weather products.

This section will clarify that relationship by providing:

- policy guidance for using aviation weather products,
- descriptions of the types of aviation weather information, and
- categorization of the sources of aviation weather information.

2.1 Use of Aviation Weather Products

With increased access to these weather products via the public Internet, the aviation community has access to an overwhelming amount of weather information and data that support self-briefing. This advisory circular (AC) describes the weather products distributed by the National Weather Service (NWS). Pilots and operators using the public Internet to access weather from a third-party vendor should request and/or review an appropriate description of services and provider disclosure. This should include, but is not limited to, the type of weather product (e.g., current weather or forecast weather), the currency of the product (i.e., product issue and valid times), and the relevance of the product. Pilots and operators should be cautious when using unfamiliar weather products and when in doubt, consult with a Flight Service Specialist.

The development of new weather products, coupled with the termination of some legacy textual and graphical products may create confusion between regulatory requirements and the new products. All flight-related aviation weather decisions must be based on all available pertinent weather products. As every flight is unique and the weather conditions for that flight vary hour by hour, day to day, multiple weather products may be necessary to meet aviation weather regulatory requirements. Many new weather products now have a Precautionary Use Statement that details the proper use or application of the specific product.

2.2 Types of Aviation Weather Information

The Federal Aviation Administration (FAA) has identified the following three distinct types of weather information that may be needed to conduct aircraft operations: observations, analyses, and forecasts.

2.2.1 Observations
Observations are raw weather data collected by some type of sensor(s). The observations can either be in situ (e.g., surface or airborne) or remote (e.g., weather radar, satellite, profiler, and lightning).

2.2.2 Analysis
Analyses of weather information are an enhanced depiction and/or interpretation of observed weather data.

2.2.3 Forecasts

Forecasts are the predictions of the development and/or movement of weather phenomena based on meteorological observations and various mathematical models.

In-flight weather advisories, including Significant Meteorological Information (SIGMET), Convective SIGMETs, Airman's Meteorological Information (AIRMET), Center Weather Advisories (CWA), and Meteorological Impact Statements (MIS), are considered forecast weather information products.

2.3 Categorizing Aviation Weather Sources

The regulations pertaining to aviation weather reflect that, historically, the Federal Government was the only source of aviation weather information. That is, the FAA and NWS, or its predecessor organizations, were solely responsible for the collection and dissemination of weather data, including forecasts. Thus, the term "approved source(s)" referred exclusively to the Federal Government. The Federal Government is no longer the only source of weather information, due to the growing sophistication of aviation operations and scientific and technological advances.

Since all three types of weather information defined in paragraph 2.2 are not available from all sources of aviation weather information, the FAA has categorized the sources as follows: Federal Government, Enhanced Weather Information System (EWINS), and commercial weather information providers.

2.3.1 Federal Government
The FAA and NWS collect weather observations. The NWS analyzes the observations, and produces forecasts, including in-flight aviation weather advisories (e.g., SIGMETs). The FAA and NWS disseminate meteorological observations, analyses, and forecast products through a variety of systems. The Federal Government is the only approval authority for sources of weather observations (e.g., contract towers and airport operators).

Commercial weather information providers contracted by the FAA to provide weather observations (e.g., contract towers, Lockheed Martin, Direct Use Access Terminal Service (DUAT/DUATS) are included in the Federal Government category of approved sources by virtue of maintaining required technical and quality assurance standards under FAA and NWS oversight.

2.3.2 Enhanced Weather Information System (EWINS)
An EWINS is a system for gathering, evaluating, and disseminating aviation weather information, and for issuing weather reports and forecasts prepared by properly trained and qualified aviation meteorologists or aircraft dispatchers. Air carriers use EWINS, which are proprietary to each carrier. In order to use an EWINS, each air carrier requires FAA approval.

To receive FAA approval, each carrier's EWINS must have sufficient procedures, personnel, and communications and data processing equipment to effectively obtain, analyze, and disseminate aeronautical weather data. For a full explanation of the requirements for EWINS approval, see the Flight Standards Information Management System (FSIMS), Order 8900.1, Volume 3, Chapter 26, Section 4, Enhanced Weather Information Systems. An EWINS source may produce weather analyses and forecasts based on meteorological observations provided by the Federal Government. Approval to use EWINS weather products is issued on a case-by-case basis and is currently only applicable to Title 14 of the Code of Federal Regulations (14 CFR) part 91K Program Managers and 14 CFR part 121/135 certificate holders, who may either act as their own EWINS or contract those services from a separate entity. These approved operators may conduct flight operations using the weather analyses and forecasts produced by their approved EWINS.

2.3.3 Commercial Weather Information Providers

Commercial weather providers are a major source of weather products for the aviation community. In general, they produce proprietary weather products based on NWS products with formatting and layout modifications but no material changes to the weather information itself. This is also referred to as "repackaging."

Commercial providers may also produce forecasts, analyses, and other proprietary weather products and substantially alter the information contained in NWS-produced products. Operators who desire to use products prepared by a commercial weather provider as opposed to using products that are simply repackaged, may require FAA approval to use an EWINS. For more information on whether an EWINS is required to use products prepared by a commercial weather provider, refer to FSIMS, Order 8900.1, Volume 3, Chapter 26, Section 2, Regulatory Sources of Aviation Weather Information. Operators and pilots contemplating using such services should request and/or review an appropriate description of services and provider disclosure. This should include, but is not limited to:

- The type of weather product (e.g., current weather or forecast weather),
- The currency of the product (i.e., product issue and valid times), and
- The relevance of the product.

Pilots and operators should be cautious when using unfamiliar products, or products not supported by FAA/NWS technical specifications.

3 OBSERVED TEXT PRODUCTS

3.1 Aviation Routine Weather Reports (METAR) and Aviation Selected Special Weather Reports (SPECI)

Surface weather observations are fundamental to all meteorological services. Observations are the basic information upon which forecasts and warnings are made in support of a wide range of weather sensitive activities within the public and private sectors, including aviation.

Although the METAR/SPECI code is used worldwide, each country is allowed to make modifications or exceptions to the code for use in their particular country. This section will focus on the U.S. modifications and exceptions. METAR/SPECIs are available online at: http://adds.aviationweather.gov/metars/

3.1.1 Aviation Routine Weather Report (METAR)
Aviation Routine Weather Report (METAR) is the primary observation code used in the U. S. to satisfy World Meteorological Organization (WMO) and International Civil Aviation Organization (ICAO) requirements for reporting surface meteorological data. A METAR report includes the airport identifier, time of observation, wind, visibility, runway visual range, present weather phenomena, sky conditions, temperature, dew point, and altimeter setting. Excluding the airport identifier and the time of observation, this information is collectively referred to as "the body of the report." As an addition, coded and/or plain language information elaborating on data in "the body of the report" may be appended to the end of the METAR in a section coded as "Remarks." The contents of the "Remarks" section vary with the type of reporting station. The METAR may be abridged at some designated stations only including a few of the mentioned elements.

3.1.2 Aviation Selected Special Weather Report (SPECI)
An Aviation Selected Special Weather Report (SPECI) is an unscheduled report taken when any of the criteria given in Table 3-1 are observed during the interim period between the hourly reports. SPECI contains all data elements found in a METAR plus additional plain language information which elaborates on data in the body of the report. All SPECIs are made as soon as possible after the relevant criteria are observed.

Whenever SPECI criteria are met at the time of the routine METAR, a METAR is issued.

Table 3-1. SPECI Criteria

1	Wind Shift	Wind direction changes by 45 degrees or more in less than 15 minutes and the wind speed is 10 knots or more throughout the wind shift.
2	Visibility	Surface visibility as reported in the body of the report decreases to less than, or if below, increases to equal or exceed: a. 3 miles b. 2 miles c. 1 mile d. The lowest standard instrument approach procedure minimum as published in the National Ocean Service (NOS) *U.S Instrument Procedures*. If none published use ½ mile.
3	Runway Visual Range (RVR)	The highest value from the designated RVR runway decreases to less than, or if below, increases to equal or exceed 2,400 feet during the preceding 10 minutes. U.S. military stations may not report a SPECI based on RVR.
4	Tornado, Funnel Cloud, or Waterspout	a. is observed. b. disappears from sight, or ends.
5	Thunderstorm	a. begins (a SPECI is not required to report the beginning of a new thunderstorm if one is currently reported). b. ends.
6	Precipitation	a. hail begins or ends. b. freezing precipitation begins, ends, or changes intensity. c. ice pellets begin, end, or change intensity
7	Squalls	When they occur
8	Ceiling	The ceiling (rounded off to reportable values) forms or dissipates below, decreases to less than, or if below, increases to equal or exceed: a. 3,000 feet. b. 1,500 feet c. 1,000 feet d. 500 feet e. The lowest standard instrument approach procedure minimum as published in the National Ocean Service (NOS) *U.S Instrument Procedures*. If none published, use 200 feet.
9	Sky Condition	A layer of clouds or obscurations aloft is present below 1,000 feet and no layer aloft was reported below 1,000 feet in the preceding METAR or SPECI.
10	Volcanic Eruption	When an eruption is first noted
11	Aircraft Mishap	Upon notification of an aircraft mishap, unless there has been an intervening observation
12	Miscellaneous	Any other meteorological situation designated by the responsible agency of which, in the opinion of the observer, is critical.

3.1.3 Format

Figure 3-1. METAR/SPECI Coding Format

A METAR/SPECI (Figure 3-1) has two major sections: the Body (consisting of a maximum of 11 groups) and the Remarks (consisting of 2 categories). Together, the body and remarks make up the complete METAR/SPECI. When an element does not occur, or cannot be observed, the corresponding group is omitted from that particular report.

3.1.3.1 Type of Report

METAR KOKC 011955Z AUTO 22015G25KT 180V250 3/4SM R17L/2600FT +TSRA BR OVC010CB 18/16 A2992 RMK AO2 TSB25 TS OHD MOV E SLP132

The type of report, **METAR** or **SPECI** precedes the body of all reports.

3.1.3.2 Station Identifier

METAR **KOKC** 011955Z AUTO 22015G25KT 180V250 3/4SM R17L/2600FT +TSRA BR OVC010CB 18/16 A2992 RMK AO2 TSB25 TS OHD MOV E SLP132

The station identifier, in ICAO format, is included in all reports to identify the station to which the coded report applies.

The ICAO airport code is a four-letter alphanumeric code designating each airport around the world. The ICAO codes are used for flight planning by air traffic controllers and airline operation departments. These codes are not the same as the International Air Transport Association (IATA) codes encountered by the general public used for reservations, baggage handling and in airline timetables. ICAO codes are also used to identify weather stations located on- or off-airport.

Unlike the IATA codes, the ICAO codes have a regional structure. For example, the first letter is allocated by continent (Figure 3-2), the second is a country within the continent; the remaining two are used to identify each airport.

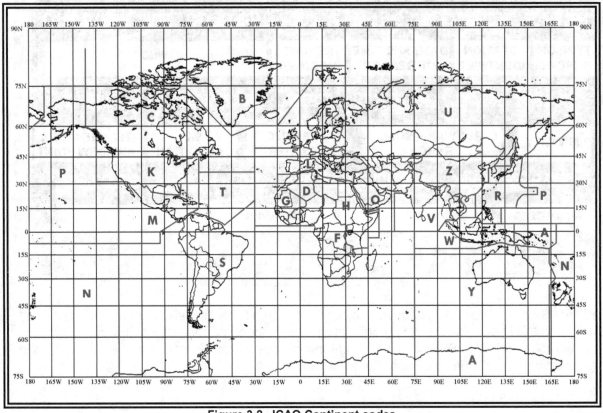

Figure 3-2. ICAO Continent codes

In the contiguous U. S., ICAO station identifiers are coded **K** followed by the three-letter IATA identifier. For example, the Seattle, Washington (IATA identifier SEA) becomes the ICAO identifier KSEA.

ICAO station identifiers in Alaska, Hawaii, and Guam begin with the continent code P, followed by the proper country code (A, H, and G respectively), and the two-letter airport identifier.

Examples:

PANC	Anchorage, AK
PAOM	Nome, AK
PHNL	Honolulu, HI
PHKO	Keahole Point, HI
PGUM	Agana, Guam
PGUA	Anderson AFB, Guam

Canadian station identifiers begin with C, followed by the country code, and the two-letter airport identifier.

Examples:

CYYZ	Toronto, Canada
CYYC	Calgary Canada
CYQB	Quebec, Canada
CYXU	London, Canada
CZUM	Churchill Falls, Canada

Mexican and western Caribbean station identifiers begin with M, followed by the proper country code and two-letter airport identifier.

Examples:

MMMX	Mexico City, Mexico
MUGM	Guantanamo Bay, Cuba
MDSD	Santo Domingo, Dominican Republic
MYNN	Nassau, Bahamas

Eastern Caribbean station identifiers begin with T, followed by the proper country code, and airport identifier.

Examples:

TJSJ	San Juan, Puerto Rico
TIST	Saint Thomas, Virgin Islands

For a list of Alaskan, Hawaiian, Canadian, Mexican, Pacific, and Caribbean ICAO identifiers see FAA Order 7350.7. For a complete worldwide listing, see ICAO Document 7910, "Location Indicators." Both are available on-line.

3.1.3.3 Date and Time of Report

```
METAR KOKC 011955Z AUTO 22015G25KT 180V250 3/4SM R17L/2600FT +TSRA BR
OVC010CB 18/16 A2992 RMK AO2 TSB25 TS OHD MOV E SLP132
```

The date and time is coded in all reports as follows: the day of the month is the first two digits (**01**) followed by the hour (**19**), and the minutes (**55**). The coded time of observations is the actual time of the report or when the criteria for a SPECI is met or noted. If the report is a correction to a previously disseminated report, the time of the corrected report is the same time used in the report being corrected. The date and time group always ends with a **Z** indicating Zulu time (or UTC). For example, METAR KOKC 011955Z would be disseminated as the 2000 hour scheduled report for station KOKC taken on the 1st of the month at 1955 UTC.

3.1.3.4 Report Modifier (As Required)

```
METAR KOKC 011955Z AUTO 22015G25KT 180V250 3/4SM R17L/2600FT +TSRA BR
OVC010CB 18/16 A2992 RMK AO2 TSB25 TS OHD MOV E SLP132
```

The report modifier, **AUTO**, identifies the METAR/SPECI as a fully automated report with no human intervention or oversight. In the event of a corrected METAR or SPECI, the report modifier, **COR**, is substituted for AUTO.

3.1.3.5 Wind Group

```
METAR KOKC 011955Z AUTO 22015G25KT 180V250 3/4SM R17L/2600FT +TSRA BR
OVC010CB 18/16 A2992 RMK AO2 TSB25 TS OHD MOV E SLP132
```

Wind is the horizontal motion of air past a given point. It is measured in terms of velocity, which is a vector that includes direction and speed. It indicates the direction the wind is coming FROM.

In the wind group, the wind direction is coded as the first three digits (**220**) and is determined by averaging the recorded wind direction over a 2-minute period. It is coded in tens of degrees relative to true north using three figures. Directions less than 100 degrees are preceded with a **0**. For example, a wind direction of 90^0 is coded as **090**.

Immediately following the wind direction is the wind speed coded in two or three digits (**15**). Wind speed is determined by averaging the speed over a 2-minute period and is coded in whole knots using the units, tens digits and, when required, the hundreds digit. When wind speeds are less than 10 knots, a leading zero is used to maintain at least a two digit wind code. For example, a wind speed of 8 knots will be coded **08KT**. The wind group is always coded with a **KT** to indicate wind speeds are reported in knots. Other countries may use kilometers per hour (KPH) or meters per second (MPS) instead of knots.

Examples:

>   **05008KT** ···········➤ Wind 50 degrees at 8 knots
>   **15014KT** ···········➤ Wind 150 degrees at 14 knots
>   **340112KT** ··········➤ Wind 340 degrees at 112 knots

3.1.3.5.1 Wind Gust
Wind speed data for the most recent 10 minutes is examined to evaluate the occurrence of gusts. Gusts are defined as rapid fluctuations in wind speed with a variation of 10 knots or more between peaks and lulls. The coded speed of the gust is the maximum instantaneous wind speed.

Wind gusts are coded in two or three digits immediately following the wind speed. Wind gusts are coded in whole knots using the units, tens, and, if required, the hundreds digit. For example, a wind out of the west at 20 knots with gusts to 35 knots would be coded **27020G35KT**.

3.1.3.5.2 Variable Wind Direction (speed 6 knots or less)
Wind direction may be considered variable when, during the previous 2-minute evaluation period, the wind speed was 6 knots or less. In this case, the wind may be coded as **VRB** in place of the 3-digit wind direction. For example, if the wind speed was recorded as 3 knots, it would be coded **VRB03KT**.

3.1.3.5.3 Variable Wind Direction (speed greater than 6 knots)
Wind direction may also be considered variable when, during the 2-minute evaluation period, it varies by 60 degrees or more and the speed is greater than 6 knots. In this case a variable wind direction group immediately follows the wind group. The directional variability is coded in a clockwise direction and consists of the extremes of the wind directions separated by a **V**. For

example, if the wind is variable from 180° to 240° at 10 <u>knots</u>, it would be coded **21010KT 180V240**.

3.1.3.5.4 Calm Wind
When no motion of air is detected, the wind is reported as calm. A calm wind is coded as **00000KT**.

3.1.3.6 Visibility Group

```
METAR KOKC 011955Z AUTO 22015G25KT 180V250 3/4SM R17L/2600FT +TSRA BR
OVC010CB 18/16 A2992 RMK AO2 TSB25 TS OHD MOV E SLP132
```

Visibility is a measure of the opacity of the atmosphere.

Prevailing visibility is the reported visibility considered representative of recorded visibility conditions at the station during the time of observation. It is the greatest distance that can be seen throughout at least half of the horizon circle, not necessarily continuous.

Surface visibility is the prevailing visibility from the surface at manual stations or the visibility derived from sensors at automated stations.

The visibility group is coded as the surface visibility in statute miles. A space is coded between whole numbers and fractions of reportable visibility values. The visibility group ends with **SM** to indicate that the visibility is in statute miles. For example, a visibility of one and a half statute miles is coded **1 1/2SM**. Other countries may use meters (no code).

Automated stations use an **M** to indicate "less than." For example, **M1/4SM** means a visibility of less than one-quarter statute mile.

3.1.3.7 Runway Visual Range (RVR) Group

```
METAR KOKC 011955Z AUTO 22015G25KT 180V250 3/4SM R17L/2600FT +TSRA BR
OVC010CB 18/16 A2992 RMK AO2 TSB25 TS OHD MOV E SLP132
```

The runway visual range (<u>RVR</u>) is an instrument-derived value representing the horizontal distance a pilot may see down the runway.

<u>RVR</u> is reported whenever the station has <u>RVR</u> equipment and prevailing visibility is 1 statute mile or less and/or the <u>RVR</u> for the designated instrument runway is 6,000 feet or less. Otherwise the <u>RVR</u> group is omitted.

Runway visual range is coded in the following format: the initial **R** is code for runway and is followed by the runway number. When more than one runway is defined with the same runway number a directional letter is coded on the end of the runway number. Next is a solidus /; followed by the visual range in feet and then **FT** completes the <u>RVR</u> report. For example, an <u>RVR</u> value for Runway 01L of 800 feet would be coded **R01L/0800FT**. Other countries may use meters.

<u>RVR</u> values are coded in increments of 100 feet up to 1,000 feet, increments of 200 feet from 1,000 feet to 3,000 feet, and increments of 500 feet from 3,000 feet to 6,000 feet. Manual <u>RVR</u>

is not reported below 600 feet. At automated stations, RVR may be reported for up to four designated runways.

When the RVR varies by more than one reportable value, the lowest and highest values will be shown with **V** between them indicating variable conditions. For example, the 10-minute RVR for runway 01L varying between 600 and 1,000 feet would be coded **R01L/0600V1000FT**.

If RVR is less than its lowest reportable value, the visual range group is preceded by **M**. For example, an RVR for runway 01L of less than 600 feet is coded **R01L/M0600FT**.

If RVR is greater than its highest reportable value, the visual range group is preceded by a **P**. For example, an RVR for runway 27 of greater than 6,000 feet will be coded **R27/P6000FT**.

3.1.3.8 Present Weather Group

```
METAR KOKC 011955Z AUTO 22015G25KT 180V250 3/4SM R17L/2600FT +TSRA BR
OVC010CB 18/16 A2992 RMK AO2 TSB25 TS OHD MOV E SLP132
```

Present weather includes precipitation, obscurations, and other weather phenomena. The appropriate notations found in Table 3-2 are used to code present weather.

Table 3-2. METAR/SPECI Notations for Reporting Present Weather[1]

QUALIFIER		WEATHER PHENOMENA		
INTENSITY OR PROXIMITY	DESCRIPTOR	PRECIPITATION	OBSCURATION	OTHER
1	2	3	4	5
- Light	**MI** Shallow	**DZ** Drizzle	**BR** Mist	**PO** Dust/Sand whirls
Moderate[2]	**PR** Partial	**RA** Rain	**FG** Fog	**SQ** Squalls
+ Heavy	**BC** Patches	**SN** Snow	**FU** Smoke	**FC** Funnel Cloud, Tornado, or Waterspout[4]
VC In the Vicinity[3]	**DR** Low Drifting	**SG** Snow Grains	**VA** Volcanic Ash	**SS** Sandstorm
	BL Blowing	**IC** Ice Crystals (Diamond Dust)	**DU** Widespread Dust	**DS** Duststorm
	SH Shower(s)	**PL** Ice Pellets	**SA** Sand	
	TS Thunderstorms	**GR** Hail	**HZ** Haze	
	FZ Freezing	**GS** Small Hail and/or Snow Pellets	**PY** Spray	
		UP Unknown Precipitation		

1. The weather groups are constructed by considering columns 1 to 5 in the table above in sequence, i.e., intensity followed by description, followed by weather phenomena, e.g., heavy rain shower(s) is coded as +SHRA.
2. To denote moderate intensity no entry or symbol is used.
3. See text for vicinity definitions.
4. Tornadoes and waterspouts are coded as +FC.

Separate groups are used for each type of present weather. Each group is separated from the other by a space. METAR/SPECI reports contain no more than three present weather groups.

When more than one type of present weather is reported at the same time, present weather is reported in the following order:

- Tornadic activity – Tornado, Funnel Cloud, or Waterspout.
- Thunderstorm(s) with and without associated precipitation.
- Present weather in order of decreasing dominance, i.e., the most dominant type is reported first.
- Left-to-right in Table 3-2 (Columns 1 through 5).

Qualifiers may be used in various combinations to describe weather phenomena. Present weather qualifiers fall into two categories: intensity (Section 3.1.3.8.1) or proximity (Section 3.1.3.8.2) and descriptors (Section 3.1.3.8.3).

3.1.3.8.1 Intensity Qualifier

The intensity qualifiers are light, moderate, and heavy. They are coded with precipitation types except ice crystals (**IC**) and hail (**GR** or **GS**) including those associated with a thunderstorm (**TS**) and those of a showery nature (**SH**). Tornadoes and waterspouts are coded as heavy (**+FC**). No intensity is ascribed to the obscurations of blowing dust (**BLDU**), blowing sand (**BLSA**), and blowing snow (**BLSN**). Only moderate or heavy intensity is ascribed to sandstorm (**SS**) and duststorm (**DS**).

When more than one form of precipitation is occurring at a time or precipitation is occurring with an obscuration, the reported intensities are not cumulative. The reported intensity will not be greater than the intensity for each form of precipitation.

3.1.3.8.2 Proximity Qualifier

Weather phenomena occurring beyond the point of observation (between 5 and 10 statute miles) are coded as in the vicinity (**VC**). VC can be coded in combination with thunderstorm (**TS**), fog (**FG**), shower(s) (**SH**), well-developed dust/sand whirls (**PO**), blowing dust (**BLDU**), blowing sand (**BLSA**), blowing snow (**BLSN**), sandstorm (**SS**), and duststorm (**DS**). Intensity qualifiers are not coded in conjunction with **VC**.

For example, **VCFG** can be decoded as meaning some form of fog is between 5 and 10 statute miles of the point of observation. If **VCSH** is coded, showers are occurring between 5 and 10 statute miles of the point of observation.

Weather phenomena occurring at the point of observation (at the station) or in the vicinity of the point of observation are coded in the body of the report. Weather phenomena observed beyond 10SM from the point of observation (at the station) is not coded in the body but may be coded in the remarks section (Section 3.1.3.12).

3.1.3.8.3 Descriptor Qualifier

Descriptors are qualifiers which further amplify weather phenomena and are used in conjunction with some types of precipitation and obscurations. The descriptor qualifiers are: shallow (**MI**), partial (**PR**), patches (**BC**), low drifting (**DR**), blowing (**BL**), shower(s) (**SH**), thunderstorm (**TS**), and freezing (**FZ**).

Only one descriptor is coded for each weather phenomena group, e.g., **FZDZ**.

The descriptors shallow (**MI**), partial (**PR**), and patches (**BC**) are only coded with **FG**, e.g., **MIFG**. Mist (**BR**) is not coded with any descriptor.

The descriptors low drifting (**DR**) and blowing (**BL**) will only be coded with dust (**DU**), sand (**SA**), and snow (**SN**), e.g., **BLSN** or **DRSN**. **DR** is coded with **DU**, **SA**, or **SN** for raised particles drifting less than six feet above the ground.

When blowing snow is observed with snow falling from clouds, both phenomena are reported, e.g., **SN BLSN**. If blowing snow is occurring and the observer cannot determine whether or not snow is also falling, then **BLSN** is reported. Spray (**PY**) is coded only with blowing (**BL**).

The descriptor for showery-type precipitation (**SH**) is coded only with one or more of the precipitation qualifiers for rain (**RA**), snow (**SN**), ice pellets (**PL**), small hail (**GS**), or large hail (**GR**). The **SH** descriptor indicates showery-type precipitation. When any type of precipitation is coded with **VC**, the intensity and type of precipitation is not coded.

The descriptor for thunderstorm (**TS**) may be coded by itself when the thunderstorm is without associated precipitation. A thunderstorm may also be coded with the precipitation types of rain (**RA**), snow (**SN**), ice pellets (**PL**), small hail and/or snow pellets (**GS**), or hail (**GR**). For example, a thunderstorm with snow and small hail and/or snow pellets would be coded as **TSSNGS**. **TS** are not coded with **SH**.

The descriptor freezing (**FZ**) is only coded in combination with fog (**FG**), drizzle (**DZ**), or rain (**RA**), e.g., **FZRA**. **FZ** is not coded with **SH**.

3.1.3.8.4 Precipitation
Precipitation is any of the forms of water particles, whether liquid or solid, that falls from the atmosphere and reaches the ground. The precipitation types are: drizzle (**DZ**), rain (**RA**), snow (**SN**), snow grains (**SG**), ice crystals (**IC**), ice pellets (**IP**), hail (**GR**), small hail and/or snow pellets (**GS**), and unknown precipitation (**UP**). **UP** is reported if an automated station detects the occurrence of precipitation but the precipitation sensor cannot recognize the type.

Up to three types of precipitation may be coded in a single present weather group. They are coded in order of decreasing dominance based on intensity.

3.1.3.8.5 Obscuration
Obscurations are any phenomenon in the atmosphere, other than precipitation, reducing the horizontal visibility. The obscuration types are: mist (**BR**), fog (**FG**), smoke (**FU**), volcanic ash (**VC**), widespread dust (**DU**), sand (**SA**), haze (**HZ**), and spray (**PY**). Spray (**PY**) is coded only as **BLPY**.

With the exception of volcanic ash, low drifting dust, low drifting sand, low drifting snow, shallow fog, partial fog, and patches (of) fog, an obscuration is coded in the body of the report if the surface visibility is less than 7 miles or considered operationally significant. Volcanic ash is always reported when observed.

3.1.3.8.6 Other Weather Phenomena
Other weather phenomena types include: well-developed dust/sand whirls (**PO**), sand storms (**SS**), dust storms (**DS**), squalls (**SQ**), funnel clouds (**FC**), and tornados and waterspouts (**+FC**).

Examples:

Code	Description
`-DZ`	Light drizzle
`-RASN`	Light rain and snow
`SN BR`	(Moderate) snow, mist
`-FZRA FG`	Light freezing rain, fog
`SHRA`	(Moderate) rain shower
`VCBLSA`	Blowing sand in the vicinity
`-RASN FG HZ`	Light rain and snow, fog, haze
`TS`	Thunderstorm (without precipitation)

+TSRA ·············► Thunderstorm, heavy rain

+FC TSRAGR BR ·············► Tornado, thunderstorm, (moderate) rain, hail, <u>mist</u>

3.1.3.9 Sky Condition Group

```
METAR KOKC 011955Z AUTO 22015G25KT 180V250 3/4SM R17L/2600FT +TSRA BR
OVC010CB 18/16 A2992 RMK AO2 TSB25 TS OHD MOV E SLP132
```

Sky condition is a description of the appearance of the sky. It is coded as: sky condition, vertical visibility, or clear skies.

The sky condition group is based on the amount of sky cover (the first three letters) followed by the height of the base of the sky cover (final three digits). No space is between the amount of sky cover and the height of the layer. The height of the layer is recorded in feet Above Ground Level (<u>AGL</u>).

Sky condition is coded in ascending order and ends at the first overcast layer. At mountain stations, if the layer is below station level, the height of the layer will be coded as *///*.

Vertical visibility is coded as **VV** followed by the vertical visibility into the indefinite ceiling. No space is between the group identifier and the vertical visibility. Figure 3-3 illustrates the effect of an obscuration on the vision from a descending aircraft.

Figure 3-3. Obscuration Effects on Slant Range Visibility
The ceiling is 500 feet in both examples, but the indefinite ceiling example (bottom) produces a more adverse impact to landing aircraft. This is because an obscuration (e.g., fog, blowing dust, snow, etc.) limits runway

acquisition due to reduced slant range visibility. **This pilot would be able to see the ground but not the runway. If the pilot was at approach minimums, the approach could not be continued and a missed approach must be executed.**

Clear skies are coded in the format, **SKC** or **CLR**. When **SKC** is used, an observer indicates no layers are present; and **CLR** is used by automated stations to indicate no layers are detected at or below 12,000 feet.

Each coded layer is separated from the others by a space. Each layer reported is coded by using the appropriate reportable contraction seen in Table 3-3. A report of clear skies (**SKC** or **CLR**) is a complete layer report within itself. The abbreviations **FEW**, **SCT**, **BKN**, and **OVC** will be followed, without a space, by the height of the layer.

Table 3-3. METAR/SPECI Contractions for Sky Cover

Reportable Contraction	Meaning	Summation Amount of Layer
VV	Vertical Visibility	8/8
SKC or CLR[1]	Clear	0
FEW[2]	Few	1/8 – 2/8
SCT	Scattered	3/8 – 4/8
BKN	Broken	5/8 – 7/8
OVC	Overcast	8/8

1. The abbreviation **CLR** will be used at automated stations when no layers at or below 12,000 feet are reported; the abbreviation **SKC** will be used at manual stations when no layers are reported.
2. Any layer amount less than 1/8 is reported as FEW.

The height is coded in hundreds of feet above the surface using three digits in accordance with Table 3-4.

Table 3-4. METAR/SPECI Increments of Reportable Values of Sky Cover Height

Range of Height Values (feet)	Reportable Increment (feet)
Less than or equal to 5,000	To nearest 100
5,001 to 10,000	To nearest 500
Greater than 10,000	To nearest 1,000

The ceiling is the lowest layer aloft reported as broken or overcast. If the sky is totally obscured with ground based clouds, the vertical visibility is the ceiling.

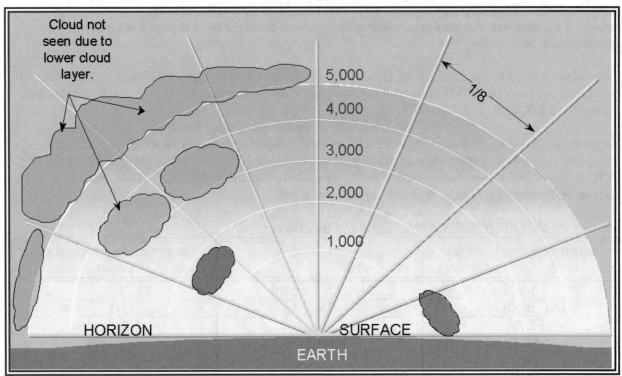

Figure 3-4. METAR/SPECI Sky Condition Coding

Clouds at 1,200 feet obscure 2/8ths of the sky (FEW). Higher clouds at 3,000 feet obscure an additional 1/8th of the sky, and because the observer cannot see above the 1,200-foot layer, he is to assume that the higher 3,000-foot layer also exists above the lower layer (SCT). The highest clouds at 5,000 feet obscure 2/8ths of the sky, and again since the observer cannot see past the 1,200 and 3,000-foot layers, he is to assume the higher 5,000-foot layer also exists above the lower layers (BKN). The sky condition group would be coded as: **FEW012 SCT030 BKN050.**

At manual stations, cumulonimbus (**CB**) or towering cumulus (**TCU**) is appended to the associated layer. For example, a scattered layer of towering cumulus at 1,500 feet would be coded **SCT015TCU** and would be followed by a space if there were additional higher layers to code.

Examples:

SKC	No layers are present
CLR	No layers are detected at or below 12,000 feet <u>AGL</u>
FEW004	Few at 400 feet <u>AGL</u>
SCT023TCU	Scattered layer of towering cumulus at 2,300 feet
BKN105	Broken layer (<u>ceiling</u>) at 10,500 feet
OVC250	Overcast layer (<u>ceiling</u>) at 25,000 feet
VV001	Indefinite <u>ceiling</u> with a vertical visibility of 100 feet
FEW012 SCT046	Few clouds at 1,200 feet, scattered layer at 4,600 feet
SCT033 BKN085	Scattered layer at 3,300 feet, broken layer (<u>ceiling</u>) at 8,500 feet
SCT018 OVC032CB	Scattered layer at 1,800 feet, overcast layer (<u>ceiling</u>) of cumulonimbus at 3,200 feet
SCT009 SCT024 BKN048	Scattered layer at 900 feet, scattered layer at 2,400 feet, broken layer (<u>ceiling</u>) at 4,800 feet

3.1.3.10 Temperature/Dew Point Group

```
METAR KOKC 011955Z AUTO 22015G25KT 180V250 3/4SM R17L/2600FT +TSRA BR
OVC010CB 18/16 A2992 RMK AO2 TSB25 TS OHD MOV E SLP132
```

Temperature is the degree of hotness or coldness of the ambient air seems as measured by a suitable instrument. Dew point is the temperature to which a given parcel of air must be cooled at constant pressure and constant water vapor content for the air to become fully saturated.

Temperature and dew point are coded as two digits rounded to the nearest whole degree Celsius. For example, a temperature of 0.3°C would be coded at **00**. Sub-zero temperatures and dew points are prefixed with an **M**. For example, a temperature of 4°C with a dew point of – 2°C would be coded as **04/M02**; a temperature of –2°C would be coded as **M02**.

If temperature is not available, the entire temperature/dew point group is not coded. If dew point is not available, temperature is coded followed by a solidus, **/,** and no entry made for dew point. For example, a temperature of 1.5°C and a missing dew point would be coded as **02/.**

3.1.3.11 Altimeter

```
METAR KOKC 011955Z AUTO 22015G25KT 180V250 3/4SM R17L/2600FT +TSRA BR
OVC010CB 18/16 A2992 RMK AO2 TSB25 TS OHD MOV E SLP132
```

The altimeter setting group codes the current pressure at elevation. This setting is then used by aircraft altimeters to determine the true altitude above a fixed plane of mean sea level.

The altimeter group always starts with an **A** (the international indicator for altimeter in inches of mercury) and is followed by the four digit group representing the pressure in tens, units, tenths, and hundredths of inches of mercury. The decimal point is not coded. For example, an altimeter setting of 29.92 inches of Mercury would be coded as **A2992**.

3.1.3.12 Remarks (RMK)

```
METAR KOKC 011955Z AUTO 22015G25KT 180V250 3/4SM R17L/2600FT +TSRA BR
OVC010CB 18/16 A2992 RMK AO2 TSB25 TS OHD MOV E SLP132
```

Remarks are included in all METAR and SPECI, when appropriate.

Remarks are separated from the body of the report by the contraction **RMK**. When no remarks are necessary, the contraction **RMK** is not required.

METAR/SPECI remarks fall into two categories: (1) Automated, Manual, and Plain Language, and (2) Additive Maintenance Data.

Table 3-5. METAR/SPECI Order of Remarks

Automated, Manual, and Plain Language				Additive and Automated Maintenance Data	
1.	Volcanic Eruptions	14.	Hailstone Size	27.	Precipitation*
2.	Funnel Cloud	15.	Virga	28.	Cloud Types*
3.	Type of Automated Station	16.	Variable Ceiling Height	29.	Duration of Sunshine*
4.	Peak Wind	17.	Obscurations	30.	Hourly Temperature and Dew Point
5.	Wind Shift	18.	Variable Sky Condition	31.	6-Hourly Maximum Temperature*
6.	Tower or Surface Visibility	19.	Significant Cloud Types	32.	6-Hourly Minimum Temperature*
7.	Variable Prevailing Visibility	20.	Ceiling Height at Second Location	33.	24-Hour Maximum and Minimum Temperature*
8.	Sector Visibility	21.	Pressure Rising or Falling Rapidly	34.	3-Hourly Pressure Tendency*
9.	Visibility at Second Location	22.	Sea-Level Pressure	35.	Sensor Status Indicators
10.	Lightning	23.	Aircraft Mishap	36.	Maintenance Indicator
11.	Beginning and Ending of Precipitation	24.	No SPECI Reports Taken	Note: Additive data is primarily used by the National Weather Service for climatological purposes.	
12.	Beginning and Ending of Thunderstorms	25.	Snow Increasing Rapidly	* These groups should have no direct impact on the aviation community and will not be discussed in this document.	
13.	Thunderstorm Location	26.	Other Significant Information		

Remarks are made in accordance with the following:

- Time entries are made in minutes past the hour if the time reported occurs during the same hour the observation is taken. Hours and minutes are used if the hour is different;

- Present weather coded in the body of the report as **VC** may be further described, i.e., direction from the station, if known. Weather phenomena beyond 10 statute miles of the point(s) of observation are coded as distant (**DSNT**) followed by the direction from the station. For example, precipitation of unknown intensity within 10 statute miles east of the station would be coded as **VCSH E**; lightning 25 statute miles west of the station would be coded as **LTG DSNT W**;

- Distance remarks are in statute miles except for automated lightning remarks which are in nautical miles;

- Movement of clouds or weather, when known, is coded with respect to the direction toward which the phenomena are moving. For example, a thunderstorm moving toward the northeast would be coded as **TS MOV NE**;

- Directions use the eight points of the compass coded in a clockwise order; and

- Insofar as possible, remarks are entered in the order they are presented in the following paragraphs (and Table 3-5).

3.1.3.13 Automated, Manual, and Plain Language Remarks
These remarks generally elaborate on parameters reported in the body of the report. Automated and manual remarks may be generated either by an automated station or observer. Plain language remarks are only provided from an observer.

3.1.3.13.1 Volcanic Eruptions (Plain Language)
Volcanic eruptions are coded in plain language and contain the following, when known:

- **Name** of volcano
- **Latitude and longitude** or the direction and approximate distance from the station
- **Date/Time** (UTC) of the eruption
- Size **description**, approximate height, and direction of movement **of the ash cloud**
- Any **other pertinent data** about the eruption

For example, a remark on a volcanic eruption would look like the following:

```
MT. AUGUSTINE VOLCANO 70 MILES SW ERUPTED AT 231505 LARGE ASH CLOUD
EXTENDING TO APRX 30000 FEET MOVING NE.
```

Pre-eruption volcanic activity is not coded. Pre-eruption refers to unusual and/or increasing volcanic activity which could presage a volcanic eruption.

3.1.3.13.2 Funnel Cloud
At manual stations, tornadoes, funnel clouds, and waterspouts are coded in the following format: Tornadic activity, **TORNADO**, **FUNNEL CLOUD**, or **WATERSPOUT,** followed by the beginning and/or ending time, followed by the location and/or direction of the phenomena from the station, and/or movement, when known. For example, **TORNADO B13 6 NE** would indicate that a tornado began at 13 minutes past the hour and was 6 statute miles northeast of the station.

3.1.3.13.3 Type of Automated Station
AO1 or **AO2** are coded in all METAR/SPECI from automated stations. Automated stations without a precipitation discriminator are identified as **AO1**; automated stations with a precipitation discriminator are identified as **AO2**.

3.1.3.13.4 Peak Wind
Peak wind is coded in the following format: the remark identifier **PK WND**, followed by the direction of the wind (first three digits), peak wind speed (next two or three digits) since the last METAR, and the time of occurrence. A space is between the two elements of the remark identifier and the wind direction/speed group; a solidus, /, (without spaces) separates the wind

direction/speed group and the time. For example, a peak wind of 45 knots from 280 degrees which occurred at 15 minutes past the hour is coded **PK WND 28045/15**.

3.1.3.13.5 Wind Shift
Wind shift is coded in the format: the remark identifier **WSHFT**, followed by the time the wind shift began. The contraction **FROPA** is entered following the time if there is reasonable data to consider the wind shift was the result of a frontal passage. A space is between the remark identifier and the time and, if applicable, between the time and the frontal passage contraction. For example, a remark reporting a wind shift accompanied by a frontal passage that began at 30 minutes after the hour would be coded as **WSHFT 30 FROPA**.

3.1.3.13.6 Tower or Surface Visibility
Tower or surface visibility is coded in the following format: tower **TWR VIS** or surface **SFC**, followed by the observed tower/surface visibility value. A space is coded between each of the remark elements. For example, the control tower visibility of 1 ½ statute miles would be coded **TWR VIS 1 1/2**.

3.1.3.13.7 Variable Prevailing Visibility
Variable prevailing visibility is coded in the following format: the remark identifier **VIS**, followed the lowest and highest visibilities evaluated separated by the letter **V**. A space follows the remark identifier and no spaces are between the letter **V** and the lowest/highest values. For example, a visibility that was varying between 1/2 and 2 statute miles would be coded **VIS 1/2V2**.

3.1.3.13.8 Sector Visibility (Plain Language)
Sector visibility is coded in the following format: the remark identifier **VIS**, followed by the sector referenced to 8 points of the compass, and the sector visibility in statute miles. For example, a visibility of 2 1/2 statute miles in the northeastern octant is coded **VIS NE 2 1/2**.

3.1.3.13.9 Visibility at Second Location
At designated automated stations, the visibility at a second location is coded in the following format: the remark identifier **VIS**, followed by the measured visibility value and the specific location of the visibility sensor(s) at the station. This remark will only be generated when the condition is lower than that contained in the body of the report. For example, a visibility of 2 1/2 statute miles measured by a second sensor located at runway 11 is coded **VIS 2 1/2 RWY11**.

3.1.3.13.10   Lightning
When lightning is observed at a manual station, the frequency, type of lightning and location is reported. The contractions for the type and frequency of lightning are based on Table 3-6, for example, **OCNL LTGICCG NW**, **FRQ LTG VC**, or **LTG DSNT W**.

When lightning is detected by an automated system:

- Within 5 nautical miles of the Airport Location Point (ALP), it is reported as **TS** in the body of the report with no remark;

- Between 5 and 10 nautical miles of the ALP, it is reported as **VCTS** in the body of the report with no remark; and

- Beyond 10 but less than 30 nautical miles of the ALP, it is reported in remarks only as **LTG DSNT** followed by the direction from the ALP.

Table 3-6. METAR/SPECI Type and Frequency of Lightning

Type of Lightning		
Type	**Contraction**	**Definition**
Cloud-ground	CG	Lightning occurring between cloud and ground.
In-cloud	IC	Lightning which takes place within the cloud.
Cloud-cloud	CC	Streaks of lightning reaching from one cloud to another.
Cloud-air	CA	Streaks of lightning which pass from a cloud to the air, but do not strike the ground.
Frequency of Lightning		
Frequency	**Contraction**	**Definition**
Occasional	OCNL	Less than 1 flash/minute.
Frequent	FRQ	About 1 to 6 flashes/minute.
Continuous	CONS	More than 6 flashes/minute.

3.1.3.13.11   Beginning and Ending of Precipitation
At designated stations, the beginning and ending time of precipitation is coded in the following format: the type of precipitation, followed by either a **B** for beginning or an **E** for ending, and the time of occurrence. No spaces are coded between the elements. The coded times of the precipitation start and stop times are found in the remarks section of the next METAR. The times are not required to be in the SPECI. The intensity qualifiers are coded. For example, if rain began at 0005 and ended at 0030 and then snow began at 0020 and ended at 0055, the remarks would be coded as **RAB05E30SNB20E55**. If the precipitation were showery, the remark is coded **SHRAB05E30SHSNB20E55**. If rain ended and snow began at 0042, the remark would be coded as **RAESNB42**.

3.1.3.13.12   Beginning and Ending of Thunderstorms
The beginning and ending of thunderstorms are coded in the following format: **TS** for thunderstorms, followed by either a **B** for beginning or an **E** for ending and the time of occurrence. No spaces are between the elements. For example, if a thunderstorm began at 0159 and ended at 0230, the remark is coded **TSB0159E30**.

3.1.3.13.13   Thunderstorm Location (Plain Language)
Thunderstorm locations are coded in the following format: the thunderstorm identifier, **TS**, followed by location of the thunderstorm(s) from the station and the direction of movement when known. For example, a thunderstorm southeast of the station and moving toward the northeast is coded **TS SE MOV NE**.

3.1.3.13.14   Hailstone Size (Plain Language)
At designated stations the hailstone size is coded in the following format: the hail identifier **GR**, followed by the size of the largest hailstone. The hailstone size is coded in ¼ inch increments. For example, **GR 1 3/4** would indicate that the largest hailstone were 1 ¾ inches in diameter. If small hail or snow pellets, **GS,** is coded in the body of the report, no hailstone size remark is required.

3.1.3.13.15 Virga (Plain Language)
Virga is coded in the following format: the identifier **VIRGA**, followed by the direction from the station. The direction of the phenomena from the station is optional, e.g., **VIRGA** or **VIRGA SW**.

3.1.3.13.16 Variable Ceiling Height
The variable ceiling height is coded in the following format: the identifier **CIG**, followed by the lowest ceiling height recorded, **V** denoting variability between two values, and ending with the highest ceiling height. A single space follows the identifier with no other spaces between the letter **V** and the lowest/highest ceiling values. For example, **CIG 005V010** would indicate a ceiling is variable between 500 and 1,000 feet.

3.1.3.13.17 Obscurations (Plain Language)
Obscurations, surface-based or aloft, are coded in the following format: the weather identifier causing the obscuration at the surface or aloft followed by the sky cover of the obscuration aloft (FEW, SCT, BKN, OVC) or at the surface (FEW, SCT, BKN), and the height. Surface-based obscurations have a height of **000**. A space separates the weather causing the obscuration and the sky cover; no space is between the sky cover and the height. For example, fog hiding 3/8 to 4/8 of the sky is coded **FG SCT000**; a broken layer at 2,000 feet composed of smoke is coded **FU BKN020**.

3.1.3.13.18 Variable Sky Condition (Plain Language)
Variable sky condition remarks are coded in the following format: the two operationally significant sky conditions (FEW, SCT, BKN, and OVC) separated by spaces and **V** denoting the variability between the two ranges. If several layers have the same condition amount, the layer height of the variable layer is coded. For example, a cloud layer at 1,400 feet varying between broken and overcast is coded **BKN014 V OVC**.

3.1.3.13.19 Significant Cloud Types (Plain Language)
Significant cloud type remarks are coded in all reports.

3.1.3.13.19.1 Cumulonimbus or Cumulonimbus Mammatus
Cumulonimbus or Cumulonimbus Mammatus not associated with thunderstorms are coded in the following format: the cloud type (**CB** or **CBMAM**) followed by the direction from the station and the direction of movement when known. The cloud type, location, direction, and direction of movement entries are separated from each other by a space. For example, a CB up to 10 statute miles west of the station moving toward the east would be coded **CB W MOV E**. If the CB was more than 10 statute miles to the west, the remark is coded **CB DSNT W**.

Cumulonimbus (CB) always evolves from the further development of towering cumulus (TCU). The unusual occurrence of lightning and thunder within or from a CB leads to its popular title, thunderstorm. A thunderstorm usually contains severe or greater turbulence, severe icing, low level wind shear (LLWS), and instrument flight rules (IFR) conditions.

Figure 3-5. Cumulonimbus (CB) Example
CB always evolves from the further development of towering cumulus (TCU). The usual occurrence of lightning and thunder within or from a CB leads to its popular title, thunderstorm. A thunderstorm usually contains severe or greater turbulence, severe icing, low level wind shear (LLWS), and instrument flight rules (IFR) conditions. (Copyright Robert A. Prentice, 1990)

Figure 3-6. Cumulonimbus Mammatus (CBMAM) Example
Cumulonimbus Mammatus (CBMAM) (also called mammatus) appears as hanging protuberances, like pouches, on the undersurface of a cloud. (Copyright Robert A. Prentice, 1993)

3.1.3.13.19.2 Towering Cumulus

Towering cumulus clouds are coded in the following format: the identifier **TCU** followed by the direction from the station. The cloud type and direction entries are separated by a space. For example, a towering cumulus cloud up to 10 statute miles west of the station is coded as **TCU W**.

Figure 3-7. Towering Cumulus (TCU) Example
Towering Cumulus (TCU). TCU is produced by strong convective updrafts and, thus, indicates turbulence. Icing is typically found above the freezing level. TCU often transforms into cumulonimbus (CB). (Copyright Charles A. Doswell, III, 1977)

3.1.3.13.19.3 Altocumulus Castellanus

Altocumulus Castellanus is coded in the following format: the identifier **ACC** followed by direction from the station. The cloud type and direction entries are separated by a space. For example, an altocumulus cloud 5 to 10 statute miles northwest of the station is coded **ACC NW**.

Figure 3-8. Altocumulus Castellanus (ACC) Example
Altocumulus Castellanus (ACC). ACC indicates convective turbulence aloft from the top of the cloud to its base and usually an undetermined height below cloud base as well. (Photo courtesy of National Severe Storms Laboratory/University of Oklahoma)

3.1.3.13.19.4Standing Lenticular or Rotor Clouds

Cirrocumulus (**CCSL**), altocumulus (**ACSL**), stratocumulus (**SCSL**), or rotor clouds are coded in the following format: the cloud type followed by the direction from the station. The cloud type and direction entries are separated by a space. For example, altocumulus standing lenticular clouds observed southwest through west of the station are coded **ACSL SW-W**; an apparent rotor cloud 5 to 10 statute miles northeast of the station is coded **APRNT ROTOR CLD NE**; and cirrocumulus clouds south of the station are coded **CCSL S**.

Figure 3-9. Standing Lenticular and Rotor Clouds Example
From top to bottom: Cirrocumulus standing lenticular (CCSL), altocumulus standing lenticular (ACSL), and rotor cloud. These clouds are characteristic of mountain waves. Mountain waves can occasionally produce violent downslope windstorms. Intense mountain waves can present a significant hazard to aviation by producing severe or even extreme turbulence that extends upward into the lower stratosphere.

3.1.3.13.20   Ceiling Height at Second Location

At designated stations, the ceiling height at a second location is coded in the following format: the identifier **CIG** followed by the measured height of the ceiling and the specific location of the ceilometer(s) at the station. This remark is only generated when the ceiling is lower than that contained in the body of the report. For example, if the ceiling measured by a second sensor located at runway 11 is broken at 200 feet, the remark would be **CIG 002 RWY11**.

3.1.3.13.21 Pressure Rising or Falling Rapidly

At designated stations, the reported pressure is evaluated to determine if a pressure change is occurring. If the pressure is rising or falling at a rate of at least 0.06 inch per hour and the pressure change totals 0.02 inch or more at the time of the observation, a pressure change remark is reported. When the pressure is rising or falling rapidly at the time of observation, the remark **PRESRR** (pressure rising rapidly) or **PRESFR** (pressure falling rapidly) is included in the remarks.

3.1.3.13.22 Sea-Level Pressure

At designated stations, the sea-level pressure is coded in the following format: the identifier **SLP** immediately followed by the sea level pressure in hectopascals. The hundreds and thousands units are not coded and must be inferred. For example, a sea-level pressure of 998.2 hectopascals is coded as **SLP982**. A sea-level pressure of 1013.2 hectopascals would be coded as **SLP132**. For a METAR, if sea-level pressure is not available, it is coded as **SLPNO**.

3.1.3.13.23 Aircraft Mishap (Plain Language)

If a SPECI report is taken to document weather conditions when notified of an aircraft mishap, the remark **ACFT MSHP** is coded in the report but the SPECI not transmitted.

3.1.3.13.24 No SPECI Reports Taken (Plain Language)

At manual stations where SPECIs are not taken, the remark **NOSPECI** is coded to indicate no changes in weather conditions will be reported until the next METAR.

3.1.3.13.25 Snow Increasing Rapidly

At designated stations, the snow increasing rapidly remark is reported, in the NEXT METAR, whenever the snow depth increases by 1 inch or more in the past hour. The remark is coded in the following format: the remark indicator **SNINCR**, the depth increase in the past hour, and the total depth of snow on the ground at the time of the report. The depth of snow increase in the past hour and the total depth on the ground are separated from each other by a solidus, /. For example, a snow depth increase of 2 inches in the past hour with a total depth on the ground of 10 inches is coded **SNINCR 2/10**.

3.1.3.13.26 Other Significant Information (Plain Language)

Agencies may add to a report other information significant to their operations, such as information on fog dispersal operations, runway conditions, **FIRST** or **LAST** reports from station, etc.

3.1.3.14 Additive and Automated Maintenance Data

Additive data groups (Table 3-5) are only reported at designated stations and are primarily used by the NWS for climatological purposes. Most have no direct impact on the aviation community but a few are discussed below.

3.1.3.14.1 Hourly Temperature and Dew Point

At designated stations, the hourly temperature and dew point group are further coded to the tenth of a degree Celsius. For example, a recorded temperature of +2.6°C and dew point of -1.5°C would be coded as **T00261015**.

The format for the coding is as follows:

T	Group indicator
0	Indicates the following number is positive; a **1** would be used if the temperature was reported as negative at the time of observation
026	Temperature disseminated to the nearest 10th and read as 02.6
1	Indicates the following number is negative; a **0** would be used if the number was reported as positive at the time of observation
015	Dew Point disseminated to the nearest 10th and read as 01.5

No spaces are between the entries. For example, a temperature of 2.6°C and dew point of –1.5°C is reported in the body of the report as **03/M01** and the hourly temperature and dew point group as **T00261015**. If the dew point is missing only the temperature is reported; if the temperature is missing the hourly temperature and dew point group is not reported.

3.1.3.14.2 Maintenance Data Groups

The following maintenance data groups, Sensor Status Indicators and the Maintenance Indicator, are only reported from automated stations.

3.1.3.14.2.1 Sensor Status Indicators

Sensor status indicators are reported as indicated below:

- If the Runway Visual Range is missing and would normally be reported, **RVRNO** is coded

- When automated stations are equipped with a present weather identifier and the sensor is not operating, the remark **PWINO** is coded

- When automated stations are equipped with a tipping bucket rain gauge and the sensor is not operating, **PNO** is coded

- When automated stations are equipped with a freezing rain sensor and the sensor is not operating, the remark **FZRANO** is coded

- When automated stations are equipped with a lightning detection system and the sensor is not operating, the remark **TSNO** is coded

- When automated stations are equipped with a secondary visibility sensor and the sensor is not operating, the remark **VISNO LOC** is coded

- When automated stations are equipped with a secondary ceiling height indicator and the sensor is not operating, the remark **CHINO LOC** is coded

3.1.3.14.2.2 Maintenance Indicator

A maintenance indicator, **$**, is coded when an automated system detects maintenance is needed on the system.

3.1.4 METAR/SPECI Examples

METAR PAHL 031836Z AUTO 07009KT 10SM CLR 13/02 A2980 RMK AO1 PNO

GROUP	CODED	TRANSLATION
Type of Report	METAR	Aviation Routine Weather Report
Station Identifier	PAHL	United States Huslia, Alaska
Date and Time of Report	031836Z	3rd day of the month, 1836 UTC
Report Modifier	AUTO	automated observation with no human augmentation
Wind	07009KT	Wind from 070 degrees (the east) at 9 knots (10 mph, 4.6 m/s)
Visibility	10SM	Visibility ten statute miles (16 kilometers)
Runway Visual Range	[omitted]	
Present Weather	[omitted]	There may or may not be significant weather present at this time
Sky Condition	CLR	Sky clear below 12,000 feet AGL
Temperature/Dewpoint	13/02	Temperature 13°C (55°F), dewpoint 2°C (36°F)
Altimeter	A2980	29.80 inches of mercury (1009.2 millibars, 1009.2 hectopascals)
Remarks	RMK	Remarks section designator
Automated, Manual, and Plain Language	A01	Automated station without a precipitation discriminator
Additive and Automated Maintenance Data	PNO	Tipping bucket rain gauge not operating

METAR KNSI 031656Z VRB03KT 5SM HZ SCT007 21/17 A2989 RMK SLP121 T02060172

GROUP	CODED	TRANSLATION
Type of Report	METAR	Aviation Routine Weather Report
Station Identifier	KNSI	United States San Nicolas Island, California
Date and Time of Report	031656Z	3rd day of the month, 1656 UTC
Report Modifier	[omitted]	Either a manual or an augmented observation
Wind	VRB03KT	Wind variable at 3 knots (4 mph, 1.5 m/s)
Visibility	5SM	Visibility five statute miles (8.0 kilometers)
Runway Visual Range	[omitted]	
Present Weather	HZ	Haze
Sky Condition	SCT007	Scattered at 700 feet AGL
Temperature/Dewpoint	21/17	Temperature 21°C (69°F), dewpoint 17°C (63°F)
Altimeter	A2989	29.89 inches of mercury (1012.3 millibars, 1012.3 hectopascals)
Remarks	RMK	Remarks section designator
Automated, Manual, and Plain Language	SLP121	Sea level pressure 1012.1 hectopascals (1012.1 millibars)
Additive and Automated Maintenance Data	T02060172	Temperature 20.6°C (69°F), dewpoint 17.2°C (63°F)

SPECI KCOT 292020Z AUTO 13009KT 3SM TSRA BR SCT011 BKN028 OVC043 23/21 A2991 RMK AO2 PK WND 13029/2000 LTG DSNT ALQDS P0020

GROUP	CODED	TRANSLATION
Type of Report	SPECI	Aviation Selected Special Weather Report
Station Identifier	KCOT	United States Cotulla, Texas
Date and Time of Report	292020Z	29th day of the month, 2020 UTC
Report Modifier	AUTO	Automated observation with no human augmentation
Wind	13009KT	Wind from 130 degrees (the southeast) at 9 knots (10 mph, 4.7 m/s)
Visibility	3SM	Visibility three statute miles (5 kilometers)
Runway Visual Range	[omitted]	
Present Weather	TSRA BR	Thunderstorm, moderate rain, mist
Sky Condition	SCT011 BKN028 OVC043	Scattered at 11,000 feet AGL, Ceiling broken at 2,800 feet AGL, Overcast at 4,300 feet AGL
Temperature/Dewpoint	23/21	Temperature 23°C (73°F), dewpoint 21°C (70°F)
Altimeter	A2991	29.91 inches of mercury (1013.0 millibars, 1013.0 hectopascals)
Remarks	RMK	Remarks section designator
Automated, Manual, and Plain Language	AO2	Automated station with a precipitation discriminator
	PK WND 13029/2000	Peak wind from 130 degrees (the southeast) at 29 knots (33 mph, 14.9 m/s) occurred at 2000 UTC
	LTG DSNT ALQDS	Lightning distant all quadrants
Additive and Automated Maintenance Data	P0020	0.20 inches of precipitation fell in the past hour

METAR KMDW 090153Z 23003KT 1/2SM R31C/4000V4500FT SN FZFG VV002 M04/M05 A3004 RMK AO2 SLP191 SNINCR 1/10 P0000 T10391050

GROUP	CODED	TRANSLATION
Type of Report	METAR	Aviation Routine Weather Report
Station Identifier	KMDW	United States Chicago (Midway), Illinois
Date and Time of Report	090153Z	9th day of the month, 0153 UTC
Report Modifier	[omitted]	Either a manual or an augmented observation
Wind	23003KT	Wind from 230 degrees (the southwest) at 3 knots (3 mph, 1.6 m/s)
Visibility	1/2SM	Visibility one-half statute miles (0.8 kilometers)
Runway Visual Range	R31C/4000V4500FT	Runway 31 center visual range variable between 4,000 and 4,5000 feet
Present Weather	SN FZFG	Snow, freezing fog
Sky Condition	VV002	Indefinite ceiling, vertical visibility 200 feet
Temperature/Dewpoint	M04/M05	Temperature -4°C (25°F), dewpoint -5°C (23°F)
Altimeter	A3004	Altimeter 30.04 inches of mercury (1017.4 hectopascals, 1017.4 millibars)
Remarks	RMK	Remarks section designator
Automated, Manual, and Plain Language	A02	Automated station with a precipitation discriminator
	SLP191	Sea level pressure 1019.1 hectopascals (1019.1 millibars)
	SNINCR 1/10	Snow increasing rapidly, snow depth increase of 1 inch in the past hour, a total depth on the ground of 10 inches
Additive and Automated Maintenance Data	P0000	Less than 1/100 of an inch of precipitation fell in the past hour
	T10391050	Temperature -3.9°C (25°F), dewpoint -5.0°C (23°F)

SPECI KMEM 091826 27013G27KT 240V310 1/2SM R36L/1000VP6000FT +TSRAGR FG FEW002 BKN023 OVC032CB 18/17 A2992 RMK A02 PK WND 31031/1802 WSHFT 1759 TSB22RAB17GRB23 PRESRR FRQ LTGIC W-NW TS W-NW GR 1/2 P0005

GROUP	CODED	TRANSLATION
Type of Report	SPECI	Aviation Selected Special Weather Report
Station Identifier	KMEM	United States Memphis, Tennessee
Date and Time of Report	091826Z	9th day of the month, 1826 UTC
Report Modifier	[omitted]	Either a manual or an augmented observation
Wind	27013G27KT 240V310	Wind from 270 degrees (the west) at 13 knots (15 mph, 6.7 m/s) gusting to 27 knots (31 mph, 13.9 m/s), wind variable between 240 degrees (the west-southwest) and 310 degrees (the northwest)
Visibility	1/2SM	Visibility one-half statute miles (0.8 kilometers)
Runway Visual Range	R36L/1000VP6000FT	Runway 36 left visual range variable between 1,000 and more than 6,000 feet
Present Weather	+TSRAGR FG	Thunderstorm, heavy rain, hail, fog
Sky Condition	FEW002 BKN023 OVC032CB	Few at 200 feet AGL, ceiling broken at 2,300 feet AGL, overcast at 3,200 feet AGL cumulonimbus
Temperature/Dewpoint	18/17	Temperature 18°C (64°F), dewpoint 17°C (63°F)
Altimeter	A2992	29.92 inches of mercury (1013.2 millibars, 1013.2 hectopascals)
Remarks	RMK	Remarks section designator
Automated, Manual, and Plain Language	AO2	Automated station with a precipitation discriminator
	PK WND 31031/1802	Peak wind from 310 degrees (the northwest) at 31 knots (36 mph, 15.9 m/s) occurred at 1802 or 2 minutes past the hour UTC
	WSHFT 1759	Wind shift occurred at 1759 UTC
	TSB22RAB17GRB23	Thunderstorm began at 22 minutes past the hour, rain began at 17 minutes past the hour, hail began at 23 minutes past the hour
	PRESRR	Pressure rising rapidly
	FRQ LTGIC W-NW	Frequent lightning in-cloud west through northwest
	TS W-NW	Thunderstorm west through northwest
	GR1/2	Largest hailstone 1/2 inches in diameter
Additive and Automated Maintenance Data	P0005	0.05 inches of precipitation fell in the past hour

SPECI KMSN 012312Z 13021G26KT 1SM -FZRAPL BR OVC011 00/M02 A2988 RMK AO2 PK WND 14031/2255 SFC VIS 1 1/2 P0005 $

GROUP	CODED	TRANSLATION
Type of Report	SPECI	Aviation Selected Special Weather Report
Station Identifier	KMSN	United States Madison, Wisconsin
Date and Time of Report	012312Z	1st day of the month, 2312 UTC
Report Modifier	[omitted]	Either a manual or an augmented observation
Wind	13021G26KT	Wind from 130 degrees (the southeast) at 21 knots (24 mph, 10.8 m/s) gusting to 26 knots (30 mph, 13.4 m/s)
Visibility	1SM	Visibility one statute mile (1.6 kilometers)
Runway Visual Range	[omitted]	
Present Weather	-FZRAPL BR	Light freezing rain, ice pellets, mist
Sky Condition	OVC011	Ceiling overcast at 1,100 feet AGL
Temperature/Dewpoint	00/M02	Temperature 0°C (32°F), dewpoint -2°C (28°F)
Altimeter	A2988	29.88 inches of mercury (1011.9 millibars, 1011.9 hectopascals)
Remarks	RMK	Remarks section designator
Automated, Manual, and Plain Language	AO2	Automated station with a precipitation discriminator
	PK WND 14031/2255	Peak wind from 140 degrees (the southeast) at 31 knots (36 mph, 15.9 m/s) occurred at 2255 UTC
	SFC VIS 1 1/2	Surface visibility one and on-half statute mile
Additive and Automated Maintenance Data	P0005	0.05 inches of precipitation fell in the past hour
	$	Maintenance is needed on the system

3.2 Pilot Weather Reports (PIREP)

No report is timelier than the one made from the flight deck of aircraft in flight. In fact, aircraft in flight are the only means of observing actual icing and turbulence conditions. Pilots welcome pilot weather reports (PIREPs) as well as pilot weather briefers and forecasters. Pilots should report any observation, good or bad, to assist other pilots with flight planning and preparation. If conditions were forecasted to occur but not encountered, a pilot should also report this inaccuracy. This will help the NWS verify forecast products and create more accurate products for the aviation community. Pilots should help themselves, the aviation public, and the aviation weather forecasters by providing PIREPs.

Pipe Up with a PIREP and help the aviation community operate more safely and effectively.

PIREPs are available in the internet at the Aviation Digital Data Service (ADDS) web page at: http://adds.aviationweather.gov/pireps/

3.2.1 Format

A PIREP is transmitted in a prescribed format (Figure 3-10). Required elements for all PIREPs are: message type, location, time, altitude/flight level, type aircraft, and at least one other element to describe the reported phenomena. The other elements will be omitted when no data is reported with them. All altitude references are mean sea level (MSL) unless otherwise noted. Distance for visibility is in statute miles and all other distances are in nautical miles. Time is reported in Universal Time Coordinated (UTC).

Figure 3-10. Pilot Weather Report (PIREP) Coding Format

3.2.1.1 Message Type (UUA/UA)
The two types of PIREPs are Urgent (**UUA**) and Routine (**UA**).

3.2.1.1.1 Urgent PIREPs
Urgent (**UUA**) PIREPs contain information about:

- Tornadoes, funnel clouds, or <u>waterspout</u>s

- Severe or extreme <u>turbulence</u> (including <u>Clear Air Turbulence</u>)

- <u>Severe icing</u>

- Hail

- Low Level Wind Shear (**LLWS**) within 2,000 feet of the surface. LLWS PIREPS are classified as **UUA** if the pilot reports air speed fluctuations of 10 <u>knot</u>s or more or if air speed fluctuations are not reported but LLWS is reported, the PIREP is classified as **UUA**.

- Volcanic ash clouds

- Any other weather phenomena reported which are considered by the briefer as being hazardous, or potentially hazardous, to flight operations.

3.2.1.1.2 Routine PIREPs
Routine PIREPs are issued after receiving a report from a pilot that does not contain any urgent information as listed in Section 3.2.1.1.1.

3.2.1.2 Location (/OV)
The Location (/**OV**) can be referenced either by geographical position or by route segment.

3.2.1.2.1 Location
Location can be referenced to a VHF NAVAID or an airport, using either the three-letter International Air Transport Association (IATA) or four letter International Civil Aviation Organization (ICAO) identifier. If appropriate, the PIREP is encoded using the identifier, then three digits to define a radial and three digits to define the distance in nautical miles.

Examples:

/OV APE	Over Appleton VOR
/OV KJFK	Over John F. Kennedy International Airport, New York City, NY
/OV APE230010	230 degrees at 10 nautical miles from the Appleton VOR
/OV KJFK107080	107 degrees at 80 nautical miles from John F. Kennedy International Airport, New York City, New York

3.2.1.2.1.1 Route Segment
A PIREP can also be referenced using two or more fixes to describe a route.

Examples:

/OV KSTL-KMKC	From Lambert-Saint Louis International Airport, Missouri to Charles B. Wheeler Downtown Airport, Kansas City, Missouri
/OV KSTL090030-KMKC045015	From 90 degrees at 30 nautical miles from Lambert-Saint Louis International Airport, Missouri to 45 degrees at 15 nautical miles from Charles B. Wheeler Downtown Airport, Kansas City, Missouri

3.2.1.3 Time (/TM)
Time (/**TM**) is the time that the reported phenomenon occurred or was encountered. It is coded in four digits UTC.

Example:

```
/TM 1315 ··············▶ 1315 UTC
```

3.2.1.4 Altitude/Flight Level (/FL)
The Altitude/Flight Level (/**FL**) is the altitude in hundreds of feet MSL where the phenomenon was first encountered. If not known, **UNKN** is entered. If the aircraft was climbing or descending, the appropriate contraction (**DURC** or **DURD**) is entered in the remarks (/**RM**). If the condition was encountered within a layer, the altitude range is entered within the appropriate element that describes the condition.

Examples:

```
/FL085 ··············▶ 8,500 feet MSL
/FL310 ············▶  Flight Level 310
/FLUNKN /RM DURC ··············▶ Flight Level unknown, remarks, during climb
```

3.2.1.5 Aircraft Type (/TP)
Aircraft Type (/**TP**) is entered. If not known, **UNKN** is entered. Icing and <u>turbulence</u> reports always include aircraft type.

Examples:

```
/TP BE20 ··············▶ Super King Air 200
/TP SR22 ··············▶ Cirrus 22
/TP P28R ··············▶ Piper Arrow
/TP UNKN ··············▶ Type unknown
```

3.2.1.6 Sky Condition (/SK)
Sky Condition (/**SK**) group is used to report height of cloud bases, tops, and cloud cover. The height of the base of a layer of clouds is coded in hundreds of feet MSL. The top of a layer is entered in hundreds of feet MSL preceded by the word **-TOP**. If reported as clear above the highest <u>cloud layer</u>, **SKC** is coded following the reported level.

Examples:

```
/BKN040-TOP065 ··············▶ Base of broken layer 4,000 feet MSL, top 6,500 feet MSL
/SK OVC100-TOP110/ SKC ············▶ Base of an overcast layer 10,000 feet MSL, top 11,000 feet MSL, clear above
/SK OVC015-TOP035/OVC230 ·······▶ Base of an overcast layer 1,500 feet MSL, top 3,500 feet MSL, base of an overcast layer 23,000 feet MSL
/SK OVC-TOP085 ··············▶ Overcast layer, top 8,500 feet MSL
```

Cloud cover amount ranges are entered with a hyphen separating the amounts; i.e., **BKN-OVC**.

Examples:

```
/SK SCT-BKN050-TOP100  ┈┈┈► Base of a scattered to broken layer 5,000 feet MSL, top
                            10,000 feet MSL
/SK BKN-OVCUNKN-TOP060/BKN120-TOP150/ SKC ┈┈┈► Base of a broken to overcast
                                               layer unknown, top 6,000 feet
                                               MSL, base of a broken layer
                                               12,000 feet MSL, top 15,000 feet
                                               MSL, clear above
```

Unknown heights are indicated by the contraction **UNKN**.

Example:

```
/SK OVC065-TOPUNKN  ┈┈┈► Base of an overcast layer 6,500 feet MSL, top unknown
```

If a pilot indicates he/she is in the clouds, **IMC** is entered.

Example:

```
/SK OVC065-TOPUNKN /RM IMC ┈┈┈► Base of an overcast layer 6,500 feet MSL, top unknown,
                                remark, in the clouds
```

When more than one layer is reported, layers are separated by a solidus (/).

3.2.1.7 Flight Visibility and Weather (/WX)
Weather conditions encountered by the pilot are reported as follows:

Flight visibility, when reported, is entered first in the **/WX** field. It is coded as **FV** followed by a two-digit visibility value rounded down, if necessary, to the nearest whole statute mile and appended with **SM** (**FV03SM**). If visibility is reported as unrestricted, **FV99SM** is entered.

Flight weather types are entered using one or more of the standard surface weather reporting symbols contained in Table 3-7.

Table 3-7. PIREP Weather Type and Symbols

Type	METAR Code
Drifting / Blowing Snow	DRSN/BLSN
Drifting Dust	DRDU
Drifting Sand	DRSA
Drizzle/Freezing Drizzle	DZ/FZDZ
Dust / Blowing Dust	DU/BLDU
Duststorm	DS
Fog (visibility less than 5/8SM)	FG
Freezing Fog	FZFG
Freezing Rain	FZRA
Funnel Cloud	FC
Hail (Approximately ¼-inch diameter or more)	GR
Hail Shower	SHGR
Haze	HZ
Ice Crystals	IC
Ice Pellets/Showers	PL/SHPL
Mist (visibility great than or equal to 5/8SM)	BR
Patchy Fog	BCFG
Patchy Fog on part of airport	PRFG
Rain/Showers	RA/SHRA
Sand/Blowing Sand	SA/BLSA
Sandstorms	SS
Shallow Fog	MIFG
Small Hail/Snow Pellet Showers	SHGS
Small Hail/Snow Pellets	GS
Smoke	FU
Snow Grains	SG
Snow / Showers	SN/SHSN
Spray	PY
Squalls	SQ
Thunderstorm	TS
Tornado/Waterspout	+FC
Unknown Precipitation	UP
Volcanic Ash	VA
Well developed Dust/Sand Whirls	PO

Intensity modifiers for precipitation (- for light, no qualifier for moderate, and + for heavy) indicates precipitation type, except ice crystals and hail, including those associated with a thunderstorm and those of a showery nature.

Intensity modifiers for obscurations are ascribed as moderate or heavy (+) for dust and sandstorms only. No intensity modifiers are used for blowing dust, blowing sand, or blowing snow.

Example:

`/WX FV01SM +DS000-TOP083/SKC /RM DURC` ········► Flight visibility 1 statute mile, base heavy duststorm layer at the surface, top 8,300 feet MSL, clear above, remarks, during climb

When more than one form of precipitation is combined in the report, the dominant type is reported first.

Examples:

`/WX FV00SM +TSRAGR` ········► Flight visibility zero statute miles, thunderstorm, heavy rain, hail

`/WX FV02SM BRHZ000-TOP083` ··········► Flight visibility 2 statute miles, base of a <u>haze</u> and mist layer at the surface, top 8,300 feet MSL

If a funnel cloud is reported, it is coded as **FC** following **/WX** group and is spelled out as **Funnel Cloud** after **/RM** group. If a tornado or <u>waterspout</u> is reported, it is coded **+FC** following **/WX** group and **TORNADO** or **WATERSPOUT** is spelled out after the **/RM** group.

Examples:

`/WX FC /RM FUNNEL CLOUD` ············► Funnel cloud, remarks, funnel cloud

`/WX +FC /RM TORNADO` ············► Tornado, remark, tornado

When the size of hail is stated, it is coded in 1/4-inch increments in remarks (**/RM**) group.

The proximity qualifier **VC** (vicinity) is only used with **TS**, **FG**, **FC**, **+FC**, **SH**, **PO**, **BLDU**, **BLSA**, and **BLSN**.

Example:

`/WX FV02SM BLDU000-TOP083 VC W` ··········► Flight visibility 2 statute miles, base of a blowing dust layer at the surface, top 8,300 feet MSL in the vicinity, west

When more than one type of weather is reported, they are reported in the following order:

- **TORNADO**, **WATERSPOUT**, or **FUNNEL CLOUD**
- Thunderstorm with or without associated precipitation
- Weather phenomena in order of decreasing predominance.

No more than three groups are used in a single PIREP.

Weather layers are entered with the base and/or top of the layer when reported. The same format as in the sky condition (**/SK**) group is used.

Example:

`/WX FU002-TOP030` ·······► Base of a smoke layer, 200 feet MSL, top 3,000 feet MSL

3.2.1.8 Air Temperature (/TA)

Outside air temperature (/TA) is reported using two digits in degrees Celsius. Negative temperatures is prefixed with an **M**; e.g., **/TA 08** or **/TA M08**.

3.2.1.9 Wind Direction and Speed (/WV)

Wind direction and speed is encoded using three digits to indicate wind direction (magnetic) and two or three digits to indicate reported wind speed. When the reported speed is less than 10 knots, a leading zero is used. The wind group will always have **KT** appended to represent the units in knots.

Examples:

```
/WV 02009KT  ········▸ Wind 20 degrees (magnetic) at 9 knots
/WV 28057KT  ········▸ Wind 280 degrees (magnetic) at 57 knots
/WV 350102KT ·······▸ Wind 350 degrees (magnetic) at 102 knots
```

3.2.1.10 Turbulence (/TB)

Turbulence intensity, type, and altitude are reported after wind direction and speed.

Duration (**INTMT**, **OCNL**, or **CONS**) is coded first (if reported by the pilot)) followed by intensity (**LGT**, **MOD**, **SEV**, or **EXTRM**). Range or variation of intensity is separated with a hyphen; e.g., MOD-SEV. If turbulence was forecasted, but not encountered, **NEG** is entered.

Type is coded second. **CAT** (Clear Air Turbulence) or **CHOP** is entered if reported by the pilot. High-level turbulence (normally above 15,000 feet AGL) not associated with clouds (including thunderstorms) is reported as CAT.

Altitude is reported (last) only if it differs from value reported in the Altitude/Flight Level (/**FL**) group. When a layer of turbulence is reported, height values are separated with a hyphen. If lower or upper limits are not defined, **BLO** or **ABV** is used.

Examples:

```
/TB LGT ·····································▸ Light turbulence
/TB LGT 040 ·····························▸ Light turbulence at 4,000 feet MSL
/TB OCNL MOD-SEV BLO 080 ·······▸ Occasional moderate to severe turbulence below 8,000
                                       feet MSL
/TB MOD-SEV CAT 350 ······▸ Moderate to severe clear air turbulence at 35,000 feet MSL
/TB NEG 120-180 ················▸ Negative turbulence between 12,000 to 18,000 feet MSL
/TB CONS MOD CHOP 220/NEG 230-280 ·······▸ Continuous moderate chop at 22,000 feet
                                              MSL, negative turbulence between 23,000
                                              to 28,000 feet MSL
/TB MOD CAT ABV 290 ·······▸ Moderate clear air turbulence above 29,000 feet MSL
```

Turbulence reports should include location, altitude, or range of altitudes, and aircraft type, and, when reported, whether in clouds or clear air. The pilot determines the degree of turbulence, intensity, and duration (occasional, intermittent, and continuous). The report should be obtained and disseminated, when possible, in conformance with the U.S. Standard Turbulence Criteria Table 3-8.

Table 3-8. PIREP Turbulence Reporting Criteria

Intensity	Aircraft Reaction	Reaction Inside Aircraft	Reporting Term-Definition
Light	Turbulence that momentarily causes slight, erratic changes in altitude and/or attitude (pitch, roll, yaw). Report as **Light Turbulence;**[1] or Turbulence that causes slight, rapid and somewhat rhythmic bumpiness without appreciable changes in altitude or attitude. Report as **Light Chop.**	Occupants may feel a slight strain against belts or shoulder straps. Unsecured objects may be displaced slightly. Food service may be conducted and little or no difficulty is encountered in walking.	Occasional – Less than 1/3 of the time. Intermittent-1/3 to 2/3 Continuous-More than 2/3
Moderate	Turbulence that is similar to Light Turbulence but of greater intensity. Changes in altitude and/or attitude occur but the aircraft remains in positive control at all times. It usually causes variations in indicated airspeed. Report as **Moderate Turbulence;**[1] or Turbulence that is similar to Light Chop but of greater intensity. It causes rapid bumps or jolts without appreciable changes in aircraft or attitude. Report as **Moderate Chop.**[1]	Occupants feel definite strains against seat belts or shoulder straps. Unsecured objects are dislodged. Food service and walking are difficult.	NOTE 1. Pilots should report location(s), time (UTC), intensity, weather in or near clouds, altitude, type of aircraft and, when applicable, duration of turbulence. 2. Duration may be based on time between two locations or over a single location. All locations should be readily identifiable. **EXAMPLES:** Over Omaha. 1232Z, Moderate Turbulence, in cloud, flight Level 310, B737. b. From 50 miles south of Albuquerque to 30 miles north of Phoenix, 1210Z to 1250Z, occasional Moderate Chop, Flight Level 330, DC8.
Severe	Turbulence that causes large, abrupt changes in altitude and/or attitude. It usually causes large variations in indicated airspeed. Aircraft may be momentarily out of control. Report as **Severe Turbulence.**[1]	Occupants are forced violently against seat belts or shoulder straps. Unsecured objects are tossed about. Food service and walking are impossible.	
Extreme	Turbulence in which the aircraft is violently tossed about and is practically impossible to control. It may cause structural damage. Report as **Extreme Turbulence.**[1]		

[1] High level turbulence (normally above 15,000 feet ASL) not associated with clouds, including thunderstorms, should be reported as CAT (clear air turbulence) preceded by the appropriate intensity, or light or moderate chop.

3.2.1.11 Icing (/IC)

Icing intensity, type and altitude is reported after turbulence.

Intensity is coded first using contractions **TRACE**, **LGT** (light), **MOD** (moderate), or **SEV** severe). Reports of a range or variation of intensity is separated with a hyphen. If icing was forecast but not encountered, **NEG** (negative) is coded.

The following table classifies icing intensity according to its operational effects on aircraft.

Table 3-9. Icing Intensities, Contractions, and Airframe Ice Accumulation

Intensity	Contraction	Airframe Ice Accumulation
Trace	TRACE	Ice becomes perceptible. Rate of accumulation slightly greater than rate of sublimation. It is not hazardous even without the use of deicing/anti-icing equipment unless encountered for an extended period of time (over 1 hour).
Light	LGT	The rate of accumulation may create a problem if flight is prolonged in this environment (over 1 hour). Occasional use of deicing/anti-icing equipment removes/prevents accumulation. It does not present a problem if the deicing/anti-icing equipment is used.
Moderate	MOD	The rate of accumulation is such that even short encounters become potentially hazardous and use of deicing/anti-icing equipment or diversion is necessary.
Severe	SEV	The rate of accumulation is such that deicing/anti-icing equipment fails to reduce or control the hazard. Immediate diversion is necessary.

Icing type is reported second. Reportable types are **RIME**, **CLR** (clear), or **MX** (mixed).

The following table classifies icing type according to it description.

Table 3-10. Icing Types, Contractions, and Descriptions

Icing Type	Contraction	Description
Rime	RM	Rough, milky, opaque ice formed by the instantaneous freezing of small super-cooled water droplets.
Clear	CLR	A glossy, clear or translucent ice formed by the relatively slow freezing of large super-cooled water droplets.
Mixed	MX	A combination of both rime and clear.

The reported icing/altitude is coded (last) only if different from the value reported in the altitude/flight level (**/FL**) group. A hyphen is used to separate reported layers of icing. **ABV** (above) or **BLO** (below) is coded when a layer is not defined.

Pilot reports of icing should also include location (**/OV**), type aircraft (**/TP**), and air temperature (**/TA**).

Examples:

```
/IC LGT-MOD MX 085   →  Light to moderate mixed icing, 8,500 feet MSL
/IC LGT RIME         →  Light rime icing
/IC MOD RIME BLO 095 →  Moderate rime icing below 9,500 feet MSL
/IC SEV CLR 035-062  →  Severe clear icing 3,500 to 6,200 feet MSL
```

3.2.1.12 Remarks (/RM)
The remarks (**/RM**) group is used to report a phenomenon which is considered important but does not fit in any of the other groups. This includes, but is not limited to, low-level wind shear

(**LLWS**) reports, thunderstorm lines, coverage and movement, size of hail (1/4-inch increments), lightning, clouds observed but not encountered, geographical or local description of where the phenomenon occurred, and contrails. Hazardous weather is reported first. LLWS is described to the extent possible.

3.2.1.12.1 Wind Shear

Ten <u>knot</u>s or more fluctuations in wind speed (+/- 10KTS), within 2,000 feet of the surface, require an Urgent (**UUA**) pilot report. When Low Level Wind Shear is entered in a pilot report, **LLWS** is entered as the first remark in the remarks (**/RM**) group.

Example:

`/RM LLWS +/-15 KT SFC-008 DURC RY22 JFK` ·······➤ Remarks, Low Level Wind Shear, air speed fluctuations of plus or minus 15 <u>knot</u>s, surface to 800 feet during climb, runway 22, John F. Kennedy International Airport, New York.

3.2.1.12.2 FUNNEL CLOUD, TORNADO, and WATERSPOUT

Funnel cloud, tornado, and <u>waterspout</u> are entered with the direction of movement when reported.

Example:

`/RM TORNADO W MOV E` ·······➤ Remarks, tornado west moving east

3.2.1.12.3 Thunderstorm

Thunderstorm coverage is coded as **ISOL** (isolated), **FEW** (few), **SCT** (scattered), **NMRS** (numerous) followed by description as **LN** (line), **BKN LN** (broken line), **SLD LN** (solid line) when reported. This is followed with **TS**, the location and movement, and the type of lightning when reported.

Example:

`/RM NMRS TS S MOV E GR1/2` ·······➤ Remarks, numerous thunderstorms south moving east, hail 1/2–inch in diameter

3.2.1.12.4 Lightning

Lightning frequency is coded as **OCNL** (occasional) or **FRQ** (frequent), followed by type as **LTGIC** (lightning in cloud), **LTGCC** (lightning cloud to cloud), **LTGCG** (lightning cloud to ground), **LTGCA** (lightning cloud to air), or combinations, when reported.

Example:

`/RM OCNL LTGICCG` ·········➤ Remarks, occasional lighting in cloud, cloud to ground

3.2.1.12.5 Electrical Discharge

For an electrical discharge, **DISCHARGE** is coded followed by the altitude.

Example:

`/RM DISCHARGE 120` ········▶ Remarks, discharge, 12,000 feet MSL

3.2.1.12.6 Clouds
Remarks are used when clouds can be seen but were not encountered and reported in the sky condition group (**/SK**)

Examples:

`/RM CB E MOV N` ·········▶ Remarks, cumulonimbus east moving north
`/RM OVC BLO` ···············▶ Remarks, overcast below

3.2.1.12.7 Plain Language
If specific phraseology is not adequate, plain language is used to describe the phenomena or local geographic locations. Remarks that do not fit in other groups like **DURC** (during climb), **DURD** (during descent), **RCA** (reach cruising altitude), **TOP**, **TOC** (top of climb), or **CONTRAILS** are included.

Examples:

`/RM BUMPY VERY ROUGH RIDE`
`/RM CONTRAILS`
`/UA/OV BIS270030/TM 1445/FL060/TP CVLT/TB LGT /RM DONNER SUMMIT PASS`

3.2.1.12.8 Volcanic Eruptions
Volcanic ash alone is an Urgent PIREP. A report of volcanic activity includes as much information as possible including the name of the mountain, ash cloud and movement, height of the top and bottom of the ash, etc., is included. If the report is received from a source other than a pilot, Aircraft **UNKN**, Flight Level **UNKN**, and **/RM UNOFFICIAL** is entered.

Example:

`/UUA/OV ANC240075/TM 2110/FL370/TP DC10/WX VA/RM VOLCANIC ERUPTION`
`2008Z MT AUGUSTINE ASH 40S MOV SSE`

Urgent Pilot Weather Report, 240 degrees at 75 nautical miles from Anchorage International Airport, Alaska, 2110 UTC, flight level 370, a DC10 reported volcanic ash, remarks, volcanic eruption occurred at 2008 UTC Mount Augustine, ash 40 nautical miles south moving south-southeast.

3.2.1.12.9 SKYSPOTTER
The SKYSPOTTER program is a result of a recommendation from the Safer Skies FAA/INDUSTRY Joint Safety Analysis and Implementation Teams. The term **SKYSPOTTER** indicates a pilot has received specialized training in observing and reporting in-flight weather phenomenon, pilot weather reports, or PIREPs.

When a PIREP is received from a pilot identifying themselves as a **SKYSPOTTER** aircraft, the additional comment "**/AWC**" is added at the end of the remarks section of the PIREP.

Example:

PIREP TEXT/RM REMARKS/AWC

3.2.2 PIREP Examples

UUA /OV ORD/TM 1235/FLUNKN/TP B727/TB MOD/RM LLWS +/- 20KT BLW 003
DURD RWY27L

Urgent Pilot Weather Report, over Chicago O'Hare Airport, Illinois, 1235 UTC, flight level
unknown, from a Boeing 727, moderate turbulence, remarks, Low Level Wind Shear, airspeed
fluctuations of plus or minus 20 knots below 300 feet AGL during descent, runway 27 left.

UUA /OV BAM260045/TM 2225/FL180/TP BE20/TB SEV/RM BROKE ALL THE
BOTTLES IN THE BAR

Urgent Pilot Weather Report, 260 degrees at 45 nautical miles from Hazen VOR, Nevada, 2225
UTC, 18,000 feet MSL, Beech Super King Air 200, severe turbulence, remarks, broke all the
bottles in the bar.

UA /OV KMRB-KPIT/TM 1600/FL100/TP BE55/SK BKN024-TOP032/BKN-OVC043-
TOPUNKN /TA M12/IC LGT-MOD RIME 055-080

Pilot Weather Report, Martinsburg, West Virginia to Pittsburgh International Airport,
Pennsylvania, 1600 UTC, 10,000 feet MSL, Beechcraft Baron, base of a broken layer 2,400 feet
MSL, top 3,200 feet MSL, base of a broken to overcast layer 4,300 feet MSL, top unknown,
temperature minus 12, light to moderate rime ice between 5,500 to 8,000 feet MSL.

UA /OV IRW090064/TM 1522/FL080/TP C172/SK SCT090-TOPUNKN/WX FV05SM
HZ/TA M04/WV 24040KT/TB LGT/RM IN CLR

Pilot Weather Report, 90 degrees and 64 nautical miles from Will Rogers VORTAC, Oklahoma
City, Oklahoma, 1522 UTC, 8,000 feet MSL, Cessna 172, base of a scattered layer 9,000 feet
MSL, top unknown, flight visibility 5 statute miles, haze, temperature minus 4, wind 240 degrees
at 40 knots, light turbulence, remarks, in clear.

```
UA /OV KLIT-KFSM/TM 0310/FL100/TP BE36/SK SCT070-TOP110/TA M03/WV
25015KT
```

Pilot Weather Report, between Little Rock and Fort Smith, Arkansas, 0310 UTC at 10,000 feet MSL. Beech 36, base of a scattered layer at 7,000 feet MSL, top 11,000 feet MSL, temperature minus 3, wind 250 degrees at 15 knots.

```
UA /OV KAEG/TM 1845/FL UNKN/TP UNKN /RM TIJERAS PASS CLSD DUE TO FG
AND LOW CLDS UNA VFR RTN KAEG.
```

Pilot Weather Report, over Double Eagle II Airport, Albuquerque, New Mexico, 1845 UTC, remarks, Tijeras Pass closed due to fog and low clouds, unable to fly VFR, returned to Double Eagle II Airport.

```
UA /OV ENA14520/TM 2200/FL310/TP B737/TB MOD CAT 350-390.
```

Pilot Weather Report, 145 degrees at 20 nautical miles from Kenai, Alaska, at 2200 UTC, at flight level 310, Boeing 737, moderate clear air turbulence between 35,000 and 39,000 feet MSL.

3.3 Radar Weather Report (SD/ROB)

A Radar Weather Report (SD/ROB) contains information about precipitation observed by weather radar. This is a textual product derived from the WSR-88D NEXRAD radar without human intervention. *The resolution of this textual product is very coarse, up to 80 minutes old, and should only be used if no other radar information is available.*

Figure 3-11. Radar Weather Report (SD/ROB) Coding Format

3.3.1 Format
Reports are transmitted hourly from WSR-88D Weather Radar sites (see figure 3-15). The SD/ROB format is presented in Figure 3-8.

3.3.1.1 Location Identifier
The location identifier is reported as the three-letter International Air Transport Association (IATA) code.

Example:

TLX ┄┄┄► Oklahoma City Twin Lakes, Oklahoma

3.3.1.2 Time
The time of the observation is reported in four-digits Universal Time Coordinated (UTC).

Example:

1935 ┄┄┄► 1935 UTC

3.3.1.3 Configuration
Three types of configurations can be reported: **CELL**, **LN** (line), and **AREA**. Multiple configurations can be reported within one Weather Radar Report.

A **CELL** is a single, isolated convective echo.

A **LN** (line) is a convective echo that meets the following criteria:

- Contains heavy or greater intensity precipitation
- Is at least 30 miles long
- Length is at least four times greater than width
- Contains at least 25 percent coverage

An **AREA** is a group of echoes of similar type, not classified as a line.

Figure 3-12 illustrates the three configurations that can be reported in a Weather Radar Report.

Figure 3-12. Radar Weather Report (SD/ROB) Configurations

3.3.1.4 Coverage
Coverage of precipitation is coded in single digits representing tenths of coverage.

For echo configurations containing multiple precipitation types, coverage is coded for each type. Total coverage is obtained by adding the individual values.

Examples:

2TRW+4R ········► 2/10 coverage TRW+, 4/10 coverage R, 6/10 total coverage

3R6S– ············► 3/10 coverage R, 6/10 coverage S-, 9/10 total coverage

3.3.1.5 Precipitation Type
Precipitation type is determined by computer model.

Reportable types are:

- Rain (**R**)
- Rain shower (**RW**)
- Snow (**S**)
- Snow shower (**SW**)
- Thunderstorm (**T**)

Multiple precipitation types can be reported within a configuration.

3.3.1.6 Precipitation Intensity

Four precipitation intensities can be reported as shown in table 3-11.

Table 3-11. SD/ROB Reportable Intensities

Symbol	Intensity	dBZ
-	Light	0-29
(no entry)	Moderate	30-40
+	Heavy	41-45
++	Heavy	46-49
X	Extreme	50-56
XX	Extreme	57 or more

Examples:

7R- → 7/10 coverage of light rain

3R-6S → 3/10 coverage light rain, 6/10 coverage moderate snow, 9/10 total coverage

2TRWX4R- → 2/10 coverage thunderstorms, extreme rain showers, 4/10 coverage light rain, 6/10 total coverage

3.3.1.7 Location

An area is coded with two end points and a width that defines a rectangle. Each end point is defined by an azimuth and range (AZRAN).

A line is also coded with two end points and a width that defines a rectangle. Each end point is defined by an AZRAN.

A cell is coded as a single point with a diameter (**D**). This point is defined by an AZRAN.

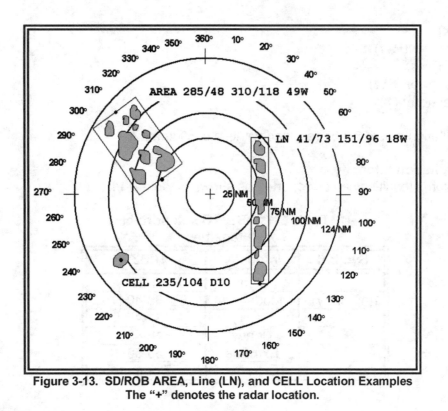

Figure 3-13. SD/ROB AREA, Line (LN), and CELL Location Examples
The "+" denotes the radar location.

3.3.1.8 Maximum Top

Maximum top (**MT** or **MTS**) denotes the altitude and location of the top of the highest precipitation echo.

All radar heights are estimates and assume <u>standard atmosphere</u> conditions and, thus, standard radar wave propagation. **MT** denotes radar data alone was used to determine the maximum top. **MTS** denotes both satellite and radar data were used to estimate the maximum top.

The maximum top is coded as a three-digit number in hundreds of feet MSL. Location is coded as an azimuth and range (AZRAN) relative to the radar site. If <u>echo top</u>s are uniform in altitude, the letter "U" precedes the altitude with no AZRAN provided.

Examples:

MT 150 19/32 ⸱⸱⸱⸱⸱⸱⸱⸱⸱⸱⸱⸱➤ Maximum top 15,000 feet MSL at 19 degrees, 32 nautical miles
MT 340 182/98 ⸱⸱⸱⸱⸱⸱⸱⸱Maximum top 34,000 feet MSL at 182 degrees, 98 nautical miles
MTS 520 5/121 ⸱⸱⸱⸱⸱⸱⸱Maximum top with satellite data 52,000 feet MSL at 5 degrees, 121
nautical miles

3.3.1.9 Cell Movement

Cell movement is the average motion of all the cells within a configuration. It is coded in the following format: the cell movement group is indicated by the letter **C** followed by four digits. The first two digits represent the direction the cell(s) is (are) moving from in tens of degrees referenced to true north. The last two digits represent the speed of the configuration in <u>knots</u>.

Movement of areas and lines is not coded.

Examples:

C0209 ················► Cell movement from 20 degrees at 9 <u>knot</u>s
C2043 ················► Cell movement from 200 degrees at 43 <u>knot</u>s
C3616 ················► Cell movement from 360 degrees at 16 <u>knot</u>s

3.3.1.10 Remarks
Remarks contain information about the radar's status and type of report. Currently, all weather radar reports are automated.

Table 3-12. Weather Radar Report Remarks and Meaning

REMARK	MEANING
PPINE	Equipment normal and operating, but no echoes observed
PPINA	Observation not available
PPIOM	Radar out for maintenance
AUTO	Report derived from an automated weather radar

3.3.1.11 Digital Section
The information contained in the digital section is used primarily to create the Radar Summary Chart. However, with the proper grid overlay chart for the corresponding radar site, the digital section code can also be used to determine precipitation location and intensity. (See Figure 3-14 for an example of a digital code plotted from the Oklahoma City, Oklahoma, Weather Radar Report.)

Each digit represents the maximum precipitation intensity found within a grid box as determined by the weather radar. Light intensity is denoted by a **1**, **2** is for moderate, **3** and **4** is for heavy, **5** and **6** is used for extreme precipitation. These digits were once commonly referred to as VIP levels because precipitation intensity, and therefore the digit, was derived using a video integrator processor (VIP). Whereas the old WSR-57 and WSR-74 weather radar video integrator processors displayed six data levels, the WSR-88D weather radar displays sixteen data levels. The data levels are still converted back to six levels for use in the Radar Weather Report. To avoid confusion, the term VIP should no longer be used to describe precipitation intensity. For example, if a grid box is coded with the number 2, it would be described as "moderate" precipitation," not "VIP 2" or "level 2" precipitation.

A grid box is identified by two letters. The first represents the row in which the box is found and the second letter represents the column. For example **MO1** identifies the box located in row M and column O as containing light precipitation. A code of **MO1234** indicates precipitation in four consecutive boxes in the same row. Working from left to right: box MO = 1, box MP = 2, MQ = 3, and box MR = 4.

A Weather Radar Report contains data about precipitation echoes only. It does not contain information about important non-precipitation echoes such as clouds, fronts, dust, etc., which can be detected by weather radar under certain circumstances.

**Figure 3-14. SD/ROB Digital Section Information Plotted on a PPI Grid Overlay Example
(See Table 3-11 for Intensity Level Codes 1 through 6.)**

3.3.2 Examples

```
GRB 1135 AREA 4TRW+ 9/101 133/76 54W MT 310 45/47 C2428 AUTO
```

Green Bay, Wisconsin, automated Radar Weather Report at 1135 UTC. An area of echoes, 4/10 coverage, contained thunderstorms and heavy rain showers. Area is defined by points (referenced from GRB radar site) at 9 degrees, 101 nautical miles and 133 degrees, 76 nautical miles. These points, plotted on a map and connected with a straight line, define the center line of the echo pattern. The width of the area was 54 nautical miles; i.e., 27 nautical miles either side of the center line. Maximum top was 31,000 feet MSL located at 45 degrees and 47 nautical miles from Green Bay. Cell movement was from 240 degrees at 28 knots.

```
ICT 1935 LN 9TRWX 274/84 216/93 22W MTS 440 260/48 C2131 AUTO
```

Wichita, Kansas, automated Radar Weather Report at 1935 UTC. A line of echoes, 9/10 coverage, contained thunderstorm with intense rain showers. The center of the line extended from 274 degrees, 84 nautical miles to 216 degrees, 93 nautical miles. The line was 22 nautical miles wide.

To display graphically, plot the center points on a map and connect the points with a straight line; then plot the width. Since the thunderstorm line was 22 nautical miles wide, it extended 11 nautical miles either side of your plotted line.

The maximum top is 44,000 feet MSL at 260 degrees, 48 nautical miles from Wichita. Cell movement was from 210 degrees at 31 knots.

```
GGW 1135 AREA 3S- 95/129 154/81 34W MT 100 130/49 0805 AUTO
```

Glasgow, Montana, automated Radar Weather Report at 1135 UTC. An area, 3/10 coverage, of light snow. The area's centerline extended from points at 95 degrees, 129 nautical miles to 154 degrees, 81 nautical miles from Glasgow. The area was 34 nautical miles wide. The maximum top was 10,000 feet MSL, at 130 degrees, 49 nautical miles from Glasgow. Cell movement was from 80 degrees at 5 knots.

```
JGX 2235 AREA 2TRW++6R- 67/130 308/45 106W MT 380 66/54 C2038 AUTO
```

Atlanta, Georgia, automated Radar Weather Report at 2235 UTC. An area of echoes, total coverage 8/10, with 2/10 of thunderstorms with very heavy rain showers and 6/10 coverage of light rain (This suggests that the thunderstorms were embedded in an area of light rain). The area was 53 nautical miles either side of the line defined by the two points, 67 degrees, 130 nautical miles and 308 degrees, 45 nautical miles from Atlanta. Maximum top was at 38,000 feet and was located on the 66 degree radial of JGX at 54 nautical miles. Cell movement was from 200 degrees at 38 knots.

```
HKM 0235 CELL TRW+ 19/22 D5 MT 270 18/23 C0414 AUTO
```

Kohala, Hawaii, automated Radar Weather Report at 0235 UTC. A cell, containing thunderstorms with very heavy rain showers, 5 miles in diameter, was located 19 degrees, 22 nautical miles from Kohala. Maximum top was 27,000 feet located at 18 degrees, 23 nautical miles from Kohala. Movement was from 40 degrees at 14 knots.

```
TLX 0435 PPINE AUTO
```

Oklahoma City, Oklahoma, automated Radar Weather Report at 0435 UTC, detected no echoes.

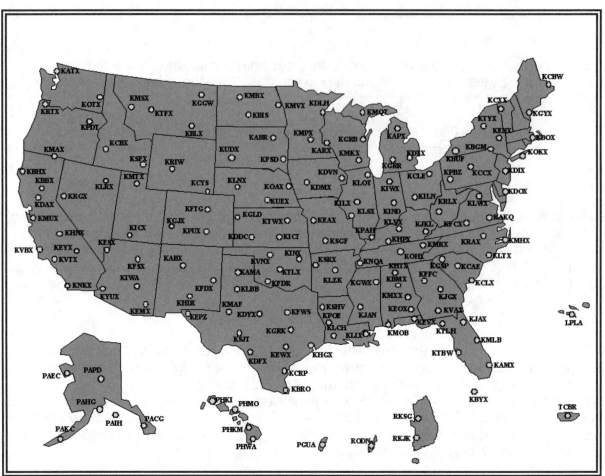

Figure 3-15. WSR-88D Weather Radar Network Sites

4 RADAR AND SATELLITE IMAGERY

4.1 Radar

4.1.1 Description
Radar images are graphical displays of precipitation and non-precipitation targets detected by weather radar. WSR-88D Doppler radar displays these targets on a variety of products which can be found on the internet on the National Weather Service (NWS) Doppler Radar Images web site at: http://radar.weather.gov/ridge/

4.1.2 Modes of Operation
The WSR-88D Doppler radar has **two** operational modes, **Clear Air** and **Precipitation**.

4.1.2.1 Clear Air Mode
In Clear Air Mode, the radar is in its most sensitive operation. This mode has the slowest antenna rotation rate which permits the radar to sample the atmosphere longer. This slower sampling increases the radar's sensitivity and ability to detect smaller objects in the atmosphere. The term "clear air" does not imply "no-precipitation" mode. Even in Clear Air Mode, the WSR-88D can detect light, stratiform precipitation (e.g., snow) due to the increased sensitivity.

Many of the radar returns in Clear Air Mode are airborne dust and particulate matter. The WSR-88D images are updated every 10 minutes when operating in this mode.

4.1.2.2 Precipitation Mode
Precipitation targets typically provide stronger return signals to the radar than non-precipitation targets. Therefore, the WSR-88D is operated in Precipitation Mode when precipitation is present although some non-precipitation echoes can still be detected in this operating mode.

The faster rotation of the WSR-88D in Precipitation Mode allows images to update at a faster rate approximately every 4 to 6 minutes.

4.1.3 Echo Intensities

Figure 4-1. WSR-88D Weather Radar Echo Intensity Legend

The colors on radar images represent different echo reflectivities (intensities) measured in dBZ (decibels of Z). The dBZ values increase based on the strength of the return signal from targets in the atmosphere. Each reflectivity image includes a color scale that represents a correlation between reflectivity value and color on the radar image. Figure 4-1 depicts these correlations. The scale ranges from -30 to greater than 75 dBZ. The scale also include **ND** correlated to black which indicates no data was measured.

Reflectivity is correlated to intensity of precipitation. For example, in Precipitation Mode, when the dBZ value reaches 15, light precipitation is present. The higher the indicated reflectivity value, the higher the rainfall rate. The interpretation of reflectivity values is the same for both Clear Air and Precipitation Modes.

Reflectivity is also correlated with intensity terminology (phraseology) for air traffic control purposes. Table 4-1 defines this correlation.

Table 4-1. WSR-88D Weather Radar Precipitation Intensity Terminology

Reflectivity (dBZ) Ranges	Weather Radar Echo Intensity Terminology
<30 dBZ	Light
30-40 dBZ	Moderate
>40-50 dBZ	Heavy
50+ dBZ	Extreme

Values below 15 dBZ are typically associated with clouds. However, they may also be caused by atmospheric particulate matter such as dust, insects, pollen, or other phenomena. The scale

cannot be used to determine the intensity of snowfall. However, snowfall rates generally increase with increasing reflectivity.

4.1.4 Products

The NWS produces numerous radar products of interest to the aviation community.   The next section will discuss Base Reflectivity and Composite Reflectivity both available through National Weather Service (NWS) Doppler Radar Images web site at: http://radar.weather.gov/ridge/

4.1.4.1 Base Reflectivity

Base Reflectivity is a display of both the location and intensity of reflectivity data. Base Reflectivity images encompass several different elevation angles (tilts) of the antenna. The Base Reflectivity image currently available on the ADDS website begins at the lowest tilt angle (0.5°), more specifically 0.5° above the horizon.

Both a short range (Figure 4-2) and long range (Figure 4-3) image is available from the 0.5° Base Reflectivity product. The maximum range of the short range Base Reflectivity product is 124 NM from the radar location. This view will not display echoes farther than 124 NM from the radar site, although precipitation may be occurring at these greater distances. Other options to view precipitation beyond 124 NM from the radar site include selecting the long-range view which increases coverage out to 248 NM, selecting adjacent radars, or viewing a radar mosaic.

Figure 4-2. WSR-88D Weather Radar Short Range (124 NM) Base Reflectivity Product Example

Figure 4-3. WSR-88D Weather Radar Long Range (248 NM) Base Reflectivity Product Example

4.1.4.1.1 Base Reflectivity Use

The <u>Base Reflectivity</u> product can be used to determine the location of precipitation and non-precipitation echoes, the intensity of liquid precipitation, and the general movement of precipitation when animating the image.

If the echo is precipitation, the product can be used to determine if it is convective or <u>stratiform</u> in nature. <u>Stratiform</u> precipitation (Figure 4-4) has the following characteristics:

- Widespread in areal coverage,
- Weak reflectivity gradients,
- Precipitation intensities are generally light or moderate (39 dBZ or less),
    - o Occasionally, precipitation intensities can be stronger
- Echo patterns change slowly when animating the image.

Figure 4-4. WSR-88D Weather Radar Stratiform Precipitation on the 0.5°Base Reflectivity Product Example

Hazards associated with <u>stratiform</u> precipitation include possible widespread icing above the <u>freezing level</u>, low <u>ceiling</u>s and reduced visibilities.

Convective precipitation (Figure 4-5) can be described using the following characteristics:

Figure 4-5. WSR-88D Weather Radar Convective Precipitation on the 0.5°Base Reflectivity Product Example

- Echoes tend to form as lines or cells,
- Reflectivity gradients are strong,

- Precipitation intensities generally vary from moderate to extreme,
  - Occasionally precipitation intensities can be light
- Echo patterns change rapidly when animating the image

Numerous hazards are associated with convective precipitation. They include: turbulence, low-level wind shear, strong and gusty surface winds, icing above the freezing level, hail, lightning, tornadoes and localized IFR conditions with heavy precipitation.

4.1.4.1.2 Strengths of Base Reflectivity
The strengths of the Base Reflectivity product include:

- The location of precipitation and non-precipitation echoes is depicted, and
- The intensity and movement of precipitation is relatively easy and straight forward to determine.

4.1.4.1.3 Limitations of Base Reflectivity
Limitations associated with the Base Reflectivity product include:

- The radar beam may overshoot targets, and
- The image may be contaminated by:
  - Beam blockage
  - Ground clutter
  - Anomalous Propagation (AP) and
  - Ghosts.

4.1.4.1.3.1 Radar Beam Overshooting
Radar beam overshooting may occur because the radar beam (typically the 0.5 degree slice) can be higher than the top of precipitation. This will most likely occur with stratiform precipitation and low-topped convection. For example, at a distance of 124 NM from the radar, the 0.5° Base Reflectivity radar beam is at an altitude of approximately 18,000 feet; at 248 NM the beam height is approximately 54,000 feet. Any precipitation with tops below these altitudes and distances will **not** be displayed on the image. Therefore, it is quite possible that precipitation may be occurring where none appears on the radar image.

4.1.4.1.3.2 Beam Blockage
Beam blockage (Figure 4-6) occurs when the radar beam is blocked by terrain and is particularly predominant in mountainous terrain. This impacts both the Composite Reflectivity and Base Reflectivity images.

Beam blockage is most easily seen on the 0.5° Base Reflectivity images where it appears as a pie-shaped area (or areas) perpetually void of echoes. When animating the imagery, the beam blockage area will remain clear of echoes even as precipitation and other targets pass through.

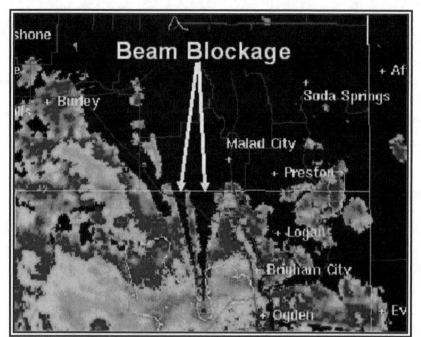

Figure 4-6. WSR-88D Weather Radar Beam Blockage on Base Reflectivity Product Example

4.1.4.1.3.3 Ground Clutter

Ground clutter (Figure 4-8) is radar echoes returns from trees, buildings, or other objects on the ground. It appears as a roughly circular region of high reflectivities at ranges close to the radar. Ground clutter appears stationary when animating images and can mask precipitation located near the radar. Most ground clutter is automatically removed from WSR-88D imagery, so typically it is does not interfere with image interpretation.

Figure 4-8. WSR-88D Weather Radar Ground Clutter Example

4.1.4.1.3.4 Ghost

A Ghost (Figure 4-9) is a diffused echo in apparently clear air caused by a "cloud" of point targets such as insects or by refraction returns of the radar beam in truly clear air.

The latter case commonly develops at sunset due to superrefraction during the warm season. The ghost develops as an area of low reflectivity echoes (typically less than 15dBZ) near the radar site and quickly expands. When animating the imagery, the ghost echo shows little movement.

Figure 4-9. WSR-88D Weather Radar Ghost Example

4.1.4.1.3.5 Angels

Angels are echoes caused by a physical phenomenon not discernible by the eye at the radar site. They are usually caused by bats, birds or insects. Angels typically appear as a donut-shaped echo with low reflectivity values (Figure 4-10). When animated, the echo expands and becomes more diffuse with time.

Angels typically only appear only when the radar is in Clear Air Mode because of their weak reflectivity. Echoes caused by birds are typically detected in the morning when they take flight for the day. Echoes caused by bats are typically detected in the evening, when they are departing from caves.

Figure 4-10. WSR-88D Weather Radar Angle Example
This angel was caused by bats departing Selman Bat Cave at Alabaster Caverns State Park, Oklahoma around sunset

4.1.4.1.3.6 Anomalous Propagation (AP)

Anomalous propagation (AP) (Figure 4-11) is an en extended pattern of ground echoes caused by superrefraction of the radar beam. Superrefraction causes the radar beam to bend downward and strike the ground. It differs from ground clutter because it can occur anywhere within the radar's range, not just at ranges close to the radar.

AP typically appears as speckled or blotchy, high reflectivity echoes. When animating images, AP tends to "bloom up" and dissipate and has no continuity of motion. AP can sometimes be misinterpreted as thunderstorms; differentiating between to two is determined by animating images. Thunderstorms move with a smooth, continuous motion while AP appears to "bloom up" and dissipate randomly.

Figure 4-11. WSR-88D Weather Radar Anomalous Propagation (AP) Example

4.1.4.2 Composite Reflectivity

Composite reflectivity is the maximum echo intensity (reflectivity) detected within a column of the atmosphere above a location. The radar scans through all of the elevation slices to determine the highest dBZ value in the vertical column (Figure 4-12) then displays that value on the product. When compared with Base Reflectivity, the Composite Reflectivity can reveal important storm structure features and intensity trends of storms.

Figure 4-12. Creation of a Composite Reflectivity product

Figure 4-13. WSR-88D Weather Radar Short Range (124 NM) Composite Reflectivity Product Example

4.1.4.2.1 Composite Reflectivity Use

The primary use of the Composite Reflectivity product, which offers the highest reflectivity value in a vertical column, is to determine the vertical structure of the precipitation. The image must be compared with the Base Reflectivity image to determine the vertical structure of the precipitation. Figure 4-14 includes the 0.5° Base Reflectivity and Composite Reflectivity images for the same location and period of time.

In Figure 4-14, within location A, the intensity of the echoes is higher on the Composite Reflectivity image. Also, within area B, many more echoes present on the Composite Reflectivity. Since the Composite Reflectivity product displays the highest reflectivity of **all** elevation scans, it is detecting these higher reflectivities at some higher altitude/elevation than the Base Reflectivity product, which is sampling closer to the ground. This often occurs when precipitation and especially thunderstorms are developing.

Figure 4-14. WSR-88D Weather Radar 0.5° Base Reflectivity versus Composite Reflectivity Comparison

4.1.4.2.2 Strengths of Composite Reflectivity

The primary strength of the Composite Reflectivity product is its three-dimensional view of reflectivity. The method used to determine this three-dimensional view is described in section 4.1.4.2.1.

4.1.4.2.3 Limitations of Composite Reflectivity

Limitations associated with the Composite Reflectivity product include:

- The radar beam may overshoot targets, and
- The image may be contaminated by:
    - Beam blockage
    - Ground clutter
    - Anomalous Propagation (AP) and
    - Ghosts.

4.1.4.2.3.1 Radar Beam Overshooting

Radar beam overshooting may occur because the lowest base reflectivity tilt (0.5) can be higher than the top of precipitation. This will most likely occur with stratiform precipitation and low-topped convection. For example, at a distance of 124 NM from the radar, the radar beam is at an altitude of approximately 18,000 feet above the radar. Any precipitation with tops below this altitude and distance will **not** be displayed on the image. Therefore, it is quite possible that precipitation may be occurring where none appears on the radar image.

4.1.4.2.3.2 Beam Blockage

Beam blockage (Figure 4-6) occurs when the radar beam is blocked by terrain and is particularly predominant in mountainous terrain. This impacts both the Composite Reflectivity and Base Reflectivity images.

Beam blockage is most easily seen on the 0.5° Base Reflectivity images where it appears as a pie-shaped area (or areas) perpetually void of echoes. When animating the imagery, the beam blockage area will remain clear of echoes even as precipitation and other targets pass through.

4.1.4.2.3.3 Ground Clutter

Ground clutter (Figure 4-8) is radar echoes returns from trees, buildings, or other objects on the ground. It appears as a roughly circular region of high reflectivities at ranges close to the radar. Ground clutter appears stationary when animating images and can mask precipitation located near the radar. Most ground clutter is automatically removed from WSR-88D imagery, so typically it is does not interfere with image interpretation.

4.1.4.2.3.4 Ghost

A Ghost (Figure 4-9) is a diffused echo in apparently clear air that is caused by a "cloud" of point targets such as insects or by refraction returns of the radar beam in truly clear air.

The latter case commonly develops at sunset due to superrefraction during the warm season. The ghost develops as an area of low reflectivity echoes (typically less than 15 dBZ) near the radar site and quickly expands. When animating the imagery, the ghost echo shows little movement.

4.1.4.2.3.5 Angels

Angels are echoes caused by a physical phenomenon not discernible by the eye at the radar site. They are usually causes by bats, birds or insects. Angels typically appear as a donut-shaped echo with low reflectivity values (Figure 4-10). When animating, the echo expends and becomes more diffuse with time.

Angels typically only appear only when the radar is in clear air mode because of their weak reflectivity. Echoes caused by birds are typically detected in the morning when they take flight for the day. Echoes caused by bats are typically detected in the evening when they take flight from caves.

4.1.4.2.3.6 Anomalous Propagation (AP)

Anomalous propagation (AP) (Figure 4-11) is an en extended pattern of ground echoes caused by superrefraction of the radar beam. Superrefraction causes the radar beam to bend downward and strike the ground. It differs from ground clutter because it can occur anywhere within the radar's range, not just at ranges close to the radar.

AP typically appears as speckled or blotchy, high reflectivity echoes. When animating images, AP tends to "bloom up" and dissipate and has no continuity of motion. AP can sometimes be misinterpreted as thunderstorms; differentiating between to two is determined by animating images. Thunderstorms move with a smooth, continuous motion while AP appears to "bloom up" and dissipate randomly.

4.1.5 Radar Mosaics

A radar mosaic consists of multiple single site radar images combined to produce a radar image on a regional or national scale. Regional and national mosaics can be found at the National Weather Service (NWS) Doppler Radar Images web site: http://radar.weather.gov/ridge/

The mosaics are located toward the bottom of the page.

4.1.5.1   0.5° Mosaics - Contiguous U.S. and Hawaii

The NWS produces a set of regional and national mosaics (Table 4-2) in the contiguous U.S. using the 124 NM 0.5° <u>Base Reflectivity</u> product (Figure 4-15).

Table 4-2. NWS Radar Mosaic Products

Pacific Northwest	Pacific Southwest
Upper Mississippi Valley	Southern Mississippi Valley
Northeast	Southeast
Southern Rockies	Northern Rockies
Southern Plains	Great Lakes
Low Resolution National	High Resolution National

Figure 4-15. Great Lakes Regional Radar Mosaic Example

The most recent image from single site radars is used to create the product. Single site data older than 15 minutes from the current time of the product are excluded from the image. Therefore, data on the mosaics will be no greater than 15 minutes old. Where radar coverage overlaps, the highest dBZ value will be plotted on the image.

4.1.5.2 0.5° Mosaics - Alaska

The Alaskan mosaic (Figure 4-16) differs from the contiguous product in only one way: it is created using the 248 NM 0.5° <u>Base Reflectivity</u> single site product.

Figure 4-16. Alaskan Regional Radar Mosaic Example

The long range <u>Base Reflectivity</u> product is used because the radar sites are located at greater distances from each other. Even with the use of the long range product, many areas of Alaskan do not have radar coverage. These areas are shaded gray on Figure 4-16.

4.2 Satellite

4.2.1 Description

Satellite is perhaps the single most important source of weather data worldwide, particularly over data sparse regions such as countries without organized weather data collection and the oceans.

GOES satellite imagery can be found on the NWS Aviation Digital Data Service (ADDS) website at: http://adds.aviationweather.noaa.gov/satellite/. Additional satellite imagery for Alaska can be found on the Alaska Aviation Weather Unit (AAWU) website at: http://aawu.arh.noaa.gov/sat.php

4.2.2 Imagery Types

Three types of satellite imagery are commonly used: Visible, infrared (IR), and water vapor. Visible imagery is available only during daylight hours. IR and water vapor imagery are available day or night.

4.2.2.1 Visible Imagery

Visible imagery (Figures 4-17 and 4-18) displays reflected sunlight from the Earth's surface, clouds, and particulate matter in the atmosphere. These images are simply black and white pictures of the Earth from space. During daylight hours, visible imagery is the most widely used image type because it has the highest resolution and approximates what is seen with the human eye.

Gray shades displayed on visible imagery can be correlated with particular features. Assuming a high sun angle, thick clouds and snow will appear white, thin clouds will appear translucent gray, land appears gray, and deep bodies of water such as lakes and oceans will appear black.

Figure 4-17. Visible Satellite Image – U.S. Example

Figure 4-18. Visible Satellite Image – Regional-Scale Example

4.2.2.1.1 Visible Image Data Legend

The data legend (Figure 4-19) on a <u>visible image</u> displays albedo, or reflectance, expressed as a percentage. For example, an albedo of 72 means 72 percent of the sunlight which struck a feature was reflected back to space.

Figure 4-19. Visible Satellite Data Legend.
The gray shades (values) represent albedo or reflectance expressed as a percentage.

4.2.2.2 Infrared (IR) Imagery

<u>Infrared</u> (IR) images (Figure 4-20 through 4-23) display temperatures of the Earth's surface, clouds, and particulate matter. Generally speaking, the warmer an object, the more infrared energy it emits. The satellite sensor measures this energy and calibrates it to temperature using a very simple physical relationship.

Clouds that are very high in the atmosphere are generally quite cold (perhaps -50°C) whereas clouds very near the earth's surface are generally quite warm (perhaps +5°C). Likewise, land may be even warmer than the lower clouds (perhaps +20°C). Those colder clouds emit much less infrared energy than the warmer clouds and the land emits more than those warm clouds.

The data measured by satellite is calibrated and colorized according to the temperature. If the temperature of the atmosphere decreases with height (which is typical), cloud-top temperature can be used to roughly determine which clouds are high-level and which are low-level.

When clouds are present, the temperature displayed on the infrared images is that of the tops of clouds. When clouds are not present, the temperature is that of the ground or the ocean.

Figure 4-20. Infrared (Color) Satellite Image – U.S. Example
The scale is in degrees Celsius. Blue/purple colors indicate colder temperatures, while orange/red colors indicate warmer temperatures.

Figure 4-21. Infrared (Color) Satellite Image – Regional-Scale Example
The scale is in degrees Celsius. Blue/purple colors indicate colder temperatures, while orange/red colors indicate warmer temperatures.

Figure 4-22. Unenhanced Infrared (black and white) Satellite Image – U.S. Example
The scale is in degrees Celsius. Lighter gray shades indicate colder temperatures, while darker gray shades indicate warmer temperatures.

Figure 4-23. Unenhanced Infrared (black and white) Satellite Image – Regional- Scale Example
The scale is in degrees Celsius. Lighter gray shades indicate colder temperatures, while darker gray shades indicate warmer temperatures.

4.2.2.2.1 Infrared Image Data Legends
The data legend (Figure 4-24 and Figure 4-25) on an infrared image is calibrated to temperature expressed in degrees Celsius. The legend may vary based on the satellite image provider.

Figure 4-24. Infrared (Color) Satellite Image Data Legend.
The colors (values) represent temperature in degrees Celsius.

Figure 4-25. Unenhanced Infrared (black and while) Satellite Image Data Legend.
The gray shades (values) represent temperature in degrees Celsius.

4.2.3.3 Water Vapor Imagery
The water vapor imagery (Figure 4-26 and Figure 4-27) displays the quantity of water vapor generally located in the middle and upper troposphere within the layer between 700 millibars (FL100) to 200 millibars (FL390). The actual numbers displayed on the water vapor images correspond to temperature in degrees Celsius. No direct relationship exists between these values and the temperatures of clouds, unlike IR imagery. Water Vapor imagery does not really "see" clouds but "sees" high-level water vapor instead.

The most useful information to be gained from the water vapor images is the locations and movements of weather systems, jet streams, and thunderstorms. Another useful tidbit is aided by the color scale used on the images. In general, regions displayed in shades of red are VERY dry in the upper atmosphere and MAY correlate to crisp blue skies from a ground perspective. On the contrary, regions displayed in shades of blue or green are indicative of lots of high-level moisture and may also indicate cloudiness. This cloudiness could simply be high-level cirrus types or thunderstorms. That determination cannot be gained from this image by itself but could easily be determined when used in conjunction with corresponding visible and infrared satellite images.

Figure 4-26. Water Vapor Satellite Image – U.S. Example
The scale is in degrees Celsius. Blue/green colors indicate moisture and/or clouds in the mid/upper troposphere, while dark gray/orange/red colors indicate dry air in the mid/upper troposphere.

Figure 4-27. Water Vapor Satellite Image – Regional-Scale Example
The scale is in degrees Celsius. Blue/green colors indicate moisture and/or clouds in the mid/upper troposphere, while dark gray/orange/red colors indicate dry air in the mid/upper troposphere.

4.2.3.3.1   Water Vapor Image Data Legend

The data legend (Figure 4-28) on a water vapor images is calibrated to temperature expressed in degrees Celsius. The actual data values on the water vapor images are not particularly useful. Interpretation of the patterns and how they change over time is more important. The legend may vary depending on the satellite image provider.

Figure 4-28. Water Vapor Satellite Image Data Legend.
The colors (values) represent temperature in degrees Celsius

5   GRAPHICAL OBSERVATIONS AND DERIVED PRODUCTS

5.1   Surface Analysis Charts

Surface Analysis charts are analyzed charts of surface weather observations. The chart depicts the distribution of several items including sea level pressure, the positions of highs, lows, ridges, and troughs, the location and character of fronts, and the various boundaries such as drylines, outflow boundaries, sea-breeze fronts, and convergence lines. Other symbols are often added depending upon the intended use of the chart. Pressure is referred to in mean sea level (MSL) on the surface analysis chart while all other elements are presented as they occur at the surface point of observation. A chart in this general form is commonly referred to as the weather map.

Figure 5-1. HPC Surface Analysis Chart Example

5.1.1   Issuance
Five National Weather Service (NWS) offices issue surface analysis charts:

- The Hydrometeorological Prediction Center (HPC) in Camp Springs, Maryland is responsible for land areas of North America. The charts are available at
    - http://www.hpc.ncep.noaa.gov/html/sfc2.shtml
    - http://www.hpc.ncep.noaa.gov/html/avnsfc.shtml

- The Ocean Prediction Center (OPC) in Camp Spring, Maryland is responsible for the Atlantic and Pacific Oceans north of 30°N latitude. The charts are available at:
  - http://www.opc.ncep.noaa.gov/

- The Tropical Prediction Center (TPC) in Miami, Florida is responsible for the tropical regions of the western hemisphere south of 30°N latitude and east of 160°E longitude. The surface analysis charts are available at:
  - http://www.nhc.noaa.gov/marine_forecasts.shtml

- The Alaskan Aviation Weather Unit (AAWU) in Anchorage, Alaska is responsible for the state of Alaska. The surface analysis chart is available at:
  - http://aawu.arh.noaa.gov/surface.php

- The Weather Forecast Office in Honolulu, Hawaii (WFO HNL) is responsible for the tropical Pacific Ocean, south of 30°N latitude and west of 160°E longitude. The charts are available at:
  - http://www.prh.noaa.gov/hnl/pages/analyses.php

Each office produces multiple versions of the surface analysis chart with varying formats.

5.1.2 HPC Surface Analysis Charts
- The Hydrometeorological Prediction Center (HPC) in Camp Springs, Maryland is responsible for land areas of North America. The charts are available at
  - http://www.hpc.ncep.noaa.gov/html/sfc2.shtml
  - http://www.hpc.ncep.noaa.gov/html/avnsfc.shtml

5.1.2.1 Issuance
The Hydrometeorological Prediction Center (HPC) issues Surface Analysis Charts for North America eight times daily (Table 5-1).

Table 5-1. HPC Surface Analysis Charts Issuance Schedule

Valid Time (UTC)	00	03	06	09	12	15	18	21

5.1.2.2 Analysis Symbols
Figure 5-2 shows analysis symbols used on HPC surface analysis charts:

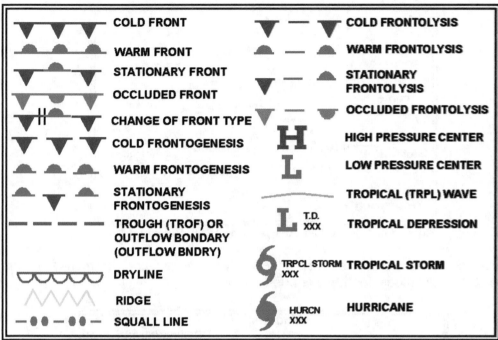

Figure 5-2. HPC Surface Analysis Chart Symbols

5.1.2.3 Station Plot Models

Land, ship, buoy, and C-MAN stations are plotted on the chart to aid in analyzing and interpreting the surface weather features. These plotted observations are referred to as station models. Some stations may not be plotted due to space limitations. However, all reporting stations are used in the analysis.

Figure 5-3 and 5-4 contain the most commonly used station plot models used in surface analysis charts:

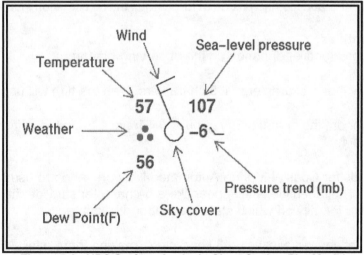

Figure 5-3. HPC Surface Analysis Chart Station Plot Model

Figure 5-4. HPC Surface Analysis Chart Ship/Buoy Plot Model

HPC also produces surface analysis charts specifically for the aviation community. Figure 5-5 contains the station plot model for these charts:

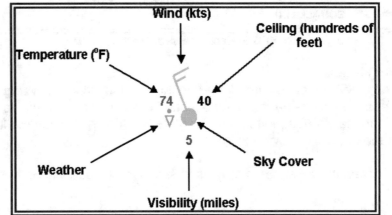

Figure 5-5. HPC Surface Analysis Chart for Aviation Interests Station Plot Model

5.1.2.3.1 Station Identifier
The format of the station identifier depends on the observing platform.

- Ship -- Typically 4 or 5 characters. If 5 characters, then the fifth will usually be a digit.

- Buoy -- Whether drifting or stationary, a buoy will have a 5-digit identifier. The first digit will always be a **4**.

- C-MAN -- Stands for Coastal-Marine Automated Network, and are usually close to coastal areas. Their identifier will appear like a 5-character ship identifier, however the 4th character will identify off which state the platform is located.

- Land -- Land stations will always be 3 characters, making them easily distinguishable from ship, buoy, and C-MAN observations.

5.1.2.3.2 Temperature
The air temperature is plotted in whole degrees <u>Fahrenheit</u>.

5.1.2.3.3 Dew Point
The dew point temperature is plotted in whole degrees Fahrenheit.

5.1.2.3.4 Weather
A weather symbol is plotted if, at the time of observation, precipitation is either occurring or a condition exists causing reduced visibility.

Figure 5-6 contains a list of the most common weather symbols:

Figure 5-6. HPC Surface Analysis Chart Common Weather Symbols

A complete list of weather symbols can be found at in Appendix I.

5.1.2.3.5 Wind
Wind is plotted in increments of 5 knots (kts). The wind direction is in "true" degrees and is depicted by a stem (line) pointed in the direction from which the wind is blowing. Wind speed is determined by adding the values of the flags (50kts), barbs (10kts), and half-barbs (5kts) found on the stem.

If the wind is calm at the time of observation, only a single circle over the station is depicted.

Figure 5-7 are some sample wind symbols:

Figure 5-7. HPC Surface Analysis Chart Wind Plotting Model

5.1.2.3.6 Ceiling
Ceiling is plotted in hundreds of feet above ground level.

5.1.2.3.7 Visibility
Surface visibility is plotted in whole statute miles.

5.1.2.3.8 Pressure
Sea-level pressure is plotted in tenths of millibars (mb), with the first two digits (generally 10 or 9) omitted. For reference, 1013 mb is equivalent to 29.92 inches of mercury. Below are some sample conversions between plotted and complete sea-level pressure values:

410: 1041.0 mb
103: 1010.3 mb
987: 998.7 mb
872: 987.2 mb

5.1.2.3.9 Pressure Trend
The pressure trend has two components, a number and a symbol, to indicate how the sea level pressure has changed during the past three hours. The number provides the 3-hour change in tenths of millibars while the symbol provides a graphic illustration of how this change occurred.

Figure 5-8 contains the meanings of the pressure trend symbols:

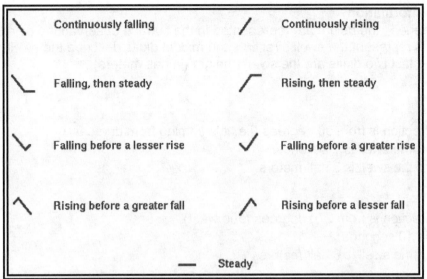

Figure 5-8. HPC Surface Analysis Chart Pressure Trends

5.1.2.3.10 Sky Cover

The approximate amount of sky cover can be determined by the circle at the center of the station plot. The amount the circle is filled reflects the amount of sky covered by clouds. Figure 5-9 contains the common cloud cover depictions:

Figure 5-9. HPC Surface Analysis Chart Sky Cover Symbols

5.1.2.3.11 Water Temperature

Water temperature is plotted in whole degrees Fahrenheit.

5.1.2.3.12 Swell Information

Swell direction, period, and height are represented in the surface observations by a 6-digit code. The first two digits represent the swell direction, the middle digits describe the swell period (in seconds), and the last two digits are the swell's height (in half meters).

```
090703
```
09 - The swell direction is from 90 degrees (i.e. it is coming from due east).
07 - The period of the swell is 7 seconds.
03 - The height of the swell is 3 half meters.

```
271006
```
27 - The swell direction is from 270 degrees (due west).
10 - The period is 10 seconds.
06 - The height of the swell is 6 half meters.

5.1.2.3.13 Wave Information

Period and height of waves are represented by a 5-digit code. The first digit is always **1**. The second and third digits describe the wave period (in seconds), and the final two digits give the wave height (in half meters).

```
10603
```
1   - A group identifier. The first digit will always be **1**.
06 - The wave period is 6 seconds.
03 - The wave height is 3 half meters.

```
10515
```
1   - The group identifier again.
05 - The wave period is 5 seconds.
15 - Wave height is 15 half meters.

In some charts by the OPC, only the wave height (in feet) is plotted.

5.1.2.4 Analyses

Isobars, pressure systems, and fronts are the most common analyses depicted on surface analysis charts.

5.1.2.4.1 Isobars

An isobar is a line of equal or constant pressure commonly used in the analysis of pressure patterns.

On a Surface Analysis Chart, isobars are solid lines usually spaced at intervals of 4 millibars (mb). Each isobar is labeled. For example, **1032** signifies 1,032.0 mb and **992** signify 992.0 mb.

METAR/SPECI (Section 2.1) reports pressure in hectopascals. However, one millibar is equivalent to one hectopascal, so no conversion is required.

5.1.2.4.2 Pressure Systems

On a Surface Analysis Chart, a High (**H**) is a maximum of atmospheric pressure, while a Low (**L**) is a minimum of atmospheric pressure. Central pressure is the atmospheric pressure located at the center of a High or Low. In general, the central pressure is the highest pressure in the center of a High and the lowest pressure at the center of a Low. The central pressure is denoted near each pressure center.

A trough or an elongated area of low atmospheric pressure is denoted by dashed lines and identified with the word **TROF.** A ridge or an elongated area of high atmospheric pressure is denoted by saw-toothed symbols. Ridges are rarely denoted on charts produced by the HPC.

Tropical storms, hurricanes, and typhoons (See Figure 5-2) are low-pressure systems with their names and central pressures denoted.

5.1.2.4.3 Fronts

The analysis shows positions and types of fronts by the symbols in Figure 5-2. The symbols on the front indicate the type of front and point in the direction toward which the front is moving. Two short lines across a front indicate a change in front type.

Figure 5-10. HPC Surface Analysis Chart – North America Example

Figure 5-11. HPC Surface Analysis Chart - Contiguous U.S. Example

Figure 5-12. HPC Surface Analysis Chart - Northeast U.S. Example

Figure 5-13. HPC Surface Analysis Chart for Aviation Interests – Contiguous U.S. Example

Figure 5-14. HPC Surface Analysis Chart for Aviation Interests – South central U.S. Example

5.1.3 OPC and WFO Honolulu Surface Analysis Charts

The Ocean Prediction Center (OPC) in Camp Spring, Maryland is responsible for the Atlantic and Pacific Oceans north of 30°N latitude. The charts are found at:

- http://www.opc.ncep.noaa.gov/

The Weather Forecast Office in Honolulu, Hawaii (WFO HNL) is responsible for the tropical Pacific Ocean, south of 30°N latitude and west of 160°E longitude. The charts are found at:

- http://www.prh.noaa.gov/hnl/pages/analyses.php

5.1.3.1 Issuance

The Ocean Prediction Center (OPC) produces surface analysis charts for the Atlantic and Pacific Oceans north of 30°N latitude four times daily (Table 5-2). The Weather Forecast Office in Honolulu, Hawaii (WFO HNL) issues surface analysis charts for the tropical Pacific Ocean, south of 30°N latitude and west of 160°E longitude four times daily. Surface analysis charts for the North Pacific are jointly issued by both offices.

Table 5-2. OPC and WFO Honolulu Surface Analysis Charts Issuance Schedule

UTC	00	06	12	18

5.1.3.2 Analysis Symbols

Figure 5-15 shows analysis symbols used on OPC and WFO HNL surface analysis charts.

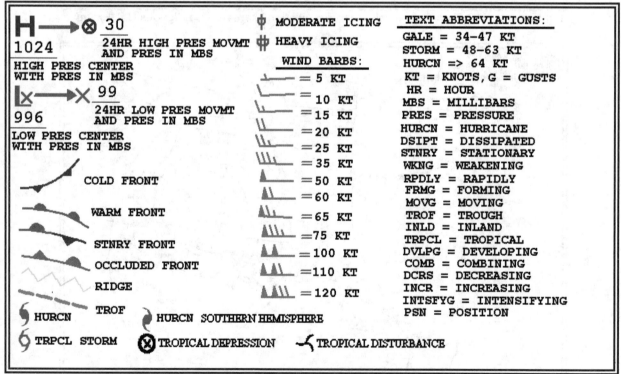

Figure 5-15. OPC and WFO HNL Surface Analysis Chart Symbols

Figure 5-16. WFO HNL Surface Analysis Chart – North Pacific Example

5.1.3.3 Wave Information

Period and height of waves are represented by a 5-digit code. The first digit is always **1**. The second and third digits describe the wave period (in seconds), and the final two digits give the wave height (in half meters). Below are two examples:

10603

1   - A group identifier. The first digit will always be **1**.

06 - The wave period is 6 seconds.

03 - The wave height is 3 half meters.

10515

1   - The group identifier again.

05 - The wave period is 5 seconds.

15 - Wave height is 15 half meters.

In certain charts by the OPC, only the wave height (in feet) is plotted.

5.1.3.4 Analyses

Isobars, pressure systems, and fronts are the most common analyses depicted on the surface analysis charts.

5.1.3.4.1 Isobars

An isobar is a line of equal or constant pressure commonly used to analyze pressure patterns.

On a Surface Analysis Chart, isobars are solid lines usually spaced at intervals of 4 millibars (mb). Each isobar is labeled. For example, **1032** signifies 1,032.0 mb and **992** signify 992.0 mb.

METAR/SPECI (Section 2.1) reports pressure in hectopascals. However, one millibar is equivalent to one hectopascal, so no conversion is required.

5.1.3.4.2 Pressure Systems

On a Surface Analysis Chart, a High (**H**) is a maximum of atmospheric pressure, while a Low (**L**) is a minimum of atmospheric pressure. Central pressure is the atmospheric pressure at the center of a High or Low -- the highest pressure in a High and the lowest pressure in a Low. The central pressure is denoted near each pressure center. Tropical storms, hurricanes, and typhoons (See Figure 5-15) are low-pressure systems with their names and central pressures denoted.

A trough or an elongated area of low atmospheric pressure is denoted by dashed lines and identified with the word **TROF**. A ridge or an elongated area of high atmospheric pressure is denoted with saw-toothed symbols. Ridges are rarely denoted on charts produced by the HPC.

5.1.3.4.3 Fronts

The analysis shows positions and types of fronts by the symbols in Figure 5-15. The symbols on the front indicate the type of front and point in the direction toward which the front is moving. Two short lines across a front indicate a change in front type.

5.1.4 TPC Surface Analysis Charts

The Tropical Prediction Center (TPC) in Miami, Florida is responsible for the tropical regions of the western hemisphere south of 30°N latitude and east of 160°E longitude. The surface analysis chart is located at:

* http://www.nhc.noaa.gov/marine_forecasts.shtml

5.1.4.1 Issuance

The Tropical Prediction Center (TPC) issues Surface Analysis Charts for tropical regions of the western hemisphere south of 30°N latitude and east of 160°E longitude four times a day (Table 5-3).

Table 5-3. TPC Surface Analysis Charts Issuance Schedule

Valid Time (UTC)	00	06	12	18

5.1.4.2 Analysis Symbols

Figure 5-17 shows analysis symbols used on TPC surface analysis charts.

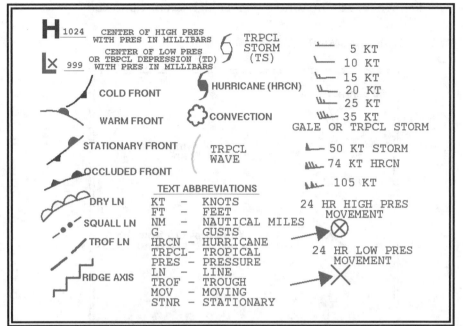

Figure 5-17. TPC Surface Analysis Chart Symbols

Figure 5-18. TPC Tropical Surface Analysis Chart Example

5.1.4.2.1 Wind

Wind is plotted in increments of 5 <u>knots</u> (kts). The wind direction is in "true" degrees and is depicted by a stem (line) pointed in the direction from which the wind is blowing. The wind speed is determined by adding up the value of the flags (50 kts), lines (10 kts), and half-lines (5 kts), each of which has the following individual values:

A single circle over the station with no wind symbol indicates a calm wind.

Figure 5-19 shows some sample wind symbols:

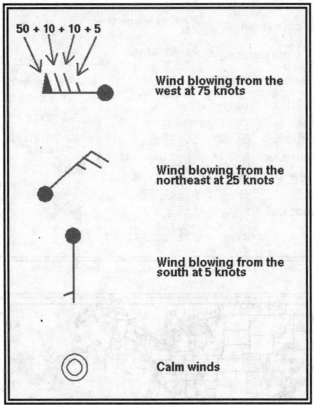

50 + 10 + 10 + 5

Wind blowing from the west at 75 knots

Wind blowing from the northeast at 25 knots

Wind blowing from the south at 5 knots

Calm winds

Figure 5-19: TPC Surface Analysis Chart Wind Plotting Model

5.1.4.3 Analyses
Isobars, pressure systems, and fronts are the most common analyses depicted on the surface analysis charts.

5.1.4.3.1 Isobars
An isobar is a line of equal or constant pressure commonly used to analyze pressure patterns.

On a Surface Analysis Chart, isobars are solid lines usually spaced at intervals of 4 millibars (mb). Each isobar is labeled. For example, **1032** signifies 1,032.0 mb and **992** signify 992.0 mb.

METAR/SPECI (Section 2.1) reports pressure in hectopascals. However, one millibar is equivalent to one hectopascal, so no conversion is required.

5.1.4.3.2 Pressure Systems
On a Surface Analysis Chart, a High (**H**) is a maximum of atmospheric pressure, while a Low (**L**) is a minimum of atmospheric pressure. Central pressure is the atmospheric pressure at the center of a High or Low -- the highest pressure in a High and the lowest pressure in a Low. The central pressure is denoted near each pressure center. Tropical storms, hurricanes, and

typhoons (See Figure 5-17) are low-pressure systems with their names and central pressures denoted.

A trough or an elongated area of low atmospheric pressure is denoted by dashed lines and identified with the word **TROF**. A ridge or an elongated area of high atmospheric pressure is denoted by saw-toothed symbols. Ridges are rarely denoted on charts produced by the TPC.

5.1.4.3.3 Fronts

The analysis shows positions and types of fronts by the symbols in Figure 5-17. The symbols on the front indicate the type of front and point in the direction toward which the front is moving. Two short lines across a front indicate a change in front type.

5.1.5 Unified Surface Analysis Chart

The Unified Surface Analysis Chart is a composite of all the surface analysis charts produced by HPC, OPC, TPC and WFO Honolulu. It contains an analysis of isobars, pressure systems and fronts.

5.1.5.1 Issuance

The chart is issued four times daily by the OPC (see Table 5-4).

Table 5-4. Unified Surface Analysis Chart Issuance Schedule

Valid Time (UTC)	00	06	12	18

06 UTC SEPTEMBER 17 2004 - NATIONAL WEATHER SERVICE

Figure 5-20. Unified Surface Analysis Chart Example

5.1.5.2 Analysis Symbols

Figure 5-21 shows analysis symbols used on the Unified Surface Analysis charts.

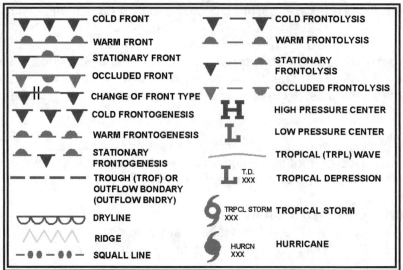

Figure 5-21. Unified Surface Analysis Chart Symbols

5.1.5.3 Analyses
Isobars, pressure systems, and fronts are the most common analyses depicted on the surface analysis charts.

5.1.5.3.1 Isobars
An isobar is a line of equal or constant pressure commonly used to analyze pressure patterns.

On a Surface Analysis Chart, isobars are solid lines usually spaced at intervals of 4 millibars (mb). Each isobar is labeled. For example, **1032** signifies 1032.0 mb and **992** signify 992.0 mb.

METAR/SPECI (Section 2.1) reports pressure in hectopascals. However, one millibar is equivalent to one hectopascal, so no conversion is required.

5.1.5.3.2 Pressure Systems
On a Surface Analysis Chart, a High (**H**) is a maximum of atmospheric pressure while a Low (**L**) is a minimum of atmospheric pressure. Central pressure is the atmospheric pressure at the center of a High or Low -- the highest pressure in a High and the lowest pressure in a Low. The central pressure is denoted near each pressure center. Tropical storms, hurricanes, and typhoons (See Figure 5-21) are low-pressure systems with their names and central pressures denoted.

On a Surface Analysis Chart, a trough is an elongated area of relatively low atmospheric pressure, while a ridge is an elongated area of relatively high atmospheric pressure. Troughs are denoted by dashed lines and identified with the word **TROF**. Ridges are denoted by saw-toothed symbols. Ridges are rarely denoted on charts produced by the HPC.

5.1.5.3.3 Fronts
The analysis shows positions and types of fronts by the symbols in Figure 5-21. The symbols on the front indicate the type of front and point in the direction toward which the front is moving. Two short lines across a front indicate a change in front type.

5.1.6 AAWU Surface Charts

The Alaskan Aviation Weather Unit (AAWU) in Anchorage, Alaska is responsible for the state of Alaska. The surface analysis chart is located at:

- http://aawu.arh.noaa.gov/surface.php

5.1.6.1 Issuance

The AAWU issues Surface Analysis Charts 4 times daily for the state of Alaska. The valid times are shown in Table 5-5.

Table 5-5. AAWU Surface Analysis Issuance Schedule

Valid Time (UTC)	00	06	12	18

5.1.6.2 Analysis Symbols

The symbols (Figure 5-22) used on the Alaskan Surface Analysis Chart are similar to those found on the HPC Surface Analysis chart. However, since the Alaskan Surface Analysis chart is in black and white all of the symbols are black and white as well.

A Key to Symbols used on the AAWU Graphic Products

- Cold Front
- Warm Front
- Occluded Front
- Stationary Front
- Trough
- Ridge

H 1032 – High Pressure Center Pressure in millibars

L 988 – Low Pressure Center Pressure in millibars

– Occasional or greater Precipitation

= – Fog	– Freezing Rain	– Mixed Rain/Snow
∞ – Haze	– Freezing Drizzle	– Rain Showers
– Smoke	⊔ – Light Icing	– Snow Showers
– Drifting Snow	⊔ – Moderate Icing	– Rain/Snow Showers
– Sandstorm	⊔ – Severe Icing	K – Thunderstorm
, – Drizzle	✳ – Snow	∧ – Light Turbulence
• – Rain	↔ – Ice Crystals	∧ – Moderate Turbulence
	△ – Ice Pellets	☆ – Severe Turbulence

Figure 5-22. AAWU Surface Analysis Chart Symbols

Figure 5-23. AAWU Alaskan Surface Chart Example

5.1.6.3 Station Plot Models

Land, ship, buoy, and C-MAN stations are plotted on the chart to aid in analyzing and interpreting the surface weather features. These plotted observations are referred to as <u>station models</u>. Some stations may not be plotted due to space limitations. However, all reporting stations are used in the analysis.

Figures 5-24 and 5-25 show the most commonly used station plot models used in surface analysis charts.

Figure 5-24. AAWU Surface Analysis Chart Station Plot Model

Figure 5-25. AAWU Surface Analysis Chart Ship/buoy Plot Model

5.1.6.3.1 Station Identifier
The format of the station identifier depends on the observing platform.

- Ship -- Typically 4 or 5 characters. If 5 characters, then the fifth will usually be a digit.

- Buoy -- Whether drifting or stationary, a buoy will have a 5-digit identifier. The first digit will always be a **4**.

- C-MAN -- Stands for Coastal-Marine Automated Network, and are usually close to coastal areas. Their identifier will appear like a 5-character ship identifier, however the 4th character will identify off which state the platform is located.

- Land -- Land stations will always be 3 characters, making them easily distinguishable from ship, buoy, and C-MAN observations.

5.1.6.3.2 Temperature
Air temperature is plotted in whole degrees Celsius on large-scale charts. Hourly surface charts may have temperatures using whole degrees Fahrenheit.

5.1.6.3.3 Dew Point
Dew point temperature is plotted in whole degrees Celsius on large-scale charts. Hourly surface charts may have dew point temperatures using whole degrees Fahrenheit.

5.1.6.3.4 Wind
Wind is plotted in increments of 5 knots (kts). The wind direction is in "true" degrees and is depicted by a stem (line) pointed in the direction from which the wind is blowing. Wind speed is determined by adding the values of the flags (50 kts), barbs (10kts), and half barbs (5 kts) found on the stem.

A single circle over the station with no wind symbol indicates a calm wind.

Figure 5-26 shows some sample wind symbols.

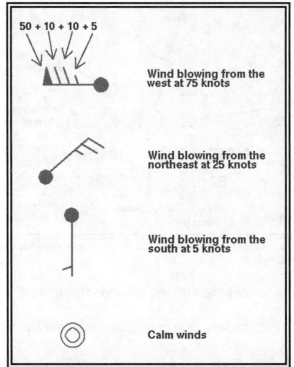

Figure 5-26: AAWU Surface Analysis Chart Wind Plotting Model

5.1.6.3.5 Ceiling
Ceiling is plotted in hundreds of feet above ground level.

5.1.6.3.6 Visibility
Surface visibility is plotted in whole statute miles.

5.1.6.3.7 Pressure
Sea-level pressure is plotted in tenths of millibars (mb), with the first two digits omitted (generally a 10 or 9). For reference, 1013 mb is equivalent to 29.92 inches of mercury. Below are some sample conversions between plotted and complete sea-level pressure values:

410: 1041.0 mb
103: 1010.3 mb
987: 998.7 mb
872: 987.2 mb

5.1.6.3.8 Pressure Trend
The pressure trend has two components, a number and symbol, to indicate how the sea-level pressure has changed during the past three hours. The number provides the 3-hour change in tenths of millibars, while the symbol provides a graphic illustration of how this change occurred.

Figure 5-27 shows the meanings of the pressure trend symbols.

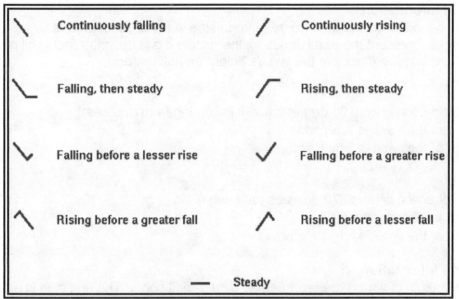

Figure 5-27. AAWU Surface Analysis Chart Pressure Trends

5.1.6.3.9 Sky Cover

The approximate amount of sky cover can be determined by the circle at the center of the station plot. The amount the circle is filled reflects the amount of sky covered by clouds. Figure 5-28 shows the common cloud cover depictions:

Figure 5-28. AAWU Surface Analysis Chart Sky Cover Symbols

5.1.6.3.10 Water Temperature

Water temperature is plotted in whole degrees Fahrenheit.

5.1.6.3.11 Swell Information

Swell direction, period, and height are represented in the surface observations by a 6-digit code. The first two digits represent the swell direction, the middle digits describe the swell period (in seconds), and the last two digits are the swell's height (in half meters).

090703

09 - The swell direction is from 90 degrees (i.e. it is coming from due east).
07 - The period of the swell is 7 seconds.
03 - The height of the swell is 3 half meters.

271006

27 - The swell direction is from 270 degrees (due west).
10 - The period is 10 seconds.
06 - The height of the swell is 6 half meters.

5.1.6.3.12 Wave Information

The period and height of waves are represented by a 5-digit code. The first digit is always **1**. The second and third digits describe the wave period (in seconds), and the final two digits give the wave height (in half meters). Below are two examples:

10603

1 - A group identifier. The first digit will always be **1**.
06 - The wave period is 6 seconds.
03 - The wave height is 3 half meters.

10515

1 - The group identifier again.
05 - The wave period is 5 seconds.
15 - Wave height is 15 half meters.

5.1.6.4 Analyses

Isobars, pressure systems, and fronts are the most common analyses depicted on surface analysis charts.

5.1.6.4.1 Isobars

An isobar is a line of equal or constant pressure commonly used to analyze pressure patterns.

On a Surface Analysis Chart, isobars are solid lines usually spaced at intervals of 4 millibars (mb). Each isobar is labeled. For example, **1032** signifies 1032.0 mb and **992** signify 992.0 mb.

METAR/SPECI (Section 2.1) reports pressure in hectopascals. However, one millibar is equivalent to one hectopascal, so no conversion is required.

5.1.6.4.2 Pressure Systems

On a Surface Analysis Chart, a High (**H**) is a maximum of atmosphere pressure, while a Low (**L**) is a minimum of atmospheric pressure. Central pressure is the atmospheric pressure at the center of a High or Low – the highest pressure in a High and the lowest pressure in a Low. The central pressure is denoted near each pressure center.

A trough or an elongated area of relatively low atmospheric pressure is denoted by dashed lines and identified with the word **TROF**. A ridge or an elongated area of relatively high atmospheric pressure is denoted by saw-toothed symbols. Ridges are rarely denoted on charts produced by the AAWU.

5.1.6.4.3 Fronts

The analysis shows positions and types of fronts by the symbols in Figure 5-22. The symbols on the front indicate the type of front and point in the direction toward which the front is moving. Two short lines across a front indicate a change in front type.

5.2 Constant Pressure Charts

Constant pressure charts are maps of selected conditions along specified constant pressure surfaces (pressure altitudes) and depict observed weather.

Constant pressure charts help to determine the three-dimensional aspect of depicted pressure systems. Each chart provides a plan-projection view at a specified pressure altitude.

Figure 5-29. Constant Pressure Chart Example

5.2.1 Issuance

Constant pressure charts are issued twice per day from observed data obtained at 00Z and 12Z. Charts are available at the NWS Fax Chart web site at:
http://weather.noaa.gov/fax/barotrop.shtml.

5.2.2 Observational Data

Observational data is plotted according to priority with some data deleted to prevent overlap. The retention priority is:

- Radiosonde observations (see Figure 5-30)
- Weather reconnaissance aircraft observations
- Aircraft observations on-time and on-level
- Aircraft observations off-time or off-level
- Satellite wind estimates

Many other data sources are used in the analysis but are not plotted. These include:

- Ships
- Buoys
- Tide gauges
- Wind profilers
- WSR-88D weather radar VAD wind profiles
- Satellite sounder

Figure 5-30. U.S. Radiosonde Network

Table 5-6 Features of Constant Pressure Charts

Constant Pressure Chart	Pressure Altitude (MSL)		Isotachs	Contour Interval (meters)	Height Plot Decoding		Examples of Height Plotting	
					Prefix	Suffix	Plotted	Height (meters, MSL)
850MB	5,000 ft	1,500 m	No	30 m	1	-	530	1,530 m
700MB	10,000 ft	3,000 m	No	30 m	2 or 3*	-	180	3,180 m
500MB	18,000 ft	5,500 m	No	60 m	-	0	582	5,820 m
300MB	30,000 ft	9,000 m	Yes	120 m	-	0	948	9,480 m
200MB	39,000 ft	12,000 m	Yes	120 m	1	0	164	11,640 m

Note: Pressure altitudes are rounded to the nearest 1,000 for feet and 500 for meters.
* Prefix a "2" or "3," whichever brings the height closer to 3,000 meters.

Table 5-7. Constant Pressure Chart Plotting Models

Radiosonde	Reconnaissance Aircraft (RECCO)	Aircraft Report (AIREP)	Satellite Wind Estimate
TT hhh / DD $h_c h_c$	TT hhh / DD R	TT $P_a P_a P_a$	$P_a P_a P_a$

SYMBOL	MEANING
	Wind plotted in standard notation. The stem points in the direction from which the wind is blowing plotted to 36 compass points, relative to true north. Wind speed is denoted by a combination of flags (50 knots), barbs (10 knots), and half barbs (5 knots).
TT	Temperature rounded to the nearest whole degree Celsius, with minus sign prefixed if negative.
hhh	Height of the constant pressure surface in meters MSL. See the Table 5-8 to see how each chart abbreviates height.
$P_a P_a P_a$	Pressure altitude in hundreds of feet MSL.
DD	Temperature-dew point spread (depression of the dew point temperature) rounded to the nearest whole degree Celsius. When DD is less than or equal to 5 degrees Celsius, the station circle is darkened so a region of high moisture content will stand out. If DD is greater than 5 degrees Celsius, the station circle is not shaded. If the DD is too large to measure, an X is plotted. For RECCO reports, DD will be missing when the temperature is colder than -41°C.
R	Reconnaissance aircraft type.

Table 5-8. Radiosonde Plotting Model Examples

TT / hhh DD h_ch_c	20 504 5 -01	08 156 6 -02	-11 582 x +01	-36 956 21 -05	-56 214 7 -02
Plotting Model	**850MB**	**700MB**	**500MB**	**300MB**	**200MB**
Wind*	190°/20 kt	190°/25 kt	270°/15 kt	240°/75 kt	250°/115 kt
TT Temperature	20°C	8°C	-11°C	-36°C	-56°C
hhh Height	1,504 m	3,156 m	5,820 m	9,560 m	12,140 m
DD Temperature -Dew Point Spread	5°C	6°C	Too dry to measure	21°C	7°C
h_ch_c Height Change	-10 m	-20 m	+10 m	-50 m	-20 m

* Wind direction assumes that north is at the top of the page. Latitude and longitude lines, as well as other geographical references, must be used to determine actual compass direction.

5.2.3 Analyses

All constant pressure charts contain analyses of height and temperature. Selected charts have an analysis of wind speed as well.

5.2.3.1 Height

Heights are analyzed with contours. Contours are lines of constant height in MSL and are used to map height variations of constant pressure surfaces. They identify and characterize pressure systems on constant pressure charts.

Contours are drawn as solid lines labeled with 3-digit numbers in decameters. Intervals at which the contours are drawn at: 30 meters for the 850 mb and 700 mb charts, 60 meters for the 500-mb chart, and 120 meters for the 300-mb and 200-mb charts. The location of a High or Low is marked with a ⊗ symbol together with a larger **H** or **L**, and the central value in decameters printed under the center location.

Contour gradient is the amount of height change over a specified horizontal distance. Gradients identify slopes of constant pressure surfaces that fluctuate in altitude. Strong gradients are denoted by closely-spaced contours which identify steep slopes. Weak gradients are denoted by widely-spaced contours which identify shallow slopes.

Wind speeds are directly proportional to contour gradients. Faster wind speeds are associated with strong contour gradients and slower wind speeds are associated with weak contour gradients. In mountainous areas, winds are often variable on constant pressure charts with altitudes near terrain elevation due to friction.

5.2.3.2 Temperature

Temperature is analyzed with isotherms which are lines of constant temperature. They are drawn as long dashed lines at intervals of 5° Celsius. They are given a two-digit label in whole degrees Celsius and are preceded with a + (positive) or – (negative) sign. The zero degree isotherm denotes the freezing level.

Temperature gradient is the amount of temperature change over a specified distance. Isotherm gradients identify the magnitude of temperature variations. Strong gradients are denoted by closely spaced isotherms and identify large temperature variations. Weak gradients are denoted by loosely spaced isotherms and identify small temperature variations.

5.2.3.3 Wind Speed
Wind speed is analyzed with isotachs. Isotachs are lines of constant wind speed. They are drawn on the 300-mb and 200-mb charts with short-dashed lines at 20-knot intervals beginning with10 knots. They are labeled with a two- or three-digit number followed by a **K** for knots. Regions of high wind speeds are highlighted by alternate bands of shading and no-shading at 40-knot intervals beginning at 70 knots. A jet stream axis is the axis of maximum wind speed in a jet stream. Jet axes are not explicitly indicated, but their positions can be inferred from the isotach pattern and plotted winds.

5.2.3.4 Use
Constant pressure charts are used to provide an overview of selected observed weather conditions at specified pressure altitudes.

Pressure patterns cause and characterize much of the weather. Typically, lows and troughs are associated with bad weather, clouds and precipitation, while highs and ridges are associated with good weather.

Table 5-9. Reconnaissance Aircraft (RECCO) Plotting Model Examples

Plotting Model	850MB	700MB	500MB	300MB	200MB
Wind*	150°/90 kt	130°/35 kt	180° /60 kt	240°/30 kt	110°/30 kt
TT Temperature	19°C	9°C	-5°C	-28°C	-53°C
hhh Height	1,366 m	3,146 m	5,800 m	9,660 m	12,420 m
DD Temperature -Dew Point Spread	1°C	1°C	2°C	3°C	Missing
R RECCO Type	AA329A	AA921A	AA923A	AA924A	AA916A

* Wind direction assumes that north is at the top of the page. Latitude and longitude lines, as well as other geographical references, must be used to determine actual compass direction.

Table 5-10. Aircraft Report (AIREP) Plotting Model Examples

TT ☐ PₐPₐPₐ	$-05\diagup060$	$12_{\square}^{100}$ LV	$-10_{\square}180$	$-38_{\square}330$	$-54_{\square}360$
Plotting Model	**850MB**	**700MB**	**500MB**	**300MB**	**200MB**
⟋ **Wind***	20°/10 kt	Light and Variable	300°/30 kt	190°/5 kt	290°/50 kt
TT **Temperature**	-5°C	12°C	-10°C	-38°C	-54°C
PₐPₐPₐ **Pressure Altitude (MSL)**	6,000 ft	10,000 ft	18,000 ft	33,000 ft	36,000 ft

* Wind direction assumes that north is at the top of the page. Latitude and longitude lines, as well as other geographical references, must be used to determine actual compass direction.

Table 5-11. Satellite Wind Estimate Plotting Model Examples

★ PₐPₐPₐ	⟍070	⌐110	⟍170	330	⟍360
Plotting Model	**850MB**	**700MB**	**500MB**	**300MB**	**200MB**
⟋ **Wind***	290°/30 kt	360°/20 kt	240°/10 kt	140°/165 kt	310°/60 kt
PₐPₐPₐ **Pressure Altitude (MSL)**	7,000 ft	11,000 ft	17,000 ft	33,000 ft	36,000 ft

* Wind direction assumes that north is at the top of the page. Latitude and longitude lines, as well as other geographical references, must be used to determine actual compass direction.

Figure 5-31. 850MB Analysis Chart Example

Figure 5-32. 700MB Analysis Chart Example

Section 5: Graphical Observations and Derived Products

Figure 5-33. 500MB Analysis Chart Example

Figure 5-34. 300MB Analysis Chart Example

D166 .. 200MB ANALYSIS HEIGHTS/ISOTACHS VALID 00Z WED 15 SEP 2004

Figure 5-35. 200MB Analysis Chart Example

5.3 Freezing-level Graphics

The freezing level is the lowest altitude in the atmosphere over a given location at which the air temperature reaches 0°C. This altitude is also known as the height of the 0°C constant-temperature surface. A freezing level chart shows the height of the 0°C constant-temperature surface.

The concept of freezing level becomes slightly more complicated when more than one altitude is determined to be at a temperature of 0°C. These "multiple freezing layers" occur when a temperature inversion at altitudes above the defined freezing level are present. For example, if the first freezing level is at 3000 ft MSL and the second is at 7000 ft MSL, a temperature inversion is between these two altitudes. This would indicate temperatures rising above freezing above 3000 ft MSL and then back below freezing at 7000 ft MSL.

The Aviation Weather Center (AWC) provides freezing level graphics available on the Aviation Digital Data Service (ADDS) web site at:
http://adds.aviationweather.noaa.gov/icing/frzg_nav.php

The ADDS Freezing Level graphics provide an initial analysis and forecasts at 3-, 6-, 9-, and 12-hours into the future. The forecasts are based on output from the National Weather Service's (NWS) Rapid Update Cycle (RUC) numerical forecast model.

5.3.1 Issuance
The initial analysis and 3-hour forecast graphics are updated hourly. The 6-, 9-, and 12-hour forecast graphics are updated every three hours.

5.3.2 Observational Data
The RUC forecast model incorporates all of the latest weather observations in order to produce the best available analysis and forecast. These observations include:

- Commercial aircraft

- Profiler related:

    o Wind profilers (404 and boundary layer 915 MHz)

    o VAD (Velocity Azimuth Display) winds from WSR-88D radars

    o RASS (Radio Acoustic Sounding System)

- Rawinsondes and special dropwinsondes

- Surface:

    o GPS total precipitable water estimates

    o GOES cloud-top data (pressure and temperature)

    o GOES total precipitable water estimates

o   SSM/I total precipitable water estimates

o   GOES high-density visible and infrared (IR) cloud drift winds

- Experimental:

    o   Radar reflectivity (3-d)

    o   Lightning

    o   Regional aircraft data with moisture (TAMDAR)

5.3.3 Format

The colors represent the height in hundreds of feet above mean sea level (MSL) of the lowest freezing level.

- Regions with white indicate the surface and the entire depth of the atmosphere are below freezing.
- Hatched regions represent areas where the surface temperature is below freezing with multiple freezing levels aloft.

- Areas where the surface temperature is above freezing with multiple freezing levels aloft are in regions where adjacent pixels change by more than one color when compared against the color scale (e.g., orange to dark blue).

The following cases illustrate the interpretation of the graphic.

Figure 5-36. RUC 00-hour Freezing Level Graphic Example

Case 1 (Figure 5-36, Case 1) represents the condition where temperature is below freezing at the surface and all levels above the surface (represented in the graphic above by white-colored pixels).

Case 2 (Figure 5-36, Case 2) represents the condition where the temperature goes above and below freezing two or more times vertically through the atmosphere while the surface temperature is less than 0°C. These regions are hatched with white. The underlying color represents the lowest height where the temperature crosses the 0°C line as shown by the blue arrow on the vertical temperature graphic.

Case 3 (Figure 5-36, Case 3) represents the condition where the temperature goes above and below freezing three or more times vertically through the atmosphere while the surface temperature is higher than 0°C. These regions are located in areas where adjacent pixels change by more than one color when compared against the color scale.

Case 4 (Figure 5-36, Case 4) is relatively simple and represents the condition where the temperature at the surface is above freezing and the air generally cools with height crossing the 0°C line once.

5.3.4 Use

Freezing level graphics are used to assess the lowest freezing level heights and their values relative to flight paths. Clear, rime and mixed icing are found in layers with below-freezing (negative) temperatures and super-cooled water droplets. Users should be aware that official forecast freezing level information is specified within the AIRMET Zulu Bulletins (Contiguous U.S. and Hawaii) and the AIRMET "ICE AND FZLVL" information embedded within the Area Forecasts (Alaska only)

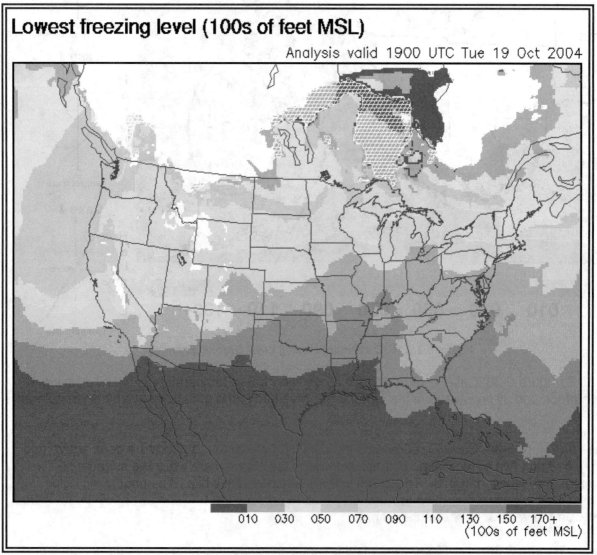

Figure 5-37. ADDS Freezing Level Graphic Example

5.4 Weather Depiction Chart

The Weather Depiction Chart (Figure 5-39) contains a plot of weather conditions at selected METAR stations and an analysis of weather flying category. It is designed primarily as a briefing tool to alert aviation interests to the location of critical or near-critical operational minimums at terminals in the conterminous US and surrounding land areas. The chart can be found at: http://weather.noaa.gov/pub/fax/QGUA00.TIF

Figure 5-39. Weather Depiction Chart Example

5.4.1 Issuance
The Weather Depiction chart is issued eight times daily at the following times:

Table 5-13. Weather Depiction Charts Issuance Schedule

Valid Time (UTC)	01	04	07	10	13	16	19	22

5.4.2 Station Plot Model
METAR elements (Section 2.1) associated with weather flying category (visibility, present weather, sky cover, and ceiling) are plotted for each station on the chart (Figure 5-41). The station is located at the center of the sky cover symbol. Most stations are not plotted due to space limitations. However, all reporting stations are used in the weather flying category analysis.

Figure 5-40. Weather Depiction Chart Station Plot Model

5.4.2.1 Visibility

When visibility is 5 miles or less, it is entered to the left of the station. Visibility is entered in statute miles and fractions of a mile.

5.4.2.2 Present Weather

Present weather symbols are entered to the left of the station. If the present weather information is obtained by an automated system, the right bracket symbol ( ]) is plotted to the right of the station.

When several types of weather and/or obstructions to visibility are reported, the most significant weather element is plotted. This is the first weather element coded in the METAR report (Section 2.1) and is usually the highest coded number in the Present Weather Symbols guide (Appendix I).

5.4.2.3 Sky Cover

Sky cover represents the summation total of the sky condition element from the METAR report. For example, if the METAR sky condition element was **SCT030 BKN060 OVC090**, the sky cover would be overcast. Sky cover symbols are listed in Figure 5-41.

5.4.2.4 Ceiling

Ceiling is the height from the base of the lowest layer aloft covering more than one-half the sky to the ground. Additionally, vertical visibility into a total surface-based obscuration is defined as a ceiling. For a METAR report, the first broken (BKN) or overcast (OVC) layer is the ceiling. For example, if the METAR sky condition element is **SCT030 BKN060 OVC090**, the ceiling is 6,000 feet.

For stations with broken to overcast layers, the ceiling height is plotted below the station. Ceilings are reported as hundreds of feet above ground level (AGL).

For a total surface-based obscuration, no ceiling is plotted and the METAR must be consulted.

Partial obscurations are not identified.

- For a partial obscuration with no layer above, the sky cover symbol will be plotted as missing (Figure 5-41).
- For a partial obscuration with a layer above, the sky cover and ceiling height will be plotted for the cloud layer only.

The METAR report should be consulted to identify the partial obscuration.

If the sky cover is clear, few, or scattered, no ceiling is plotted.

5.4.3 Weather Flying Category Analysis
Instrument Flight Rules (IFR) indicated on the Weather Depiction Chart represents ceilings less than 1,000 feet and/or visibility less than 3 statute miles and IFR operations must be in place. IFR areas are outlined on the chart with a solid line and are shaded. IFR areas are typically shaded red in colorized versions of the chart.

Marginal Visual Flight Rules (MVFR) indicated on the Weather Depiction Chart represents ceiling 1,000 to 3,000 feet and/or visibility 3 to 5 statute miles and VFR operations can take place. MVFR areas are outlined with a solid line, but the area is not shaded. MVFR areas are typically shaded blue in colorized versions of the chart.

Visual Flight Rules (VFR) indicated on the Weather Depiction Chart represents a ceiling greater than 3,000 feet or clear skies and visibility greater than 5 statute miles and VFR operations can take place. VFR conditions are not analyzed. This does not necessarily imply that the sky is clear.

5.4.4 Use
The Weather Depiction Chart is an ideal place to begin flight planning or to prepare for a weather briefing. This chart provides an overview of weather flying categories and other adverse weather conditions for the chart valid time. The chart, though, may not completely represent the en route conditions because of terrain variations and the possibility of weather occurring between reporting stations. This chart should be used in addition to the current METAR reports, pilot weather reports, and radar and satellite imagery for a complete look at the latest flying conditions.

5.5 Alaska Weather Depiction Charts

The Alaska Weather Depiction Charts (Figure 5-43) display color coded station plots which show: temperature, dew point, ceiling, visibility and wind direction/speed. A key to the station plots is found on each map.

Figure 5-41. AAWU Alaska Weather Depiction Chart Example

Thirteen charts cover Alaska (except for the Aleutians) and adjacent areas of Canada.

Table 5-14. AAWU Alaska Weather Depiction Charts Coverage

Chart Coverage	Scale
Entire State of Alaska	(1:12 million)
All of Southeast Alaska	(1:5 million)
Southern Southeast Alaska	(1:3 million)
Northern Southeast Alaska	(1:3 million)
North Gulf Coast	(1:5 million)
South Central Alaska	(1:5 million)
Cook Inlet/Susitna Valley	(1:2 million)
Southwest Alaska	(1:6 million)
Western Interior	(1:5 million)
Central Interior	(1:5 million)
Northern Alaska	(1:6 million)
Southwest British Columbia	(1:7 million)
Yukon Territory/Northern British Columbia	(1:8 million)

5.5.1 Issuance

The charts are issued hourly and can be found on the Alaska Aviation Weather Unit (AAWU) web site at: http://aawu.arh.noaa.gov/Sigwx.php. The charts will first appear at about 10 minutes past the hour, with a second update at about 25 minutes past the hour.

5.5.2 Legends

The Alaska Weather Depiction Charts depict numerous parameters including the flying category, sky cover and wind.

5.5.2.1 Flying Category

Each station plot is color-coded according to the weather flying category reported (Table 5-16). Red indicates instrument flight rules (IFR), blue indicates marginal visual flight rules (MVFR), and black is plotted for stations reporting visual flight rules (VFR).

Table 5-15 AAWU Alaska Weather Flying Categories and Criteria

FLYING CATEGORY	CEILING (feet)	VISIBILITY (miles)
VFR (black)	Greater than 3,000 feet	Greater than 5 miles
MVFR (blue)	1,000 to 3,000 feet	3 to 5 miles
IFR (red)	Less than 1,000 feet	Less than 3 miles

5.5.2.2 Station Plot

METAR elements are plotted for each station on the chart (Figure 5-45). Some stations are not plotted due to space limitations, notably on the chart which covers the entire state of Alaska.

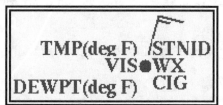

Figure 5-42. AAWU Alaska Weather Depiction Chart Station Plot Legend

5.5.2.3 Sky Cover
The sky cover symbol is plotted at the station location and is filled according to the summation total of the sky condition element from the METAR report. For example, if the METAR sky condition element was **SCT030 BKN060 OVC090**, the sky cover would be overcast. Sky cover symbols are listed in Figure 5-41.

5.5.2.4 Station Identifier (STNID)
The four-letter ICAO station identifier is entered to the upper right of the station.

5.5.2.5 Wind
Wind is plotted in increments of 5 knots (kts). The wind direction is referenced to "true" north and is depicted by a stem (line) pointed in the direction from which the wind is blowing. Wind speed is determined by adding the values of the flags (50 kts), barbs (10kts), and half barbs (5 kts) found on the stem.

A single circle over the station with no wind symbol indicates a calm wind.

Some sample wind symbols are shown on Figure 5-46.

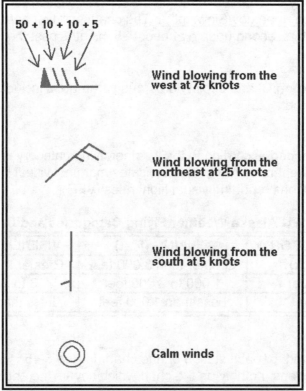

Figure 5-43. AAWU Alaska Weather Depiction Chart Wind Symbols

5.5.2.6 Temperature (TMP deg F)
Temperature in degrees Fahrenheit is plotted to the upper left of the sky cover symbol.

5.5.2.7 Visibility (VIS)
Visibility in statute miles is plotted to the left of the sky cover symbol. Decimals are used to represent tenths of miles when necessary.

5.5.2.8 Dew Point Temperature (DEWPT deg F)
Dew point temperature in degrees Fahrenheit is plotted to the lower left of the sky cover symbol.

5.5.2.9 Ceiling (CIG)
Ceiling is the height from the base of the lowest layer aloft covering more than one-half the sky. Additionally, vertical visibility into a total surface-based obscuration is defined as a ceiling. For a METAR report, the first broken (BKN) or overcast (OVC) layer is the ceiling. For example, if the METAR sky condition element is **SCT030 BKN060 OVC090**, the ceiling is 6,000 feet.

For a total surface-based obscuration, no ceiling is plotted and the METAR must be consulted.

If the sky cover is clear, few, or scattered, no ceiling is plotted.

The ceiling is plotted to the lower right of the station circle. Ceilings are reported as hundreds of feet above ground level (AGL). If no ceiling is present, the code **999** will be plotted.

5.5.2.10 Present Weather (WX)
Present weather symbols are entered to the left of the station. Note that the older Surface Aviation Observation (SAO) code is used instead Surface Analysis Chart symbols or the modern METAR code.

Table 5-16 Alaska Weather Depiction Charts Precipitation Symbols

Symbol	Meaning
T	Thunderstorm
R	Rain
RW	Rain Shower
L	Drizzle
ZR	Freezing Rain
ZL	Freezing Drizzle
A	Hail
IP	Ice Pellets
IPW	Ice Pellet Showers
S	Snow
SW	Snow Showers
SP	Snow Pellets
SG	Snow Grains
IC	Ice Crystals

Table 5-17 Alaska Weather Depiction Charts Obstruction to Visibility Symbols

Symbol	Meaning
BD	Blowing Dust
BN	Blowing Sand
BS	Blowing Snow
BY	Blowing Spray
D	Dust
F	Fog
GF	Ground Fog
H	Haze
IF	Ice Fog
K	Smoke

Table 5-18 Alaska Weather Depiction Charts Precipitation Intensity Symbols

Symbol	Meaning
-	Light
(No symbol)	Moderate
+	Heavy

5.5.3 Use

The Alaska Weather Depiction Charts provide an overview of weather flying categories and other adverse weather conditions for the chart valid time. The chart often does not completely represent the en route conditions because of terrain variations and the possibility of weather occurring between reporting stations. These charts should be used in addition to the latest METAR/SPECIs, pilot weather reports, and radar and satellite imagery for a complete look at the latest flying conditions.

Figure 5-44. AAWU Alaska Weather Depiction Chart – South Central Alaska Example

5.6 Radar Summary Chart

The Radar Summary Chart (Figure 5-49) is a computer-generated mosaic of radar echo intensity contours based on Radar Weather Reports (Section 2.3) over the contiguous U.S. Possible precipitation types, cell movements, maximum tops, locations of line echoes, and remarks are plotted on this chart. Much of this information is often truncated due to space limitations. Severe thunderstorm and tornado watches are plotted if they are in effect when the chart is valid. The Radar Summary Chart is available on the National Weather Service (NWS) Fax Charts web site at: http://weather.noaa.gov/pub/fax/QAUA00.TIF

Figure 5-45. Radar Summary Chart Example

5.6.1 Issuance
The chart is issued hourly. Figure 5-50 depicts the WSR-88D weather radar network from which the chart is produced.

5.6.2 Format
The Radar Summary Chart depicts precipitation type, intensity, coverage, movement, echoes, and maximum tops.

5.6.2.1 Precipitation Type
The precipitation type, determined by a computer model, is indicated on the chart by symbols located adjacent to the precipitation areas. These symbols (Table 5-20) are not in METAR

format. Freezing precipitation is not reported in Radar Weather Reports and, thus, not plotted on the Radar Summary Chart.

**Table 5-19. Radar Summary Chart
Precipitation Type Symbols**

SYMBOL	MEANING
R	Rain
RW	Rain shower
S	Snow
SW	Snow shower
T	Thunderstorms

5.6.2.2 Precipitation Intensity

The six precipitation intensity levels coded in the Radar Weather Report are consolidated into three contour intervals for the Radar Summary Chart (Figure 5-47). Precipitation intensity is correlated only for liquid precipitation, not solid precipitation (e.g., snow).

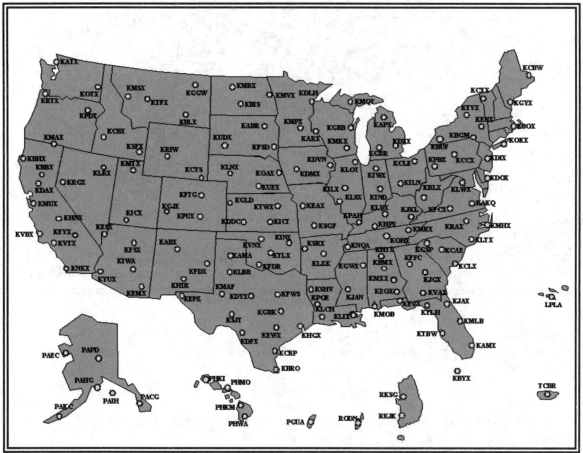

Figure 5-46. WSR-88D Weather Radar Network

ATC Weather Radar Echo Terminology	Precipitation Description	Reflectivity (dBZ)
Light	Trace to light rain	<30 dBZ
Moderate	Light to moderate rain	30-40 dBZ
Heavy	Heavy rain; possible small granules	>40-50 dBZ
Extreme	Very heavy rain; hail; pea/marble or greater size hail	50+ dBZ

450   Highest echo top in area in hundreds of feet MSL (45,000 feet MSL).

Figure 5-47. Radar Summary Chart Precipitation Intensity

5.6.2.3 Echo Coverage

All of the shaded areas within the contours are assumed to contain precipitation. However, actual precipitation coverage is less. This is because only a fraction of a grid box needs to be covered with echoes for the entire grid box to be plotted as precipitation on the chart.

5.6.2.4 Line Echoes

When precipitation echoes are reported as a **LINE**, a line will be drawn through them on the chart (see Table 5-21). Where there is 8/10ths or more coverage, the line is labeled as solid (**SLD**) at both ends.

Table 5-20. Radar Summary Chart Echo Configuration Symbols

SYMBOL	MEANING
SLD	8/10ths or greater coverage in a line.
/	Line of echoes.
SLD TRW SLD	Solid line of thunderstorms with intense to extreme precipitation.

5.6.2.5 Cell Movement

Cell movement is the average motion of all cells within a configuration. An arrow indicates direction of cell movement. Speed in knots is entered near the arrowhead. **LM** identifies little movement. Movement of areas and lines can be significantly different from the motion of the individual cells that comprise these configurations.

Table 5-21. Radar Summary Chart Cell Movement Examples

SYMBOL	MEANING
↗ 35	Cell movement to the northeast at 35 knots
→ 24	Cell movement to the east at 24 knots
↓ 18	Cell movement to the south at 18 knots
↙ 12	Cell movement to the southwest at 12 knots
LM	Little cell movement

5.6.2.6 Maximum Top

Figure 5-48. Radar Summary Chart Maximum Top Example

A maximum top is the altitude of the highest precipitation echo as coded on a Weather Radar Report (Section 2.3). Altitudes are sometimes augmented by satellite data. Individual Radar Weather Reports should be used to determine if satellite data was used for precipitation echo tops.

Tops are plotted in 3-digit groups representing height in hundreds of feet MSL and are underlined. Where it is necessary to offset a top for reasons of insufficient space, a line is drawn from one end of the underline to a small black square which represents the location of the top.

Maximum echo top does not equal maximum cloud top. The maximum echo top is the altitude of the highest light precipitation echo, not highest cloud top. Also, all radar heights are approximations due to radar wave propagation variations depending on atmosphere conditions.

5.6.2.7 Weather Watch Areas

Heavy dashed lines outline Tornado (**WT**) (Section 5.5.2) and Severe Thunderstorm (**WS**) Watch (Section 5.4.2) areas. The type of watch and the watch number are enclosed in a rectangle and positioned as closely as possible to the northeast corner of the watch. If there is no room at the northeast corner of the watch, the watch information is offset and connected to the watch by a thin line. The watch number is also printed at the bottom of the chart (in Mexico) together with the issuance time and expiration time under a label reading "**WEATHER WATCH AREAS**". In case no weather watch is in effect, "**NONE**" is printed at the bottom of the chart.

Table 5-22. Radar Summary Chart Weather Watch Area Examples

SYMBOL	MEANING
WS210	Severe Thunderstorm Watch number 210
WT457	Tornado Thunderstorm Watch number 457

5.6.2.8 Operational Contractions

Radar sites which report **PPINA**, **PPINE**, and **PPIOM** in their Weather Radar Reports (Section 2.3.1.10) are abbreviated to **NA**, **NE**, and **OM** respectively and plotted over the radar sites on the chart.

Table 5-23. Radar Summary Chart
Operational Contractions

SYMBOL	MEANING
NA	Not available
NE	No echoes
OM	Out for maintenance

5.6.3 Use

The Radar Summary Chart aids in preflight planning by identifying areas of precipitation and highlighting its characteristics. This chart displays precipitation only; it does not display clouds, fog, fronts, or other boundaries. Therefore, the absence of echoes does not equal clear weather. Cloud tops will be somewhat higher than precipitation tops detected by radar. The chart must be used in conjunction with other charts, reports, and forecasts.

The radar summary chart is for <u>preflight</u> planning only and should always be cross-checked and updated by current WSR-88D images. Once airborne, the pilot must evade individual storms by in-flight observations. This can be done by using visual sighting or airborne radar as well as by requesting weather radar information from En route Flight Advisory Service "Flight Watch" briefers at <u>Automated Flight Service Station (AFSS)</u>. AFSS Flight Watch briefers have access to current weather radar imagery.

Figure 5-49. Radar Summary Chart Example

5.7 Alaska Initial Geopotential Heights and Winds Charts

The Alaska Initial Geopotential Heights and Winds Charts (Figure 5-54) display an analysis of the observed height contours and winds at selected constant pressure surfaces (flight levels).

Figure 5-50. Alaskan Initial Geopotential Heights and Winds Chart Example

Table 5-24. Pressure Altitudes of Alaska Initial Geopotential
Heights and Winds Charts

CHART	PRESSURE ALTITUDE (Feet, MSL)	PRESSURE ALTITUDE (Meters, MSL)
200 MB	39,000 ft	12,000 m
300 MB	30,000 ft	9,000 m
500 MB	18,000 ft	5,500 m
700 MB	10,000 ft	3,000 m
850 MB	5,000 ft	1,500 m

5.7.1 Issuance

The charts are issued twice daily with valid times of 00z and 12z and can be found on the Alaska Aviation Weather Unit (AAWU) web site at: http://aawu.arh.noaa.gov/upperwinds.php.

5.7.2 Analysis
The analysis of both <u>height</u> contours and winds are based on output from the North American Mesoscale (NAM) computer forecast model.

5.7.2.1 Height Contours
<u>Height</u> contours are lines of constant <u>height</u> referenced to MSL and are used to map the <u>height</u> variations of constant pressure surfaces. They identify and characterize pressure systems on <u>constant pressure chart</u>s.

Contours are drawn as solid lines and labeled in meters. The intervals at which the contours are drawn are 60 meters on all of the charts.

5.7.2.2 Winds
Wind is plotted in increments of 5 <u>knot</u>s (kts). The wind direction is referenced to "true" north and is depicted by a stem (line) pointed in the direction from which the wind is blowing. Wind speed is determined by adding the values of the flags (50 kts), barbs (10kts), and half barbs (5 kts) found on the stem.

A single circle over the station with no wind symbol indicates a calm wind.

Figure 5-55 contains some examples wind symbols.

Figure 5-51. Alaskan Initial Geopotential Heights and Winds Chart Wind Plotting Model

5.7.3 Use
The Alaska Initial <u>Geopotential Heights</u> and Winds Charts are used to provide an overview of <u>height</u>s, pressure patterns and winds at specified pressure altitudes. Pressure patterns cause

and characterize much of the weather. Typically, lows and troughs are associated with bad weather, clouds and precipitation, while highs and ridges are associated with good weather.

Figure 5-52. Alaskan Initial Geopotential Heights and Winds Chart - 200MB Winds and Contours Chart Example

Figure 5-53. Alaskan Initial Geopotential Heights and Winds Chart - 300MB Winds and Contours Chart Example

Figure 5-54. Alaskan Initial Geopotential Heights and Winds Chart - 500MB Winds and Contours Chart Example

Figure 5-55. Alaskan Initial Geopotential Heights and Winds Chart - 700MB Winds and Contours Chart Example

Figure 5-56. Alaskan Initial Geopotential Heights and Winds Chart - 850MB Winds and Contours Chart Example

6 PRODUCTS FOR AVIATION HAZARDS

6.1 Significant Meteorological Information (SIGMET)

A SIGMET is a concise description of the occurrence or expected occurrence of specified en route weather phenomena which may affect the safety of aircraft operations. SIGMETs are intended for dissemination to all pilots in flight to enhance safety. SIGMETs are issued by the responsible MWO as soon as practical to give notice to operators and aircrews of potentially hazardous en-route conditions.

- SIGMETs are available on the Aviation Digital Data Service (ADDS) web site at:
  http://adds.aviationweather.noaa.gov/airmet/

  - Alaska SIGMETs are also available on the Alaska Aviation Weather Unit (AAWU) web site at: http://aawu.arh.noaa.gov/

  - Hawaii SIGMETs are also available on the NWS WFO Honolulu web site at: http://www.prh.noaa.gov/hnl/pages/aviation.php

6.1.1 SIGMET Issuance
SIGMETs are issued from Meteorological Watch Offices (MWO). The U.S. has three MWOs: the Aviation Weather Center (AWC), the Alaska Aviation Weather Unit (AAWU), and the Weather Forecast Office (WFO) in Honolulu. Their areas of responsibility are as follows:

- The AWC:

  - Twenty (20) domestic Air Route Traffic Control Center (ARTCC) Flight Information Regions (FIRs) covering the conterminous U.S. (CONUS) and adjacent coastal waters (Figure 6-1).

  - The New York, Houston, Miami, and San Juan Oceanic FIRs (Figure 6-2).

  - The Oakland Oceanic FIR north of 30 north latitude, and the portion east of 140 west longitude which is between the equator and 30 north latitude (Figure 6-3).

- The AAWU is responsible for the Anchorage Continental FIR and Anchorage Oceanic FIR (Figure 6-3).

- WFO Honolulu is responsible for the Oakland Oceanic FIR south of 30 north latitude and between 140 west and 130 east longitude (Figure 6-3).

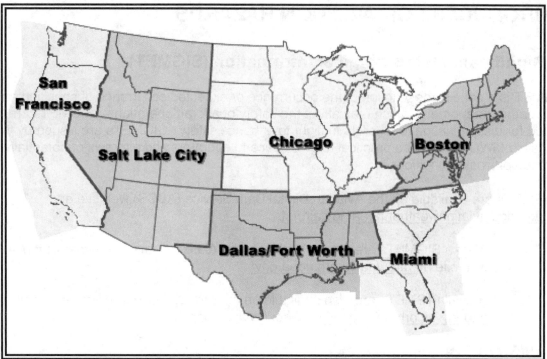

Figure 6-1. AWC SIGMET Areas of Responsibility - Conterminous U.S.

Figure 6-2. AWC SIGMET Areas of Responsibility – Atlantic Basin

Figure 6-3. SIGMET Areas of Responsibility – Pacific Basin

6.1.1.1 SIGMET Identification
When a SIGMET is issued, it is assigned a unique series identifier:

- AWC for CONUS
  - **NOVEMBER** through **YANKEE**, excluding **SIERRA** and **TANGO**

- AWC for Oakland Oceanic FIR
  - **ALFA** through **HOTEL**

- Honolulu MWO for Oakland Oceanic FIR
  - **NOVEMBER** through **ZULU**

- AAWU for Anchorage FIR
  - **INDIA** through **MIKE**

A number is assigned sequentially with each issuance until the phenomenon ends. At 0000 UTC each day, all continuing SIGMETs are renumbered to one (1) regardless of a continuation of the phenomena. (e.g., YANKEE 1, YANKEE 2, YANKEE 3, etc.)

6.1.2 SIGMET Standardization

SIGMETs follow these standards:

- All heights or altitudes are referenced to above mean sea level (AMSL), unless otherwise noted, and annotated using the height in hundreds of feet, consisting of three digits (e.g., 040). For heights at or above 18,000 feet, the level is preceded by FL to represent flight levels (e.g., FL180).

- References to latitude and longitude are in whole degrees and minutes following the model: Nnn[nn] or Snn[nn], Wnnn[nn] or Ennn[nn] with a space between latitude and longitude and a hyphen between successive points. Example: N3106 W07118 – N3011 W7209

- Messages are prepared in abbreviated plain language using contractions from the Federal Aviation Administration (FAA) Order 7340.2 for domestic products and International Civil Aviation Organization (ICAO) document 8400 for international products issued for Oceanic FIRs. A limited number of non-abbreviated words, geographical names and numerical values of a self-explanatory nature may also be used.

- Weather and obstructions to visibility are described using the weather abbreviations for surface weather observations (METAR/SPECI). See the Federal Meteorological Handbook (FMH) No. 1 – Surface Observations or Section 3.1 of this document.

Note: Refer to Appendix A for definitions of common terms used in SIGMETs.

6.1.3 SIGMET (Non-Convective) – Conterminous U.S.

6.1.3.1 SIGMET (Non-Convective) Issuance Criteria – Contiguous U.S.

A SIGMET may be issued in the Contiguous U.S. when any of the following conditions are affecting or, in the judgment of the forecaster, are expected to affect an area of at least 3,000 square miles or an area judged to have a significant impact on the safety of aircraft operations.

- Severe or greater Turbulence (SEV TURB)

- Severe Icing (SEV ICE)

- Widespread Duststorm (WDSPR DS)

- Widespread Sandstorm (WDSPR SS)

- Volcanic Ash (VA)

6.1.3.2 SIGMET (Non-Convective) Issuance Time and Valid Period – Conterminous U.S.
A SIGMET is an unscheduled product issued any time conditions reaching SIGMET criteria are occurring or expected to occur within a 4-hour period. A SIGMET can have a valid period up to, but not exceeding, four (4) hours. SIGMETs for continuing phenomena will be reissued at least every 4 hours as long as SIGMET conditions continue to occur in the area for responsibility.

6.1.3.3 SIGMET (Non-Convective) Format – Conterminous U.S.
The content and order of elements in the SIGMET are as follows:

- series name and number

- valid beginning and ending time (UTC)

- list of states affected by the phenomena

- location of phenomena delineated by high-altitude VOR coordinates covering the affected area during the SIGMET valid time

- phenomena description (e.g., SEV ICE)

- vertical extent (base and top), if appropriate

- movement, if appropriate

- intensity change (INTSF – intensifying, WKN – weakening, NC – no change)

- Indication that the whether the condition will continue during the 4 hours beyond the valid time of the SIGMET

LINE

1 — SFOR UWS 100130
2 — SIGMET ROMEO 1 VALID UNTIL 100530
3 — OR WA
4 — FROM SEA TO PDT TO EUG TO SEA
5 — OCNL MOGR CAT BTN FL280 AND FL350 EXP DUE TO
     JTSTR.   CONDS BGNG AFT 0200Z CONTG BYD 0530Z AND
     SPRDG OVR CNTRL ID BY 0400Z.

Figure 6-4. SIGMET for the Conterminous U.S. Decoding Example

Table 6-1. Decoding a SIGMET (Non-Convective) for the Conterminous U.S.

Line	Content	Description
1	SFO	SIGMET area identifier
	R	SIGMET series
	WS	Product identifier
	100130	Issuance date/time UTC
2	SIGMET	Product type
	ROMEO	SIGMET series name
	1	Series issuance number
	VALID UNTIL 100530	Ending valid date/time UTC
3	OR WA	Phenomenon location (states)
4	FROM SEA TO PDT TO EUG TO SEA	Phenomenon location (high-altitude VOR coordinates)
5	OCNL MOGR CAT BTN FL280 AND FL350 EXP DUE TO JTSTR. CONDS BGNG AFT 0200Z CONTG BYD 0530Z AND SPRDG OVR CNTRL ID BY 0400Z.	Phenomenon description

The SIGMET in Figure 6-4 is decoded as the following:

(Line 1) *SIGMET ROMEO series issued for the San Francisco Area at 0130 UTC on the 10th day of the month.*

(Line 2) *This is the first issuance of the SIGMET ROMEO series and is valid until the 10th day of the month at 0530 UTC.*

(Line 3) *The affected states within the SFO area are Oregon and Washington.*

(Line 4) *From Seattle, WA; to Pendleton, OR; to Eugene, OR; to Seattle, WA;*

(Line 5) Occasional moderate or greater clear air <u>turbulence</u> between Flight Level 280 and Flight Level 350, expected due to <u>jet stream</u>. Conditions beginning after 0200Z continuing beyond 0530Z and spreading over central Idaho by 0400Z.

6.1.3.4 SIGMET (Non-Convective) Cancellations – Conterminous U.S.
A CONUS non-convective SIGMET is canceled when the phenomena is no longer occurring or no longer expected to occur or has moved out of the area of responsibility.

6.1.3.5 SIGMET (Non-Convective) Amendments – Conterminous U.S.
Amendments to CONUS non-convective SIGMETs are NOT issued. Instead, a new SIGMET is issued using the next series number.

6.1.3.6 SIGMET (Non-Convective) Corrections – Conterminous U.S.
Corrections to CONUS non-convective SIGMETs are issued as necessary. The corrected SIGMET is identified by a "COR" located at the end of the first line after the issuance UTC date/time.

6.1.3.7 SIGMET (Non-Convective) Example – Conterminous U.S.

```
WSUS01 KKCI 050600
WS1R
BOSR WS 050600
SIGMET ROMEO 2 VALID UNTIL 051000
ME NH VT
FROM CAR TO YSJ TO CON TO MPV TO CAR
SEV TURB OBS AND FCST BLW 080. CONDS CONTG BYD 1000Z.
```

SIGMET (WSUS01) issued by the Meteorological Watch Office (WMO) (Aviation Weather Center) in Kansas City, Missouri (KKCI) on the 5th day of the month at 0600 UTC. The National Weather Service AWIPS communication header for this product is WSR1. SIGMET issued for the Boston Area Forecast region on the 5th day of the month at 0600 UTC. This is the second (2nd) issuance of SIGMET series Romeo and is valid until the 5th day of the month at 1000 UTC. The affected states are Maine (ME), New Hampshire (NH) and Vermont (VT). Within an area bounded from Caribou, Maine (CAR) to St. Johns, New Brunswick (YSJ); to Concord, New Hampshire (CON); to Montpelier, Vermont (MPV); to Caribou, Maine (CAR). Severe <u>turbulence</u> observed and forecast below 8,000 feet. Conditions continuing beyond 1000 UTC.

6.1.4 Convective SIGMET
Convective SIGMETs are issued for the conterminous U.S. (CONUS) instead of SIGMETs for thunderstorms. Any Convective SIGMET implies severe or greater turbulence, severe icing, and low level wind shear.

6.1.4.1 Convective SIGMET - Routine Issuance Criteria
A Convective SIGMET will be issued when any of the following conditions are occurring or, in the judgment of the forecaster, are expected to occur:

- A line of thunderstorms at least 60 miles long with thunderstorms affecting at least 40 percent of its length.

- An area of active thunderstorms affecting at least 3,000 square miles covering at least 40 percent of the area concerned and exhibiting a very strong radar reflectivity intensity or a significant satellite or lightning signature.

- Embedded or severe thunderstorm(s) expected to occur for more than 30 minutes during the valid period regardless of the size of the area.

6.1.4.2 Convective SIGMET - Special Issuance Criteria

A special Convective SIGMET may be issued when any of the following criteria are occurring or, in the judgment of the forecaster, are expected to occur for more than 30 minutes of the valid period.

- Tornado, hail greater than or equal to ¾ inch (at the surface), or wind gusts greater than or equal to 50 knots (at the surface) are reported.

- Indications of rapidly changing conditions, if in the forecaster's judgment, they are not sufficiently described in existing Convective SIGMETs.

- Special issuance is not required for a valid Convective SIGMET.

6.1.4.3 Convective SIGMET Issuance Time and Valid Period

Convective SIGMET bulletins for the eastern, central and western regions of the conterminous U.S. (Figure 6-5) are issued on a scheduled basis, hourly at 55 minutes past the hour. Each bulletin contains all valid Convective SIGMETs within the region. Convective SIGMETs are valid for two (2) hours or until superseded by the next hourly issuance. A Convective SIGMET bulletin must be transmitted each hour for each region. When conditions do not meet or are not expected to meet Convective SIGMET criteria within a region at the scheduled time of issuance a "CONVECTIVE SIGMET...NONE" message is transmitted.

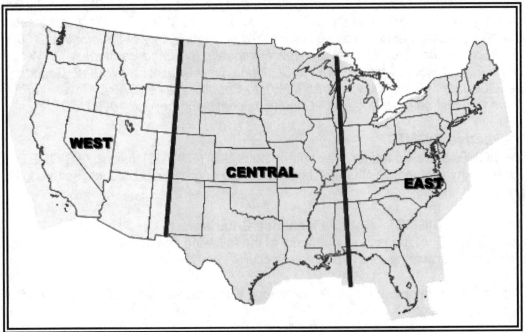

Figure 6-5. AWC Convective SIGMET Areas of Responsibility

6.1.4.4 Convective SIGMET Format

Each Convective SIGMET bulletin includes one or more individually numbered Convective SIGMETs for the region. The content and order of each bulletin is as follows:

- CONVECTIVE SIGMET series number and region letter (E, W or C)

- Valid ending time (UTC)

- list of states affected by the phenomena

- location of phenomena delineated by high-altitude VOR coordinates covering the affected area during the SIGMET valid time

- phenomena description (e.g., AREA SEV EMBD TS)

- movement (e.g., MOV FROM 26030KT)

- cloud top (e.g., TOPS ABV FL450)

- remarks (e.g., TORNADOES...HAIL TO 2.5 IN...WIND GUSTS TO 70KT POSS)

Note: Tropical Cyclone information will be added to remarks section of the CONUS Convective SIGMETs when appropriate.

Note: Refer to Appendix A for definitions of common terms used in Convective SIGMETs.

Figure 6-6. Convective SIGMET Decoding Example

Table 6-2. Decoding a Convective SIGMET

Line	Content	Description
1	MKC	Issuing Office (AWC)
	C	Region (East, Central or West)
	WST	Product Identifier
	221855	Issuance date/time (DDHHMM)
2	CONVECTIVE SIGMET	Product type
	20	Issuance number
	C	Region (East, Central or West)
3	VALID UNTIL 2055Z	Valid ending time (UTC)
4	ND SD	States/areas affected
5	FROM 90W MOT-GFK-ABR-90W MOT	Phenomenon location (high altitude VOR coordinates)
6	INTSFYG AREA SEV TS MOVG FROM 24045KT. TOPS ABV FL450. WIND GUSTS TO 60KTS RPRTD. TORNADOES...HAIL TO 2 IN... WIND GUSTS TO 65KTS POSS ND PTN	Phenomenon description, movement, cloud top, remarks

The Convective SIGMET in Figure 6-6 is decoded as the following:

(Line 1) *Convective SIGMET issued for the central portion of the United States on the 22nd at 1855Z.*

(Line 2) *This is the 20th Convective SIGMET issued on the 22nd for the central United States as indicated by "20C."*

(Line 3) *Valid until 2055Z*

(Line 4) *The affected states are North and South Dakota.*

(Line 5) *From 90 nautical miles west of Minot, ND; to Grand Forks, ND; to Aberdeen, SD; to 90 nautical miles west of Minot, ND.*

(Line 6) *An intensifying area of severe thunderstorms moving from 240 degrees at 45 knots (to the northeast). Thunderstorm tops above Flight Level 450. Wind gusts to 60 knots reported. Tornadoes, hail to 2 inches in diameter, and wind gusts to 65 knots possible in the North Dakota portion.*

6.1.4.5 Convective SIGMET Outlook

Each Convective SIGMET bulletin includes a 2- to 6-hour outlook at the end of the bulletin. The content and order of each bulletin is as follows:

- Beginning and ending valid times

- Location of expected Convective SIGMET issuances delineated by high-altitude VOR coordinates for the outlook valid time.

- Discussion of forecast

6.1.4.6 Convective SIGMET Cancellations

Convective SIGMETs are not cancelled but are superseded by the next Convective SIGMET in the series.

6.1.4.7 Convective SIGMET Amendments

Amended Convective SIGMETs are NOT issued. Instead, a new Convective SIGMET is issued for that region.

6.1.4.8 Convective SIGMET Corrections

Corrections to Convective SIGMETs are issued as necessary. The corrected Convective SIGMET is identified by a "COR" located at the end of the first line after the issuance UTC date/time.

6.1.4.9 Convective SIGMET Bulletin Examples

```
WSUS33 KKCI 091855
SIGW
CONVECTIVE SIGMET...NONE
.
OUTLOOK VALID 092055-100055
TS ARE NOT EXPD.
```

Convective SIGMET bulletin for the western region of the conterminous U.S.(WSUS33) issued by the Meteorological Watch Office (WMO) (Aviation Weather Center) in Kansas City, Missouri (KKCI) on the 9th day of the month at 1855 UTC. The National Weather Service AWIPS communication header for this product is SIGW.

No Convective SIGMETs are in effect.

The outlook portion of the Convective SIGMET bulletin is valid from the 9th day of the month at 2055 UTC to the 10th day of the month at 0055 UTC. Thunderstorms are not expected.

```
WSUS32 KKCI 091855
SIGC
MKCC WST 091855
CONVECTIVE SIGMET 21C
VALID UNTIL 2055Z
AR OK
FROM 20S RZC-40SSW FSM
DMSHG LINE TS 25 NM WIDE MOV FROM 27025KT. TOPS TO FL320.
.
OUTLOOK VALID 092055-100055
FROM 40NE BUM-60SE SGF-50WSW LIT-40W GGG-60ENE ABI-ADM-50WNW
BUM-40NE BUM
WST ISSUANCES EXPD. REFER TO MOST RECENT ACUS01 KWNS FROM STORM
PREDICTION CENTER FOR SYNOPSIS AND METEOROLOGICAL DETAILS.
```

Convective SIGMET bulletin for the central region of the conterminous U.S.(WSUS32) issued by the Meteorological Watch Office (Aviation Weather Center) in Kansas City, Missouri (KKCI) on the 9th day of the month at 1855 UTC. The National Weather Service AWIPS communication header for this product is SIGC.

Convective SIGMET (WST) for the central region of the conterminous U.S. issued by the Aviation Weather Center in Kansas City, Missouri (MKCC) on the 9th day of the month at 1855 UTC. Convective SIGMET 21C is the 21st Convective SIGMET issued for the central region of the conterminous US on the 9th day of the month. Valid until 2055 UTC. States affected are Arkansas (AR) and Oklahoma (OK). Bounded within an area from 20 nautical miles south of Razorback, Arkansas (RZC), to 40 nautical miles south-southwest of Fort Smith, Arkansas (FSM). A diminishing line of thunderstorms 25 nautical miles wide moving from 270 degrees (to the east) at 25 <u>knots</u>. Thunderstorms tops to FL320 (approximately 32,000 ft MSL).

The outlook portion of the Convective SIGMET bulletin is valid from the 9th day of the month at 2055 UTC to the 10th day of the month at 0055 UTC. Within an area bounded from 40 nautical miles northeast of Butler, Missouri (BUM), to 60 nautical miles southeast of Springfield, MO (SGF), to 50 nautical miles west-southwest of Little Rock, Arkansas (LIT), to 40 nautical miles west of Longview, Texas (GGG), to 60 nautical miles east-northeast of Abilene, Texas (ABI), to Ardmore, Oklahoma (ADM), to 50 nautical miles west-northwest of Butler, Missouri (BUM), to 40 nautical miles northeast of (BUM). Convective SIGMET issuances are expected. Refer to the most recent Day 1 <u>Convective Outlook</u> (ACUS01 KWNS) from the Storm Prediction Center (SPC) for a synopsis and meteorological details.

6.1.4.9.1 Convective SIGMET Bulletin – Tropical Cyclone Example

```
WSUS31 KKCI 211355
SIGE
MKCE WST 211355
CONVECTIVE SIGMET 1E
VALID UNTIL 1555Z
NC SC FL GA AND CSTL WTRS
```

```
FROM 30SSE CLT-160SE ILM-140ENE OMN-60E TLH-ABY-30SSE CLT
AREA SEV EMBD TS MOV FROM 21015KT. TOPS ABV FL450.
TORNADOES...WIND GUSTS TO 60KT POSS.
TS ASSOCD WITH TROPICAL STORM ALBERTO.
.
OUTLOOK VALID 211555-211955
FROM 30E RDU-180SE ECG-140SSE ILM-180E PBI-40SE PBI-40S
EYW-90SW EYW-70W SRQ-50N CTY-40N MCN-30NW SPA-30E RDU
REF WW 475.
WST ISSUANCES EXPD. REFER TO MOST RECENT ACUS01 KWNS FROM STORM
PREDICTION CENTER FOR SYNOPSIS AND METEOROLOGICAL DETAILS. REFER TO
MOST RECENT WTNT21 KNHC FROM TROPICAL PREDICTION CENTER FOR
DETAILS ON TROPICAL STORM ALBERTO.
```

Convective SIGMET bulletin for the eastern region of the conterminous U.S.(WSUS31) issued by the Meteorological Watch Office (Aviation Weather Center) in Kansas City, Missouri (KKCI) on the 21st day of the month at 1355 UTC. The National Weather Service AWIPS communication header for this product is SIGE.

Convective SIGMET (WST) for the eastern region of the conterminous U.S. issued by the Aviation Weather Center in Kansas City, Missouri (MKCE) on the 21st day of the month at 1355 UTC. Convective SIGMET 1E is the 1st Convective SIGMET issued for the eastern region of the conterminous US on the 21st day of the month. Valid until 1555 UTC. States affected are North Carolina (NC), South Carolina (SC), Florida (FL), Georgia (GA) and adjacent coastal waters. Within an area bounded from 30 nautical miles south-southeast of Charlotte, North Carolina (CLT) to 160 nautical miles southeast of Wilmington, North Carolina (ILM) to 140 nautical miles east-northeast of Ormond Beach, Florida (OMN) to 60 nautical miles east of Tallahassee, Florida (TLH) to Albany, Georgia (ABY) to 30 nautical miles south-southeast of Charlotte, North Carolina (CLT). An area of severe embedded thunderstorms moving from 210 degrees at 15 knots. Cumulonimbus tops above flight level 450 (approximately 45,000 feet MSL) Tornadoes and surface wind gust to 60 knots are possible. The thunderstorms are associated with Tropical Storm Alberto.

The outlook portion of the Convective SIGMET bulletin is valid from the 21st day of the month at 1555 UTC to the 21st day of the month at 1955 UTC. Within an area bounded from 30 nautical miles east of Raleigh-Durham, North Carolina (RDU) to 180 nautical miles southeast of Elizabeth City, North Carolina (ECG) to 140 south-southeast of Wilmington, North Carolina (ILM) to 180 nautical miles east of (PBI) to 40 nautical miles southeast of West Palm Beach, Florida (PBI) to 40 nautical miles south of Key West, Florida (EYW) to 90 nautical miles southwest of Key West, Florida (EYW) to 70 nautical miles west of Sarasota, Florida (SRQ) to 50 nautical miles north of Cross City, Florida (CTY) to 40 nautical miles north of Macon, Georgia (MCN) to 30 nautical miles northwest of Sparta, Georgia (SPA) to 30 nautical miles east of Raleigh-Durham, North Carolina (RDU). Refer to Weather Watch Notification Message 475. Convective SIGMET issuances are expected. Refer to the most recent Day 1 Convective Outlook (ACUS01 KWNS) from the Storm Prediction Center (SPC) for a synopsis and meteorological details. Refer to the most recent Tropical Cyclone Forecast/Advisory (WTNT21 KNHC) from the Tropical Prediction Center (TPC) for details on Tropical Storm Alberto.

6.1.5 SIGMET – Outside the Conterminous U.S. (O-CONUS)

6.1.5.1 SIGMET Issuance Criteria – Outside the Conterminous U.S. (O-CONUS)

SIGMETs outside the Conterminous U.S. (O-CONUS SIGMETs) are issued when any of the following is occurring or expected to occur affecting an area greater than 3,000 square miles or, in the judgment of the forecaster, an area having the potential to have a significant effect on the safety of aircraft operations.

- Thunderstorm - of type below*

  - Obscured (OBSC TS)
  - Embedded (EMBD TS)
  - Widespread (WDSPR TS)
  - Squall line (SQL TS)
  - Isolated severe (ISOL SEV TS)

- Severe Turbulence (SEV TURB)

- Severe Icing (SEV ICE)

  - With Freezing rain (SEV ICE (FZRA)

- Widespread Duststorm (WDSPR DS)

- Widespread Sandstorm (WDSPR SS)

- Volcanic Ash (VA)

- Tropical Cyclone (TC)

NOTE: Obscured, embedded, or squall line thunderstorms do not have to reach 3,000 square miles criteria.

*Tornado (TDO), Funnel Cloud (FC), Waterspout (WTSPT), and Heavy Hail (HVY GR) may be used as a further description of the thunderstorm as necessary.

6.1.5.2 SIGMET Issuance Time and Valid Period – Outside the Conterminous U.S. (O-CONUS)

A SIGMET is an unscheduled product issued any time conditions reaching SIGMET criteria are occurring or expected to occur within a 4-hour period. A SIGMET outside the conterminous U.S. (O-CONUS) can have a valid period up to, but not exceeding, four (4) hours, except for volcanic ash (VA) and tropical cyclone (TC) which can be valid up to six (6) hours. SIGMETs for continuing phenomena will be reissued at least every 4 (or 6) hours as long as SIGMET conditions continue to occur in the area for responsibility.

6.1.5.3 SIGMET Format – Outside the Conterminous U.S. (O-CONUS)

O-CONUS SIGMETs contain the following information, related to the specific phenomena and in the order indicated:

- Phenomenon and its description (e.g., SEV TURB).

- An indication whether the information is observed, using OBS and/or FCST. The time of observation will be given in UTC.

- Location of the phenomenon referring, where possible to latitude and longitude, and flight levels (altitude) covering the affected area during the SIGMET valid time. SIGMETs for volcanic ash cloud and tropical cyclones contain the positions of the ash cloud, tropical cyclone center and radius of convection at the start of the validity time of the SIGMET.

- Movement towards or expected movement using sixteen points of the compass, with speed in knots, or stationary, if appropriate.

- Thunderstorm maximum height as FL.

- Changes in intensity; using as appropriate, the abbreviations Intensifying (INTSF), Weakening (WKN), or No Change (NC).

- Forecast position of volcanic ash cloud or the center of the tropical cyclone at the end of the validity period of the SIGMET message.

Figure 6-7. SIGMET Outside the Conterminous U.S. Decoding Example

Table 6-3. Decoding a SIGMET Outside of the Conterminous U.S. (O-CONUS)

Line	Content	Description
1	WSPA07	ICAO communication header
	PHFO	Issuance MWO
	010410	Issuance UTC date/time
2	SIGPAT	NWS AWIPS communication header
3	KZOA	Area Control Center
	SIGMET	Product type
	TANGO	SIGMET series
	2	Issuance number
	VALID 010410/010800	Valid period UTC date/time
	PHFO	Issuance office
4	OAKLAND OCEANIC FIR	Flight Information Region (FIR)
	FRQ TS OBS AND FCST WI 200NM N3006 W14012 - N2012 W15016 CB TOP FL400 MOV W 10KT WKN.	Phenomenon description

The SIGMET in Figure 6-7 is decoded as the following:

(Line 1) The WMO product header is WSPA07. Issued by the PHFO on the 1st day of the month at 0410 UTC.

(Line 2) The NWS AWIPS communication header is SIGPAT.

(Line 3) For the Oakland (KZOA) Area Control Center. This is the 2nd issuance of SIGMET Tango series, valid from the 1st day of the month at 0410 UTC until the 1st day of the month at 0800 UTC, issued by the Honolulu Meteorological Watch Office.

(Line 4) Concerning the Oakland Oceanic Flight Information Region (FIR), frequent thunderstorms observed and forecast within 200 nautical miles of 30 degrees and 6 minutes north; 140 degrees and 12 minutes west; to 20 degrees and 12 minutes north, 150 degrees and 16 minutes west, cumulonimbus tops to flight level 400 moving west at 10 knots, weakening.

6.1.5.4 SIGMETs for Volcanic Ash

A SIGMET for volcanic ash cloud is issued for volcanic eruptions. A volcanic eruption is any volcanic activity including the emission of volcanic ash, regardless of the eruption's magnitude. Initial Volcanic Ash SIGMETs may be issued based on credible pilot reports in the absence of a Volcanic Ash Advisory (VAA), but are updated once a VAA is issued. Volcanic ash SIGMETs will continue to be issued until the ash cloud is no longer occurring or expected to occur over the area of responsibility.

SIGMETs for volcanic ash cloud are valid up to six (6) hours and provide an observed or forecast location of the ash cloud at the beginning of the SIGMET. A six-hour forecast position for the ash cloud, valid at the end of the validity period of the SIGMET message, is also included. SIGMETs are reissued at least every six (6) hours while the volcanic ash cloud hazard exists or is expected to exist.

6.1.5.5 SIGMETs for Tropical Cyclone

A SIGMET for a tropical cyclone may be issued for non-frontal synoptic-scale cyclones meeting the following criteria.

- Originates over tropical or sub-tropical waters with organized convection and definite cyclonic surface wind circulation.

- Wind speeds reach 35 knots independent of the wind averaging time used by the Tropical Cyclone Advisory Center (TCAC).

SIGMETs for tropical cyclones will be valid up to six (6) hours. SIGMETs for tropical cyclones will include two positions. The first position included will be the TCAC advisory position. The second position will be the forecast position valid at the end of the SIGMET period.

In addition to the two storm positions, SIGMETs will include associated convection when applicable. SIGMETs will be reissued at least every six (6) hours while the tropical cyclone wind remains or are expected to remain above 34 knots.

6.1.5.6 SIGMET Cancellation– Outside the Conterminous U.S. (O-CONUS)

SIGMETs are cancelled when the phenomena is no longer occurring or expected to occur in the area of responsibility.

6.1.5.7 SIGMET Amendments– Outside the Conterminous U.S. (O-CONUS)

SIGMET amendments will NOT be issued. Instead, the next SIGMET in the series is issued to accomplish the update. The valid time of the new SIGMET is reset to reflect the new 4-hour valid period (6-hour for VA and TC SIGMETs).

6.1.5.8 SIGMET Corrections– Outside the Conterminous U.S. (O-CONUS)

Corrections to SIGMETs are issued as necessary. This is done by issuing a new SIGMET in the series which advances the SIGMET number and cancels the previous SIGMET.

6.1.5.9 SIGMET Example– Outside the Conterminous U.S. (O-CONUS)

```
WSPA07 PHFO 010358
SIGPAT
KZOA SIGMET TANGO 1 VALID 010400/010800 PHFO-
OAKLAND OCEANIC FIR. EMBD TS OBS BY SATELLITE WITHIN AREA BOUNDED BY
N2055 W15000 - N1950 W14945 - N1922 W15130 - N2027 W15048 - N2055
W15000. CB TOP FL400. MOV W 10KT. WKN.
```

SIGMET (SWPA07) issued by the Meteorological Watch Office (Weather Forecast Office) in Honolulu, Hawaii (PHFO) on the 1ˢᵗ day of the month at 0358 UTC. The National Weather Service AWIPS communication header for this product is SIGPAT. This SIGMET concerns the Oakland Oceanic FIR. This is the first (1) issuance of SIGMET series Tango valid from the 1ˢᵗ day of the month at 0400 UTC until the 1ˢᵗ day of the month at 0800 UTC. Within the WFO Honolulu portion of the Oakland Oceanic FIR, embedded thunderstorms observed by satellite within an area bounded by 20 degrees/55 minutes north, 150 degrees/00 minutes west to 19 degrees/50 minutes north, 14 degrees/45 minutes west to 19 degrees/22 minutes north, 151 degrees/30 minutes west to 20 degrees/27 minutes north, 150 degrees/48 minutes west to 20 degrees/55 minutes north, 150 degrees/00 minutes west. Cumulonimbus tops to flight level 400 (approximately 40,000 feet MSL). The thunderstorms are moving west at 10 knots and weakening.

6.1.5.9.1 SIGMET for Volcanic Ash Example

```
WVNT06 KKCI 082030
TJZS SIGMET FOXTROT 2 VALID 082030/090230 KKCI-
SAN JUAN FIR VA FROM SOUFRIERE HILLS LOC 1642N06210W
VA CLD OBS AT 2030Z SFC/060 WI N1730 W06400 - N1700 W06300 - N1650
W06300 - N1710 W06400 - N1730 W06400. MOV W 15KT. FCST 0230Z VA CLD
APRX N1730 W06500 - N1700 W06300 - N1650 W06300 - N1710 W06500 - N1730
W06500.
```

The ICAO communication header for this product is WVNT06. It is a SIGMET issued by the Aviation Weather Center (KKCI) in Kansas City, Missouri on the 8ᵗʰ day of the month at 2030 UTC. This is the second (2) issuance of SIGMET series Foxtrot valid from the 8ᵗʰ day of the month at 2030 UTC until the 9ᵗʰ day of the month at 0230 UTC. Within the San Juan Oceanic FIR, volcanic ash from Soufriere Hills volcano located at 16 degrees/42 minutes north, 62 degrees/10 minutes west. Volcanic ash cloud observed at 2030 UTC from the surface to 6,000 feet MSL within an area bounded by 17 degrees/30 minutes north, 64 degrees/00 minutes west to 17 degrees/00 minutes north, 63 degrees/00 minutes west to 16 degrees/50 minutes north, 63 degrees/00 minutes west to 17 degrees/10 minutes north, 64 degrees/00 minutes west to 17 degrees/30 minutes north, 64 degrees/00 minutes west. Moving to the west at 15 knots. Forecast at 0230 UTC, volcanic ash cloud located approximately at 17 degrees/30 minutes north, 65 degrees/00 minutes west to 17 degrees/00 minutes north, 63 degrees/00 minutes west to 16 degrees/50 minutes north, 63 degrees/00 minutes west to 17 degrees/10 minutes north, 65 degrees/00 minutes west to 17 degrees/30 minutes north, 65 degrees/00 minutes west.

6.1.5.9.2 SIGMET for Tropical Cyclone Example

```
WSNT03 KKCI 081451
SIGA0C
```

```
KZNY SIGMET CHARLIE 11 VALID 081500/082100 KKCI-
NEW YORK OCEANIC FIR TC KYLE OBS N3106 W07118 AT 1500Z CB TOP FL500 WI
120NM OF CENTER MOV WSW 5 KT NC FCST 2100Z TC CENTER N3142 W07012
```

The ICAO communication header for this product is WSNT03. It is a SIGMET issued by the Aviation Weather Center (KKCI) in Kansas City, Missouri on the 8th day of the month at 1451 UTC. The National Weather Service AWIPS communication header for this product is SIGPAT. This is the eleventh (11) issuance of SIGMET series Charlie valid from the 8th day of the month at 1500 UTC until the 8th day of the month at 2100 UTC. Within the New York Oceanic FIR, Tropical Cyclone Kyle observed at 31 degrees/6 minutes north, 71 degrees/18 minutes west at 1500 UTC, cumulonimbus tops to flight level 500 (approximately 50,000 feet MSL), within 120 nautical miles of the center, moving from west-southwest at 5 knots, no change in intensity is forecast, at 2100 UTC the tropical cyclone center will be at 31 degrees/42 minutes north, 70 degrees/12 minutes west.

6.2 Airmen's Meteorological Information (AIRMET)

An <u>AIRMET</u> is a concise description of the occurrence or expected occurrence of specified en route weather phenomena which may affect the safety of aircraft operations, but at intensities lower than those which require the issuance of a SIGMET. <u>AIRMET</u>s are intended for dissemination to all pilots in flight to enhance safety and are of particular concern to operators and pilots of aircraft sensitive to the phenomena described and to pilots without instrument ratings. <u>AIRMET</u>s are issued by the responsible Meteorological Watch Office (MWO) to give notice to operators and aircrews of potentially hazardous en route conditions.

- <u>AIRMET</u>s are available for the conterminous U.S. (CONUS) on the Aviation Digital Data Service (ADDS) web site at: <u>http://adds.aviationweather.noaa.gov/airmets/</u>

- <u>AIRMET</u>s are available for Alaska on the Alaska Aviation Weather Unit (AAWU) web site at: <u>http://aawu.arh.noaa.gov/</u>

- <u>AIRMET</u>s are available for Hawaii on the NWS WFO Honolulu web site at: <u>http://www.prh.noaa.gov/hnl/pages/aviation.php</u>

6.2.1 AIRMET Issuance

<u>AIRMET</u>s are issued from the three Meteorological Watch Offices (MWO) located at the Aviation Weather Center (AWC), the Alaska Aviation Weather Unit (AAWU), and the Weather Forecast Office (WFO) in Honolulu. Their areas of responsibility are:

- AWC: The conterminous U.S. and adjacent coastal waters (CONUS) (Figure 6-8)

- AAWU: Alaska and adjacent coastal waters (Figure 6-9)

- WFO Honolulu: Hawaii and adjacent waters (Figure 6-10)

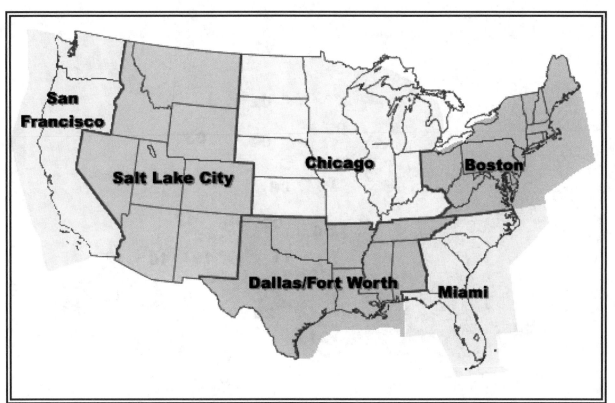

Figure 6-8 AWC AIRMET Areas of Responsibility – Conterminous U.S.

Figure 6-9. AAWU Flight Advisory and Area Forecast Zones - Alaska

Table 6-4. AAWU Flight Advisory and Area Forecast Zones – Alaska

1	Arctic Coast Coastal	14	Southern Southeast Alaska
2	North Slopes of the Brooks Range	15	Coastal Southeast Alaska
3	Upper Yukon Valley	16	Eastern Gulf Coast
4	Koyukuk and Upper Kobuk Valley	17	Copper River Basin
5	Northern Seward Peninsula-Lower Kobuk Valley	18	Cook Inlet-Susitna Valley
6	Southern Seward Peninsula-Eastern Norton Sound	19	Central Gulf Coast
7	Tanana Valley	20	Kodiak Island
8	Lower Yukon Valley	21	Alaska Peninsula-Port Heiden to Unimak Pass
9	Kuskowim Valley	22	Unimak Pass to Adak
10	Yukon-Kuskowim Delta	23	St. Lawrence Island-Bering Sea Coast
11	Bristol Bay	24	Adak to Attu
12	Lynn Canal and Glacier Bay	25	Pribilof Islands and Southeast Bering Sea
13	Central Southeast Alaska		

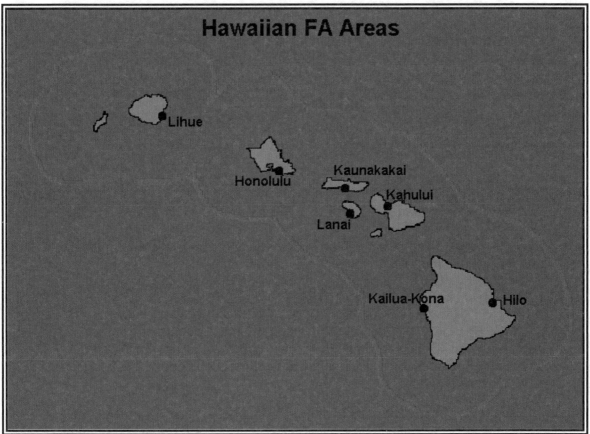

Figure 6-10. WFO Honolulu AIRMET Areas of Responsibility - Hawaii

6.2.2 AIRMET Issuance Criteria

An <u>AIRMET</u> may be issued when any of the following weather phenomena are occurring or expected to occur over an area of at least 3,000 square miles:

- Ceiling less than 1,000 feet and/or visibility less than 3 statute miles (IFR)

  - o Weather phenomena restricting the visibility including, but not limited to, precipitation (PCPN), smoke (FU), haze (HZ), mist (BR), fog (FG), and blowing snow (BS).

- Widespread mountain obscuration (MTN OBSCN)

  - o Weather phenomena causing the obscurement are included, but limited to clouds (CLDS), precipitation (PCPN), smoke (FU), haze (HZ), mist (BR), and fog (FG).

- Moderate turbulence (MOD TURB)

  - o Top and bottom of MOD TURB layer are specified.

- Sustained surface wind greater than 30 knots (STG SFC WND)

- Moderate icing (MOD ICE)

o Top and bottom of MOD ICE are specified.
o The range of freezing level altitudes is given when the bottom altitude of MOD ICE is the freezing level (FRZLVL).
o Areas with multiple freezing levels are specified.
o Range of freezing levels over the area is specified.
o Lowest freezing levels above ground level (AGL) at intervals of 4,000 feet AMSL (or SFC as appropriate) are specified.

- Non-convective low-level wind shear potential below 2,000 feet AGL (LLWS POTENTIAL).

6.2.3 AIRMET Standardization
All AIRMETs follow these standards:

- All heights or altitudes are referenced to above mean sea level (AMSL), unless otherwise noted, and annotated using the height in hundreds of feet, consisting of three digits (e.g., 040). For heights at or above 18,000 feet, the level is preceded by FL to represent flight levels (e.g., FL180).

- Messages are prepared in abbreviated plain language using contractions from the Federal Aviation Administration (FAA) Order 7340.2. A limited number of non-abbreviated words, geographical names and numerical values of a self-explanatory nature may also be used.

- Weather and obstructions to visibility are described using the weather abbreviations for surface weather observations (METAR/SPECI). See the Federal Meteorological Handbook (FMH) No. 1 – Surface Observations or Section 3.1 of this document.

Note: Refer to Appendix A for definitions of common terms used in AIRMETs.

6.2.4 AIRMET Bulletins, Issuance Times, and Valid Period
AIRMETs are issued as bulletins containing one or more AIRMET messages following the schedule listed below. Unscheduled AIRMETs are issued when conditions are occurring or expected to occur, but were not forecast.

Table 6-5. AIRMET Issuance Schedule

	1st Scheduled Issuance (UTC)	2nd Scheduled Issuance (UTC)	3rd Scheduled Issuance (UTC)	4th Scheduled Issuance (UTC)
CONUS	0255	0855	1455	2055
Alaska	0145 (DT)/ 0245 (ST)	0745 (DT)/ 0845 (ST)	1345 (DT)/ 1445 (ST)	1945 (DT)/ 2045 (ST)
Hawaii	0400	1000	1600	2200
Note: DT - Daylight Time, ST - Standard Time				

AIRMETs are valid for no more than 6 hours. The valid period of an AIRMET message cannot exceed the valid time of the AIRMET bulletin. However, note that each AIRMET contains remarks concerning the continuance of the phenomenon during the six (6) hours following the AIRMET ending time. Also, AIRMET bulletins can contain a separate outlook when conditions meeting AIRMET criteria are expected to occur during the 6-hour period after the valid time of the AIRMET bulletin.

6.2.5 AIRMET Format

An AIRMET message includes the following information as appropriate and in the order indicated:

- Reference to appropriate active SIGMETs affecting the area at the time of AIRMET issuance (e.g., SEE SIGMET BRAVO SERIES).

- Beginning time of the AIRMET phenomenon if different from the AIRMET beginning valid time.

- AIRMET name (SIERRA, TANGO or ZULU), update number, weather phenomenon, and ending valid time (Note: the AIRMET number is reset to one (1) after 0000 UTC each day).

    o AIRMET Sierra describes IFR conditions and/or extensive mountain obscurations

    o AIRMET Tango describes moderate turbulence, sustained surface winds of 30 knots or greater and non-convective low-level wind shear.

    o AIRMET Zulu describes moderate icing and provides freezing level heights

- List of affected states (CONUS only).

- Location of phenomenon using VORs

- Description of phenomenon for the AIRMET issuance.

- Vertical extent (bases and tops), as appropriate.

- Ending time of phenomenon if different from the AIRMET ending time.

- Remarks concerning the continuance of the phenomenon during the six (6) hours following the AIRMET ending time.

- CONUS and Hawaii AIRMETs: A separate AIRMET outlook is included in the AIRMET bulletin when conditions meeting AIRMET criteria are expected to occur during the 6-hour period after the valid time of the AIRMET bulletin.

- Alaska AIRMETs: Outlook information is included in the appropriate Area Forecast zone when conditions are expected to occur during the 6-hour period after the valid time of the AIRMET bulletin.

LINE

```
1 → BOSS WA 211945
2 → AIRMET SIERRA UPDT 3 FOR IFR AND MTN OBSCN VALID
    UNTIL 220200
    .
3A→ AIRMET IFR..ME NH VT MA CT RI NY NJ AND CSTL WTRS
4A→ FROM CAR TO YSJ TO 150E ACK TO EWR TO YOW TO CAR
5A→ OCNL CIG BLW 010/VIS BLW 3SM PCPN/BR. CONDS CONT
    BYD 02Z THRU 08Z.
    .
3B→ AIRMET MTN OBSCN..ME NH VT MA NY PA
4B→ FROM CAR TO MLT TO CON TO SLT TO SYR TO CAR
5B→ MTNS OCNLY OBSCD BY CLDS/PCPN/BR. CONDS CONT BYD
    02Z THRU 08Z.
```

Figure 6-11. AIRMET Bulletin Decoding Example

Table 6-6. Decoding an AIRMET Bulletin

Line	Content	Description
1	BOS	AIRMET area identifier
	S	AIRMET series
	WA	Product type
	211945	Issuance UTC date/time
2	AIRMET	Product type
	SIERRA	AIRMET series
	UPDT 3	Update number
	FOR IFR AND MTN OBSCN	Product description
	VALID UNTIL 220200	Ending UTC date/time
3A	AIRMET IFR..ME NH VT MA CT RI NY NJ AND CSTL WTRS	Product type/series... Phenomenon location (states)
3B	AIRMET MTN OBSCN..ME NH VT MA NY PA	
4A	FROM CAR TO YSJ TO 150E ACK TO EWR TO YOW TO CAR	Phenomenon location (VOR locations)
4B	FROM CAR TO MLT TO CON TO SLT TO SYR TO CAR	
5A	CIG BLW 010/VIS BLW 3SM PCPN/BR. CONDS CONT BYD 02Z THRU 08Z.	Phenomenon description
5B	MTNS OBSCD BY CLDS/PCPN/BR. CONDS CONT BYD 02Z THRU 08Z.	

The AIRMET bulletin in Figure 6-11 is decoded as follows:

(Line 1) AIRMET SIERRA issued for the Boston area at 1945Z on the 21st day of the month. "SIERRA" *contains information on Instrument Flight Rules (IFR) and/or mountain obscurations.*

(Line 2) This is the third updated issuance of this Boston AIRMET series as indicated by "SIERRA UPDT 3" *and is valid until 0200Z on the 22nd.*

(Line 3A) The affected states within the BOS area are: Maine, New Hampshire, Vermont, Massachusetts, Connecticut, Rhode Island, New York, New Jersey, and coastal waters.

(Line 3B) The affected states within the BOS area are: Maine, New Hampshire, Vermont, Massachusetts, New York, and Pennsylvania.

(Line 4A) Within an area bounded by: Caribou, ME; to Saint Johns, New Brunswick; to 150 nautical miles east of Nantucket, MA; to Newark, NJ; to Ottawa, Ontario; to Caribou, ME

(Line 4B) Within an area bounded by: Caribou, ME to Millinocket, ME to Concord, NH to Slate Run, PA to Syracuse, NY to Caribou, ME

(Line 5A) Ceiling below 1,000 feet/visibility below 3 statute miles, precipitation/mist. Conditions continuing beyond 0200Z through 0800Z.

(Line 5B) Mountains Obscured by clouds, precipitation and mist. Conditions continuing beyond 0200Z through 0800Z.

6.2.5.1 AIRMET Updates and Amendments

If an AIRMET is amended, **AMD** is added after the date/time group on the FAA product line. The update number will be incremented, **UPDT** is added to end of the line containing the list of affected states (CONUS only). The issuance time of the AIRMET bulletin is updated to reflect the time of the amendment. The ending valid time remains unchanged.

6.2.5.2 AIRMET Corrections

AIRMETs containing errors are corrected by adding COR after the date/time group on the FAA product line. The issuance time of the AIRMET bulletin is updated to reflect the time of the correction. The ending valid time remains unchanged.

6.2.6 AIRMET Examples

6.2.6.1 CONUS AIRMET Example

```
WAUS43 KKCI 091445
CHIZ WA 091445
AIRMET ZULU UPDT 4 FOR ICE AND FRZLVL VALID UNTIL 092100
AIRMET ICE...KS IA MO IL
FROM 30WSW FOD TO DBQ TO 50NW DEC TO 50SW FAM TO OSW TO MKC TO
30WSW FOD
MOD ICE BTN FRZLVL AND FL200. FRZLVL 060-100. CONDS ENDG BY 21Z.
.
OTLK VALID 2100-0300Z...ICE IA MO WI IL IN KY
BOUNDED BY BAE-BVT-PXV-50SW FAM-50NW DEC-DBQ-BAE
MOD ICE BTN FRZLVL AND FL200. FRZLVL 080-100. CONDS CONTG THRU
```

```
03Z.
.
FRZLVL...RANGING FROM SFC-120 ACRS AREA
MULT FRZLVL 015-085 BOUNDED BY 40W INL-YQT-SSM-70NNE
ASP-YVV-DXO-40NE FWA-40SSE BJI-40W INL
SFC ALG 50NNW ISN-70W FAR-GFK-40NE ODI-40SW DXO
040 ALG ISN-70S BIS-30W ABR-30E ABR-60S FAR-30SW BRD-30NE FWA
080 ALG GLD-SLN-30W BDF-50S JOT-40SE IND-30SW CVG-40SW LOZ
```

AIRMET (WAUS43) issued by the Meteorological Watch Office (Aviation Weather Center) in Kansas City, Missouri on the 9th day of the month at 1445 UTC. This AIRMET (WA) is the Zulu series bulletin for the Chicago Area Forecast region (CHIZ) issued on the 9th day of the month at 1445 UTC. This is the 4th update to the Zulu series bulletin for icing and freezing levels and is valid until the 9th day of the month at 2100 UTC.

The first (and only) AIRMET noted within the bulletin is for icing affecting Kansas, Iowa, Missouri and Illinois. Within an area bounded from 30 nautical miles west-southwest of Fort Dodge, Iowa (FOD) to Dubuque, Iowa (DBQ) to 50 nautical miles northwest of Decatur, Illinois (DEC) to 50 nautical miles southwest of Farmington, Missouri (FAM) to Oswego, Kansas (OSW) to Kansas City, Missouri (MKC) to 30 nautical miles west-southwest of Fort Dodge, Iowa (FOD). Moderate icing between the freezing level and flight level 200 (approximately 20,000 feet MSL). The freezing level is between 6,000 feet MSL and 10,000 feet MSL. Conditions ending by 2100 UTC.

An outlook for icing between 2100 UTC to 0300 UTC exists over: Iowa, Missouri, Wisconsin, Illinois, Indiana and Kentucky. Within an area bounded by Milwaukee, Wisconsin (BAE) to Lafayette, Indiana (BVT) to Pocket City, Indiana (PXV) to 50 nautical miles southwest of Farmington, Missouri (FAM) to 50 nautical miles northwest of Decatur, Illinois (DEC) to Dubuque, Iowa (DBQ) to Milwaukee, Wisconsin (BAE). Moderate icing between the freezing level and flight level 200 (approximately 20,000 feet MSL). The freezing level is between 8,000 feet MSL and 10,000 feet MSL. Conditions continuing through 0300 UTC.

The freezing level ranges from the surface to 12,000 feet MSL across the Chicago Area Forecast region. Multiple freezing levels exist between 1,500 feet MSL and 8,500 feet MSL within an area bounded by 40 nautical miles west of International Falls, Minnesota (INL) to Thunder Bay, Ontario, Canada to Sault Saint Marie, Michigan (SSM) to 70 nautical miles north-northeast of Oscoda, Michigan (ASP) to Wiarton, Ontario, Canada to Detroit, Michigan (DXO) to 40 nautical miles northeast of Fort Wayne, Indiana (FWA) to 40 nautical miles south-southeast of Bemidji, Minnesota (BJI) to 40 nautical miles west of International Falls, Minnesota (INL). The freezing level is at the surface along a line from 50 nautical miles north-northwest of Williston, North Dakota (ISN) to 70 nautical miles west of Fargo, North Dakota (FAR) to Grand Forks, North Dakota (GFK) to 40 nautical miles northeast of Nodine, Minnesota (ODI) to 40 nautical miles southwest of Detroit, Michigan (DXO). The freezing level is at 4,000 feet MSL along a line from Williston, North Dakota (ISN) to 70 nautical miles south of Bismarck, North Dakota (BIS) to 30 nautical miles west of Aberdeen, South Dakota (ABR) to 30 nautical miles east of Aberdeen, South Dakota (ABR) to 60 nautical miles south of Fargo, North Dakota (FAR) to 30 nautical miles southwest of Brainerd, Minnesota (BRD) to 30 nautical miles northeast of Fort Wayne, Indiana. The freezing level is 8,000 feet MSL along a line from Goodland, Kansas (GLD) to Salina, Kansas (SLN) to 30 nautical miles west of Bradford, Illinois (BDF) to 50 nautical miles south of Joliet, Illinois to 40 nautical miles southeast of Indianapolis, Indiana (IND) to 30 nautical miles southwest of Covington, Kentucky (CVG) to 40 nautical miles southwest of London, Kentucky (LOZ).

6.2.6.2 Hawaii AIRMET Example

```
WAHW31 PHFO 090945
WA0HI
HNLT WA 091000
AIRMET TANGO UPDATE 1 FOR TURB VALID UNTIL 091600
AIRMET TURB...KAUAI OAHU MOLOKAI LANAI MAUI
OVR AND IMDT N THRU E OF MTS.
MOD TURB BLW 100. CONDS CONTG BYD 1600Z.
```

AIRMET (WAHW31) issued by the Meteorological Watch Office (Weather Forecast Office) in Honolulu, Hawaii on the 9th day of the month at 0945 UTC. The National Weather Service AWIPS communication code for this product is WA0HI. This AIRMET (WA) is the Tango series bulletin for the Hawaii Area Forecast region (HNLT) issued on the 9th day of the month at 1000 UTC. This is the 1st update to the Tango series bulletin for turbulence and is valid until the 9th day of the month at 1600 UTC.

The first (and only) AIRMET noted within the bulletin is for turbulence affecting the islands of Kauai, Oahu, Molokai, Lanai and Maui, over and immediately north through east of the mountains. Moderate turbulence below 10,000 feet MSL. Conditions continuing beyond 1600 UTC.

6.2.6.3 Alaska AIRMET Example

```
WAAK47 PAWU 011740
WA7O
JNUS WA 011740
AIRMET SIERRA FOR IFR AND MT OBSC VALID UNTIL 012100
.
LYNN CANAL AND GLACIER BAY JB
W OF LYNN CANAL..MTS OCNL OBSC IN CLDS/PCPN.
SPRDG E. INTSF.
.
CNTRL SE AK JC
PAOH-PAFE LN W..MTS OCNL OBSC IN CLDS/PCPN. SPRDG
E. INTSF.
.
ERN GLF CST JE
MTS OCNL OBSC IN CLDS/PCPN. IMPRG.
.
SE AK CSTL WTRS JF
OCNL CIG BLW 010 VIS BLW 3SM SN BLSN. NC.
```

AIRMET (WAAK47) issued by the Meteorological Watch Office (Alaska Aviation Weather Unit) in Anchorage, Alaska on the 1st day of the month at 1740 UTC. The National Weather Service AWIPS communication code for this product is WA7O. This AIRMET (WA) is the Sierra series bulletin for the Juneau forecast area issued on the 1st day of the month at 1740 UTC. This is the AIRMET Sierra series for IFR and mountain obscuration valid until the 1st day of the month at 2100 UTC.

For the Lynn Canal and Glacier Bay forecast regions, Juneau region B...west of Lynn Canal...mountains occasionally obscured in clouds and precipitation. Conditions spreading east and intensifying during the forecast period.

For the Central Southeast Alaska forecast region, Juneau region C...from a Hoonan, Alaska (PAOH) to Kake, Alaska (PAFE) line westward, mountains occasionally obscured in clouds and precipitation. Conditions spreading east and intensifying during the forecast period.

For the Eastern Gulf Coast forecast region, Juneau region E...Mountains occasionally obscured in clouds and precipitation. Conditions improving during the forecast period.

For the Southeast Alaska Coastal Waters, Juneau region F...Occasional ceiling below 1,000 feet AGL, visibility below 3 statute miles in snow and blowing snow. No change in conditions is expected during the forecast period.

6.3 Graphical Airman's Meteorological Advisory (G-AIRMET)

The Graphical-AIRMET product, known as the "G-AIRMET," is a decision-making tool based on weather "snapshots" displayed at short time intervals. The G-AIRMET identifies hazardous weather in space and time more precisely than text products, enabling pilots to maintain high safety margins while flying more efficient routes.

The National Weather Service's (NWS) goal is to maximize aviation safety and air space efficiency by providing the most accurate and timely weather information possible to enhance both pre-flight and in-flight decision making. For decades, NWS has issued text-based AIRMETs that have provided broad-scale descriptions of hazardous weather. Often referred to as a time "smear", the text-based AIRMET requires meteorologists to describe hazardous weather over large geographical areas for six-hour periods. G-AIRMET provides more precise, and informative weather hazard depictions than the text only AIRMET.

Aviation weather users have found that pictures are worth a thousand contractions. G-AIRMETs provide a better path from the aviation meteorologist to the weather user, by providing precise, interactive and easy to understand graphical displays. Meteorologists can put their energy into creating and updating G-AIRMET weather graphics, while the traditional text AIRMET is generated from G-AIRMET information.

G-AIRMETs are available for the conterminous U.S. (CONUS) and adjacent coastal waters only and can be viewed on Aviation Digital Data Service (ADDS) web site using the G-AIRMET display tools at: http://aviationweather.gov/products/gairmet/

6.3.1 G-AIRMET Issuance

G-AIRMETs are issued by the Aviation Weather Center (AWC) every 6 hours and updated/amended as necessary, coincident with the text AIRMET products.

Table 6-7. G-AIRMET Issuance Schedule

	1st Scheduled Issuance (UTC)	2nd Scheduled Issuance (UTC)	3rd Scheduled Issuance (UTC)	4th Scheduled Issuance (UTC)
CONUS	0255	0855	1455	2055

6.3.2 G-AIRMET Content

Graphical AIRMET Snapshots (G-AIRMET) are graphical forecasts of en-route weather hazards valid at discrete times no more than 3 hours apart for a period of up to 12 hours into the future (00, 03, 06, 09 and 12 hours). 00 hour represents the initial conditions, and the subsequent 3-hourly graphics depict the area affected by the particular hazard at that valid time. G-AIRMET snapshots may be viewed as static (single) images, combined, and looped using the tools provided on the web page.

G-AIRMET depicts the following en-route aviation weather hazards:

- Instrument flight Rule conditions (IFR)

  o Areas of cloud ceilings with bases less than 1000 feet above ground level (AGL) and/or areas of surface visibilities below 3 statute miles, including the weather causing the visibility restriction. The cause of the visibility restriction includes only PCPN, FU, HZ, BR, FG, and BLSN.

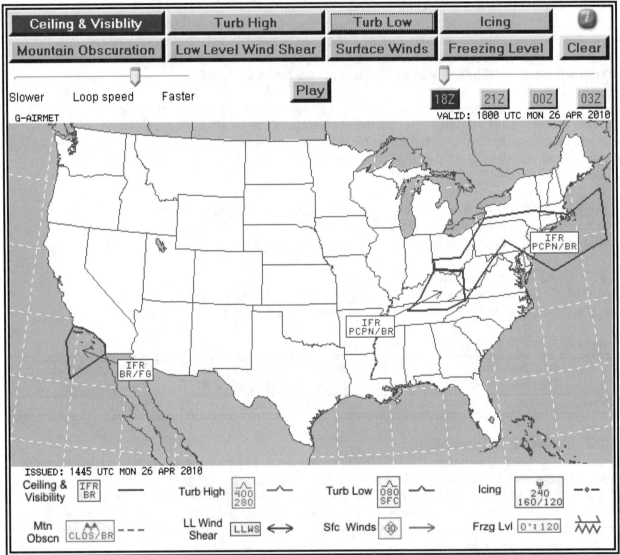

Figure 6-12. G-AIRMET – Ceiling and Visibility (IFR) Snapshot Example

- Mountain Obscuration

  - Areas of widespread mountain obscuration where Visual Meteorological Conditions (VMC) cannot be maintained, including the weather causing the obscuration. The weather causing the obscuration includes only CLDS, PCPN, FU, HZ, BR, and FG.

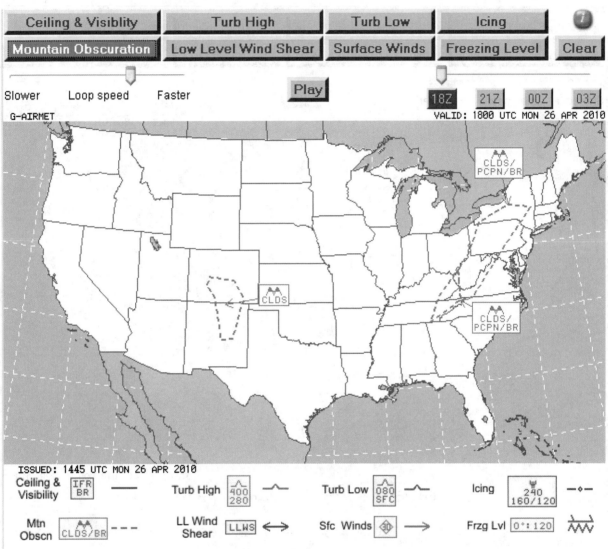

Figure 6-13. G-AIRMET – Mountain Obscuration Snapshot Example

- Icing

  o Areas of moderate airframe icing, other than convectively induced, including the vertical extent (base and top). Altitude variations in the base of icing layers may be denoted (e.g., "080 / 060" indicates the altitude varies between 6,000 and 8,000 feet above mean seal level (AMSL)).

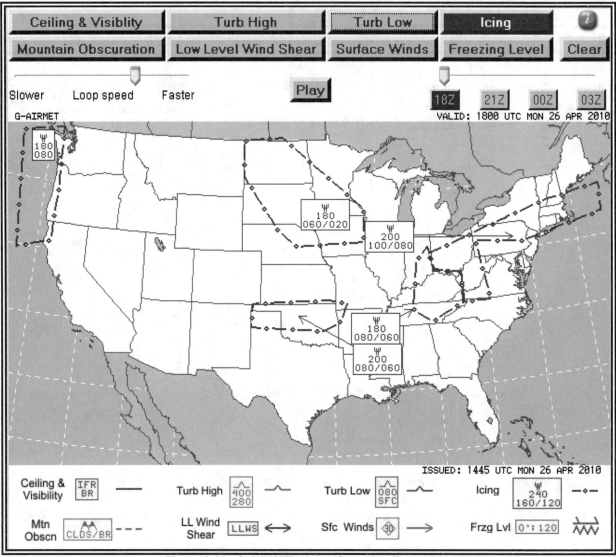

Figure 6-14. G-AIRMET – Icing Snapshot Example

- Freezing Level

  o Freezing level is defined as the lowest freezing level above the ground or at the SFC as appropriate. Freezing levels above the ground are delineated at 4000 feet intervals above mean sea level (AMSL). Areas with multiple freezing levels above the ground are delineated including the vertical extent (base and top).

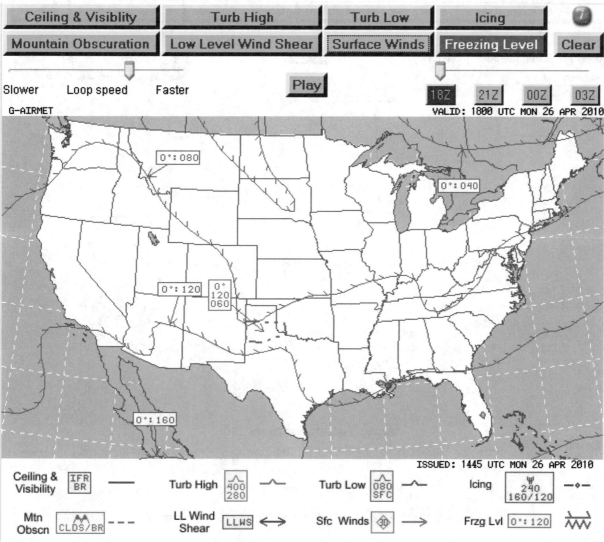

Figure 6-15. G-AIRMET – Freezing Level Snapshot Example

- Turbulence

   o Areas of moderate turbulence, other than convectively induced, including the vertical extent (base and top).

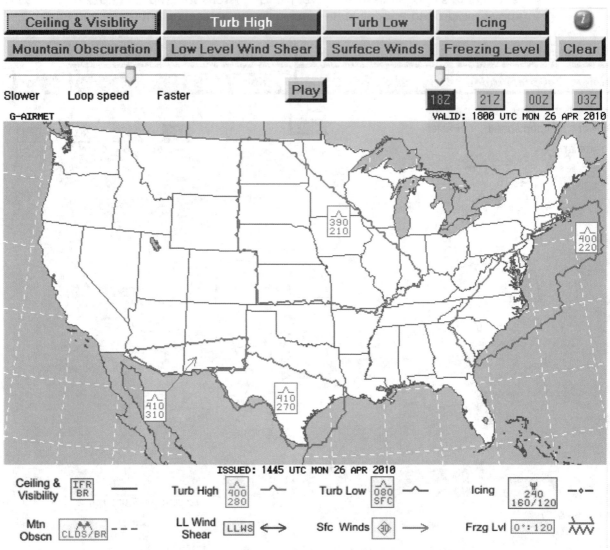

Figure 6-16. G-AIRMET – Turbulence-High Snapshot Example

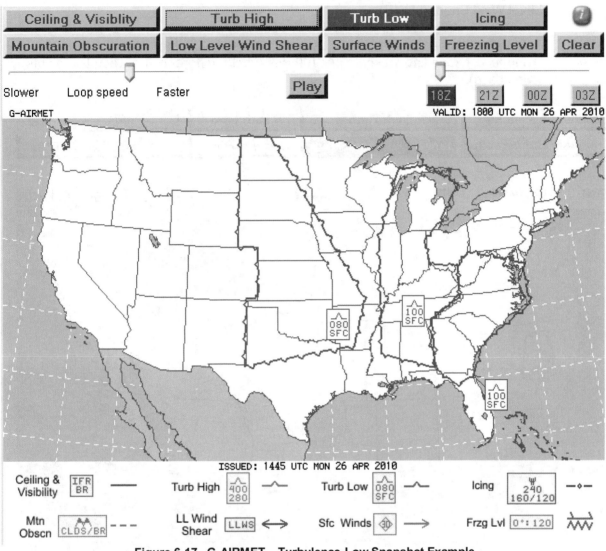

Figure 6-17. G-AIRMET – Turbulence-Low Snapshot Example

- Low Level Wind Shear (LLWS)

  o LLWS is defined as wind shear below 2000 feet AGL, other than convectively induced, exceeding 10 knots per 100 feet (vector difference between two points in space).

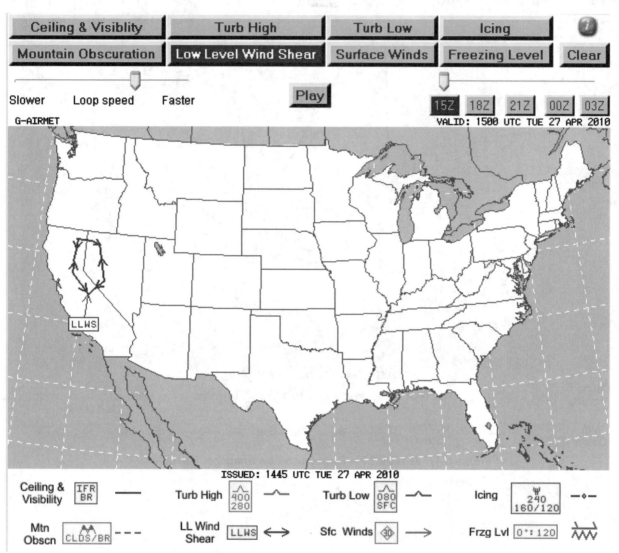

Figure 6-18. G-AIRMET – Low-Level Wind Shear (LLWS) Snapshot Example

- Strong Surface Winds

  o Areas of sustained surface winds greater than 30 knots. The direction and speed of winds are not depicted; only the area where sustained surface winds greater than 30 knots will occur.

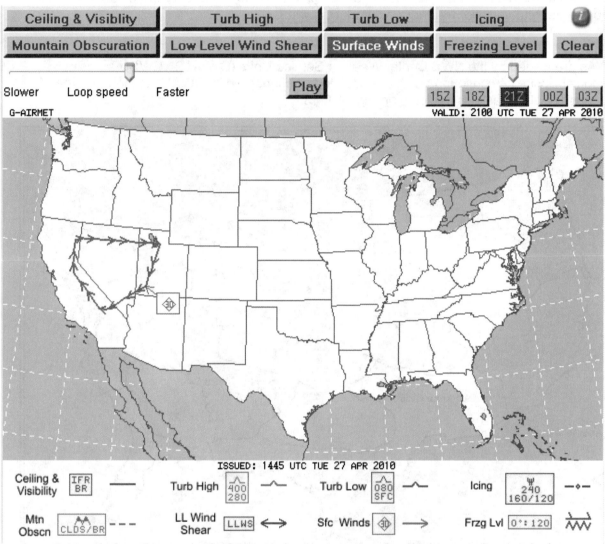

Figure 6-19. G-AIRMET – Strong Surface Winds Snapshot Example

6.4 Center Weather Advisory (CWA)

A Center Weather Advisory (CWA) is an aviation weather warning for conditions meeting or approaching national in-flight advisory (AIRMET, SIGMET or Convective SIGMET) criteria. The CWA is primarily used by aircrews to anticipate and avoid adverse weather conditions in the en route and terminal environments. CWAs are available on the Aviation Weather Center (AWC) web site at: http://aviationweather.gov/products/cwsu/.

6.4.1 CWA Issuance

CWAs are issued by the NWS Center Weather Service Units (CWSUs). CWSU areas of responsibility in the contiguous U.S. are depicted on Figure 6-12. CWSU Anchorage area of responsibility for Alaska is depicted on Figure 6-13.

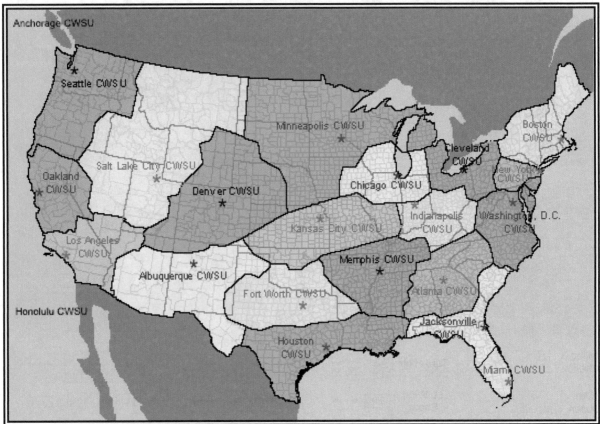

Figure 6-20. Center Weather Service Unit (CWSU) Areas of Responsibility, Contiguous U.S.

Figure 6-21. CWSU Anchorage, AK (PAZA) Area of Responsibility

CWAs are valid for up to two (2) hours and may include forecasts of conditions expected to begin within two (2) hours of issuance. If conditions are expected to persist after the advisory's valid period, a statement to that effect is included in the last line of the text. Additional CWAs will subsequently be issued as appropriate. Notice of significant changes in the phenomenon described in a CWA is provided by a new CWA issuance for that phenomenon. If the forecaster deems it necessary, CWAs may be issued hourly for convective activity.

6.4.2 CWA Criteria

CWAs are used in the four (4) following situations:

- **Precede an Advisory**
  - When the AWC has not yet issued an advisory, but conditions meet or will soon meet advisory criteria.

- **Refine an existing Advisory**
  - To supplement an existing AWC advisory for the purpose of refining or updating the location, movement, extent, or intensity of the weather event relevant to the ARTCC's area of responsibility.

- **Highlight significant conditions not meeting Advisory criteria**
  - When conditions do not meet advisory criteria, but conditions, in the judgment of the CWSU meteorologist, will adversely impact air traffic within the ARTCC area of responsibility.

- **To cancel a CWA when the phenomenon described in the CWA is no longer expected.**

6.4.3 CWA Format

LINE

1 — ZDV2 CWA 032140

2 — ZDV CWA 202 VALID UNTIL 032340

3 — FROM FMN TO 10N FMN TO 20NE FMN TO 10E
FMN TO FMN

4 — ISOLD SEV TS NR FMN MOVG NEWD 10KTS.
TOP FL410. WND GSTS TO 55KTS. HAIL TO
1 INCH RPRTD AT FMN. SEV TS CONTG BYD
2340Z.

Figure 6-22. Center Weather Advisory (CWA) Decoding Example

Table 6-8. Decoding a Center Weather Advisory (CWA)

Line	Content	Description
1	ZDV	ARTCC Identification
	2	Phenomenon Number (single digit, 1-6)
	CWA	Product Type (UCWA/CWA)
	032140	Beginning and/or issuance UTC date/time
2	ZDV	ARTCC Identification
	CWA	Product Type
	2	Phenomenon Number (single digit, 1-6)
	02	Issuance Number (issued sequentially for each Phenomenon Number)
	VALID TIL 032340Z	Ending valid UTC date/time
3	FROM FMN TO 10N FMN TO 20NE FMN TO 10E FMN TO FMN	Phenomenon Location
4	ISOLD SEV TS NR FMN MOVG NEWD 10KTS. TOP FL410. WND GSTS TO 55KTS. HAIL TO 1 INCH RPRTD AT FMN. SEV TS CONTG BYD 2340Z	Phenomenon Description

Time permitting, any CWA overlapping into another center's airspace is coordinated and a statement is included in the text, e.g., **SEE ZOB CWA 201 FOR TS CONDS IN ZOB CTA** (CTA is control area). If issuance prior to coordination is necessary, a statement regarding the area(s) affected is included in the text, e.g., **LINE TS EXTDS NW INTO ZOB CTA**.

AIRMETs/SIGMETs being augmented by the CWA will be referenced in a text remark, e.g. **SEE CONVECTIVE SIGMET 8W**.

The CWA in Figure 6-14 is decoded as follows:

(Line 1) Center Weather Advisory issued for the Denver ARTCC (ZDV) CWSU. The "2" after ZDV in the first line denotes this is the second meteorological event of the local calendar day. This CWA was issued/begins on the 3rd day of the month at 2140 UTC.

(Line 2) The Denver ARTCC (ZDV) is identified again. The "202" in the second line denotes the phenomena number again (2) and the issuance number (02) for this phenomenon. This CWA is the valid until the 3rd day of the at 2340 UTC.

(Line 3) From Farmington, New Mexico to 10 nautical miles north of Farmington, New Mexico to 20 nautical miles northeast of Farmington, NM to 10 nautical mile east of Farmington, New Mexico to Farmington, New Mexico.

(Line 4) Isolated severe thunderstorms near Farmington moving northeastward at 10 knots. Tops to Flight Level 410. Wind gusts to 55 knots. Hail to one inch reported at Farmington. Severe thunderstorms continuing beyond 2340 UTC.

6.4.4 Examples

```
ZME1 CWA 081300

ZME CWA 101 VALID TIL 081500
FROM MEM TO JAN TO LIT TO MEM
OCNL TS MOV FM 26025KT. TOPS TO FL450.
```

Center Weather Advisory issued for the Memphis, Tennessee ARTCC on the 8th day of the month at 1300 UTC. The 1 after the ZME in the first line denotes this CWA has been issued for the first weather phenomenon to occur for the local calendar day. The 101 in the second line denotes the phenomenon number again (1) and the issuance number (01) for this phenomenon. The CWA is valid until the 8th of the month at 1500 UTC. From Memphis, Tennessee to Jackson, Mississippi to Little Rock, Arkansas to Memphis, Tennessee. Occasional thunderstorms moving from 260 degrees at 25 knots. Tops to flight level 450.

```
ZLC3 CWA 271645

ZLC CWA 303 VALID TIL 271745
CNL CWA 302.
SEE CONVECTIVE SIGMET 8W.
```

Center Weather Advisory issued for the Salt Lake City, Utah ARTCC on the 27th day of the month at 1645 UTC. The 3 after the ZLC in the first line denotes this CWA has been issued for the third weather phenomenon to occur for the local calendar day. The 303 in the second line denotes the phenomenon number again (3) and the issuance number (03) for this phenomenon. The CWA is valid until the 27th day of the month at 1745 UTC. CWA number 302 has been cancelled. See Convective SIGMET 8W.

```
ZME1 CWA 040100

ZME CWA 101 VALID TIL 040300
VCY MEM
SEV CLR ICE BLW 020 DUE TO FZRA. NUMEROUS ACFT REP RAPID
```

```
ACCUMULATION OF ICE DRG DES TO MEM. NO ICE REPS ABV 020. CONDS CONTG
AFT 03Z. NO UPDATES AFT 040200Z.
```

Center Weather Advisory issued for the Memphis, Tennessee ARTCC on the 4th day of the month at 0100 UTC. The 1 after the ZLC in the first line denotes this CWA has been issued for the first weather phenomenon to occur for the local calendar day. The 101 in the second line denotes the phenomenon number again (1) and the issuance number (01) for this phenomenon. The CWA is valid until the 4th day of the month at 0300 UTC. For the Memphis, Tennessee vicinity. Severe clear icing below 2,000 feet MSL due to freezing rain. Numerous aircraft report rapid accumulation of icing during descent to Memphis. No icing reports above 2,000 feet MSL. Conditions continuing after 0300 UTC. No updates after 4th day of the month at 0200 UTC.

```
ZNY5 UCWA 021400

ZNY CWA 502 VALID TIL 021600
FROM BGM TO 18WNW JFK TO HAR TO SLT TO BGM
NUMEROUS ACFT REP SEV TURB AND WS BLW 020.
CONDS EXTD NE INTO ZBW CTA. CONDS EXP TO CONT AFT 16Z.
```

Center Weather Advisory issued for the New York ARTCC on the 2nd day of the month at 1400 UTC. The 5 after the ZNY in the first line denotes this CWA has been issued for the fifth weather phenomenon to occur for the local calendar day. The 502 in the second line denotes the phenomenon number again (5) and the issuance number (02) for this phenomenon. The CWA is valid until the 2nd day of the month at 1600 UTC. From Binghamton, New York; to 18 nautical miles west-northwest of New York (JFK Airport), New York; to Harrisburg, Pennsylvania; to Slate Run, Pennsylvania; to Binghamton, New York. Numerous aircraft report severe turbulence and wind shear below 2,000 feet MSL. Conditions extending northeast into Nashua, New Hampshire control area. Conditions expected to continue after 1600 UTC.

```
ZNY4 UCWA 041500

ZNY CWA 401 VALID TIL 041700
40N SLT TO 18WNW JFK
DEVELOPING LINE TS 25 NM WIDE MOV 24020KT. TOPS ABV FL350.
LINE TS EXTDS NW INTO ZOB CTA.
```

Urgent Center Weather Advisory issued for the New York ARTCC on the 4th day of the month at 1500 UTC. The 4 after the ZNY in the first line denotes this CWA has been issued for the fourth weather phenomenon to occur for the local calendar day. The 401 in the second line denotes the phenomenon number again (4) and the issuance number (01) for this phenomenon. The CWA is valid until the 4th day of the month at 1700 UTC. From 40 nautical miles north of Slate Run, Pennsylvania; to 18 nautical miles west-northwest of New York (JFK Airport), New York. Developing line of thunderstorms 25 nautical miles wide moving from 240 degrees at 20 knots. Tops above flight level 350. The line of thunderstorms extends northwest into the Oberlin, Ohio control area.

6.5 Additional Products for Convection

The National Weather Service (NWS) in addition to the SIGMETs, Convective SIGMETs, and CWAs already discussed, offers a few more products informing the aviation community about the potential for convective weather.

6.5.1 Convective Outlooks (AC)

The NWS Storm Prediction Center (SPC) issues narrative and graphical convective outlooks to provide the contiguous U.S. NWS Weather Forecast Offices (WFOs), the public, media and emergency managers with the potential for severe (tornado, wind gusts 50 knots or greater, or hail 1 inch diameter size or greater) and non-severe (general) convection and specific severe weather threats during the following three days. The Convective Outlook defines areas of slight risk (**SLGT**), moderate risk (**MDT**) or high risk (**HIGH**) of severe thunderstorms for a 24-hour period beginning at 1200 UTC. The Day 1 and Day 2 Convective Outlooks also depict areas of general thunderstorms (**GEN TSTMS**), while the Day 1, Day 2, and Day 3 Convective Outlooks may use **SEE TEXT** for areas where convection may approach or slightly exceed severe criteria. The outlooks are available on the SPC web site at: http://www.spc.noaa.gov/products/outlook/.

6.5.1.1 Issuance

Convective Outlooks are scheduled products issued at the following times:

Table 6-9. Convective Outlook Issuance Schedule

Convective Outlook	Issuance Time (UTC)	Valid Period (UTC)
Day 1	0600	1200 – 1200
	1300	1300 – 1200
	1630	1630 – 1200
	2000	2000 – 1200
	0100	0100 – 1200
Day 2	0600 (Daylight Savings Time) 0700 (Standard Time)	Day 2/1200 – 1200
	1730	Day 2/1200 – 1200
Day 3	0730 (Daylight Savings Time) 0830 (Standard Time)	Day 3/1200 – 1200

SPC corrects outlooks for format and grammatical errors and amends outlooks when the current forecast does not or will not reflect the ongoing or future convective development.

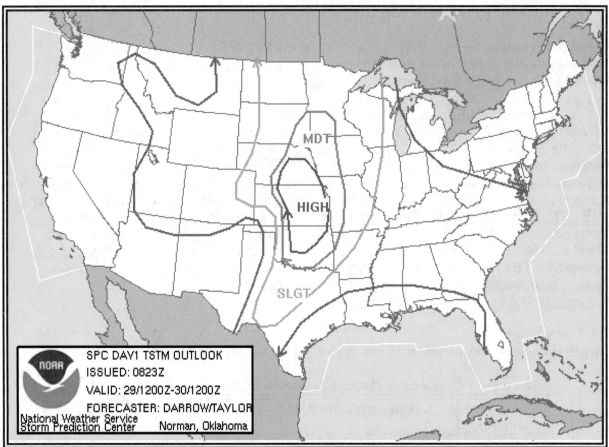

Figure 6-23. Day 1 Categorical Convective Outlook Graphic Example

6.5.1.2 Format of the Categorical Convective Outlook Narrative

SPC AC ddhhmm [SPC - issuing office, AC – product type, ddhhmm – date and time the product was issued

DAY (**ONE, TWO OR THREE**) CONVECTIVE OUTLOOK
NWS STORM PREDICTION CENTER NORMAN OK
time am/pm time zone day mon dd yyyy

VALID DDHHMM - DDHHMMZ

THERE IS A (SLIGHT, MODERATE, HIGH) RISK OF SEVERE THUNDERSTORMS TO
THE RIGHT OF LINE (LIST OF ANCHOR POINTS AND DIRECTION AND DISTANCE IN
STATUTE MILES FROM THE LINE). THE LINE WILL ENCLOSE THE AREA OF RISK.
THERE MAY BE ONE OR MORE AREAS OF RISK AT THE APPROPRIATE LEVEL OF
RISK. WHEN A MODERATE OR HIGH RISK IS FORECAST, THE INDIVIDUAL STATES
ARE ALSO LISTED WITH THE TWO LETTER POSTAL STATE IDENTIFIERS.

GEN TSTMS ARE FCST TO THE RIGHT OF A LINE FROM (LIST OF ANCHOR POINTS
AND DIRECTION AND DISTANCE IN STATUTE MILES FROM THE LINE). THERE MAY
BE ONE OR MORE AREAS OF GEN TSTMS LISTED.

...AREA OF CONCERN #1...

```
AREAS OF HIGHEST RISK ARE DISCUSSED FIRST (HIGH SEVERE RISK,
MODERATE SEVERE RISK, SLIGHT SEVERE RISK, APPROACHING SEVERE
LIMITS). THE FORECAST PROVIDES A NARRATIVE TECHNICAL DISCUSSION.

...AREA OF CONCERN #2...
NARRATIVE TECHNICAL DISCUSSION

$$

...FORECASTER NAME... MM/DD/YY
```

6.5.2 Watch Notification Messages

The NWS Storm Prediction Center (SPC) issues Watch Notification Messages to alert the aviation community, NWS offices (WFOs), the public, media and emergency managers to organized thunderstorms forecast to produce tornadic and/or severe weather in the conterminous U.S.

SPC issues three types of Watch Notification Messages: Aviation Watch Notification Message, Public Severe Thunderstorm Watch Notification Message and Public Tornado Watch Notification Message. They are available on the SPC web site at: http://www.spc.noaa.gov/products/watch/.

6.5.2.1 Aviation Watch Notification Message

SPC issues Aviation Watch Notification Messages to alert the aviation community to organized thunderstorms forecast to produce tornadic and/or severe weather as indicated in Public Watch Notification Messages.

6.5.2.1.1 Format of an Aviation Watch Notification Message

```
SPC AWW ddhhmm
WWnnnn SEVERE TSTM ST LO DDHHMMZ - DDHHMMZ
AXIS...XX STATUTE MILES EITHER SIDE OF A LINE
XXDIR CCC/LOCATION ST/ - XXDIR CCC/LOCATION ST
..AVIATION COORD.. XX NM EITHER SIDE /XXDIR CCC - XXDIR CCC
HAIL SURFACE AND ALOFT..X X/X INCHES. WIND GUSTS..XX KNOTS.
MAX TOPS TO XXX. MEAN STORM MOTION VECTOR DIR/SPEED
```

Figure 6-24. Aviation Watch Notification Message Decoding Example

Table 6-10. Decoding a Severe Weather Watch Bulletin

Line	Content	Description
1	SPC AWW 132101	Issuing office Product Type Issuance date/time
2	WW568 TORNADO OK 132130Z – 140300Z	Watch number Watch Type States affected Valid date/time period
3	AXIS..80 STATUTE MILES EAST AND WEST OF A LINE...	Watch axis
4	50SSE FSI/FORT SILL OK/ – 20NW PNC/PONCA CITY OK/	Anchor points
5	...AVIATION COORDS.. 70NM E/W/ 21E SPS – 43S ICT/	Aviation coordinates
6	HAIL SURFACE AND ALOFT...3 INCHES. WIND GUSTS..70 KNOTS. MAX TOPS TO 550. MEAN STORM MOTION VECTOR 26030.	Type, intensity, max tops, and mean storm motion using standard contractions.

The Severe Weather Watch Bulletin in Figure 6-16 is decoded as follows:

(Line 1) *Alert Severe Weather Watch Bulletin (AWW), issued by the Storm Prediction Center on the 13th at 2101Z,*

(Line 2) *for Tornado Watch number 568 (WW568) for Oklahoma, valid from the 13th at 2130Z until the 14th at 0300Z.*

(Line 3) *The Tornado Watch area is along and 80 statute miles east and west of a line from*

(Line 4) *50 statute miles south southeast of Fort Sill (Lawton), OK to 20 statute miles northwest of Ponca City, OK.*

(Line 5) *Aviation coordinates for this Tornado Watch are 70 nautical miles east and west of a line from 21 nautical miles east of Sheppard AFB (Wichita Falls), TX to 43 nautical miles south of Wichita, KS.*

(Line 6) *Hail surface and aloft to 3 inches in diameter, wind gusts to 70* knots, *max tops to Flight Level 550, mean storm motion from 260 degrees at 30* knots

6.5.2.1.2 Issuance

Watch Notification Messages are non-scheduled, event driven products valid from the time of issuance to expiration or cancellation time. Valid times are in UTC. SPC will correct watches for format and grammatical errors.

When tornadoes or severe thunderstorms have developed, the local NWS Weather Forecast Offices (WFOs) will issue the warnings for the storms.

SPC forecasters may define the watch area as a rectangle (some number of miles either side of line from point A to point B) or as a parallelogram (some number of miles north and south or east and west of line from point A to point B). The axis coordinates are measured in statute miles. The aviation coordinates are measured in nautical miles and referenced to VHF Omni-Directional Range (VOR) navigational aid locations. The watch half-width is in statute miles. The Aviation Watch Notification Message contains hail size in inches or half inches at the surface and aloft, surface convective wind gusts in knots, maximum tops, and the Mean Storm Motion Vector. Forecasters have discretion in including hail size for tornado watches associated with hurricanes.

6.5.3 Public Severe Thunderstorm Watch Notification Message

SPC issues a Public Severe Thunderstorm Watch Notification Message when forecasting six or more hail events of 1 inch (quarter) diameter or greater or damaging winds of 50 knots (58 mph) or greater. The forecast event minimum threshold is at least 2 hours over an area at least 8,000 square miles. Below these thresholds, SPC, in collaboration with affected NWS offices may issue convective watches along coastlines, near the Canadian and Mexican borders, and for any ongoing organized severe convection.

A Public Severe Thunderstorm Watch Notification Message contains the area description and axis, watch expiration time, a description of hail size and thunderstorm wind gusts expected, the definition of the watch, a call to action statement, a list of other valid watches, a brief discussion of meteorological reasoning, and technical information for the aviation community.

SPC includes the term "adjacent coastal waters" when the watch affects coastal waters adjacent to the Pacific/Atlantic coast, Gulf of Mexico, or Great Lakes. Adjacent coastal waters refers to a WFO's near-shore responsibility (out to 20 miles for oceans), except for convective watches which include portions of the Great Lakes.

SPC issues a watch cancellation message when **no** counties, parishes, independent cities and/or marine zones remaining are in the watch area prior to the expiration time. The text of the message will specify the number and area of the cancelled watch.

6.5.3.1 Format of Public Severe Thunderstorm Watch Notification Message

`WWUS20 KWNS ddhhmm` (*ICAO communication header*)

```
URGENT - IMMEDIATE BROADCAST REQUESTED
SEVERE THUNDERSTORM WATCH NUMBER nnnn
NWS STORM PREDICTION CENTER NORMAN OK
time am/pm time zone day mon dd yyyy

THE STORM PREDICTION CENTER HAS ISSUED A
SEVERE THUNDERSTORM WATCH FOR PORTIONS OF

                PORTION OF STATE
                PORTION OF STATE
                AND ADJACENT COASTAL WATERS (IF REQUIRED)

EFFECTIVE (TIME PERIOD) UNTIL hhmm am/pm time zone.

...THIS IS A PARTICULARLY DANGEROUS SITUATION (IF FORECAST)...

HAIL TO X INCHES IN DIAMETER...THUNDERSTORM WIND GUSTS TO XX MPH...AND
DANGEROUS LIGHTNING ARE POSSIBLE IN THESE AREAS.
```

NARRATIVE DESCRIPTION OF WATCH AREA USING A LINE AND ANCHOR
POINTS. DISTANCES TO EITHER SIDE OF THE LINE WILL BE IN STATUTE MILES.

CALL TO ACTION STATEMENTS

```
OTHER WATCH INFORMATION...OTHER WATCHES IN EFFECT AND IF THIS
WATCH REPLACES A PREVIOUS WATCH.
```

NARRATIVE DISCUSSION OF REASON FOR THE WATCH.

```
AVIATION...BRIEF DESCRIPTION OF SEVERE WEATHER THREAT TO AVIATORS.
HAIL SIZE WILL BE GIVEN IN INCHES AND WIND GUSTS IN KNOTS. MAXIMUM
STORM TOPS AND A MEAN STORM VECTOR WILL ALSO BE GIVEN.

$$

..FORECASTER NAME.. MM/DD/YY
```

6.5.3.2 Example of a Public Severe Thunderstorm Watch Notification Message

```
WWUS20 KWNS 161711 (ICAO communication header)
SPC WW 161710

URGENT - IMMEDIATE BROADCAST REQUESTED
SEVERE THUNDERSTORM WATCH NUMBER 647
NWS STORM PREDICTION CENTER NORMAN OK
1210 PM CDT FRI JUL 16 2004

THE NWS STORM PREDICTION CENTER HAS ISSUED A
SEVERE THUNDERSTORM WATCH FOR PORTIONS OF

        EASTERN IOWA
        NORTHERN ILLINOIS
```

```
       NORTHWEST INDIANA
       LAKE MICHIGAN

EFFECTIVE THIS FRIDAY AFTERNOON FROM 1210 PM UNTIL 500 PM CDT.

HAIL TO 2 INCHES IN DIAMETER...THUNDERSTORM WIND GUSTS TO 70
MPH...AND DANGEROUS LIGHTNING ARE POSSIBLE IN THESE AREAS.

THE SEVERE THUNDERSTORM WATCH AREA IS ALONG AND 75 STATUTE MILES
EITHER SIDE OF A LINE FROM 40 MILES SOUTHEAST OF SOUTH BEND
INDIANA TO 35 MILES SOUTHWEST OF CEDAR RAPIDS IOWA.

REMEMBER...A SEVERE THUNDERSTORM WATCH MEANS CONDITIONS ARE
FAVORABLE FOR SEVERE THUNDERSTORMS IN AND CLOSE TO THE WATCH AREA.
PERSONS IN THESE AREAS SHOULD BE ON THE LOOKOUT FOR THREATENING
WEATHER CONDITIONS AND LISTEN FOR LATER STATEMENTS AND POSSIBLE
WARNINGS. SEVERE THUNDERSTORMS CAN AND OCCASIONALLY DO PRODUCE
TORNADOES.

OTHER WATCH INFORMATION...CONTINUE...WW 646...

DISCUSSION...THUNDERSTORMS WILL CONTINUE TO INCREASE ACROSS WATCH
AREA WHERE AIR MASS HAS BECOME STRONGLY UNSTABLE AND UNCAPPED.
VEERING SHEAR PROFILE SUPPORT STORMS EVOLVING INTO SHORT LINE
SEGMENTS ENHANCING WIND DAMAGE POTENTIAL

AVIATION...A FEW SEVERE THUNDERSTORMS WITH HAIL SURFACE AND ALOFT
TO 2 INCHES. EXTREME TURBULENCE AND SURFACE WIND GUSTS TO 60
KNOTS. A FEW CUMULONIMBI WITH MAXIMUM TOPS TO 500. MEAN STORM
MOTION VECTOR 33025.

...HALES
```

6.5.4 Public Tornado Watch Notification Message

SPC issues a Public Tornado Watch Notification Message when forecasting three or more tornadoes or any tornado which could produce F2 or greater damage. The forecast event minimum thresholds are at least 2 hours over an area at least 8,000 square miles. Below these thresholds, SPC, in collaboration with affected NWS offices, may issue convective watches along coastlines, near the Canadian and Mexican borders and for any ongoing organized severe convection.

A Public Tornado Watch Notification Message contains the area description and axis, watch expiration time, the term "damaging tornadoes", a description of the largest hail size and strongest thunderstorm wind gusts expected, the definition of the watch, a call to action statement, a list of other valid watches, a brief discussion of meteorological reasoning, and technical information for the aviation community.

SPC includes the term "adjacent coastal waters" when the watch affects coastal waters adjacent to the Pacific/Atlantic coast, Gulf of Mexico, or Great Lakes. Adjacent coastal waters refers to a WFO's near shore responsibility (out to 20 nautical miles for oceans), except for convective watches which include portions of the Great Lakes.

SPC issues a watch cancellation message whenever it cancels a watch prior to the expiration time. The text of the message will specify the number and area of the cancelled watch.

6.5.4.1 Format of a Public Tornado Watch Notification Message

```
WWUS20 KWNS ddhhmm (ICAO communication header)

URGENT - IMMEDIATE BROADCAST REQUESTED
TORNADO WATCH NUMBER nnnn
NWS STORM PREDICTION CENTER NORMAN OK
time am/pm time zone day mon dd yyyy

THE STORM PREDICTION CENTER HAS ISSUED A
TORNADO WATCH FOR PORTIONS OF

          PORTION OF STATE
          PORTION OF STATE
          AND ADJACENT COASTAL WATERS (IF REQUIRED)

EFFECTIVE (TIME PERIOD) UNTIL hhmm am/pm time zone.

...THIS IS A PARTICULARLY DANGEROUS SITUATION (IF FORECAST)...

DESTRUCTIVE TORNADOES...HAIL TO X INCHES IN DIAMETER...THUNDERSTORM
WIND GUSTS TO XX MPH...AND DANGEROUS LIGHTNING ARE POSSIBLE IN THESE
AREAS.

NARRATIVE DESCRIPTION OF WATCH AREA USING A LINE AND ANCHOR POINTS.
DISTANCES TO EITHER SIDE OF THE LINE WILL BE IN STATUTE MILES.

CALL TO ACTION STATEMENTS

OTHER WATCH INFORMATION...OTHER WATCHES IN EFFECT AND IF THIS WATCH
REPLACES A PREVIOUS WATCH.

NARRATIVE DISCUSSION OF REASON FOR THE WATCH.

AVIATION...BRIEF DESCRIPTION OF SEVERE WEATHER THREAT TO AVIATORS.
HAIL SIZE WILL BE GIVEN IN INCHES AND WIND GUSTS IN KNOTS. MAXIMUM
STORM TOPS AND A MEAN STORM VECTOR WILL ALSO BE GIVEN.

$$

..FORECASTER NAME.. MM/DD/YY
```

6.5.4.2 Example of a Public Tornado Watch Notification Message

```
WWUS20 KWNS 050550 (ICAO communication header)

URGENT - IMMEDIATE BROADCAST REQUESTED
TORNADO WATCH NUMBER 243
NWS STORM PREDICTION CENTER NORMAN OK
```

```
1250 AM CDT MON MAY 5 2003

THE NWS STORM PREDICTION CENTER HAS ISSUED A
TORNADO WATCH FOR PORTIONS OF

          WESTERN AND CENTRAL ARKANSAS
          SOUTHERN MISSOURI
          FAR EASTERN OKLAHOMA

EFFECTIVE THIS MONDAY MORNING FROM 1250 AM UNTIL 600 AM CDT.

...THIS IS A PARTICULARLY DANGEROUS SITUATION...

DESTRUCTIVE TORNADOES...LARGE HAIL TO 2 INCHES IN DIAMETER...
THUNDERSTORM WIND GUSTS TO 70 MPH...AND DANGEROUS LIGHTNING ARE
POSSIBLE IN THESE AREAS.

THE TORNADO WATCH AREA IS ALONG AND 100 STATUTE MILES EAST AND
WEST OF A LINE FROM 15 MILES WEST NORTHWEST OF FORT LEONARD WOOD
MISSOURI TO 45 MILES SOUTHWEST OF HOT SPRINGS ARKANSAS.

REMEMBER...A TORNADO WATCH MEANS CONDITIONS ARE FAVORABLE FOR
TORNADOES AND SEVERE THUNDERSTORMS IN AND CLOSE TO THE WATCH AREA.
PERSONS IN THESE AREAS SHOULD BE ON THE LOOKOUT FOR THREATENING
WEATHER CONDITIONS AND LISTEN FOR LATER STATEMENTS AND POSSIBLE
WARNINGS.

OTHER WATCH INFORMATION...THIS TORNADO WATCH REPLACES TORNADO
WATCH NUMBER 237. WATCH NUMBER 237 WILL NOT BE IN EFFECT AFTER
1250 AM CDT. CONTINUE...WW 239...WW 240...WW 241...WW 242...

DISCUSSION...SRN MO SQUALL LINE EXPECTED TO CONTINUE EWD...WHERE
LONG/HOOKED HODOGRAPHS SUGGEST THREAT FOR EMBEDDED
SUPERCELLS/POSSIBLE TORNADOES. FARTHER S...MORE WIDELY SCATTERED
SUPERCELLS WITH A THREAT FOR TORNADOES WILL PERSIST IN VERY STRONGLY
DEEP SHEARED/LCL ENVIRONMENT IN AR.

AVIATION...TORNADOES AND A FEW SEVERE THUNDERSTORMS WITH HAIL
SURFACE AND ALOFT TO 2 INCHES. EXTREME TURBULENCE AND SURFACE WIND
GUSTS TO 60 KNOTS. A FEW CUMULONIMBI WITH MAXIMUM TOPS TO 500. MEAN
STORM MOTION VECTOR 26045.
.
..CORFIDI
```

6.6   Products for Tropical Cyclones

The NWS issues SIGMETs, Convective SIGMETs and CWAs to inform the aviation community about the potential or existence of tropical cyclones and the adverse conditions associated with them.   These above listed products are the primary source of information.   The NWS also issues other products pertaining to Tropical Cyclones. These additional products are defined in this section.

6.6.1   Aviation Tropical Cyclone Advisory (TCA)

The Aviation Tropical Cyclone Advisory (TCA) is intended to provide short-term tropical cyclone forecast guidance for international aviation safety and routing purposes. It is prepared by the National Hurricane Center (NHC) and the Central Pacific Hurricane Center (CPHC) in Honolulu, Hawaii, for all on-going tropical cyclone activity in their respective areas of responsibility.   This requirement is stated in the World Meteorological Organization Region IV hurricane plan. Any valid TCA in the Atlantic or eastern Pacific is available on the NHC web site at: http://www.nhc.noaa.gov. Any valid TCA for the central Pacific is available on the CPHC web site at: http://www.prh.noaa.gov/hnl/cphc/

6.6.1.1   Issuance

TCAs are issued at 0300, 0900, 1500, and 2100 UTC and are valid from the time of issuance until the next scheduled issuance or update.

6.6.1.2   Content

TCAs list the current tropical cyclone position, motion and intensity, and 12-, 18- and 24-hour forecast positions and intensities. It is an alphanumeric text product produced by hurricane forecasters and consists of information extracted from the official forecasts. This forecast is produced from subjective evaluation of current meteorological and oceanographic data as well as output from numerical weather prediction models, and is coordinated with affected NWS offices, the NWS National Centers, and the Department of Defense.

6.6.1.3   Format

The format of the Aviation Tropical Cyclone Advisory is as follows:

```
FKaa2i cccc ddhhmm (ICAO communication header)

(TROPICAL CYCLONE TYPE) (NAME) ICAO ADVISORY NUMBER ##
(ISSUING OFFICE CITY STATE) BBCCYYYY
time UTC day of week mon dd yyyy

TEXT
$$
```

NOTE: As part of the header, a coded string is appended at the end of the "ISSUING OFFICE CITY STATE" line. (Example: NWS TPC/NATIONAL HURRICANE CENTER MIAMI FL BBCCYYY)

Where: (BB) is the basin AL – North Atlantic, EP – East Pacific, or CP – Central Pacific
Where: (CC) is the cyclone number (01, 02, 03,…49)
Where: (YYYY) is the 4 digit year.

6.6.1.4 Aviation Tropical Cyclone Advisory (TCA) Example

```
FKNT25 KNHC 210900
TCANT5

TROPICAL STORM ICAO ADVISORY NUMBER 27
NWS TPC/NATIONAL HURRICANE CENTER MIAMI FL AL092007
0900 UTC SUN OCT 21 2007

TC ADVISORY
DTG:                      20071021/0900Z
TCAC:                     KNHC
TC:                       ERNESTO
NR:                       027
PSN:                      N3000 W08012
MOV:                      N 13KT
C:                        0998HPA
MAX WIND:                 045KT
FCST PSN + 06 HR:         211200 N3106 W07951
FCST MAX WIND + 06 HR: 045KT
FCST PSN + 12 HR:         211800 N3206 W07930
FCST MAX WIND + 12 HR: 050KT
FCST PSN + 18 HR:         220000 N3321 W07903
FCST MAX WIND + 18 HR: 045KT
FCST PSN + 24 HR:         220600 N3436 W07836
FCST MAX WIND + 24 HR: 040KT
NXT MSG:                  20071021/1500Z

$$
```

6.6.2 Tropical Cyclone Public Advisory (TCP)

A Tropical Cyclone Public Advisory (TCP) is the primary tropical cyclone information product issued to the public. The TCP provides critical tropical cyclone watch, warning, and forecast information for the protection of life and property.

6.6.2.1 TCP Responsibility

The National Hurricane Center (NHC), as a part of the Tropical Prediction Center (TPC); the Central Pacific Hurricane Center (CPHC); and Weather Forecast Office (WFO) Tiyan, Guam, issue TCPs. In the Atlantic and central Pacific, NHC and CPHC issue TCPs for all tropical cyclones respectively. In the eastern Pacific, NHC will issue public advisories when watches or warnings are required, or the tropical cyclone is otherwise expected to impact nearby land areas. In the western Pacific, WFO Guam will issue public advisories generally based on the tropical cyclone bulletins of the Joint Typhoon Warning Center (JTWC) for all tropical cyclones expected to affect land within 48 hours.

Valid TCP in the Atlantic or eastern Pacific is available on the NHC web site at: http://www.nhc.noaa.gov.

Valid TCP for the central Pacific is available on the CPHC web site at: http://www.prh.noaa.gov/hnl/cphc/.

TCPs issued by WFO Guam for the western Pacific are available at: http://www.prh.noaa.gov/pr/guam/cyclone.php.

6.6.2.2 TCP Issuance

The initial advisory may be issued when data confirm a tropical cyclone has developed. The title of the advisory will depend upon the intensity of the tropical cyclone as listed below.

- A tropical depression advisory refers to a tropical cyclone with 1-minute sustained winds up to 33 knots (38 mph).

- A tropical storm advisory will refer to tropical cyclones with 1-minute sustained surface winds 34 to 63 knots (39 to 73 mph).

- A hurricane/typhoon advisory will refer to tropical cyclones with winds 64 knots (74 mph) or greater.

Public advisories are discontinued when the tropical cyclone:

- Ceases to be a tropical cyclone; that is, it becomes extratropical, a remnant low, or dissipates, or

- Is centered over land, is below tropical storm strength, and is not forecast to move back over water as a tropical cyclone, and no coastal tropical cyclone watches or warnings are in effect.

- For Guam when the tropical cyclone moves out of the WFO area of responsibility.

Tropical Cyclone Public Advisories are issued according to the schedule below and are valid from the time of issuance until the next scheduled issuance or update. Valid position times correspond to the advisory time.

Table 6-11. Tropical Cyclone Public Advisory Issuance Schedule

TPC/CPHC ISSUANCE TIME (UTC)	WFO GUAM ISSUANCE TIME (UTC)
0300	0400
0900	1000
1500	1600
2100	2200

Times in advisories are local time of the affected area; however, local time and UTC are used when noting the storm's location. All advisories use statute miles and statute miles per hour. The Tropical Cyclone Center (TPC and CPHC) and WFO Guam, at their discretion, may use nautical miles/knots in parentheses immediately following statute miles/mph. Advisories include the metric units of kilometers and kilometers per hour following the equivalent English units except when the United States is the only country threatened.

NHC, CPHC and WFO Guam issue tropical storm/hurricane/typhoon watches if tropical storm/hurricane/typhoon conditions are possible over land areas within 36 hours, except 48 hours in the western north Pacific. Tropical storm watches are not issued if the tropical cyclone is forecast to reach hurricane/typhoon intensity within the watch period.

Tropical storm/hurricane/typhoon warnings are issued when tropical storm/hurricane/typhoon conditions along the coast are expected within 24 hours. Tropical storm warnings are issued at the discretion of the hurricane specialist when gale warnings, not related to the pending tropical storm, are already in place. Tropical storm warnings may be issued on either side of a hurricane/typhoon warning area.

6.6.2.2.1 TCP Intermediate Issuances

Intermediate Public Advisories are issued on a 2- to 3-hourly interval between scheduled advisories (see times of issuance below). 3-hourly intermediate advisories are issued whenever a tropical storm or hurricane watch/warning is in effect. 2-hourly intermediates are issued whenever tropical storm or hurricane warnings are in effect and coastal radars are able to provide responsible Tropical Cyclone Centers with a reliable hourly center position. For clarity, when intermediate public advisories are issued, a statement is included at the end of the scheduled public advisory informing users when an intermediate advisory may be issued, i.e., "AN INTERMEDIATE ADVISORY WILL BE ISSUED BY THE CENTRAL PACIFIC HURRICANE CENTER AT 2 PM HST FOLLOWED BY THE NEXT COMPLETE ADVISORY ISSUANCE AT 5 PM HST."

Table 6-12. Intermediate Tropical Cyclone Public Advisory Issuance Schedule

	TPC/CPHC ISSUANCE TIME (UTC)	WFO GUAM ISSUANCE TIME (UTC)
3-Hourly Issuances	0000	0100
	0600	0700
	1200	1300
	1800	1900
2-Hourly Issuances	2300	0000
	0100	0200
	0500	0600
	0700	0800
	1100	1200
	1300	1400
	1700	1800
	1900	2000

Intermediate advisories are not used to issue tropical cyclone watches or warnings. They can be used to clear all, or parts of, a watch or warning area. Content is similar to the scheduled advisory.

6.6.2.3 TCP Content

Advisories list all tropical cyclone watches and warnings in effect. The first advisory in which watches or warnings are mentioned will give the effective time of the watch or warning, except when it is being issued by other countries and the time is not known. Except for tropical storms and hurricanes/typhoons forming close to land, a watch will precede a warning. Once a watch is in effect, it will either be replaced by a warning or remain in effect until the threat of the tropical cyclone conditions has passed. A hurricane/typhoon watch and a tropical storm warning can be in effect for the same section of coast at the same time.

All advisories include the location of the center of the tropical cyclone by its latitude and longitude, and distance and direction from a well known point, preferably downstream from the tropical cyclone. If the forecaster is unsure of the exact location of a depression, the position may be given as within 50, 75, etc., miles of a map coordinate. When the center of the tropical cyclone is over land, its position is given referencing the state or country in which it is located and in respect to some well known city, if appropriate.

Movement forecasts apply to the tropical cyclone's center. The present movement is given to 16 points of the compass when possible. A 24-hour forecast of movement in terms of a continuance or departure from the present movement and speed is also included. This can be reduced to a 12-hour forecast. Uncertainties in either the tropical cyclone's location or movement will be explained in the advisory. An outlook beyond 24 hours (out to 72 hours when appropriate) may be included in the text of the advisory.

Maximum observed 1-minute sustained surface wind speed rounded to the nearest 5 mph is given. During landfall threats, specific gust values and phrases like "briefly higher in squalls" may be used. The area (or radius) of both tropical and hurricane/typhoon force winds is given. The storm may also be compared to some memorable hurricane or referred to by relative intensity. Where appropriate, the Saffir/Simpson Hurricane Scale (SSHS) is used in public releases.

Central pressure values in millibars and inches are provided as determined by available data.

The inland impacts of tropical cyclones will be highlighted in advisories. This includes the threat of strong winds, heavy rainfall, flooding, and tornadoes. The extent and magnitude of the inland winds is included as well as anticipated rainfall amounts and the potential for flooding and tornadoes. Tornado and flood watches will be mentioned as appropriate.

6.6.2.4 TCP Format
The format of the Tropical Cyclone Public Advisory is as follows:

```
WTaaii cccc ddhhmm
TCPxxx

BULLETIN
(TROPICAL CYCLONE TYPE) (NAME) ADVISORY NUMBER XX.
(ISSUING OFFICE CITY STATE) BBCCYYYY
time am/pm time zone day month dd YYYY

...HEADLINE...

TEXT
$$

FORECASTER NAME
```

NOTE: As part of the header, a coded string is appended at the end of the "ISSUING OFFICE CITY STATE" line (Example: NWS TPC/NATIONAL HURRICANE CENTER

MIAMI FL BBCCYYYY)

Format:
where: (BB) is the basin AL - North Atlantic, EP - East Pacific, CP - Central Pacific
         WP – western Pacific
where: (CC) is the cyclone number (01, 02, 03,...49)
where: (YYYY) is the 4 digit year.

6.6.2.5 Tropical Storm Public Advisory (TCP) Example

```
WTNT34 KNHC 260359
MIATCPAT4
BULLETIN
TROPICAL STORM DEBBY ADVISORY NUMBER 18
NWS TPC/NATIONAL HURRICANE CENTER MIAMI FL AL042006
1100 PM AST FRI AUG 25 2006


...DEBBY BARELY HANGING ON AS A TROPICAL STORM...

AT 1100 PM AST...0300Z...THE CENTER OF TROPICAL STORM DEBBY WAS
LOCATED NEAR LATITUDE 25.2 NORTH...LONGITUDE 45.6 WEST OR ABOUT 1400
MILES...2255 KM...SOUTHWEST OF THE AZORES.

DEBBY IS MOVING TOWARD THE WEST-NORTHWEST NEAR 14 MPH...22 KM/HR...
AND A TURN TO THE NORTHWEST AND THEN NORTH-NORTHWEST IS EXPECTED
OVER THE NEXT 24 HOURS.

MAXIMUM SUSTAINED WINDS ARE NEAR 40 MPH...65 KM/HR...WITH HIGHER
GUSTS. LITTLE CHANGE IN STRENGTH IS FORECAST DURING THE NEXT 24
HOURS.

TROPICAL STORM FORCE WINDS EXTEND OUTWARD UP TO 105 MILES...165 KM
FROM THE CENTER.

ESTIMATED MINIMUM CENTRAL PRESSURE IS 1008 MB...29.77 INCHES.

REPEATING THE 1100 PM AST POSITION...25.2 N...45.6 W. MOVEMENT
TOWARD...WEST-NORTHWEST NEAR 14 MPH. MAXIMUM SUSTAINED WINDS...40
MPH. MINIMUM CENTRAL PRESSURE...1008 MB.

THE NEXT ADVISORY WILL BE ISSUED BY THE NATIONAL HURRICANE CENTER
AT
500 AM AST.
$$
FORECASTER KNABB
```

6.6.2.6 Hurricane/Typhoon Public Advisory Example

```
WTNT32 KNHC 282058
TCPAT2
```

```
BULLETIN
HURRICANE KATRINA ADVISORY NUMBER 24
NWS TPC/NATIONAL HURRICANE CENTER MIAMI FL
4 PM CDT SUN AUG 28 2005

...POTENTIALLY CATASTROPHIC HURRICANE KATRINA HEADED FOR THE
NORTHERN GULF COAST...

A HURRICANE WARNING IS IN EFFECT FOR THE NORTH CENTRAL GULF COAST
FROM MORGAN CITY LOUISIANA EASTWARD TO THE ALABAMA/FLORIDA
BORDER...INCLUDING THE CITY OF NEW ORLEANS AND LAKE PONTCHARTRAIN.
PREPARATIONS TO PROTECT LIFE AND PROPERTY SHOULD BE COMPLETED THIS
EVENING.

A TROPICAL STORM WARNING AND A HURRICANE WATCH ARE IN EFFECT FROM
EAST OF THE ALABAMA/FLORIDA BORDER TO DESTIN FLORIDA...AND FROM
WEST OF MORGAN CITY TO INTRACOASTAL CITY LOUISIANA.

A TROPICAL STORM WARNING IS ALSO IN EFFECT FROM DESTIN FLORIDA
EASTWARD TO INDIAN PASS FLORIDA...AND FROM INTRACOASTAL CITY
LOUISIANA WESTWARD TO CAMERON LOUISIANA.

FOR STORM INFORMATION SPECIFIC TO YOUR AREA...INCLUDING POSSIBLE
INLAND WATCHES AND WARNINGS...PLEASE MONITOR PRODUCTS ISSUED
BY YOUR LOCAL WEATHER OFFICE.

AT 4 PM CDT...2100Z...THE CENTER OF HURRICANE KATRINA WAS LOCATED
NEAR LATITUDE 26.9 NORTH...LONGITUDE 89.0 WEST OR ABOUT 150 MILES
SOUTH OF THE MOUTH OF THE MISSISSIPPI RIVER.

KATRINA IS MOVING TOWARD THE NORTHWEST NEAR 13 MPH...AND A GRADUAL
TURN TO THE NORTH IS EXPECTED OVER THE NEXT 24 HOURS. ON THIS
TRACK THE CENTER OF THE HURRICANE WILL BE NEAR THE NORTHERN GULF
COAST EARLY MONDAY. HOWEVER...CONDITIONS ARE ALREADY BEGINNING TO
DETERIORATE ALONG PORTIONS OF THE CENTRAL AND NORTHEASTERN GULF
COAST...AND WILL CONTINUE TO WORSEN THROUGH THE NIGHT.

MAXIMUM SUSTAINED WINDS ARE NEAR 165 MPH...WITH HIGHER GUSTS.
KATRINA IS A POTENTIALLY CATASTROPHIC CATEGORY FIVE HURRICANE ON
THE SAFFIR-SIMPSON SCALE. SOME FLUCTUATIONS IN STRENGTH ARE LIKELY
UNTIL LANDFALL. KATRINA IS EXPECTED TO MAKE LANDFALL AT CATEGORY
FOUR OR FIVE INTENSITY. WINDS AFFECTING THE UPPER FLOORS OF
HIGH-RISE BUILDINGS WILL BE SIGNIFICANTLY STRONGER THAN THOSE NEAR
GROUND LEVEL.

KATRINA IS A LARGE HURRICANE. HURRICANE FORCE WINDS EXTEND
OUTWARD UP TO 105 MILES FROM THE CENTER...AND TROPICAL STORM FORCE
WINDS EXTEND OUTWARD UP TO 230 MILES. SUSTAINED TROPICAL STORM FORCE
WINDS ARE OCCURRING OVER THE SOUTHEAST LOUISIANA COAST. SOUTHWEST
PASS...NEAR THE MOUTH OF THE MISSISSIPPI RIVER...RECENTLY REPORTED
SUSTAINED WINDS OF 48 MPH WITH GUSTS TO 53 MPH.
```

A NOAA HURRICANE HUNTER PLANE REPORTED A MINIMUM CENTRAL
PRESSURE OF 902 MB...26.64 INCHES.

COASTAL STORM SURGE FLOODING OF 18 TO 22 FEET ABOVE NORMAL TIDE
LEVELS...LOCALLY AS HIGH AS 28 FEET...ALONG WITH LARGE AND DANGEROUS
BATTERING WAVES...CAN BE EXPECTED NEAR AND TO THE EAST OF WHERE THE
CENTER MAKES LANDFALL. SOME LEVEES IN THE GREATER NEW ORLEANS
AREA COULD BE OVERTOPPED. SIGNIFICANT STORM SURGE FLOODING WILL OCCUR
ELSEWHERE ALONG THE CENTRAL AND NORTHEASTERN GULF OF MEXICO
COAST.

RAINFALL TOTALS OF 5 TO 10 INCHES...WITH ISOLATED MAXIMUM AMOUNTS OF
15 INCHES...ARE POSSIBLE ALONG THE PATH OF KATRINA ACROSS THE GULF
COAST AND THE TENNESSEE VALLEY. RAINFALL TOTALS OF 4 TO 8 INCHES
ARE POSSIBLE ACROSS THE OHIO VALLEY INTO THE EASTERN GREAT LAKES
REGION TUESDAY AND WEDNESDAY.

ISOLATED TORNADOES WILL BE POSSIBLE BEGINNING THIS EVENING OVER
SOUTHERN PORTIONS OF LOUISIANA...MISSISSIPPI...AND ALABAMA...AND
OVER THE FLORIDA PANHANDLE.

REPEATING THE 4 PM CDT POSITION...26.9 N... 89.0 W. MOVEMENT
TOWARD...NORTHWEST NEAR 13 MPH. MAXIMUM SUSTAINED WINDS...165 MPH.
MINIMUM CENTRAL PRESSURE... 902 MB.

AN INTERMEDIATE ADVISORY WILL BE ISSUED BY THE NATIONAL HURRICANE
CENTER AT 7 PM CDT FOLLOWED BY THE NEXT COMPLETE ADVISORY AT
10 PM CDT.

FORECASTER PASCH

$$

6.6.2.7 Intermediate Public Advisory Example

WTNT33 KNHC 221858
TCPAT3

BULLETIN
HURRICANE RITA INTERMEDIATE ADVISORY NUMBER 20A
NWS TPC/NATIONAL HURRICANE CENTER MIAMI FL
1 PM CDT THU SEP 22 2005

...RITA WEAKENS A LITTLE FURTHER...REMAINS AN EXTREMELY DANGEROUS
HURRICANE...

A HURRICANE WARNING IS IN EFFECT FROM PORT O'CONNOR TEXAS TO
MORGAN CITY LOUISIANA. A HURRICANE WARNING MEANS THAT HURRICANE
CONDITIONS ARE EXPECTED WITHIN THE WARNING AREA WITHIN THE NEXT 24
HOURS. PREPARATIONS TO PROTECT LIFE AND PROPERTY SHOULD BE RUSHED TO
COMPLETION.

A TROPICAL STORM WARNING REMAINS IN EFFECT FROM SOUTH OF PORT
O'CONNOR TO PORT MANSFIELD TEXAS AND FOR THE SOUTHEASTERN COAST OF
LOUISIANA EAST OF MORGAN CITY TO THE MOUTH OF THE MISSISSIPPI
RIVER. A TROPICAL STORM WARNING MEANS THAT TROPICAL STORM
CONDITIONS ARE EXPECTED WITHIN THE WARNING AREA WITHIN THE NEXT 24
HOURS.

A TROPICAL STORM WATCH IS IN EFFECT FROM NORTH OF THE MOUTH OF THE
MISSISSIPPI RIVER TO THE MOUTH OF THE PEARL RIVER INCLUDING
METROPOLITAN NEW ORLEANS AND LAKE PONTCHARTRAIN...FROM SOUTH OF
PORT MANSFIELD TO BROWNSVILLE TEXAS...AND FOR THE NORTHEASTERN
COAST OF MEXICO FROM RIO SAN FERNANDO NORTHWARD TO THE RIO
GRANDE. A TROPICAL STORM WATCH MEANS THAT TROPICAL STORM CONDITIONS
ARE POSSIBLE WITHIN THE WATCH AREA...GENERALLY WITHIN 36 HOURS.

FOR STORM INFORMATION SPECIFIC TO YOUR AREA...INCLUDING POSSIBLE
INLAND WATCHES AND WARNINGS...PLEASE MONITOR PRODUCTS ISSUED
BY YOUR LOCAL WEATHER OFFICE.

AT 1 PM CDT...1800Z...THE CENTER OF HURRICANE RITA WAS LOCATED NEAR
LATITUDE 25.5 NORTH...LONGITUDE 89.2 WEST OR ABOUT 435 MILES...700
KM...SOUTHEAST OF GALVESTON TEXAS AND ABOUT 430 MILES...695 KM...
SOUTHEAST OF PORT ARTHUR TEXAS.

RITA IS MOVING TOWARD THE WEST-NORTHWEST NEAR 9 MPH...15 KM/HR. A
GRADUAL TURN TO THE NORTHWEST IS EXPECTED DURING THE NEXT 24 TO 36
HOURS.

DATA FROM A NOAA RECONNAISSANCE AIRCRAFT INDICATE THAT MAXIMUM
SUSTAINED WINDS HAVE DECREASED TO NEAR 150 MPH...240 KM/HR... WITH
HIGHER GUSTS. RITA IS NOW A STRONG CATEGORY FOUR HURRICANE ON
THE SAFFIR-SIMPSON SCALE. SOME SLIGHT WEAKENING IS FORECAST DURING
THE NEXT 24 HOURS BUT RITA IS EXPECTED TO REMAIN AN EXTREMELY
DANGEROUS HURRICANE.

HURRICANE FORCE WINDS EXTEND OUTWARD UP TO 85 MILES...140 KM...
FROM THE CENTER...AND TROPICAL STORM FORCE WINDS EXTEND OUTWARD
UP TO 185 MILES...295 KM.

LATEST MINIMUM CENTRAL PRESSURE REPORTED BY A NOAA HURRICANE
HUNTER PLANE WAS 915 MB...27.01 INCHES.

COASTAL STORM SURGE FLOODING OF 15 TO 20 FEET ABOVE NORMAL TIDE
LEVELS...ALONG WITH LARGE AND DANGEROUS BATTERING WAVES...CAN BE
EXPECTED NEAR AND TO THE EAST OF WHERE THE CENTER MAKES LANDFALL.
TIDES ARE CURRENTLY RUNNING ABOUT 2 FOOT ABOVE NORMAL ALONG THE
MISSISSIPPI AND LOUISIANA COASTS IN THE AREAS AFFECTED BY KATRINA.
TIDES IN THOSE AREAS WILL INCREASE UP TO 3 TO 4 FEET AND BE
ACCOMPANIED BY LARGE WAVES...AND RESIDENTS THERE COULD EXPERIENCE
SOME COASTAL FLOODING.

RAINFALL ACCUMULATIONS OF 8 TO 12 INCHES WITH ISOLATED MAXIMUM 15
INCH TOTAL ARE POSSIBLE ALONG THE PATH OF RITA PARTICULARLY OVER
SOUTHEAST TEXAS AND WESTERN LOUISIANA. IN ADDITION...RAINFALL
AMOUNTS OF 3 TO 5 INCHES ARE POSSIBLE OVER SOUTHEASTERN LOUISIANA
INCLUDING NEW ORLEANS. BASED ON THE FORECAST TRACK...RAINFALL
TOTALS IN EXCESS OF 25 INCHES ARE POSSIBLE AFTER RITA MOVES INLAND.

REPEATING THE 1 PM CDT POSITION...25.5 N... 89.2 W. MOVEMENT
TOWARD...WEST-NORTHWEST NEAR 9 MPH. MAXIMUM SUSTAINED WINDS...150
MPH. MINIMUM CENTRAL PRESSURE...915 MB.

THE NEXT ADVISORY WILL BE ISSUED BY THE NATIONAL HURRICANE CENTER
AT 4 PM CDT.

FORECASTER AVILA

$$

6.6.2.8 Special Public Advisory Example

WTNT33 KNHC 241309
TCPAT3

BULLETIN
HURRICANE ANDREW SPECIAL ADVISORY NUMBER 25
NWS TPC/NATIONAL HURRICANE CENTER MIAMI FL AL011992
900 AM EDT MON AUG 24 1992

...HURRICANE ANDREW MOVING INTO THE GULF OF MEXICO...

HURRICANE WARNINGS REMAIN POSTED FOR THE FLORIDA WEST COAST SOUTH
OF VENICE TO FLAMINGO AND FOR LAKE OKEECHOBEE. AT 9 AM EDT A
HURRICANE WATCH WILL GO INTO EFFECT FOR THE NORTHERN GULF COAST
FROM MOBILE ALABAMA TO SABINE PASS TEXAS. ALL OTHER POSTED
WATCHES AND WARNINGS ARE DISCONTINUED.

WIND GUSTS TO HURRICANE FORCE CONTINUE TO OCCUR ALONG THE
SOUTHEAST FLORIDA COAST BUT WILL GRADUALLY DIMINISH DURING THE
DAY. SMALL CRAFT ADVISORIES REMAIN IN EFFECT. RESIDENTS IN THESE
AREAS SHOULD MONITOR LOCAL NWS OFFICES FOR THE LATEST FORECASTS
AND CONDITIONS IN THEIR AREA.

AT 9 AM EDT THE CENTER OF HURRICANE ANDREW WAS LOCATED NEAR
LATITUDE 25.6 NORTH AND LONGITUDE 81.8 WEST OR APPROXIMATELY 45 MILES
SOUTH OF NAPLES FLORIDA.

HURRICANE ANDREW IS MOVING TOWARD THE WEST AT 18 MPH. THIS MOTION
IS EXPECTED TO CONTINUE THIS MORNING WITH A GRADUAL TURN TO THE
WEST NORTHWEST LATER TODAY.

MAXIMUM SUSTAINED WINDS ARE NEAR 140 MPH. LITTLE CHANGE IN

STRENGTH IS LIKELY DURING THE NEXT 24 HOURS.

HURRICANE FORCE WINDS EXTEND OUTWARD TO 30 MILES...50 KM FROM THE
CENTER WITH TROPICAL STORM FORCE WINDS EXTENDING OUTWARD TO 140
MILES. ESTIMATED MINIMUM CENTRAL PRESSURE IS 945 MB...27.91 INCHES.

STORM SURGES OF 5 TO 8 FEET ARE POSSIBLE ON THE FLORIDA WEST COAST
NEAR AND TO THE SOUTH OF THE CENTER FOLLOWING PASSAGE OF THE
HURRICANE. ALONG THE SOUTHEAST COAST OF FLORIDA STORM SURGE TIDES
ARE DECREASING. PRELIMINARY REPORTS FROM THE SOUTH FLORIDA WATER
MANAGEMENT DISTRICT INDICATE A STORM SURGE OF 8 FEET ABOVE NORMAL
WAS RECORDED IN BISCAYNE BAY NEAR HOMESTEAD FLORIDA.

RAINFALL AMOUNTS OF 5 TO 8 INCHES AND ISOLATED TORNADOES ARE
POSSIBLE ACROSS SOUTHERN AND CENTRAL FLORIDA TODAY.

FOR STORM INFORMATION SPECIFIC TO YOUR AREA...PLEASE MONITOR
PRODUCTS ISSUED BY YOUR LOCAL WEATHER OFFICE.

REPEATING THE 9 AM EDT POSITION...LATITUDE 25.6 NORTH AND LONGITUDE
81.8 WEST AND MOVING TOWARD THE WEST AT 18 MPH. MAXIMUM SUSTAINED
WINDS NEAR 140 MPH. MINIMUM CENTRAL PRESSURE OF 945 MB...27.91 INCHES.

THE NEXT SCHEDULED ADVISORY WILL BE ISSUED BY THE NATIONAL
HURRICANE CENTER AT 11 AM EDT MON.

$$

6.6.2.9 Public Advisory Correction Example

HURRICANE ANDREW ADVISORY NUMBER 25...**CORRECTED**
NWS TPC/NATIONAL HURRICANE CENTER MIAMI FL
500 AM EDT MON AUG 24 1992

CORRECTED FOR CENTRAL PRESSURE...

BODY OF TEXT

$$

6.7 Volcanic Ash Advisory Products

In addition to SIGMETs, the NWS issues products to notify the aviation community of volcanic ash.

6.7.1 Volcanic Ash Advisory Center (VAAC)

A Volcanic Ash Advisory Center (VAAC) is a meteorological office designated by ICAO regional air navigation agreement to provide advisory volcanic ash information to Meteorological Watch Offices (MWOs), World Area Forecast Centers (WAFCs), area control centers, flight information centers and international operational meteorological (OPMET) data banks regarding the lateral and vertical extent and forecast movement of volcanic ash in the atmosphere following a volcanic eruption. There are nine VAACs worldwide (Figure 6-17). The duties of a VAAC include:

- Monitoring relevant geostationary and polar-orbiting satellite data to detect the existence and extent of volcanic ash in the atmosphere in the area concerned

- Activating the volcanic ash numerical trajectory/dispersion model in order to forecast the movement of any ash cloud which has been detected or reported

- Issuing advisory information regarding the extent and forecast movement of the volcanic ash cloud.

Figure 6-25. Volcanic Ash Advisory Centers (VAACs) Area of Responsibility

The U.S. has two VAACs with responsibilities defined in ICAO Annex 3. The Washington VAAC is jointly managed by the National Environmental Satellite Data and Information Service (NESDIS) Satellite Analysis Branch (SAB) and the NWS National Centers for Environmental

Prediction (NCEP) Central Operations (NCO). The Anchorage VAAC is managed by the AAWU. The areas of responsibility for each VAAC are:

- Washington VAAC

  o FIRs in CONUS and adjacent coastal waters (Figures 6-1 and 6-18)
  o The Oakland Oceanic FIR over the Pacific Ocean (Figures 6-3 and 6-18)
  o The New York FIR over the western Atlantic Ocean (Figures 6-2 and 6-18)
  o FIRs over and adjacent to the Caribbean, and Central and South America north of 10 degrees south latitude (Figure 6-2 and 6-18)

- Anchorage VAAC
  o The Anchorage FIR (Figures 6-3 and 6-18).
  o Russian FIRs north of 60 degrees north latitude and east of 150 degrees east longitude (Figure 6-18).

6.7.2 Volcanic Ash Advisory Statement (VAAS)

A Volcanic Ash Advisory Statement (VAAS) provides information on hazards to aircraft flight operations caused by a volcanic eruption.

6.7.2.1 Issuance

Volcanic Ash Advisory Centers (VAACs) are responsible for providing ash movement and dispersion guidance to Meteorological Watch Offices (MWOs) and neighboring VAACs. There are nine VAACs worldwide, two of which are located in the US (Figure 6-18). Each VAAC issues Volcanic Ash Advisory Statements and provide guidance to Meteorological Watch Offices (MWOs) for SIGMETs involving volcanic ash.

A VAAS may be issued within 6 hours of an eruption and every 6 hours thereafter. However, it can be issued more frequently if new information about the eruption is received.

6.7.2.2 Format

A VAAS summarizes the known information about an eruption. It may include the location of the volcano, height of the volcano summit, height of the ash plume, a latitude/longitude box of the ash dispersion cloud, and a forecast of ash dispersion. The height of the ash cloud is estimated by meteorologists analyzing satellite imagery and satellite cloud drift winds combined with any pilot reports, volcano observatory reports, and upper-air wind reports.

6.7.2.3 VAAS Issued by the Washington VAAC Example

```
VOLCANIC ASH ADVISORY
ISSUED: 2003JUL10/1300Z      VAAC: WASHINGTON

VOLCANO: ANATAHAN 0804-20
LOCATION: N1621E14540    AREA: MARIANA ISLANDS

SUMMIT ELEVATION: 2585 FT (788 M)

ADVISORY NUMBER: 2003/251

INFORMATION SOURCE: GOES 9 IMAGERY. GFS MODEL WINDS FORECAST
```

```
ERUPTION DETAILS: ASH AND GAS EMISSIONS SINCE MAY 10.

OBS ASH DATE/TIME: 09/1202Z.

OBS ASH CLOUD: ASH NOT IDENTIFIABLE FROM SATELLITE DATA.

WINDS SFC/FL080 MOVING SW 10-15 KNOTS.

FCST ASH CLOUD +6H: SEE SIGMETS.

REMARKS: THE ASH PLUME OBSERVED IN VISIBLE IMAGERY IS TOO THIN AND
DIFFUSE TO BE SEEN IN INFRARED AND MULTISPECTRAL IMAGAERY. ANY ASH UP
TO FL080 SHOULD MOVE TOWARDS THE SW AT 10-15 KNOTS.

NEXT ADVISORY: WILL BE ISSUED BY 2003JUL10/1900Z.
```

6.7.3 Volcanic Ash Advisory (VAA)

The Volcanic Ash Advisory (VAA) is advisory information on volcanic ash cloud issued in abbreviated plain language, using approved ICAO abbreviations and numerical values of self explanatory nature.

6.7.3.1 VAA Issuance

Volcanic Ash Advisory Centers (VAACs) are responsible for providing ash movement and dispersion guidance to Meteorological Watch Offices (MWOs) and neighboring VAACs. There are nine VAACs worldwide, two of which are located in the US (Figure 6-18). Each VAAC issues Volcanic Ash Advisory Statements and provide guidance to Meteorological Watch Offices (MWOs) for SIGMETs involving volcanic ash.

VAAs are issued as necessary, but at least every six hours until such time as the volcanic ash cloud is no longer identifiable from satellite data, no further reports of volcanic ash are received from the area, and no further eruptions of the volcano are reported.

6.7.3.2 VAA Format

The VAA format conforms to the "Template for advisory message for volcanic ash" included in ICAO Annex 3.

6.7.3.3 Volcanic Ash Advisory (VAA) Example

```
FVAK21 PAWU 190615
VOLCANIC ASH ADVISORY
ISSUED:                 20030419/0615Z
VAAC:                   ANCHORAGE
VOLCANO:                CHIKURACHKI, 900-36
LOCATION:               N5019 E15527
AREA:                   KAMCHATKA NORTHERN KURIL ISLANDS
SUMMIT ELEVATION:       7674 FT (2339 M)
ADVISORY NUMBER:        2003-02
INFORMATION SOURCE:     SATELLITE
AVIATION COLOR CODE:    NOT GIVEN
ERUPTION DETAILS:       NEW ERUPTION OCCURRED APPROX 190500 UTC.
                        HEIGHT IS ESTIMATED AT FL300. ESTIMATE IS BASED
```

```
                           ON OBSERVEDAND MODEL WINDS. MOVEMENT
                           APPEARS TO BE E AT 75 KTS.
OBS ASH DATA/TIME:         19/0500Z
OBS ASH CLOUD:             VA EXTENDS FM NEAR VOLCANO EWD TO N50 E160.
FCST ASH CLOUD +6HR:       30NM EITHER SIDE OF LN FM NIPPI N49 E159 - N50
                           E175.
FCST ASH CLOUD +12HR:      30NM EITHER SIDE OF LN FM N50 E168 - N50 E180.
FCST ASH CLOUD +18HR:      30NM EITHER SIDE OF LN FM N51 E175 - N50 E185.
NEXT ADVISORY:             20030419/1500Z
REMARKS:                   UPDATES AS SOON AS INFO BECOMES AVAILABLE.
```

7 FORECAST TEXT PRODUCTS

7.1 Area Forecasts (FA)

An Area Forecast (FA) is a forecast in an abbreviated plain language of specified weather phenomena covering a flight information region (FIR) or other area designated by the meteorological authority. The Area Forecast (in conjunction with AIRMETs, SIGMETs, Convective SIGMETs, CWAs, etc.), is used to determine forecast en route weather and to interpolate conditions at airports which do not have a Terminal Aerodrome Forecast (TAF). As such, it serves as a flight planning and pilot weather briefing aid for use by general aviation pilots, civil and military aviation operations, and Federal Aviation Administration (FAA) weather briefers. Area forecasts are not intended for use in operational decision- making or as a substitute for a TAF in 14 CFR part 121 Air Carrier operations. In these operations, an FA may only be used to enhance situational awareness.

Note: Hazardous weather (e.g., IFR, icing, turbulence, etc.) meeting AIRMET or SIGMET criteria are not forecast in the CONUS or Hawaii FAs. Valid AIRMETs and SIGMETs must be used in conjunction with the FA to determine hazardous weather information for the flight.

All Area Forecasts are available on the Aviation Weather Center (AWC) web site at: http://aviationweather.gov/products/fa/.

Alaska Area Forecasts can also be found on the Alaska Aviation Weather Unit (AAWU) web site at: http://aawu.arh.noaa.gov/areaforecasts.php.

7.1.1 Area Forecast Issuance
Area forecasts are issued by the following offices for the following areas:

- The Aviation Weather Center (AWC)

  - Conterminous U.S. (CONUS) - Six (6) FAs covering separate geographical areas of the CONUS, excluding the Gulf of Mexico coastal waters west of 85W (Figure 7-1).

  - Gulf of Mexico: The northern Gulf of Mexico, including the Houston Oceanic FIR, the Gulf of Mexico portion of the Miami Oceanic FIR, and the coastal waters west of 85W longitude (Figures 7-1 and 7-2).

  - Caribbean Sea: Portions of the Gulf of Mexico (south of the Houston Oceanic FIR to approximately 22N latitude), the Caribbean Sea and adjacent portions of the North Atlantic (Figure 7-3).

- The Alaskan Aviation Weather Unit (AAWU)

  - Alaska: Seven (7) FAs covering separate geographical areas of Alaska and the adjacent coastal waters, including the Pribilof Islands and Southeast Bering Sea (Figure 7-5).

- WFO Honolulu, Hawaii

o Hawaii: The main Hawaiian Islands and adjacent coastal waters extending out 40 nautical miles from the coastlines (Figure 7-4).

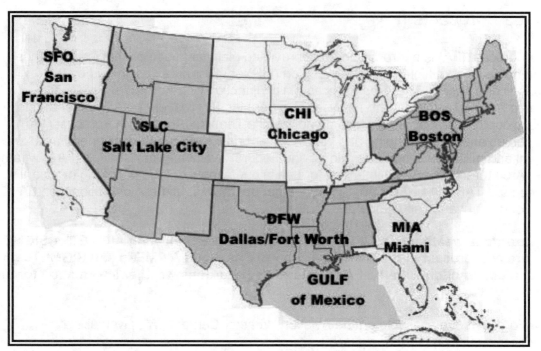

Figure 7-1. AWC Area Forecast Regions- Contiguous U.S.

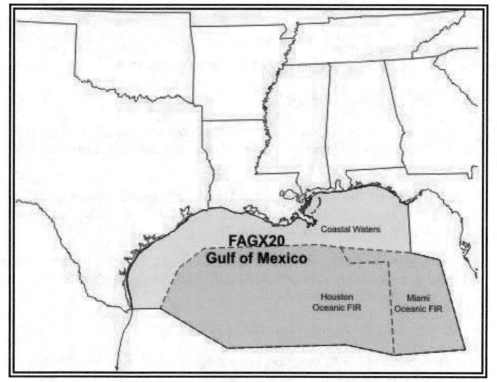

Figure 7-2. AWC Area Forecast Region and WMO Header - Gulf of Mexico

Figure 7-3. AWC Area Forecast Region and WMO Header - Caribbean

Figure 7-4. WFO Honolulu Area Forecast Region and WMO header - Hawaii

Figure 7-5. AAWU Flight Advisory and Area Forecast Zones - Alaska

Table 7-1. AAWU Area Forecast Zones – Alaska

1	Arctic Coast Coastal	14	Southern Southeast Alaska
2	North Slopes of the Brooks Range	15	Coastal Southeast Alaska
3	Upper Yukon Valley	16	Eastern Gulf Coast
4	Koyukuk and Upper Kobuk Valley	17	Copper River Basin
5	Northern Seward Peninsula-Lower Kobuk Valley	18	Cook Inlet-Susitna Valley
6	Southern Seward Peninsula-Eastern Norton Sound	19	Central Gulf Coast
7	Tanana Valley	20	Kodiak Island
8	Lower Yukon Valley	21	Alaska Peninsula-Port Heiden to Unimak Pass
9	Kuskowim Valley	22	Unimak Pass to Adak
10	Yukon-Kuskowim Delta	23	St. Lawrence Island-Bering Sea Coast
11	Bristol Bay	24	Adak to Attu
12	Lynn Canal and Glacier Bay	25	Pribilof Islands and Southeast Bering Sea
13	Central Southeast Alaska		

7.1.2   Area Forecast Standardization

All Area Forecasts follow these standards:

- All heights or altitudes are referenced to above mean sea level (AMSL), unless otherwise noted (i.e., prefaced by AGL or CIG), and annotated using the height in hundreds of feet, consisting of three digits (e.g., 040). For heights at or above 18,000 feet, the level is preceded by FL to represent flight levels (e.g., FL180). Tops are always referenced to AMSL.

- References to latitude and longitude are in whole degrees and minutes following the model: Nnn[nn] or Snn[nn], Wnnn[nn] or Ennn[nn] with a space between latitude and longitude and a hyphen between successive points. Example: N3106 W07118 – N3011 W7209

- Messages are prepared in abbreviated plain language using contractions from the **Federal Aviation Administration (FAA) Order 7340.2** for domestic products and International Civil Aviation Organization (ICAO) document 8400 for international products issued for Oceanic FIRs. A limited number of non-abbreviated words, geographical names, and numerical values of a self-explanatory nature may also be used.

- Weather and obstructions to visibility are described using the weather abbreviations for surface weather observations (METAR/SPECI). See the Federal Meteorological Handbook (FMH) No. 1 – Surface Observations or Section 3.1 of this document.

Note: For AWC FAs, "CSTL WTRS" refer to water areas that extend from the coastline to the FIR boundary. "CSTL SXNS" refer to land areas along and near the coastline.

Note: Refer to Appendix A for definitions of common terms used in Area Forecasts.

7.1.3   Area Forecast Issuance Schedule

Area forecasts are scheduled products issued at the following times.

Table 7-2. Area Forecast (FA) Issuance Schedule

	Boston and Miami (UTC)	Chicago and Fort Worth (UTC)	San Francisco and Salt Lake City (UTC)	Gulf of Mexico (UTC)	Caribbean (UTC)	Hawaii (UTC)	Alaska (UTC)
1st Issuance	0845 DT 0945 ST	0945 DT 1045 ST	1045 DT 1145 ST	0130	0330	0340	0145 DT 0245 ST
2nd Issuance	1745 DT 1845 ST	1845 DT 1945 ST	1945 DT 2045 ST	1030	0930	0940	0745 DT 0845 ST
3rd Issuance	0045 DT 0145 ST	0145 DT 0245 ST	0245 DT 0345 ST	1830	1530	1540	0145 DT 1445 ST
4th Issuance					2130	2140	1945 DT 2045 ST

Note: DT – daylight Time, ST – Standard Time, UTC – Coordinated Universal Time

7.1.4   Area Forecast Amendments

Amendments are issued whenever the weather significantly improves or deteriorates based upon the judgment of the forecaster. These updates are those required to keep forecasts of _non-AIRMET_ conditions representative of existing or expected conditions. "AMD" is included after the date/time group on the FAA product line. The date/time group on the WMO and FAA lines is updated to indicate the time of the correction. The ending valid time remains unchanged.

7.1.5   Area Forecast Corrections

Area Forecasts containing errors will be corrected. "COR" is included after the date/time group on the FAA product line. The date/time group on the WMO and FAA lines is updated to indicate the time of the correction. The ending valid time remains unchanged.

7.1.6   Area Forecast Format – Conterminous U.S. (CONUS)

Area forecasts issued for the conterminous U.S. (CONUS) cover the airspace between the surface and 45,000 feet AMSL and include the following forecast sections:

- Synopsis: A short description of significant synoptic weather systems affecting the area during the 18 hour valid period. This includes the location and movement of pressure systems and fronts. Air mass descriptions may be used in the absence of significant weather systems. References to low ceilings and/or visibilities, strong winds, or any other phenomena that the forecaster considers useful may also be included.

- VFR Clouds/Weather: A 12-hour specific clouds and weather forecast, followed by a 6-hour categorical outlook giving a total forecast period of 18 hours. This section gives a general description of clouds and weather which cover an area greater than

3,000 square miles and are significant to VFR flight operations. The forecasts are referenced to states or geographic areas. States are presented in the order listed within the header of the FA, however, portions of adjacent states may be grouped together when they are forecast to have similar conditions. The following weather elements, if applicable, are included in the following order for each 12-hour specific forecast:

o   Sky condition (coverage, cloud base, and tops) if bases are higher than or equal to 1,000 feet AGL and at or below FL180. Heights are referenced to MSL unless preceded by AGL or CIG. Sky condition is not repeated for each new time group unless it is forecast to change.

o   Surface visibilities and associated obstructions when visibility is between 3 and 5 statute miles and coverage is 3,000 square miles or greater. When no visibility value is forecast, it is implied to be greater than 5 statute miles.

o   Weather (precipitation, including thunderstorms, fog, haze, blowing dust, etc.) if it results in visibilities of 3 to 5 statute miles.

o   Significant wind information (direction and speed) if the surface wind is sustained at 20 knots or greater and/or gusts are greater than or equal to 25 knots.

A 6-hour categorical outlook follows the 12-hour specific clouds and weather forecast. At a minimum, the category of the expected prevailing condition (IFR, MVFR, VFR) is stated in the outlook. If IFR or MVFR, the cause is listed (e.g., CIG, FG, BR, etc.). VFR stands alone except for wind (WND), thunderstorms (TSRA) and precipitation types (without intensities). The contraction "WND" is appended to any category if the sustained surface wind is expected to be 20 knots or more or surface wind gusts are expected to be 25 knots or more during the majority of the 6-hour outlook period.

LINE	
1	DFWC FA 120945
2	SYNOPSIS AND VFR CLDS/WX
3	SYNOPSIS VALID UNTIL 130400
4	CLDS/WX VALID UNTIL 122200...OTLK VALID 122200-130400
5	OK TX AR TN MS AL

Figure 7-6. Area Forecast – CONUS Communication and Product Header Example

Table 7-3. Decoding a CONUS Area Forecast Communication and Product Header

Line	Content	Description
1	DFW	Area Forecast region identifier
	C	Indicates VFR clouds and weather forecast
	FA	Product type
	120945	Issuance and beginning of valid date/time (UTC)
2	SYNOPSIS AND VFR CLDS/WX	Statement of weather information contained in this forecast message
3	SYNOPSIS VALID UNTIL 130400	Synopsis valid date and time
4	CLDS/WX VALID UNTIL 122200...OTLK VALID 122200-130400	The clouds and weather section valid time. The valid date and time of the outlook.
5	OK TX AR TN MS AL	Description of the area for which the FA is valid.

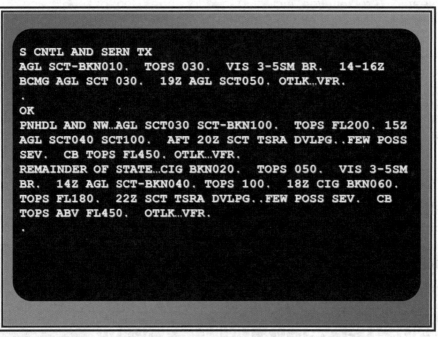

```
S CNTL AND SERN TX
AGL SCT-BKN010.   TOPS 030.  VIS 3-5SM BR.   14-16Z
BCMG AGL SCT 030.   19Z AGL SCT050. OTLK...VFR.
.
OK
PNHDL AND NW...AGL SCT030 SCT-BKN100.   TOPS FL200. 15Z
AGL SCT040 SCT100.   AFT 20Z SCT TSRA DVLPG..FEW POSS
SEV.  CB TOPS FL450. OTLK...VFR.
REMAINDER OF STATE...CIG BKN020.   TOPS 050.  VIS 3-5SM
BR.  14Z AGL SCT-BKN040. TOPS 100.  18Z CIG BKN060.
TOPS FL180.  22Z SCT TSRA DVLPG..FEW POSS SEV.  CB
TOPS ABV FL450.  OTLK...VFR.
.
```

Figure 7-7. Area Forecast - Clouds and Weather Element Example

The "Clouds and Weather" section above is decoded as follows:

South central and southeast Texas:
Scattered to broken bases at 1,000 feet above ground level (AGL). Tops at 3,000 feet above mean sea level (MSL). Visibility 3 to 5 statute miles in mist. Between 1400 and 1600 UTC...clouds bases becoming scattered at 3,000 feet AGL. 1900 UTC...scattered bases at 5,000 feet AGL. 12 to 18 hour categorical outlook...VFR.

Oklahoma:
Panhandle and northwest...scattered bases at 3,000 feet AGL, scattered to broken bases at 10,000 feet AGL. Tops at flight level 20,000 feet MSL. 1500 UTC...scattered bases at 4,000 feet AGL, scattered bases at 10,000 feet AGL. After 2000 UTC...scattered thunderstorms with rain

showers developing…a few possible severe. Cumulonimbus tops to flight level 45,000 feet MSL. Outlook…VFR.

Remainder of the state…Ceilings broken at 2,000 feet AGL. Tops at 5,000 feet MSL. Visibilities 3 to 5 statute miles in mist. 1400 UTC…scattered to broken bases at 4,000 feet AGL. Tops at 10,000 feet MSL. 1800 UTC…ceilings broken 6,000 feet AGL. Tops to flight level 18,000 feet MSL. 2200 UTC…scattered thunderstorm with rain showers developing…a few possibly severe. Cumulonimbus tops above flight level 45,000 feet MSL. 12-18 hour categorical outlook…VFR.

7.1.6.1   Area Forecast – Conterminous U.S. (CONUS) Examples

7.1.6.1.1   Area Forecast – BOS Example

```
FAUS41 KKCI 081745  (ICAO product header)
FA1W  (NWS AWIPS Communication header)
BOSC FA 081745  (Area forecast region, product type, issuance date/time)
SYNOPSIS AND VFR CLDS/WX
SYNOPSIS VALID UNTIL 091200


CLDS/WX VALID UNTIL 090600...OTLK VALID 090600-091200
ME NH VT MA RI CT NY LO NJ PA OH LE WV MD DC DE VA AND CSTL WTRS
.
SEE AIRMET SIERRA FOR IFR CONDS AND MTN OBSCN.
TS IMPLY SEV OR GTR TURB SEV ICE LLWS AND IFR CONDS.
NON MSL HGTS DENOTED BY AGL OR CIG.
.
SYNOPSIS...18Z CDFNT 30N PQI-40E MPV-ALB-20N JHW LN. STNR FNT 20N
JHW-ECK LN. STNR FNT EWC-ROD-IND LN. TROF 210SE SIE-170SE ECG LN
CONTG SWD. HIGH WRN NC. 12Z STNR FNT FM LOW NR FWA ALG 20N CLE-
JHW-ALB-30NNE BOS LN. CDFNT 30NNE BOS-120SE BGR LN. CDFNT FM LOW
NR FWA ALG PXV-50SE FAM LN CONTG SWWD. HIGH NR ODF.
.
ME NH VT
NRN ME...SCT040 BKN060 TOP FL250. OCNL BKN040. SCT -SHRA/ISOL
-TSRA. CB TOP FL350. 21Z BKN040. ISOL -SHRA. WND W G25KT. 03Z
SKC. OTLK...VFR.
VT/NRN NH/RMNDR ME MTNS...SCT-BKN040 BKN060 TOP FL250. SCT
SHRA/ISOL TSRA. CB TOP FL350. 03Z BKN040. OCNL VIS 3-5SM BR.
OTLK...MVFR CIG BR.
SRN NH/RMNDR ME...SCT040 BKN100 TOP FL250. OCNL BKN040 IN WDLY
SCT -SHRA/ISOL -TSRA BECMG AFT 19Z SCT TSRA. TS POSS SEV. CB TOP
FL400. 04Z BKN020. WDLY SCT -SHRA. OTLK...MVFR CIG SHRA BR.
.
MA RI CT
CT CSTL PLAIN/RI/SERN MA...SKC. 21Z SCT040. ISOL TSRA. CB TOP
FL400. 03Z SKC. OCNL VIS 3-5SM BR. OTLK...IFR CIG BR.
RMNDR...SCT100. 19Z SCT040 BKN100 TOP 160. SCT TSRA POSS SEV. CB
TOP FL450. 02Z BKN040. WDLY SCT SHRA. OTLK...MVFR CIG BR.
.
NY LO
LO/N CNTRL-NERN NY...SCT-BKN040 BKN060 TOP 160. SCT SHRA/ISOL
TSRA. CB TOP FL350. 03Z BKN040. WDLY SCT -SHRA. OTLK...MVFR CIG
SHRA.
WRN-S CNTRL NY...BKN040 OVC060 TOP 160. SCT -TSRA. CB TOP FL450.
```

03Z BKN030. SCT SHRA. OTLK...MVFR CIG SHRA.
EXTRM SERN NY-LONG ISLAND...SKC. 21Z SCT040. ISOL TSRA. 03Z SKC.
OCNL VIS 3-5SM BR. OTLK...IFR CIG BR.
RMNDR NY...BKN050 TOP 160. SCT TSRA POSS SEV. CB TOP FL450. 03Z
BKN040. SCT SHRA. OTLK...MVFR CIG SHRA.
.

PA NJ
WRN-N CNTRL PA...BKN040 OVC060 TOP FL220. SCT TSRA. CB TOP FL400.
03Z BKN060. SCT SHRA NWRN/N CNTRL PA. OTLK...VFR SWRN PA...MVFR CIG SHRA
NWRN/N CNTRL PA.
S CNTRL-NERN PA...BKN060 TOP FL220. ISOL TSRA BECMG AFT 20Z SCT
TSRA. CB TOP FL400. 03Z OVC060. SCT SHRA NERN PA. OTLK...MVFR CIG
SHRA NERN PA. MVFR CIG BR S CNTRL PA.
SERN PA-NRN NJ...SCT060. AFT 21Z ISOL TSRA. CB TOP FL400. 03Z SKC
OR SCT CI. OTLK...VFR.
SRN NJ...SKC OR SCT CI. OTLK...VFR.
.

OH LE
LE/NRN 1/2 OH...BKN030 OVC060 TOP FL220. SCT TSRA POSS SEV. CB
TOP FL450. OTLK...MVFR CIG TSRA.
SWRN 1/4 OH...SCT040 BKN100 TOP FL220. SCT TSRA POSS SEV. CB TOP
FL450. 03Z BKN060. WDLY SCT TSRA. OTLK...MVFR CIG TSRA.
SERN 1/4 OH...SCT050 BKN100 TOP FL220. OCNL BKN050 IN WDLY SCT TSRA.
TS POSS SEV. CB TOP FL400. 03Z BKN060. OTLK...VFR.
.

WV
W WV PNHDL-NWRN...SCT100...19Z BKN060 TOP FL220. TIL 03Z SCT
SHRA/WDLY SCT TSRA. CB TOP FL450. OTLK...VFR.
SW...SCT080. AFT 20Z ISOL TSRA. CB TOP FL400. 01Z
SCT100 SCT CI. OTLK...VFR.
SERN WV...SCT070. 01Z SKC. OTLK...VFR BECMG 09Z IFR BR.
RMNDR...SCT080. 20Z SCT080 BKN100 TOP FL220. ISOL TSRA. CB TOP
FL400. 03Z SCT-BKN CI. OTLK...VFR BECMG 09Z IFR BR.
.

MD DC DE VA
NRN 1/2 APLCNS...SCT080. 20Z SCT080 BKN100 TOP FL220. ISOL TSRA.
CB TOP FL400. 03Z SCT-BKN CI. OTLK...VFR BECMG 09Z IFR BR.
SRN 1/2 APLCNS...SCT070. 01Z SKC. OTLK...VFR BECMG 09Z IFR HZ BR.
SERN VA CSTL SXNS...SCT040. 04Z SCT-BKN100 TOP FL250. OTLK...VFR.
DC/DE/RMNDR MD/RMNDR VA...SCT040. 00Z SKC OR SCT CI. OTLK...VFR.
.

CSTL WTRS
ME/NH...SCT040 BKN100 TOP FL250. WDLY SCT SHRA/TSRA DVLPG 20-22Z.
CB TOP FL400. OTLK...VFR SHRA.
RMNDR N OF ACK...SKC. BECMG 2123 SCT040 BKN100 TOP FL250. WDLY
SCT SHRA/TSRA. CB TOP FL400. OTLK...VFR SHRA.
S OF 30NE ORF-150SE SIE LN...SCT040 SCT CI. 03Z SCT-BKN100 TOP
FL250. OTLK...VFR.
RMNDR...SCT060. 00Z SKC OR SCT CI. OTLK...VFR.
. . . .

7.1.6.1.2 Area Forecast – SFO (FA) Example

FAUS46 KKCI 210245 *(ICAO product header)*

```
FA6W  (NWS AWIPS Communication header)
SFOC FA 210245  (Area forecast region, product type, issuance date/time)
SYNOPSIS AND VFR CLDS/WX
SYNOPSIS VALID UNTIL 212100
CLDS/WX VALID UNTIL 211500...OTLK VALID 211500-212100
WA OR CA AND CSTL WTRS
.
SEE AIRMET SIERRA FOR IFR CONDS AND MTN OBSCN.
TS IMPLY SEV OR GTR TURB SEV ICE LLWS AND IFR CONDS.
NON MSL HGTS DENOTED BY AGL OR CIG.
.
SYNOPSIS...SFC...03Z OCFNT SE AB-LOW PRES SCNTRL MT-NCNTRL UT-
BTY-SRN CA. TROF SRN NV-SW AZ. TROF NERN PTNS WA CSTL WTRS-WRN
PTNS OR CSTL WTRS. HI PRES RDG ECNTRL OR-NRN CA CSTL WTRS. 21Z
CDFNT NERN MT-SERN WY-SRN CA. HI PRES RDG NCNTRL MT-SW OR. TROF
NCNTRL CA-NR 60E SAC-SRN SIERNEV. ALF...03Z UPR LVL TROF NCNTRL
WA-CNTRL CA. NWLY JTST OR CSTL WTRS-NW CA CSTLN. 21Z UPR LVL TROF
SW BC-SW UT-SW AZ. NWLY JTST WRN WA-NERN CA-SERN CA-WRN AZ.
.
WA CASCDS WWD
CSTL...BKN015-025 OVC060 TOP 140. WDLY SCT -SHRA. 10Z OVC015 TOP
100. OTLK...MVFR CIG.
MTNS...OVC040-050 TOP FL180. VIS 3-5SM -RA/-SN ABV 040.
OTLK...IFR CIG SHSN SHRA BECMG MVFR CIG SHSN SHRA 19Z.
RMNDR...BKN035-045 TOP 150. 05Z BKN015-025 OVC050 TOP 160. WDLY
SCT -SHRA. OTLK...MVFR CIG SHRA BECMG VFR 19Z.
.
WA E OF CASCDS
CNTRL WA...SCT-BKN CI. BECMG 0709 BKN110 TOP 150. OTLK...VFR.
ERN WA...OVC050 TOP FL180. ISOL -SHRA. 04Z SCT090 SCT-BKN CI. 10Z
BKN050 OVC100 TOP 120. ISOL -SHRA. OTLK...MVFR CIG BECMG VFR SHRA
19Z.
.
OR CASCDS WWD
CSTL...BKN015-025 OVC060 TOP 140. WDLY SCT -SHRA. 10Z OVC015 TOP
100. OTLK...MVFR CIG.
NW INTR...BKN040 TOP 140. TIL 11Z WDLY SCT -SHRA. 12Z OVC025.
OTLK...MVFR CIG BECMG VFR SHRA 19Z.
N CASCDS...OVC040-050 TOP FL180. VIS 3-5SM -RA/-SN ABV 040.
OTLK...IFR CIG SHSN SHRA BECMG MVFR CIG SHSN SHRA 19Z.
SW INTR...SCT060. 12Z SCT-BKN040 BKN060 TOP 120. OTLK...VFR.
S CASCDS...SCT-BKN080 TOP 150. TIL 04Z ISOL -SHRA/-TSRA. CB TOP
FL250. 05Z SCT090. OTLK...VFR.
.
OR E OF CASCDS
NW...SCT CI. WND NW 20G30KT. 08Z SCT-BKN080 BKN110 TOP 150. WND
WLY G25KT. OTLK...VFR.
SW...BKN080 TOP 150. TIL 04Z ISOL -SHRA/-TSRA. CB TOP FL250. 05Z
SCT090. OTLK...VFR...20Z WND.
NERN...BKN060 TOP 160. WDLY SCT -SHRA. 06Z SCT100. 11Z BKN050
OVC100 TOP 120. ISOL -SHRA. OTLK...VFR SHRA.
SE...SCT-BKN090 OVC120 TOP FL250. WDLY SCT -SHRA/ISOL -TSRA. CB
TOP FL260. WND W G25KT. 07Z BKN090 TOP 150. OTLK...VFR...16Z WND.
.
```

```
NRN CA...STS-SAC-TVL LN NWD
CSTL SXNS N OF 40SSE FOT...BKN025 TOP 120. 09Z OVC010-020 TOP
100. OTLK...MVFR CIG BECMG VFR 18Z.
RMNDR CSTL SXNS...SKC. OTLK...VFR.
SHASTA-SISKIYOUS-NERN CA...SCT-BKN080 TOP 150. TIL 04Z ISOL
-SHRA/-TSRA. CB TOP FL250. WND NW G25KT. 05Z SCT090. OTLK...VFR.
SAC VLY...SKC. TIL 06Z WND W G25KT. OTLK...VFR WND 16Z.
NRN SIERNEV...SCT100. ISOL -SHRA/-TSRA. CB TOP FL300. WND SW G25-
30KT. 09Z SCT120. OTLK...VFR.
.

CNTRL CA
CSTL SXNS
CSTLN N OF SNS...OVC010-015 TOP 020. WND W G25KT. 07Z SKC.
OTLK...VFR.
CSTLN SNS SWD...OVC010-015 TOP 020. 08Z SCT010. 10Z SKC.
OTLK...VFR...16Z.
INLAND...SKC. TIL 09Z WND NW G25-30KT. OTLK...VFR WND 16Z.
SAN JOAQUIN VLY...SKC. WND NW 20G30KT. OCNL BLDU. OTLK...VFR WND.
SRN SIERNEV...SKC. WND W 25G35KT. OTLK...VFR WND.
.

SRN CA...VBG-NID-60NNW BIH LN SWD
CSTL SXNS
CSTLN N OF LAX...SCT015. 10Z OVC015 TOP 025. 14Z SCT015.
OTLK...VFR...18Z WND.
CSTLN LAX SWD...OVC015-025 TOP 030. OTLK...VFR.
INLAND N OF LAX...SKC. OTLK...VFR.
INLAND LAX SWD...SKC. 07Z OVC010 TOP 030. VIS 3SM BR. OTLK...MVFR
CIG HZ BECMG 20Z VFR WND.
COLORADO RIVER VLY...SKC. WND SW G25KT. OTLK...VFR WND BECMG 18Z MVFR
BLDU BLSA WND.
INTR MTNS-DESERTS...SKC. WND NW 25G30-35KT. OCNL BLDU. OTLK...VFR
WND.
.

CSTL WTRS
WA/OR/NRN CA...BKN015-025 OVC060 TOP 140. WDLY SCT -SHRA. WND
NW G25KT. 10Z OVC015 TOP 100. OTLK...MVFR CIG.
CNTRL-SRN CA...SCT-BKN015 TOP 025. OCNL VIS 3-5SM BR. WND NW 20G30-
40KT. OTLK...VFR WND CNTRL CA...MVFR CIG WND SRN CA.
....
```

7.1.7   Area Forecast Format – Gulf of Mexico (FAGX)

Area Forecasts issued for the Gulf of Mexico (FAGX) cover the airspace between the surface and 45,000 feet AMSL (Above Mean Sea Level) and include the following elements with each geographical section having an entry even if it is negative.

- Synopsis: This is a brief discussion of the significant synoptic weather affecting the FAGX area during the entire 24-hour valid period.

- Significant Clouds and Weather: This is a description of the significant clouds and weather for the first 12-hours including the following elements.

   o   Cloud amount (SCT, BKN or OVC) for clouds with bases below FL180
   o   Cloud bases and tops associated with the above bullet

- o Precipitation and thunderstorms
- o Visibility below 7 SM and obstruction(s) to visibility
- o Sustained surface winds greater than or equal to 20 knots
- o 12- to 24-hour categorical outlook (LIFR, IFR, MVFR or VFR)

- Icing and Freezing Level: Moderate or severe icing and freezing level. For the coastal waters portion of the FAGX, users will be referred to the appropriate CONUS AIRMET.

- Turbulence: Moderate or greater turbulence. For the coastal waters portion of the FAGX, users will be referred to the appropriate CONUS AIRMET.

7.1.7.1   Area Forecast – Gulf of Mexico (FAGX) Example

```
FAGX20 KKCI 091812  (ICAO product header)
OFAGX  (NWS AWIPS Communication header)
SYNOPSIS VALID TIL 101900Z
FCST...091900Z-100700Z
OTLK...100700Z-101900Z
INTERNATIONAL OPERATIONS BRANCH
AVIATION WEATHER CENTER KANSAS CITY MISSOURI
.
CSTL WATERS FROM COASTLINE OUT TO HOUSTON OCEANIC FIR AND GLFMEX MIAMI
OCEANIC FIR AND W OF 85W. HOUSTON OCEANIC FIR AND GLFMEX MIAMI OCEANIC
FIR.
.
TS IMPLY SEV OR GTR TURB SEV ICE LLWS AND IFR CONDS. HGTS MSL.
.
01 SYNOPSIS...HIGH PRES OVR NRN GLFMEX.
.
02 SIGNIFICANT CLD/WX...
.
CSTL WATERS...
SCT020. OTLK...VFR.
.
HOUSTON OCEANIC FIR...
SCT020. OTLK...VFR.
.
GLFMEX MIAMI OCEANIC FIR...
SCT020. OTLK...VFR.
.
03 ICE AND FRZLVL...
CSTL WATERS...SEE AIRMETS ZULU WAUS44 KKCI AND WAUS42 KKCI.
HOUSTON OCEANIC FIR... NO SGFNT ICE EXP OUTSIDE CNVTV ACT.
GLFMEX MIAMI OCEANIC FIR...NO SGFNT ICE EXP OUTSIDE CNVTV ACT.
FRZLVL...140 THRUT.
.
04 TURB...
CSTL WATERS...SEE AIRMETS TANGO WAUS44 KKCI AND WAUS42 KKCI.
HOUSTON OCEANIC FIR... NO SGFNT TURB EXP OUTSIDE CNVTV ACT.
GLFMEX MIAMI OCEANIC FIR...NO SGFNT TURB EXP OUTSIDE CNVTV ACT.
```

7.1.8   Area Forecast Format – Caribbean (FACA)

Area forecasts issued for the Caribbean (FACA) cover the airspace between the surface and 24,000 feet AMSL and include the following elements. Each geographical section will have an entry even if it is negative.

- Synopsis: brief discussion of the synoptic weather affecting the FACA area during the 24-hour valid period.

- Significant Clouds and Weather: description of the significant clouds and weather for the first 12 hours including the following elements.

  o Cloud amount (SCT, BKN or OVC) for cloud bases below FL180
  o Cloud bases and tops associated with the above bullet
  o Precipitation and thunderstorms
  o Visibility below 7 SM and obstruction(s) to visibility
  o Sustained surface winds greater than or equal to 20 knots
  o 12- to 24-hour categorical outlook (IFR, MVFR or VFR)

- Icing and Freezing Level: moderate or greater icing and freezing level

- Turbulence: moderate or greater turbulence

7.1.8.1   Area Forecast – Caribbean (FACA) Example

```
FACA20 KKCI 121530 (ICAO product header)
OFAMKC (NWS AWIPS Communication header)
INTERNATIONAL OPERATIONS BRANCH
AVIATION WEATHER CENTER KANSAS CITY MISSOURI
VALID 121600-130400
OUTLOOK...130400-131600
.
ATLANTIC S OF 32N W OF 57W...CARIBBEAN...GULF OF MEXICO BTN 22N AND
24N.
.
TS IMPLY SEV OR GTR TURB SEV ICE LLWS AND IFR CONDS. SFC TO 400 MB.
.
SYNOPSIS...WK CDFNT EXTDS FM NR 28N60W TO 23N63W TO THE MONA
PASSAGE. CDFNT WL MOV EWD AND WKN TODAY. EXP NARROW BAND OF
CLDS WITH ISOL SHRA INVOF CDFNT.
.
SIGNIFICANT CLD/WX...
ERN MONTERREY FIR...NRN MERIDA FIR
SCT025 SCT060. OTLK...VFR.
.
ATLC SWRN NEW YORK FIR...SAN JUAN FIR
NW OF CDFNT...SCT025 SCT060. LYR OCNL BKN. TOP 120. ISOL SHRA.
OTLK...VFR.
VCNTY CDFNT...SCT025 BKN060. OCNL BKN025. TOP 120. WDLY SCT
SHRA. ISOL TSRA TIL 20Z. OTLK...VFR SHRA.
SE OF CDFNT...SCT025 SCT060. ISOL SHRA. OTLK...VFR.
.
ATLC MIAMI FIR
```

```
SCT025 SCT060. LYR OCNL BKN. TOP 120. ISOL SHRA. OTLK...VFR.
.
WRN PIARCO FIR...NRN MAIQUETIA FIR...CURACAO FIR
BTN 61W-63W...SCT025 BKN060. OCNL BKN025. TOP 120. WDLY SCT
SHRA. OTLK...VFR SHRA.
RMNDR...SCT025 SCT060. ISOL SHRA. OTLK...VFR.
.
SANTO DOMINGO FIR...PORT-AU-PRINCE FIR
SCT025 SCT060. LYR OCNL BKN. TOP 120. ISOL SHRA. OTLK...VFR.
.
NRN BARRANQUILLA FIR...NRN PANAMA FIR
SCT025 SCT060. ISOL SHRA. SFC WND NE 20-25KT. OTLK...VFR.
.
KINGSTON FIR...NERN CNTRL AMERICAN FIR...HABANA FIR
SCT025 SCT060. ISOL SHRA. OTLK...VFR.
.
ICE AND FRZLVL...
NO SGFNT ICE EXP OUTSIDE CNVTV ACT.
FRZLVL... 145-170.
.
TURB...
NO SGFNT TURB EXP OUTSIDE CNVTV ACT.
```

7.1.9 Area Forecast Format - Hawaii

Area forecasts issued for Hawaii cover the airspace between the surface and 45,000 feet AMSL and include the following elements.

- Synopsis: brief discussion of the significant synoptic weather affecting the FA area during the 18-hour valid period.

- Clouds and Weather: description of the clouds and weather for the first 12-hour period including the following elements.
  - Cloud amount (SCT, BKN or OVC) with bases and tops
  - Visibilities of 6 SM or less with obstruction(s) to visibility
  - Precipitation and thunderstorms
  - Sustained surface winds 20 knots or greater

- 12- to 18-hour categorical outlook: IFR, marginal MVFR, or VFR, including expected precipitation and/or obstructions to visibility

7.1.9.1 Area Forecast – Hawaii Example

```
FAHW31 PHFO 080940 (ICAO product header)
FA0HI (NWS AWIPS Communication header)
.
HNLC FA 080940 (Area forecast region, product type, issuance date/time)
SYNOPSIS AND VFR CLD/WX
SYNOPSIS VALID UNTIL 090400
CLD/WX VALID UNTIL 082200...OUTLOOK VALID 082200-090400
.
SEE AIRMET SIERRA FOR IFR CLD AND MT OBSC.
TS IMPLY SEV OR GREATER TURB SEV ICE LOW LEVEL WS AND IFR COND.
```

NON MSL HGT DENOTED BY AGL OR CIG.
.
SYNOPSIS...SFC HIGH FAR N PHNL NEARLY STNR.
.
BIG ISLAND ABOVE 060.
SKC. 20Z SCT090. OUTLOOK...VFR.
.
BIG ISLAND LOWER SLOPES...COAST AND ADJ WATERS FROM UPOLU POINT TO CAPE
KUMUKAHI TO APUA POINT.
SCT030 BKN050 TOPS 080 ISOL BKN030 VIS 3-5SM -SHRA BR. 21Z SCT030 SCT-
BKN050 TOPS 080 ISOL BKN030 5SM -SHRA. OUTLOOK...VFR.
.
BIG ISLAND LOWER SLOPES...COAST AND ADJ WATERS FROM APUA POINT TO SOUTH CAPE
TO UPOLU POINT. SKC. 21Z SCT-BKN060 TOPS 080. 23Z SCT030 SCT-BKN060 TOPS
080 ISOL BKN030 -SHRA. OUTLOOK...VFR.
.
BIG ISLAND LOWER SLOPES...COAST AND ADJ WATERS FROM SOUTH CAPE TO PHKO TO
UPOLU POINT.
SCT050 ISOL BKN050 TOPS 080. 18Z FEW050. 23Z SCT-BKN050 TOPS 080.
OUTLOOK...VFR.
.
N AND E FACING SLOPES...COAST AND ADJ WATERS OF THE REMAINING ISLANDS.
SCT020 BKN045 TOPS 070 TEMPO BKN020 VIS 3-5SM -SHRA...FM OAHU EASTWARD
ISOL CIG BLW 010 AND VIS BLW 3SM SHRA BR WITH TOPS 120. 22Z SCT025
SCT-BKN050 TOPS 070 ISOL BKN025 3-5SM -SHRA. OUTLOOK...VFR.
.
REST OF AREA.
SCT035 SCT-BKN050 TOPS 070 ISOL BKN030 -SHRA. 20Z SCT050 ISOL SCT030
BKN045 TOPS 070 -SHRA. OUTLOOK...VFR.

7.1.10 Area Forecast Format - Alaska

Area forecasts issued for Alaska cover the airspace between the surface and 45,000 feet AMSL and include the following elements. Clouds and weather, turbulence and icing information is included in each geographical zone.

- Synopsis: a brief description of the significant synoptic weather affecting the FA area during the first 18 hours of the forecast period.

- Clouds and Weather: a description of the clouds and weather for each geographical zone during the first 12 hours of the forecast period including the following elements:

  o AIRMET information for IFR ceiling and visibility, mountain obscuration, and strong surface winds
  o Cloud amount (SCT, BKN or OVC) with bases and tops
  o Visibilities of 6 SM or less with obstruction(s) to visibility
  o Precipitation and thunderstorms
  o Surface wind greater than 20 knots
  o Mountain pass conditions using categorical terms (for selected zones only)
  o 12- to 30-hour categorical outlook (VFR, MVFR, and IFR)

- Turbulence: a description of expected turbulence conditions including the following elements.

- o AIRMET information for turbulence or low level wind shear
- o Turbulence not meeting SIGMET or AIRMET criteria during the 6- to 12-hour period
- o If no significant turbulence is forecast, NIL SIG will be entered.

- Icing and freezing level: a description of expected icing conditions including the following elements.

  - o AIRMET information for icing and freezing precipitation
  - o Icing not meeting SIGMET or AIRMET criteria during the 6- to 12-hour period
  - o Freezing level
  - o If no significant icing is forecast, NIL SIG will be entered followed by the freezing level.

7.1.10.1 Area Forecast – Alaska Example

```
FAAK48 PAWU 251345 (ICAO product header)
FA8H (NWS AWIPS Communication header)
ANCH FA 251345 (Area forecast region, product type, issuance date/time)
AK SRN HLF EXC SE AK...
.
AIRMETS VALID UNTIL 252000
TS IMPLY POSSIBLE SEV OR GREATER TURB SEV ICE LLWS AND IFR CONDS.
NON MSL HEIGHTS NOTED BY AGL OR CIG.
.
SYNOPSIS VALID UNTIL 260800
972 MB BRISTOL BAY LOW WL MOV N TO 50 S PAOM AT 987 MB BY END OF PD.
ASSOCIATED OCCLUDED FRONT FM PALJ..KENNEDY ENTRANCE..SE WL MOV NE TO
PAMH..PACV..SE BY 08Z.
.
COOK INLET AND SUSITNA VALLEY AB...VALID UNTIL 260200
...CLOUDS/WX...
***AIRMET IFR/MT OBSC***AK RANGE/W SIDE COOK INLET..OCNL CIGS BLW 10 VIS
BLW 3SM -RA BR. NC...
OTHERWISE..AK RANGE/W SIDE INLET..SCT005 OVC020 VIS 3-5SM -RA BR.
ELSEWHERE..SCT025 BKN045 OVC080 LYR ABV TO FL250. OCNL BKN025 OVC045 -RA.
COOK INLET..SFC WND NE 20G30 KTS. THRU TERRAIN GAPS..ERN MTS/AK RANGE..SFC
WND E 30G60 KTS.
OTLK VALID 260200-262000...MVFR CIG RA WND.
PASSES...LAKE CLARK..MERRILL..RAINY..IFR CIG RA WND. WINDY..MVFR CIG RA.
PORTAGE..IFR CIG RA WND.
...TURB...
***SIGMET***KILO 1 VALID 251607/252000 PANC-
OCNL SEV TURB FCST BLW 080 WI AN AREA FM TKA-JOH-MDO-AKN-SQA-TKA.
THIS IS THE AREA S OF A PAHZ-PATK LN.
***AIRMET TURB/LLWS***OCNL MOD TURB BLW 120. LLWS. NC...
...ICE AND FZLVL...
***AIRMET ICE***OCNL MOD RIME/MX ICEIC 050-160. FZLVL 050. NC...
.
COPPER RIVER BASIN AC...VALID UNTIL 260200
...CLOUDS/WX...
FEW045 SCT090 BKN-OVC180 TOP FL250.
SFC WND SE G 25 KTS.
```

Page 7-17

```
WRN MTS..ISOL BKN025 OVC045 4SM -SHRA.
OTLK VALID 260200-262000...VFR.
PASS...TAHNETA..MVFR CIG.
...TURB...
NIL SIG.
...ICE AND FZLVL...
NIL SIG. FZLVL 050.
.
CNTRL GLF CST AD...VALID UNTIL 260200
...CLOUDS/WX...
***AIRMET MT OBSC***MTS OBSCD IN CLDS/PRECIPITATION. NC...
SCT020 OVC040 LYRD ABV TO FL250 -RA.
OCNL SCT005 OVC020 VIS 3-5SM -RA BR.
SFC WND E 20G35 KTS. THRU TRRN GAPS WND E-NE 25G50 KTS.
ALONG KENAI PENINSULA..ISOL CIGS BLW 10 VIS BLW 3SM RA BR.
OTLK VALID 260200-260200..MVFR CIG RA WND.
...TURB...
***SIGMET***KILO 1 VALID 251607/252000 PANC-
OCNL SEV TURB FCST BLW 080 WI AN AREA FM TKA-JOH-MDO-AKN-SQA-TKA.
THIS IS THE AREA E OF A JOH-PAMD LN.
***AIRMET TURB/LLWS***OCNL MOD TURB BLW 120. LLWS NR TRRN. NC...
...ICE AND FZLVL...
***AIRMET ICE***OCNL MOD RIME ICEIC 050-160. FZLVL 050. NC...
.
KODIAK ISLAND AE...VALID UNTIL 260200
...CLOUDS/WX...
***AIRMET MT OBSC***MTS OBSCD IN CLDS/PRECIPITATION. NC...
SCT020 OVC040 LYRD ABV TO FL250 -RA.
OCNL SCT005 OVC020 VIS 3-5SM -RA BR.
E SIDE..ISOL CIGS BLW 10 VIS BLW 3SM RA BR.
SFC WND SE G 25 KT.
OTLK VALID 260200-262000...MVFR CIG SHRA WND. AFT 06Z..VFR.
...TURB...
NIL SIG.
...ICE AND FZ LVL...
ISOL MOD RIME ICEIC 030-120. FZLVL 030.
```

7.2 Terminal Aerodrome Forecast (TAF)

A Terminal Aerodrome Forecast (TAF) is a concise statement of the expected meteorological conditions significant to aviation for a specified time period within 5 statute miles (SM) of the center of the airport's runway complex (terminal). The TAFs use the same weather codes found in METAR weather reports (Section 2) and can be viewed on the National Weather Service (NWS) Aviation Digital Data Service (ADDS) web site at: http://adds.aviationweather.noaa.gov/tafs/.

7.2.1 Responsibility
TAFs are issued by NWS Weather Forecast Offices (WFOs). A map of WFO areas of responsibility can be found at: http://www.srh.noaa.gov/.

7.2.2 Generic Format of the Forecast Text of a NWS-Prepared TAF

Table 7-4. Generic Format of NWS TAFs

TAF or **TAF AMD** or **TAF COR** *Type of report*			
CCCC *Location identifier*	**YYGGggZ** *Date/time of forecast origin group*	$Y_1Y_1G_1G_1/Y_2Y_2G_2G_2$ *Valid period*	**dddffGf$_m$f$_m$KT** *Wind group*
VVVV *Visibility group*	**w'w'** or **NSW** *Significant weather group*	$N_sN_sN_sh_sh_sh_s$ or $VVh_sh_sh_s$ or **SKC** *Cloud and vertical obscuration groups*	**WSh$_{ws}$h$_{ws}$h$_{ws}$/dddftKT** *Non-convective low-level wind shear (LLWS) group*
TTGGgg *Forecast change indicator groups*			
FMY$_1$Y$_1$GGgg *From group*	**TEMPO Y$_1$Y$_1$GG/Y$_e$Y$_e$G$_e$G$_e$** *Temporary group*	**PROB30 Y$_1$Y$_1$GG/Y$_e$Y$_e$G$_e$G$_e$** *Probability group*	

7.2.2.1 Type of Report (TAF or TAF AMD or TAF COR)

The report-type header always appears as the first element in the TAF and is produced in three forms: a routine forecast, **TAF**, an amended forecast, **TAF AMD**, or a corrected forecast, **TAF COR**.

TAFs are amended whenever they become, in the forecaster's judgment, unrepresentative of existing or expected conditions, particularly regarding those elements and events significant to aircraft and airports. An amended forecast is identified by **TAF AMD** (in place of **TAF**) on the first line of the forecast text.

7.2.2.2   Location Identifier (CCCC)

After the line containing either **TAF**, **TAF AMD**, or **TAF COR**, each TAF begins with its four-letter International Civil Aviation Organization (ICAO) location identifier.

Examples:
KDFW – Dallas-Fort Worth
PANC – Anchorage, Alaska
PHNL – Honolulu, Hawaii

7.2.2.3   Date/Time of Forecast Origin Group (YYGGggZ)

The date/time of forecast origin group (**YYGGggZ**) follows the terminal's location identifier. It contains the day of the month in two (2) digits (**YY**) and time in four (4) digits (**GGgg** in hours and minutes) the forecast is completed and ready for transmission, with a **Z** appended to denote UTC. This time is entered by the forecaster. A routine forecast, TAF, is issued 20 to 40 minutes before the beginning of its valid period.

Examples
061737Z
The TAF was issued on the 6th day of the month at 1737 UTC.

121123Z
The TAF was issued on the 12th day of the month at 1123 UTC.

7.2.2.4   Valid Period (Y₁Y₁G₁G₁/Y₂Y₂G₂G₂)

The TAF valid period ($Y_1Y_1G_1G_1/Y_2Y_2G_2G_2$) follows the date/time of forecast origin group. Scheduled 24- and 30-hour TAFs are issued four (4) times per day, at 0000, 0600, 1200, and 1800Z. The first two digits (Y_1Y_1) are the day of the month for the start of the TAF. The next two digits (G_1G_1) are the starting hour (UTC). Y_2Y_2 is the day of the month for the end of the TAF, and the last two digits (G_2G_2) are the ending hour (UTC) of the valid period. A forecast period that begins at midnight UTC is annotated as **00**. If the end time of a valid period is at midnight UTC, it is annotated as **24**. For example, a 00Z TAF issued on the 9th of the month and valid for 24 hours would have a valid period of **0900/0924**.

Whenever an amended TAF (**TAF AMD**) is issued, it supersedes and cancels the previous TAF. That is, users should not wait until the start of the valid period indicated within the TAF AMD to begin using it.

Examples:
1512/1612
The TAF is valid from the 15th day of the month at 1200 UTC until the 16th day of the month at 1200 UTC.

2306/2412

This is a 30-hour TAF valid from the 23rd day of the month at 0600 UTC until the 24th day of the month at 1200 UTC.

0121/0218

This is an amended TAF valid from the 1st day of the month at 2100 UTC until the 2nd day of the month at 1800 UTC.

0600/0624

This TAF is valid from the 6th day of the month at 0000 UTC until the 6th day of the month at 2400 UTC (or 7th day of the month at 0000 UTC).

7.2.2.5 Wind Group (dddffGf$_m$f$_m$KT)

The initial time period and any subsequent **FM** groups begin with a mean surface wind forecast (**dddffGf$_m$f$_m$KT**) for that period. Wind forecasts are expressed as the mean three-digit direction (**ddd** - relative to true north) from which the wind is blowing, rounded to the nearest 10 degrees and the mean wind speed in knots (**ff**) for the time period. If wind gusts are forecast (gusts are defined as rapid fluctuations in wind speeds with a variation of 10 knots or more between peaks and lulls), they are indicated immediately after the mean wind speed by the letter **G**, followed by the peak gust speed expected. **KT** is appended to the end of the wind forecast group. Any wind speed of 100 knots or more will be encoded in three digits. Calm winds are encoded as **00000KT**.

The prevailing wind direction is forecast for any speed greater than or equal to 7 knots. When the prevailing surface wind direction is variable (variations in wind direction of 30 degrees or more), the forecast wind direction is encoded as **VRBffKT**. Two conditions where this can occur are very light winds and convective activity. Variable wind direction for very light winds must have a wind speed of 1 through 6 knots inclusive. For convective activity, the wind group may be encoded as **VRBffGf$_m$f$_m$KT**, where **Gf$_m$f$_m$** is the maximum expected wind gusts. **VRB** is not used in the non-convective LLWS group.

Squalls are forecast in the wind group as gusts (**G**), but must be identified in the significant weather group with the code **SQ**.

Examples:
23010KT
Wind from 230 degrees "true" (southwest) at 10 knots.

28020G35KT
Wind from 280 degrees "true" (west) at 20 knots gusting to 35 knots.

VRB05KT
Wind variable at 5 knots. This example depicts a forecast for light winds that are expected to variable in direction.

VRB15G30KT
Wind variable at 15 knots gusting to 30 knots. This example depicts winds that are forecast to be variable with convective activity.

00000KT
Wind calm

090105KT
Wind from 90 degrees at 105 knots

7.2.2.6   Visibility Group (VVVV)

The initial time period and any subsequent FM groups include a visibility forecast (**VVVV**) in statute miles appended by the contraction SM.

When the prevailing visibility is forecast to be less than or equal to 6 SM, one or more significant weather groups are included in the TAF. However, drifting dust (**DRDU**), drifting sand (**DRSA**), drifting snow (**DRSN**), shallow fog (**MIFG**), partial fog (**PRFG**), and patchy fog (**BCFG**) may be forecast with prevailing visibility greater than or equal to 7 statute miles.

When a whole number and a fraction are used to forecast visibility, a space is included between them (e.g., **1 1/2SM**). Visibility greater than 6 statute miles is encoded as **P6SM**.

If the visibility is not expected to be the same in different directions, prevailing visibility is used.

When volcanic ash (**VA**) is forecast in the significant weather group, visibility is included in the forecast, even if it is unrestricted (**P6SM**). For example, an expected reduction of visibility to 10 statute miles by volcanic ash is encoded in the forecast as **P6SM VA**.

Although not used by the National Weather Service in U.S. domestic TAFs, the contraction "CAVOK" (Ceiling and Visibility OK) may replace the visibility, weather, and sky condition groups if all of the following conditions are forecast: Visibility of 10 kilometer (6 statute miles) or more, no clouds below 1500 meters (5,000 feet) or below the highest minimum sector altitude (whichever is greater), no cumulonimbus, and no significant weather phenomena.

Examples

P6SM
Visibility unrestricted

1 1/2SM
Visibility 1 and ½ statute miles

4SM
Visibility 4 statute miles

7.2.2.7   Significant Weather Group (w'w' or NSW)

The significant weather group (**w'w'** or **NSW**) consists of the appropriate qualifier(s) and weather phenomenon contraction(s) or **NSW** (No significant weather).

If the initial forecast period and subsequent **FM** groups are not forecast to have explicit significant weather, the significant weather group is omitted. **NSW** is **not** used in the initial forecast time period or **FM** groups.

One or more significant weather group(s) is (are) required when the visibility is forecast to be 6SM or less. The exceptions are: volcanic ash (**VA**), low drifting dust (**DRDU**), low drifting sand (**DRSA**), low drifting snow (**DRSN**), shallow fog (**MIFG**), partial fog (**PRFG**), and patchy fog

(**BCFG**). Obstructions to vision are only forecast when the prevailing visibility is less than 7 statute miles or, in the opinion of the forecaster, is considered operationally significant.

Volcanic ash (**VA**) is always forecast when expected. When **VA** is included in the significant weather group, visibility is included in the forecast as well, even if the visibility is unrestricted (**P6SM**).

NSW is used in place of significant weather only in a **TEMPO** group to indicate when significant weather (including in the vicinity (**VC**)) included in a previous sub-divided group is expected to end.

Multiple precipitation elements are encoded in a single group (e.g., -TSRASN). If more than one type of precipitation is forecast, up to three appropriate precipitation contractions can be combined in a single group (with no spaces) with the predominant type of precipitation being first. In this single group, the intensity refers to the total precipitation and can be used with either one or no intensity qualifier, as appropriate. In TAFs, the intensity qualifiers (light, moderate, and heavy) refer to the intensity of the precipitation and not to the intensity of any thunderstorms associated with the precipitation.

Intensity is coded with precipitation types, except ice crystals and hail, including those associated with thunderstorms and those of a showery nature (**SH**). No intensity is ascribed to blowing dust (**BLDU**), blowing sand (**BLSA**), or blowing snow (**BLSN**). Only moderate or heavy intensity is ascribed to sandstorm (**SS**) and duststorm (**DS**).

7.2.2.7.1 Exception for Encoding Multiple Precipitation Types

When more than one type of precipitation is forecast in a time period, any precipitation type associated with a descriptor (e.g., **FZRA**) is encoded first in the precipitation group, regardless of the predominance or intensity of the other precipitation types. Descriptors are not encoded with the second or third precipitation type in the group. The intensity is associated with the first precipitation type of a multiple precipitation type group. For example, a forecast of moderate snow and light freezing rain is coded as **-FZRASN** although the intensity of the snow is greater than the freezing rain.

Examples:

Combinations of one precipitation and one non-precipitation weather phenomena:

`-DZ FG`
Light drizzle and fog (obstruction which reduces visibility to less than 5/8 SM)

`RA BR`
Moderate rain and mist

`-SHRA FG`
Light rain showers and fog

`+SN FG`
Heavy snow and fog

Combinations of more than one type of precipitation:

```
-RASN FG HZ
```
Light rain and snow (light rain predominant), fog and haze

```
TSSNRA
```
Thunderstorm with moderate snow and rain (moderate snow predominant)

```
FZRASNPL
```
Moderate freezing rain, snow, and ice pellets (freezing rain mentioned first due to the descriptor, followed by other precipitation types in order of predominance)

```
SHSNPL
```
Moderate snow showers and ice pellets

7.2.2.7.2 Thunderstorm Descriptor

The TS descriptor is treated differently than other descriptors in the following cases:

- When non-precipitating thunderstorms are forecast, TS may be encoded as the sole significant weather phenomenon; and

- When forecasting thunderstorms with freezing precipitation (**FZRA** or **FZDZ**), the **TS** descriptor is included first, followed by the intensity and weather phenomena.

Example:
```
TS -FZRA
```
When a thunderstorm is included in the significant weather group (even using vicinity - **VCTS**), the cloud group ($N_sN_sN_sh_sh_sh_s$) includes a forecast cloud type of CB. See the following example for encoding **VCTS**.

Example
```
-FZRA VCTS BKN010CB
```

7.2.2.7.3 Fog Forecast

A visibility threshold must be met before a forecast for fog (FG) is included in the TAF. When forecasting a fog-restricted visibility from 5/8SM to 6SM, the phenomena is coded as **BR** (mist). When a fog-restricted visibility is forecast to result in a visibility of less than 5/8SM, the code **FG** is used. The forecaster never encodes weather obstruction as mist (**BR**) when the forecast visibility is greater than 6 statute miles (P6SM).

The following fog-related terms are used as described below:

Table 7-5. TAF Fog Terms

TERM	DESCRIPTION
Freezing Fog (**FZFG**)	Any fog (visibility less than 5/8 SM) consisting predominantly of water droplets at temperatures less than or equal to 32° F/0°C, whether or not rime ice is expected to be deposited. **FZBR** is not a valid significant weather combination and will not be used in TAFs.
Shallow Fog (**MIFG**)	The visibility at 6 feet above ground level is greater than or equal to 5/8 SM and the apparent visibility in the fog layer is less than 5/8 SM.
Patchy Fog (**BCFG**)	Fog patches covering part of the airport. The apparent visibility in the fog patch or bank is less than 5/8 SM, with the foggy patches extending to at least 6 feet above ground level.
Partial Fog (**PRFG**)	A substantial part of the airport is expected to be covered by fog while the remainder is expected to be clear of fog (e.g., a fog bank). NOTE: **MIFG**, **PRFG** and **BCFG** may be forecast with prevailing visibility of P6SM.

Examples:

```
1/2SM FG
```
Fog is reducing visibilities to less than 5/8SM, therefore FG is used to encode the fog.

```
3SM BR
```
Fog is reducing visibilities to between 5/8 and 6SM, therefore BR is used to encode the fog.

7.2.2.8   Vicinity (VC)

In the United States, vicinity (**VC**) is defined as a donut-shaped area between 5 and 10SM from the center of the airport's runway complex. The FAA requires TAFs to include certain meteorological phenomena which may directly affect flight operations to and from the airport. Therefore, NWS TAFs may include a prevailing condition forecast of fog, showers and thunderstorms in the airport's vicinity. A prevailing condition is defined as a greater than or equal to 50% probability of occurrence for more than ½ of the sub-divided forecast time period. **VC** is not included in **TEMPO** or **PROB** groups.

The significant weather phenomena in Table 7-5 are valid for use in prevailing portions of NWS TAFs in combination with **VC**:

Table 7-6: TAF Use of Vicinity (VC)

Phenomenon	Coded
Fog*	VCFG
Shower(s)**	VCSH
Thunderstorm	VCTS
* Always coded as **VCFG** regardless of visibility in the obstruction, and without qualification as to intensity or type (frozen or liquid) ** The **VC** group, if used, should be the last entry in any significant weather group (**w'w'**)	

7.2.2.9 Cloud and Vertical Obscuration Groups ($N_sN_sN_sh_sh_sh_s$ or $VVh_sh_sh_s$ or SKC)

The initial time period and any subsequent **FM** groups include a cloud or obscuration group ($N_sN_sN_sh_sh_sh_s$ or $VVh_sh_sh_s$ or **SKC**), used as appropriate to indicate the cumulative amount ($N_sN_sN_s$) of all cloud layers in ascending order and height ($h_sh_sh_s$), to indicate vertical visibility ($VVh_sh_sh_s$) into a surface-based obstructing medium, or to indicate a clear sky (**SKC**). All cloud layers and obscurations are considered opaque

7.2.2.9.1 Cloud Group ($N_sN_sN_sh_sh_sh_s$)

The cloud group ($N_sN_sN_sh_sh_sh_s$) is used to forecast cloud amount in Table 7-6.

Table 7-7. TAF Sky Cover

SKY COVER CONTRACTION	SKY COVERAGE
SKC	0 oktas
FEW	0 to 2 oktas
SCT	3 to 4 oktas
BKN	5 to 7 oktas
OVC	8 oktas

When zero (0) oktas of sky coverage is forecast, the cloud group is replaced by **SKC**. The contraction **CLR**, which is used in the METAR code, is not used in TAFs. TAFs for sites with ASOS/AWOS contain the cloud amount and/or obscurations which the forecaster expects, not what is expected to be reported by an ASOS/AWOS.

Heights of clouds ($h_sh_sh_s$) are forecast in hundreds of feet AGL.

The lowest level at which the cumulative cloud cover equals 5/8 or more of the celestial dome is understood to be the forecast ceiling. For example, **VV008**, **BKN008,** or **OVC008** all indicate an 800 ft ceiling.

7.2.2.9.2 Vertical Obscuration Group ($VVh_sh_sh_s$)

The vertical obscuration group ($VVh_sh_sh_s$) is used to forecast, in hundreds of feet AGL, the vertical visibility (**VV**) into a surface-based total obscuration. $VVh_sh_sh_s$ is this ceiling at the height indicated in the forecast. TAFs do not include forecasts of partial obscurations (i.e., **FEW000**, **SCT000**, or **BKN000**).

Example:
```
1SM BR VV008
```
Ceiling is 800 feet due to vertical visibility into fog

7.2.2.9.3 Cloud Type (CB)

The only cloud type included in the TAF is **CB**. **CB** follows cloud or obscuration height ($h_sh_sh_s$) without a space whenever thunderstorms are included in significant weather group (**w'w'**), even if thunderstorms are only forecast in the vicinity (**VCTS**). **CB** can be included in the cloud group ($N_sN_sN_sh_sh_sh_s$) or the vertical obscuration group ($VVh_sh_sh_s$) without mentioning thunderstorm in the significant weather group (**w'w'**). Therefore, situations may occur where nearly identical $N_sN_sN_sh_sh_sh_s$ or $VVh_sh_sh_s$ appear in consecutive time periods, with the only change being the addition or elimination of **CB** in the forecast cloud type.

Examples:
```
1/2SM TSRA OVC010CB
```
Thunderstorms are forecast at the airport

7.2.2.10 Non-Convective Low-Level Wind Shear (LLWS) Group (WSh$_{ws}$h$_{ws}$h$_{ws}$/dddffKT)

Wind Shear (**WS**) is defined as a rapid change in horizontal wind speed and/or direction, with distance and/or a change in vertical wind speed and/or direction with height. A sufficient difference in wind speed, wind direction, or both, can severely impact airplanes, especially within 2,000 feet AGL because of limited vertical airspace for recovery.

Forecasts of LLWS in the TAF refer only to non-convective LLWS from the surface up to and including 2,000 feet AGL. LLWS is always assumed to be present in convective activity. LLWS is included in TAFs on an "as-needed" basis to focus the aircrew's attention on LLWS problems which currently exist or are expected. Non-convective LLWS may be associated with the following: frontal passage, inversion, low-level jet, lee side mountain effect, sea breeze front, Santa Ana winds, etc.

When LLWS conditions are expected, the non-convective LLWS code **WS** is included in the TAF as the last group (after cloud forecast). Once in the TAF, the **WS** group remains the prevailing condition until the next **FM** change group or the end of the TAF valid period if there are no subsequent **FM** groups. Forecasts of non-convective LLWS are not included in **TEMPO** or **PROB** groups.

The format of the non-convective low-level wind shear group is:

```
WShwshwshws/dddffKT
```
WS – Indicator for non-convective LLWS
hwshwshws – Height of the top of the WS layer in hundreds of feet AGL
ddd – True direction in 10 degree increments at the indicated height
-- VRB is not used for direction in the non-convective LLWS forecast group.
ff – Speed in knots of the forecast wind at the indicated height
KT – Unit indicator for wind

Example:
```
TAF…13012KT…WS020/27055KT
```
Wind shear from the surface to 2,000 feet. Surface winds from 130 (southeast) at 12 knots changes to 270 (west) at 55 knots at 2,000 feet.

In this example the indicator **WS** is followed by a three-digit number which is the top of the wind shear layer. LLWS is forecast to be present from the surface to this level. After the solidus /, the five digit wind group is the wind direction and speed at the top of the wind shear layer. It is not a value for the amount of shear.

A non-convective LLWS forecast is included in the initial time period or a **FM** group in a TAF whenever:

- One or more PIREPs are received of non-convective LLWS within 2,000 feet of the surface, at or in the vicinity of the TAF airport, causing an indicated air speed loss or gain of 20 knots or more, and the forecaster determines the report(s) reflect a valid non-convective LLWS event rather than mechanical turbulence, or

- When non-convective vertical **WS** of 10 knots or more per 100 feet in a layer more than 200 feet thick are expected or reliably reported within 2,000 feet of the surface at, or in the vicinity of, the airport.

7.2.2.11 Forecast Change Indicator Groups

Forecast change indicator groups are contractions which are used to sub-divide the forecast period (24-hours for scheduled TAFs; less for amended or delayed forecasts) according to significant changes in the weather.

The forecast change indicators, FM, TEMPO, and PROB, are used when a change in any or all of the elements forecast is expected:

7.2.2.11.1 From (FM) Group (FMYYGGgg)

The change group **FMYYGGgg** (voiced as "from") is used to indicate when prevailing conditions are expected to change significantly over a period of less than 1 hour. In these instances, the forecast is sub-divided into time periods using the contraction **FM**, followed, without a space, by six digits, the first two of which indicate the day of the month and the final four which indicate the time (in hours and minutes Z) the change is expected to occur. While the use of a four-digit time in whole hours (e.g. 2100Z) is acceptable, if a forecaster can predict changes and/or events with higher resolution, then more precise timing of the change to the minute will be indicated. All forecast elements following **FMYYGGgg** relate to the period of time from the indicated date and time (**YYGGgg**) to the end of the valid period of the terminal forecast, or to the next **FM** if the terminal forecast valid period is divided into additional periods.

The **FM** group will be followed by a complete description of the weather (i.e., self-contained) and all forecast conditions given before the **FM** group are superseded by those following the group. All elements of the TAF (surface wind, visibility, significant weather, clouds, obscurations, and when expected, non-convective LLWS) will be included in each **FM** group, regardless if they are forecast to change or not. For example, if forecast cloud and visibility changes warrant a new **FM** group but the wind does not, the new **FM** group will include a wind forecast, even if it is the same as the most recently forecast wind.

The only exception to this involves the significant weather group. If no significant weather is expected in the **FM** time period group, then significant weather group is omitted. A TAF may include one or more **FM** groups, depending on the prevailing weather conditions expected. In the interest of clarity, each **FM** group starts on a new line of forecast text, indented five spaces.

Examples:
```
TAF
KDSM 022336Z 0300/0324 20015KT P6SM BKN015
FM030230 29020G35KT 1SM +SHRA OVC005
     TEMPO 0303/0304 30030G45KT 3/4SM -SHSN
     FM030500 31010G20KT P6SM SCT025...
```
A change in the prevailing weather is expected on the **3**rd day of the month at **0230** UTC and the **3**rd day of the month at **0500** UTC.

```
TAF
KAPN 312330Z 0100/0124 13008KT P6SM SCT030
FM010320 31010KT 3SM -SHSN BKN015
FM010500 31010KT 1/4SM +SHSN VV007...
```
Note the wind in the **FM010500** group is the same as the previous **FM** group, but is repeated since all elements are required to be included in a **FM** group.

7.2.2.11.2 TEMPO (YYGG/YₑYₑGₑGₑ) Group

The change-indicator group **TEMPO YYGG/YₑYₑGₑGₑ** is used to indicate temporary fluctuations to forecast meteorological conditions which are expected to:

- Have a high percentage (greater than 50%) probability of occurrence,

- Last for 1 hour or less in each instance and,

- In the aggregate, cover less than half of the period **YYGG** to **YₑYₑGₑGₑ**

The first two digits (**YY**) are the day of the month for the start of the TEMPO. The next two digits (**GG**) are the starting hour (UTC). After the solidus (**/**), the next two digits (**YₑYₑ**) are the ending day of the month, while the last two digits (**GₑGₑ**) are the ending hour (UTC) of the TEMPO period.

Each **TEMPO** group is placed on a new line in the TAF. The **TEMPO** identifier is followed by a description of all the elements in which a temporary change is forecast. A previously forecast element which has not changed during the **TEMPO** period is understood to remain the same and will not be included in the **TEMPO** group. Only those weather elements forecast to temporarily change are required to be included in the **TEMPO** group.

TEMPO groups will not include forecasts of either significant weather in the vicinity (**VC**) or non-convective LLWS.

Examples:
```
TAF
KDDC 221130Z 2212/2312 29010G25KT P6SM SCT025
TEMPO 2215/2217 30025G35KT 1 1/2SM SHRA BKN010...
```
In the example, all forecast elements in the TEMPO group are expected to be different than the prevailing conditions. The TEMPO group is valid on the 17 from 1500 UTC to 1700 UTC.

```
TAF
KSEA 091125Z 0912/1012 19008KT P6SM SCT010 BKN020 OVC090
TEMPO 0912/0915 -RA SCT010 BKN015 OVC040...
```

In this example the visibility is **not** forecast in the TEMPO group. Therefore, the visibility is expected to remain the same (P6SM) as forecast in the prevailing conditions group. Also, note that in the TEMPO 0912/0915 group, all three cloud layers are included, although the lowest layer is not forecast to change from the initial time period.

7.2.2.11.3 PROB30 (YYGG/$Y_eY_eG_eG_e$) Group

The probability group, **PROB30 YYGG/$Y_eY_eG_eG_e$,** is only used by NWS forecasters to forecast a low probability occurrence (30% chance) of a thunderstorm or precipitation event and its associated weather and obscuration elements (wind, visibility, and/or sky condition) at an airport.

The **PROB30** group is the forecaster's assessment of probability of occurrence of the weather event which follows it. The first two digits (**YY**) are the day of the month for the start of the PROB30. The next two digits (**GG**) are the starting hour (UTC). After the solidus (/), the next two digits (Y_eY_e) are the ending day of the month, while the last two digits (G_eG_e) are the ending hour (UTC) of the PROB30 period. PROB30 is the only PROB group used in NWS TAFs. Note that U.S. military and international TAFs may use the PROB40 (40% chance) group as well.

The **PROB30** group is located within the same line of the prevailing condition group, continuing on the line below if necessary.

The **PROB30** group may not be used in the first 9 hours of the TAF's valid period, including amendments. Also, only one **PROB30** group may be used in the initial forecast period and in any subsequent **FM** groups. Note that U.S. military and international TAFs do not have these restrictions.

PROB30 groups do not include forecasts of significant weather in the vicinity (**VC**) or non-convective LLWS.

Example:

```
FM012100 18015KT P6SM SCT050 PROB30 0123/0201 2SM TSRA OVC020CB
```
In this example, the PROB30 group is valid on the 1st day of the month at 2300 UTC to the 2nd day of the month at 0100 UTC.

7.2.2.12 TAF Examples

```
TAF
KPIR 111140Z 1112/1212 13012KT P6SM BKN100 WS020/35035KT
TEMPO 1112/1114 5SM BR
FM111500 16015G25KT P6SM SCT040 BKN250
FM120000 14012KT P6SM BKN080 OVC150 PROB30 1200/1204 3SM TSRA
BKN030CB
FM120400 14008KT P6SM SCT040 OVC080 TEMPO 1204/1208 3SM TSRA
OVC030CB
TAF ─────────────▶ Terminal Aerodrome Forecast
KPIR ────────────▶ Pierre, South Dakota
111140 ──────────▶ prepared on the 11th at 1140 UTC
1112/1212────────▶ valid from the 11th at 1200 UTC until the 12th at 1200
UTC
```

13012KT ················▶ wind 130 at 12 knots
P6SM ·········▶visibility greater than 6 statute miles
BKN100 ··········▶ceiling 10,000 broken
WS020/35035KT ·····▶wind shear at 2,000 feet, wind from 350 at 35 knots
TEMPO 1112/1114 ▶temporary conditions between the 11th day of the month at 1200 UTC and the 11th day of the month at 1400 UTC
5SM ···············▶visibility 5 statute miles
BR ···················▶mist
FM111500···········▶from the 11th day of the month at 1500 UTC
16015G25KT ···········▶wind 160 at 15 knots gusting to 25 knots
P6SM ·········▶visibility greater than 6 statute miles
SCT040 BKN250 ·····▶4,000 scattered, ceiling 25,000 broken
FM120000···········▶from the 12th day of the month at 0000Z
14012KT ·············▶wind 140 at 12 knots
P6SM ·········▶visibility greater than 6 statute miles
BKN080 OVC150·····▶ ceiling 8,000 broken, 15,000 overcast
PROB30 1200/1204▶   30% probability between the 12th day of the month at 0000 UTC and the 12th day of the month at 0400 UTC
3SM ···········▶visibility 3 statute miles
TSRA ··········▶thunderstorm with moderate rain showers
BKN030CB ··········▶ceiling 3,000 broken with cumulonimbus
FM120400···········▶from the 12th day of the month at 0400 UTC
14008KT ·············▶wind 140 at 8 knots
P6SM ·········▶visibility greater than 6 statute miles
SCT040 OVC080 ·····▶4,000 scattered, ceiling 8,000 overcast
TEMPO 1204/1208 ▶temporary conditions between the 12th day of the month at 0400 UTC and the 12th day of the month at 0800 UTC
3SM ···········▶visibility 3 statute miles
TSRA ··········▶thunderstorms with moderate rain showers
OVC030CB ···········▶ceiling 3,000 overcast with cumulonimbus

TAF AMD
KEYW 131555Z 1316/1412 VRB03KT P6SM VCTS SCT025CB BKN250
TEMPO 1316/1318 2SM TSRA BKN020CB
FM131800 VRB03KT P6SM SCT025 BKN250 TEMPO 1320/1324 1SM TSRA
OVC010CB
FM140000 VRB03KT P6SM VCTS SCT020CB BKN120 TEMPO 1408/1412
BKN020CB

TAF AMD ·········▶ Amended Terminal Aerodrome Forecast
KEYW ············▶Key West, Florida
131555Z ············▶prepared on the 13th at 1555 UTC
1316/1412···········▶valid from the 13th at 1600 UTC until the 14th at 1200 UTC
VRB03KT ············▶wind variable at 3 knots
P6SM ·········▶visibility greater than 6 statute miles
VCTS ············▶thunderstorms in the vicinity
SCT025CB BKN250 ▶2,500 scattered with cumulonimbus, ceiling 25,000 broken
TEMPO 1316/1318 ▶temporary conditions between the 13th day of the month at 1600 UTC and the 13th day of the month at 1800 UTC
2SM ············▶visibility 2 statute miles
TSRA ··········▶thunderstorms with moderate rain showers
BKN020CB ··········▶ceiling 2,000 broken with cumulonimbus
FM131800···········▶from the 13th day of the month at 1800 UTC

VRB03KT ················➤ wind variable at 3 knots
P6SM ···················➤ visibility greater than 6 statute miles
SCT025 BKN250 ·····➤ 2,500 scattered, ceiling 25,000 broken
TEMPO 1320/1324 ➤ temporary conditions between the 13th day of the month at 2000 UTC and the 14th day of the month at 0000 UTC
1SM ····················➤ visibility 1 statute mile
TSRA ··················➤ thunderstorms with moderate rain showers
OVC010CB ···········➤ ceiling 1,000 overcast with cumulonimbus
FM140000···········➤ from the 14th day of the month at 0000 UTC
VRB03KT ·············➤ variable wind at 3 knots
P6SM ··················➤ visibility greater than 6 statute miles
VCTS ··················➤ thunderstorms in the vicinity
SCT020CB BKN120 ➤ 2,000 scattered with cumulonimbus, ceiling 12,000 broken
TEMPO 1408/1412 ➤ temporary conditions between the 14th day of the month at 0800 UTC and the 14th day of the month at 1200 UTC
BKN020CB ···········➤ ceiling 2,000 broken with cumulonimbus
TAF
KCRP 111730Z 1118/1218 19007KT P6SM SCT030
TEMPO 1118/1120 BKN040
FM112000 16011KT P6SM VCTS FEW030CB SCT250
FM120200 14006KT P6SM FEW025 SCT250
FM120800 VRB03KT 5SM BR SCT012
FM121500 17007KT P6SM SCT025
TAF ···················➤ Terminal Aerodrome Forecast
KCRP ·················➤ Corpus Christi, Texas
111730Z ·············➤ prepared on the 11th at 1730 UTC
1118/1218 ··········➤ valid from the 11th at 1800 UTC until the 12th at 1800 UTC
19007KT ·············➤ wind 190 at 7 knots
P6SM ·················➤ visibility greater than 6 statute miles
SCT030 ··············➤ 3,000 scattered
TEMPO 1118/1120 ➤ temporary conditions between 1800 UTC and 2000 UTC on the 11th.
BKN040 ··············➤ ceiling 4,000 broken
FM112000···········➤ from the 11th day of the month at 2000 UTC
16011KT ·············➤ wind 160 at 11 knots
P6SM ·················➤ visibility greater than 6 statute miles
VCTS ·················➤ thunderstorms in the vicinity
FEW030CB SCT250 ➤ 3,000 few with cumulonimbus, 25,000 scattered
FM120200···········➤ from the 12th day of the month at 0200 UTC
14006KT ·············➤ wind 140 at 6 knots
P6SM ·················➤ visibility greater than 6 statute miles
FEW025 SCT250 ····➤ 2,500 few, 25,000 scattered
FM120800 ··········➤ from the 12th day of the month at 0800 UTC
VRB03KT···········➤ wind variable at 3 knots
5SM ··················➤ visibility 5 statute miles
BR ····················➤ mist
SCT012 ··············➤ 1,200 scattered
FM121500···········➤ from the 12th day of the month at 1500 UTC
17007KT ·············➤ wind 170 at 7 knots
P6SM ·················➤ visibility greater than 6 statute miles
SCT025 ··············➤ 2,500 scattered

7.2.3 Issuance

Scheduled TAFs prepared by NWS offices are issued four times a day, every 6 hours, according to the following schedule:

Table 7-8. TAF Issuance Schedule

SCHEDULED ISSUANCE	VALID PERIOD	ISSUANCE WINDOW
0000 UTC	0000 to 2400 UTC	2320 to 2340 UTC
0600 UTC	0600 to 0600 UTC	0520 to 0540 UTC
1200 UTC	1200 to 1200 UTC	1120 to 1140 UTC
1800 UTC	1800 to 1800 UTC	1720 to 1740 UTC

7.2.3.1 Minimum Observational Requirements for Routine TAF Issuance and Continuation

The NWS WFO aviation forecaster must have certain information for the preparation and scheduled issuance of each individual TAF. Although integral to the TAF writing process, a complete surface (METAR/SPECI) observation is not required. Forecasters use the "total observation concept" to write TAFs with data including nearby surface observations, radar, satellite, radiosonde, model data, aircraft, and other sources.

If information sources, such as surface observations, are missing, unreliable, or not complete, forecasters will append **AMD NOT SKED** to the end of a TAF. The use of AMD NOT SKED indicates the forecaster has enough data, using the total observation concept, to issue a forecast but will not provide updates. This allows airport operations to continue using a valid TAF.

In rare situations where observations have been missing for extended periods of time (i.e., more than one TAF cycle of 6 hours), and the total observation concept cannot provide sufficient information, the TAF may be suspended by the use of **NIL TAF**.

7.2.3.2 Sites with Scheduled Part-Time Observations

For TAFs with less than 24-hour observational coverage, the TAF will be valid to the end of the routine scheduled forecast period even if observations cease prior to that time. The time observations are scheduled to end and/or resume will be indicated by expanding the **AMD NOT SKED** statement. Expanded statements will include the observation ending time (**AFT Y_1Y_1HHmm**, e.g., AFT 120200), the scheduled observation resumption time (**TIL Y_1Y_1HHmm**, e.g., TIL 171200Z) or the period of observation unavailability (**Y_1Y_1HH/Y_eY_ehh**, e.g., 2502-2512). TIL will be used only when the beginning of the scheduled TAF valid period coincides with the time of the last observation or when observations are scheduled to resume prior to the next scheduled issuance time. When used, these remarks will immediately follow the last forecast group. If a routine TAF issuance is scheduled to be made after observations have ceased, but before they resume, the remark **AMD NOT SKED** will immediately follow the valid period group of the scheduled issuance. After sufficient data using the total observation concept has been received, the **AMD NOT SKED** remark will be removed.

7.2.3.2.1 Examples of Scheduled Part-Time Observations TAFs

```
TAF AMD
KRWF 150202Z 1502/1524 {TAF text}
AMD NOT SKED 1505Z-1518Z=
```
No amendments will be available between the 15th day of the month at 0500 UTC and the 15th day of the month at 1800 UTC due to lack of a complete observational set between those times.

```
TAF AMD
KPSP 190230Z 1903/1924 {TAF text}
AMD NOT SKED=
```
Amendments are not scheduled.

7.2.3.3   Automated Observing Sites Requiring Part-Time Augmentation

TAFs for AWOS-III sites which have part-time augmentation are prepared using the procedures for part-time manual observation sites detailed in the previous section, with one exception. This exception is the remark used when the automated system is unattended. Specifically, the time an augmented automated system is scheduled to go into unattended operation and/or the time augmentation resumes is included in a remark unique to automated observing sites: **AMD LTD TO CLD VIS AND WIND (AFT YYHHmm, or TIL YYhhmm, or YYHH-YYhh)**, where **YY** is the date, **HHm**m is the time, in hours and minutes, of last augmented observation and **hhmm** is the time, in hours and minutes, the second complete observation is expected to be received. This remark, which does not preclude amendments for other forecast elements, is appended to the last scheduled TAF issued prior to the last augmented observation. It will also be appended to all subsequent amendments until augmentation resumes.

The **AMD LTD TO** (elements specified) remark is a flag for users and differs from the **AMD NOT SKED AFT Z** remark for part-time manual observation sites. **AMD LTD TO** (elements specified) means users should expect amendments only for those elements and the times specified.

Example:
```
TAF AMD
KCOE 150202Z 1502/1524 text
AMD LTD TO CLD VIS AND WIND 1505-1518=
```
The amended forecast indicates that amendments will only be issued for wind, visibility, and clouds, between the 15th day of the month at 0500Z and the 15th day of the month at 1800Z.

An amendment includes forecasts for all appropriate TAF elements, even those not reported when the automated site is not augmented. If unreported elements are judged crucial to the TAF and cannot be adequately determined (e.g., fog versus moderate snow), the TAF will be suspended (i.e. an amended TAF stating **"AMD NOT SKED"**).

AWOS-III systems with part-time augmentation, which the forecaster suspects are providing unreliable information when not augmented, will be reported for maintenance and treated the same as part-time manual observation sites. In such cases, the **AMD NOT SKED AFT YY/aaZ** remark will be used.

7.2.3.4 Non-Augmented Automated Observing Sites

The TAF issued for a non-augmented ASOS site may be suspended in the event the forecaster is notified of, or strongly suspects, an outage or unrepresentative data. Forecasters may also suspend TAF amendments when an element the forecaster judges to be critical is missing from the observation and cannot be obtained using the total observation concept. The term **AMD NOT SKED** will be appended, on a separate line and indented five spaces, to the end of an amendment to the existing TAF when appropriate.

7.3 International Aviation Route Forecasts (ROFOR)

International ROFORs are prepared and issued several hours in advance of regularly scheduled flights. The only NWS office which routinely issues ROFORs is the Weather Forecast Office (WFO) in Honolulu due to its designation as an ICAO Meteorological Watch Office (MWO).

7.3.1 ROFOR Criteria
WFO Honolulu will honor all ROFOR requests for flights within the Pacific Region beginning or ending in, or having most of the flight path within its area of responsibility, which is the Oakland Oceanic FIR south of 30N, between 140W and 130E.

7.3.2 Issuance
ROFORs are issued for prescribed times, several hours in advance, for regularly scheduled flights. ROFOR requests for unscheduled flights are prepared as soon as time allows.

7.3.2.1 ROFOR Amendments

ROFORs are not required to be amended.

7.3.2.2 ROFOR Corrections

ROFOR corrections are issued as soon as possible when erroneous data has been transmitted.

7.3.3 ROFOR Content
ROFORs contain some or all of the following forecast parameters:

- Winds and temperatures aloft

- Significant en-route weather

- Zone weather

- Weather Synopsis

At a minimum, ROFORs include the first two bullets. They may contain data for multiple altitudes and include TAFs for destination points and/or alternates.

The core of a ROFOR is formatted as follows: **0iQLL 4hhhTT ddFFF**

Where   i = 1 for zone up to latitude **L**
         i = 2 for zone up to longitude LL
         Q = 1 east of the dateline in the northern hemisphere
         Q = 2 west of the dateline in the northern hemisphere
         Q = 6 east of the dateline in the southern hemisphere
         Q = 7 west of the dateline in the southern hemisphere
      hhh = height to which the temperature and wind refer
       TT = air temperature in whole degrees Celsius at hhh
       dd = true direction in tens of degrees from which the wind will blow at hhh
       fff = wind speed in know at hhh

01104 4300M31 10010

Decoded as: The 30,000 foot wind (10010) and temperature (M31) are for that zone along the flight path from the equator to 05N east of the dateline.

Note: Refer to Appendix A for definitions of common terms used in ROFORs.

7.3.4   ROFOR Examples

7.3.4.1   Santa Barbara and San Francisco to Honolulu Route ROFOR Example

```
FRPN31 PHFO 301857
RFRKSF
WINDS/TEMPERATURES AND WEATHER BY ZONE FOR
ROUTE SFO/HNL VIA 31.3N/140W VALID AT 311200Z
FLIGHT LEVELS
ZONE   FL050 FL100 FL180 FL240 ZONE WEATHER
25     3315 P16    3208 P11    3109 M07    3216 M19    6-8 STSC 010/030
26     3316 P13    3211 P09    3117 M06    3023 M18    4-6 STSC 015/045
27     3013 P12    3212 P09    3020 M06    3024 M18    6-8 MERGING LYR TO 200
ISOL VIS 3-5SM RA
ISOL TCU TOPS FL220
28     3008 P14    3008 P08    2815 M06    2918 M18    DO
29     9905 P14    9905 P08    2609 M06    2612 M18    4-6 CUSC 020/050
30     0506 P14    9905 P08    9905 M06    2406 M18    DO
31     0818 P15    0613 P09    0307 M06    9905 M18    4-6 CUSC 020/080
ISOL -SHRA
32     0822 P15    0719 P09    0711 M05    9905 M17    DO
OVERALL COMPONENTS
P4     P2     M4     M10
ROUTE SBA/HNL VIA 29.5N/140W VALID AT 311200Z
FLIGHT LEVELS
ZONE FL050 FL100 FL180 FL240 ZONE WEATHER
25     3509 P17    3108 P11    3011 M07    3015 M19    6-8 STSC 010/030
26     3416 P14    3312 P09    3218 M05    3123 M18    4-6 STSC 015/045
27     0111 P13    3510 P10    3017 M05    3021 M18    2-4 CUSC 020/045
28     0307 P14    3606 P09    2713 M05    2717 M18    DO
29     0406 P14    9905 P08    2507 M05    2610 M18    4-6 CUSC 020/050
30     0815 P15    0610 P09    9905 M05    9905 M17    DO
31     0821 P15    0616 P09    0408 M05    9905 M18    4-6 CUSC 020/080
ISOL -SHRA
32     0822 P15    0719 P09    0812 M06    9905 M18    DO
OVERALL COMPONENTS
P10    P5     M4     M7
SYNOPSIS...1024MB HIGH CENTERED NEAR N3000 W15600.
```

7.4 Wind and Temperature Aloft Forecast (FB)

Wind and Temperature Aloft Forecasts (FB) are computer prepared forecasts of wind direction, wind speed, and temperature at specified times, altitudes, and locations. Forecasts are based on the North American Mesoscale (NAM) forecast model run. FBs are available on the Aviation Weather Center (AWC) web site at: http://aviationweather.gov/products/nws/winds/.

7.4.1 Forecast Altitudes
The following table contains the altitudes for which winds are forecast. Altitudes up to 15,000 feet are referenced to Mean Sea Level (MSL). Altitudes at or above 18,000 feet are references to flight levels (FL).

Table 7-9. Wind and Temperature Aloft Forecast Levels

Actual Altitudes (MSL)
1,000 feet*
1,500 feet*
2,000 feet*
3,000 feet
6,000 feet
9,000 feet
12,000 feet
15,000 feet*
Pressure Altitudes (Hectopascals)
18,000 feet (500 Hectopascals)
24,000 feet (400 Hectopascals)
30,000 feet (300 Hectopascals)
34,000 feet (250 Hectopascals)
39,000 feet (200 Hectopascals)
45,000 feet (150 Hectopascals)#
53,000 feet (100 Hectopascals)#
* Hawaii and Western Pacific only.
# Not available for selected locations in the Contiguous US.

Wind forecasts are not issued for altitudes within 1,500 feet of a location's elevation. Temperature forecasts are not issued for altitudes within 2,500 feet of a location's elevation. Forecasts for intermediate levels are determined by interpolation.

7.4.2 Format
The symbolic form of the forecasts is **DDff+TT** in which **DD** is the wind direction, **ff** the wind speed, and **TT** the temperature.

Wind direction is indicated in tens of degrees (two digits) with reference to true north and wind speed is given in knots (two digits). Light and variable wind or wind speeds of less than 5 knots are expressed by **9900**. Forecast wind speeds of 100 through 199 knots are indicated by subtracting 100 from the speed and adding 50 to the coded direction. For example, a forecast of 250 degrees, 145 knots, is encoded as **7545**. Forecast wind speeds of 200 knots or greater are indicated as a forecast speed of 199 knots. For example, **7799** is decoded as 270 degrees at 199 knots or greater.

Temperature is indicated in degrees Celsius (two digits) and is preceded by the appropriate algebraic sign for the levels from 6,000 through 24,000 feet. Above 24,000 feet, the sign is omitted since temperatures are always negative at those altitudes.

The product header includes the date and time observations were collected, the forecast valid date and time, and the time period during which the forecast is to be used.

Examples
```
1312+05
```
The wind direction is from 130 degree (i.e. - southeast), the wind speed is 12 knots and the temperature is 5 degrees Celsius.

```
9900+10
```
Wind light and variable, temperature +10 degrees.

```
7735-07
```
The wind direction is from 270 degrees (i.e. west), the wind speed is 135 knots, and the temperature is minus 7 degrees Celsius.

7.4.2.1   Coding Example

Sample winds aloft text message:

```
DATA BASED ON 010000Z
VALID 010600Z FOR USE 0500-0900Z. TEMPS NEG ABV 24000
FT 3000 6000 9000 12000 18000 24000 30000 34000 39000
MKC 9900 1709+06 2018+00 2130-06 2242-18 2361-30 247242 258848 550252
```

Sample message decoded:

(Line 1) `DATA BASED ON 010000Z`
Forecast data is based on computer forecasts generated the first day of the month at 0000 UTC.

(Line 2) `VALID 010600Z FOR USE 0500-0900Z. TEMPS NEG ABV 24000`
The valid time of the forecast is the 1st day of the month at 0600 UTC. The forecast winds and temperature are to be used between 0500 and 0900 UTC. Temperatures are negative above 24,000 feet.

(Line 3)
`FT 3000 6000 9000 12000 18000 24000 30000 34000 39000`
FT indicates the altitude of the forecast.

(Line4)
`MKC 9900 1709+06 2018+00 2130-06 2242-18 2361-30 247242 258848 550252`
MKC indicates the location of the forecast. The rest of the data is the winds and temperature aloft forecast for the respective altitudes.

The following table shows data for MKC (Kansas City, MO).

Table 7-10. Wind and Temperature Aloft Forecast Decoding Examples

FT 3000 6000 9000 12000 18000 24000 30000 34000 39000			
MKC 9900 1709+06 2018+00 2130-06 2242-18 2361-30 247242 258848 550252			
Altitude (feet)	**Coded**	**Wind**	**Temperature (°C)**
3,000 FT	9900	Light and variable	Not forecast
6,000 FT	1709+06	170 degrees at 9 knots	+06 degrees Celsius
9,000 FT	2018+00	200 degrees at 18 knots	Zero degrees Celsius
12,000 FT	2130-06	210 degrees at 30 knots	-06 degrees Celsius
18,000 FT	2242-18	220 degrees at 42 knots	-18 degrees Celsius
24,000 FT	2361-30	230 degrees at 61 knots	-30 degrees Celsius
30,000 FT	247242	240 degrees at 72 knots	-42 degrees Celsius
34,000 FT	258848	250 degrees at 88 knots	-48 degrees Celsius
39,000 FT	750252	250 degrees at 102 knots	-52 degrees Celsius

7.4.2.2   Example for the Contiguous US and Alaska

```
DATA BASED ON 091200Z
VALID 091800Z FOR USE 1400-2100Z. TEMPS NEG ABV 24000
FT 3000 6000 9000 12000 18000 24000 30000 34000 39000
ABI 1931+10 1929+10 2024+06 2331-10 2448-23 235239 246348 256056
ABQ 2213+03 2327-04 2253-17 2263-27 227242 236946 245749
ABR 2017 2312+14 2308+09 2615+02 2724-13 2527-26 273641 274051 274562
AGC (etc.)
FT 45000 53000
ABI 301049 281149
ABQ 235061 244859
ABR 224559 243756
AGC (etc.)
```

Note: 45,000- and 53,000-foot winds are not available for selected locations in the conterminous US.

7.4.2.3   Example for Hawaii and the Western Pacific

```
DATA BASED ON 091200Z
VALID 091800Z FOR USE 1400-2100Z. TEMPS NEG ABV 24000
FT 1000 1500 2000 3000 6000 9000 12000 15000 18000 24000
LIH 9900 9900 1705 1806 1711+13 2216+10 2520+05 2523+01 2833-07 2937-19
HNL 9900 9900 9900 9900 1407+14 1908+11 2410+05 2612+01 2928-07 2930-18
LNY 9900 9900 9900 9900 1208+14 9900+11 9900+06 2909+01 3024-07 3027-18
OGG (etc.)
FT 30000 34000 39000 45000 53000
LIH 040734 990044 241055 281666 990072
HNL 051234 010543 250654 301066 990072
LNY 041433 010743 230754 260966 990072
OGG (etc)
```

Note: The altitudes forecast in the Hawaii and western Pacific bulletins are different than those forecast in the Contiguous US and Alaska

Note: The Hawaii and western Pacific bulletins are separated at the 24,000-foot level instead of 39,000 feet because of the additional, lower levels noted in Table 7-8.

7.4.3   Issuance

The NWS National Centers for Environmental Prediction (NCEP) produces scheduled Wind and Temperature Aloft Forecasts (**FB**) 4 times daily for specified locations in the Continental United States (CONUS), the Hawaiian Islands, Alaska and coastal waters, and the western Pacific Ocean (Figures 7-8 through 7-11).

Amendments are not issued to the forecasts.

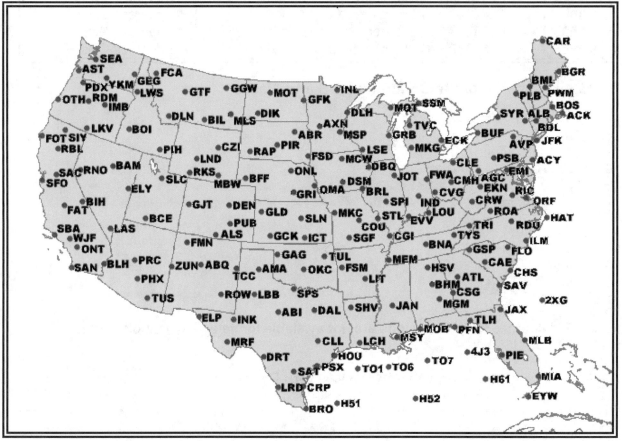

Figure 7-8. Wind and Temperature Aloft Forecast Network - Contiguous US

Figure 7-9. Wind and Temperature Aloft Forecast Network - Alaska

Figure 7-10. Wind and Temperature Aloft Forecast Network - Hawaii

Figure 7-11. Wind and Temperature Aloft Forecast Network - Western Pacific

Table 7-11. Wind and Temperature Aloft Forecast (FB) Periods

Model Run	Product Available	6 hour Forecast		12 hour Forecast		24 hour Forecast	
		Valid	For Use	Valid	For Use	Valid	For Use
0000Z	~0200Z	0600Z	0200-0900Z	1200Z	0900-1800Z	0000Z	1800-0600Z
0600Z	~0800Z	1200Z	0800-1500Z	1800Z	1500-0000Z	0600Z	0000-1200Z
1200Z	~1400Z	1800Z	1400-2100Z	0000Z	2100-0600Z	1200Z	0600-1800Z
1800Z	~2000Z	0000Z	2000-0300Z	0600Z	0300-1200Z	1800Z	1200-0000Z

7.4.4 Delayed Forecasts

If the scheduled forecast transmission is delayed, the existing valid forecast based on the earlier 6-hourly data can be used until a new forecast is transmitted.

8 FORECAST CHARTS

8.1 Short-Range Surface Prognostic (Prog) Charts

Short-Range Surface Prognostic (Prog) Charts (Figure 8-1) provide a forecast of surface pressure systems, fronts and precipitation for a 2-day period. The forecast area covers the 48-contiguous states, the coastal waters and portions of adjacent countries. The forecasted conditions are divided into four forecast periods, 12-, 24-, 36-, and 48-hours. Each chart depicts a "snapshot" of weather elements expected at the specified valid time.

The Surface Prognostic (Prog) Charts are available at the Aviation Digital Data Services (ADDS) web site at: http://adds.aviationweather.noaa.gov/progs/.

Figure 8-1. Surface Prog Chart Example

8.1.1 Content

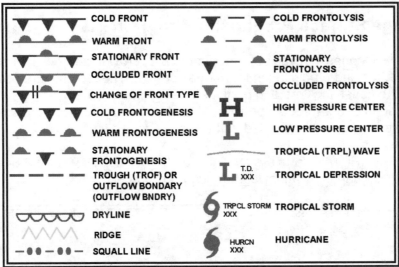

Figure 8-2. Surface Prog Chart Symbols

8.1.1.1 Pressure Systems

Pressure systems are depicted by pressure centers, troughs, isobars, drylines, tropical waves, tropical storms and hurricanes using standard symbols (Figure 8-2). Isobars are denoted by solid thin gray lines and labeled with the appropriate pressure in millibars. The central pressure is plotted near the respective pressure center.

8.1.1.2 Fronts

Fronts are depicted using the standard symbols in Figure 8-2.

8.1.1.3 Squall Lines

Squall lines are denoted using the standard symbol in Figure 8-2.

8.1.1.4 Precipitation

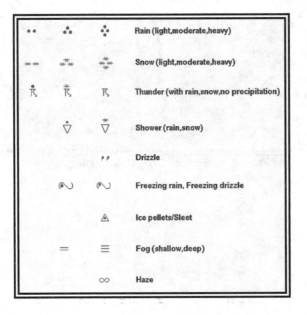

Figure 8-3. Surface Prog Chart Precipitation Symbols

Precipitation areas are enclosed by thick, solid, green lines (Figure 8-4). Standard precipitation symbols are used to identify precipitation types (Figure 8-3). These symbols are positioned within or adjacent to the associated area of precipitation. If adjacent to the area, an arrow will point to the area with which they are associated. A mix of precipitation is indicated by the use of two pertinent symbols separated by a slash (Figure 8-4). A bold, dashed, grey line is used to separate precipitation within an outlined area with contrasting characteristics (Figure 8-4). For instance, a dashed line would be used to separate an area of snow from an area of rain.

Figure 8-4. Surface Prog Chart Precipitation Example

Precipitation characteristic are further described by the use of shading (Figure 8-5). Shading or lack of shading indicates the expected coverage of the precipitation. Shaded areas indicate the precipitation is expected to have more than 50% (broken) coverage. Unshaded areas indicate 30-50% (scattered) coverage.

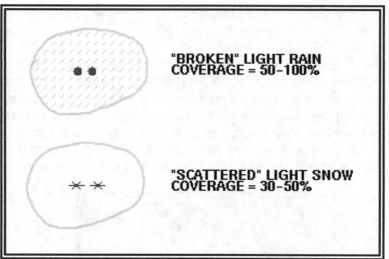

Figure 8-5. Surface Prog Chart Precipitation Coverage

8.1.2 Issuance

Short-Range Surface Prognostic (Prog) Charts are issued by the Hydrometeorological Prediction Center (HPC) in Camp Springs, MD. Table 8-1 provides the product schedule. The 12- and 24-Hour Surface Prognostic (Prog). Charts are issued four times a day and are termed "Day 1" progs. The 36- and 48- Hour Surface Prog Charts are issued twice daily and are termed "Day 2" progs. They are available on the HPC web site at: http://adds.aviationweather.noaa.gov/progs/.

Table 8-1. Short-Range Surface Prog Charts Schedule

	Issuance Time (UTC)			
	~1720	~2310	~0530	~0935
	Valid Time (UTC)			
12-Hour Surface Prog	0000	0600	1200	1800
24-Hour Surface Prog	1200	1800	0000	0600
36-Hour Surface Prog	0000	NA	1200	NA
48-Hour Surface Prog	1200	NA	0000	NA

8.1.3 Use

Short-Range Surface Prognostic (Prog) Charts can be used to obtain an overview of the progression of surface weather features during the next 48 hours. The progression of weather is the change in position, size, and intensity of weather with time. Progression analysis is accomplished by comparing charts of observed conditions to the 12-, 24-, 36-, and 48-hour progs. Short-Range Surface Prognostic (PROG) Charts make the comprehension of weather details easier and more meaningful. For example, in Figures 8-6 through 8-9, the cold front located from the eastern Great Lakes to Missouri is forecast to move southeastward and the High pressure center just north of the Minnesota/North Dakota boarder is also forecast to move southeast and weaken.

Figure 8-6. 12-hour Surface Prog Chart Example

Figure 8-7. 24-hour Surface Prog Chart Example

Figure 8-8. 36-hour Surface Prog Chart Example

Figure 8-9. 48-hour Surface Prog Chart Example

8.2 Low-Level Significant Weather (SIGWX) Charts

The Low-Level Significant Weather (SIGWX) Charts (Figure 8-10) provide a forecast of aviation weather hazards primarily intended to be used as guidance products for pre-flight briefings. The forecast domain covers the 48 contiguous states and the coastal waters for altitudes 24,000 ft MSL (Flight Level 240 or 400 millibars) and below. Each chart depicts a "snapshot" of weather expected at the specified valid time.

Figure 8-10. 12-Hour Low-Level SIGWX Chart Example

8.2.1 Content

Low-Level Significant Weather (SIGWX) Charts depict weather flying categories, turbulence, and freezing levels (Figure 8-11). Icing is not specifically forecast.

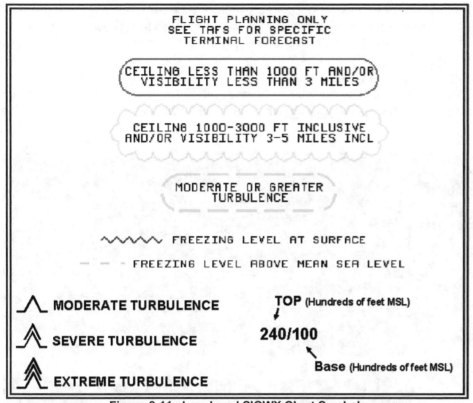

Figure 8-11. Low-Level SIGWX Chart Symbols

8.2.1.1 Flying Categories

Instrument Flight Rules (IFR) areas are outlined with a solid red line, Marginal Visual Flight Rules (MVFR) areas are outlined with a scalloped cyan (light blue) line, Visual Flight Rules (VFR) areas are not depicted (Figure 8-12).

Figure 8-12. Low-Level SIGWX Chart Flying Categories Example

8.2.1.2 Turbulence

Areas of moderate or greater turbulence are enclosed by bold, dashed, yellow lines (Figure 8-13). Turbulence intensities are identified by standard symbols (Figure 8-11). The vertical extent of turbulence layers is specified by top and base heights separated by a slant. The intensity symbols and height information may be located within or adjacent to the forecasted areas of turbulence. If located adjacent to an area, an arrow will point to the associated area. Turbulence height is depicted by two numbers separated by a solidus /. For example, an area on the chart with turbulence indicated as **240/100** indicates the turbulence can be expected from the top at FL240 to the base at 10,000 feet MSL. When the base height is omitted, the turbulence is forecast to reach the surface. For example, **080/** identifies a turbulence layer from the surface to 8,000 feet MSL. Turbulence associated with thunderstorms is not depicted on the chart.

Figure 8-13. Low-Level SIGWX Chart Turbulence Forecast Example

8.2.1.3 Freezing Levels

The freezing level at the surface is depicted by a blue, saw-toothed symbol (Figure 8-11). The surface freezing level separates above-freezing from below-freezing temperatures at the Earth's surface.

Freezing levels above the surface are depicted by fine, green, dashed lines labeled in hundreds of feet MSL beginning at 4,000 feet using 4,000 foot intervals (Figure 8-11). If multiple freezing levels exist, these lines are drawn to the highest freezing level. For example, **80** identifies the 8,000-foot freezing level contour (Figure 8-14). The lines are discontinued where they intersect the surface.

The freezing level for locations between lines is determined by interpolation. For example, the freezing level midway between the 4,000 and 8,000 foot lines is 6,000 feet.

Figure 8-14. Low-Level SIGWX Chart Freezing Level Forecast Example

Multiple <u>freezing level</u>s occur when the temperature is zero degrees Celsius at more than one altitude aloft. Multiple <u>freezing level</u>s can be forecasted on the Low-Level Significant Weather Prog Charts in situations where the temperature is below-freezing (negative) at the surface with multiple <u>freezing level</u>s aloft.

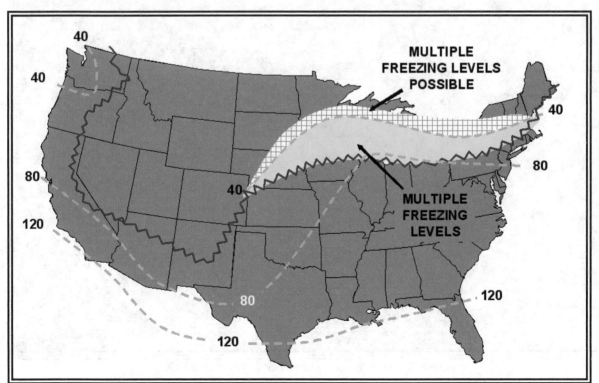

Figure 8-15. Low-Level SIGWX Chart Multiple Freezing Levels Example

On the chart, areas with multiple freezing levels are located on the below-freezing side of the surface freezing level contour and bounded by the 4,000 foot freezing level. Multiple freezing levels are **possible** beyond the 4,000 feet freezing level (i.e., below 4,000 feet MSL), but the exact cutoff cannot be determined (Figure 8-15).

8.2.2 Issuance

Low-Level Significant Weather (SIGWX) Charts are issued four times per day by the Aviation Weather Center (AWC) in Kansas City, Missouri (Table 8-2). Two charts are issued; a 12-hour and a 24-hour prog. Both are available on the AWC web site: http://aviationweather.gov/products/swl/.

Table 8-2. Low-Level SIGWX Chart Issuance Schedule

	Issuance Time			
	~1720Z	~2310Z	~0530Z	~0935Z
Chart	Valid Time			
12-Hour Prog	00Z	06Z	12Z	18Z
24-Hour Prog	12Z	18Z	00Z	06Z

8.2.3 Use

The Low-Level Significant Weather (SIGWX) Charts provide an overview of selected aviation weather hazards up to 24,000 feet MSL (FL240 or 400 millibars) at 12- and 24-hours into the future.

Figure 8-16. 12-Hour Low-Level SIGWX Chart Example

Figure 8-17. 24-hour Low-Level SIGWX Chart Example

8.3 Mid-Level Significant Weather (SIGWX) Chart

The Mid-Level Significant Weather (SIGWX) Chart (Figure 8-18) provides a forecast of significant en route weather phenomena over a range of flight levels from 10,000 ft MSL to FL450, and associated surface weather features. The chart depicts a "snapshot" of weather expected at the specified valid time.

The Mid-Level Significant Weather (SIGWX) Chart is available on the Aviation Weather Center web site at: http://aviationweather.gov/products/swm/.

Figure 8-18. Mid-Level SIGWX Chart Example

8.3.1 Content
The Mid-Level Significant Weather (SIGWX) Chart depicts numerous weather elements that can be hazardous to aviation.

8.3.1.1 Thunderstorms
The abbreviation **CB** is only included where it refers to the expected occurrence of an area of widespread cumulonimbus clouds, cumulonimbus along a line with little or no space between individual clouds, cumulonimbus embedded in cloud layers, or cumulonimbus concealed by haze. It does not refer to isolated or scattered cumulonimbus not embedded in cloud layers or concealed by haze.

Each cumulonimbus area is identified with **CB** and characterized by coverage, bases and tops.

Table 8-3. Mid-Level SIGWX Chart Cumulonimbus Coverage

CODED	CHARACTERIZATION	MEANING
ISOL	Isolated	Less than 1/8th coverage
OCNL	Occasional	1/8th to 4/8^{ths} coverage
FRQ	Frequent	More than 4/8^{ths} coverage
EMBD	Embedded	CBs concealed by other cloud layers, haze, dust, etc.

Coverage, Table 8-3, is identified as isolated (**ISOL**) meaning less than 1/8th, occasional (**OCNL**) meaning 1/8th to 4/8^{ths}, and frequent (**FRQ**) meaning more than 4/8^{ths} coverage. Isolated and occasional **CB**s are further characterized as embedded (**EMBD**). The chart does not display isolated or scattered cumulonimbus clouds unless they are embedded in other clouds, haze, or dust.

The vertical extent of cumulonimbus layer is specified by top and base heights. Bases that extend below 10,000 feet (the lowest altitude limit of the chart) are encoded **XXX**.

Cumulonimbus clouds (**CB**s) are depicted by enclosed (red) scalloped lines (Figure 8-19). The identification and characterization of each cumulonimbus area appears within or adjacent to the outlined area. If the identification and characterization is adjacent to an outlined area, an arrow points to the appropriate cumulonimbus area.

On significant weather (SIGWX) charts, the inclusion of **CB** or the thunderstorm symbol (Figure 8-3) should be understood to include all weather phenomena normally associated with cumulonimbus or thunderstorm, namely, moderate or severe icing, moderate or severe turbulence, and hail.

Figure 8-19. Mid-Level SIGWX Chart Thunderstorm Examples

8.3.1.2 Jet Streams

A jet stream axis with a wind speed of more than 80 knots is identified by a bold green line (Figure 8-21). An arrowhead is used to indicate wind direction. Double-hatched, light green lines positioned along a jet stream axis identify 20 knot wind speed changes.

Symbols and altitudes are used to further characterize a jet stream axis. A standard wind symbol (light green) is placed at each pertinent position to identify wind velocity. The flight level "FL" in hundreds of feet MSL is placed adjacent to each wind symbol to identify the altitude of the jet stream axis.

Jet stream vertical depth (jet depth) forecasts are included when the maximum speed is 120 knots or more. Jet depth is defined as the vertical depths to the 80 knot wind field above and below the jet stream axis using flight levels.

Figure 8-21. Mid-Level SIGWX Chart Jet stream Example.
Forecast maximum speeds of 100 knots at FL310 at one location and 120 knots at FL290 at another location. At the latter location, the base of the 80 knot wind field is FL210, and the top of the 80 knot wind field is FL340.

8.3.1.3 Tropopause Heights

Tropopause heights are plotted at selected locations on the chart (Figure 8-22). They are enclosed by rectangles and plotted in hundreds of feet MSL. Centers of high (**H**) and low (**L**) tropopause heights are enclosed by polygons and plotted in hundreds of feet MSL.

Figure 8-22. Mid-Level SIGWX Chart Tropopause Height Examples

8.3.1.4 Tropical Cyclones

Tropical cyclones are depicted by the appropriate symbol (Figure 8-23) with the storm's name positioned adjacent to the symbol. Cumulonimbus clouds meeting chart criteria are identified and characterized relative to each storm.

Figure 8-23. Mid-Level SIGWX Chart Tropical Cyclone Examples

8.3.1.5 Moderate or Severe Icing

Areas of moderate or severe icing are depicted by enclosed (red) scalloped lines (Figure 8-24). The identification and characterization of each area appears within or adjacent to the outlined area. If the identification and characterization is adjacent to an outlined area, an arrow points to the appropriate area.

The identification box uses the standard icing symbol (Appendix J). The vertical extent of the icing layer is specified by top and base heights. Bases which extend below the layer of the chart are identified with **XXX**.

Figure 8-24. Mid-Level SIGWX Chart Icing Examples

8.3.1.6 Moderate or Severe Turbulence (in cloud or in clear air)

Forecast areas of moderate or severe turbulence associated with wind shear zones and/or mountain waves are enclosed by bold yellow dashed lines (Figure 8-25). Intensities are identified by standard symbols (Appendix J).

The vertical extent of a turbulence layer is specified by top and base heights, separated by a horizontal line. A turbulence base which extends below the layer of the chart is identified with **XXX**.

Thunderstorm turbulence is not identified.

Figure 8-25. Mid-Level SIGWX Chart Turbulence Examples

Areas of moderate or severe turbulence are also depicted by enclosed (red) scalloped lines (Figure 8-24). The identification and characterization of each area appears within or adjacent to the outlined area. If the identification and characterization is adjacent to an outlined area, an arrow points to the associated area.

Standard turbulence symbols are used (Appendix J). The vertical extent of the turbulence layer is specified by top and base heights. Bases which extend below the layer of the chart are identified with **XXX**.

8.3.1.7 Cloud Coverage (non-cumulonimbus)

Clouds are enclosed within (red) scalloped lines (Figure 8-26). Cloud coverage (non-cumulonimbus) appears within or adjacent to the outlined area. If the cloud coverage is adjacent to an outlined area, an arrow points to the appropriate area.

The cloud coverage symbols are listed in Table 8-4. See Table 8-3 for cumulonimbus cloud coverage.

Table 8-4. Mid-Level SIGWX Chart Cloud Coverage (Non-cumulonimbus)

CODED	MEANING	COVERAGE
SKC	Sky Clear	$0/8^{ths}$
FEW	Few clouds	$1/8^{th}$ to $2/8^{ths}$
SCT	Scattered	$3/8^{ths}$ to $4/8^{ths}$
BKN	Broken	$5/8^{ths}$ to $7/8^{ths}$
OVC	Overcast	$8/8^{ths}$

8.3.1.8 Cloud Type

Table 8-5 shows the contractions used to identify cloud type.

Table 8-5. Mid-Level SIGWX Chart Cloud Types

CODED	MEANING
CI	Cirrus
CC	Cirrocumulus
CS	Cirrostratus
AC	Altocumulus
AS	Altostratus
NS	Nimbostratus
SC	Stratocumulus
ST	Stratus
CU	Cumulus
CB	Cumulonimbus

DEPICTION	MEANING
BKN OVC AS AC 210 ⋀ XXX 190 Ψ XXX	BROKEN ALTOSTRATUS AND OVERCAST ALTOCUMULUS CLOUDS. MODERATE TURBULENCE FROM FL210 TO BELOW FL100. MODERATE ICING FROM FL190 TO BELOW FL100.

Figure 8-26. Mid-Level SIGWX Chart - Example of Moderate or Severe Icing, Moderate or Severe Turbulence (in cloud or in clear air), Clouds, and Cloud Types

8.3.1.9 Volcanic Eruptions

Volcanic eruption sites are identified by a trapezoidal symbol (Figure 8-27). The dot on the base of the trapezoid identifies the location of the volcano. The name of the volcano, as well as the latitude and longitude are noted adjacent to the symbol.

ETNA
37.7N 15.0E

Figure 8-27. Mid-Level SIGWX Chart Volcanic Eruption Example

8.3.1.10 Release of Radioactive Materials

Radioactive materials in the atmosphere are depicted by the standard symbol shown in Figure 8-28. Information on the chart regarding the radioactive material includes the latitude/longitude of the accident site, the date and time of the accident, and a reference to check NOTAMs for further information.

Figure 8-28. Mid-Level SIGWX Chart Release of Radioactive Materials Example

8.3.2 Issuance

The Aviation Weather Center (AWC) in Kansas City has the responsibility, as part of the World Area Forecast Center (WAFC), Washington, to provide global weather forecasts of significant weather phenomena. The AWC issues a 24-hour Mid-Level Significant Weather chart, four times daily, for the North Atlantic Ocean Region (NAT) (Table 8-6). The Mid Level Significant (WIGWX) Chart is found online at: http://aviationweather.gov/products/swm/

Table 8-6. Mid-Level SIGWX Chart Issuance Schedule

North Atlantic Ocean Region (NAT)	Valid Times (UTC)			
	Issued 0800	Issued 1400	Issued 2000	Issued 0200
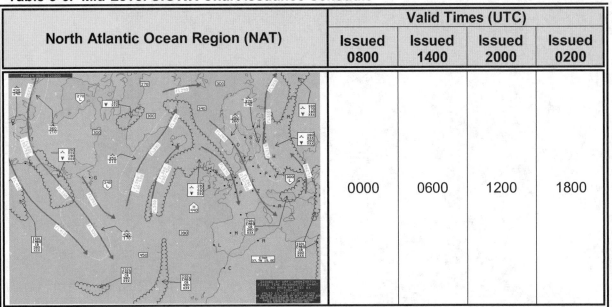	0000	0600	1200	1800

8.3.3 Use

The Mid-Level Significant Weather (SIGWX) Chart is used to determine an overview of selected flying weather conditions between 10,000 feet MSL and FL450. It can be used by airline dispatchers for flight planning and weather briefings before departure and by flight crew members during flight.

Figure 8-29. Mid-Level SIGWX Chart Example

8.4 High-Level Significant Weather (SIGWX) Charts

High-Level Significant Weather (SIGWX) Charts (Figure 8-30) provide a forecast of significant en route weather phenomena over a range of flight levels from FL250 to FL630, and associated surface weather features. Each chart depicts a "snap-shot" of weather expected at the specified valid time. They are available on the Aviation Weather Center (AWC) web site at: http://aviationweather.gov/products/swh/.

Figure 8-30. High-level SIGWX Chart Example

8.4.1 Content

8.4.1.1 Thunderstorms and Cumulonimbus Clouds

The abbreviation **CB** is only included where it refers to the expected occurrence of an area of widespread cumulonimbus clouds, cumulonimbus along a line with little or no space between individual clouds, cumulonimbus embedded in cloud layers, or cumulonimbus concealed by haze. It does not refer to isolated or scattered cumulonimbus not embedded in cloud layers or concealed by haze.

Each cumulonimbus area is identified with **CB** and characterized by coverage, bases and tops. Coverage (Table 8-3) is identified as isolated (**ISOL**) meaning less than 1/8th, occasional (**OCNL**) meaning 1/8th to 4/8ths, and frequent (**FRQ**) meaning more than 4/8ths coverage. Isolated and occasional CBs are further characterized as embedded (**EMBD**). The chart will not display isolated or scattered cumulonimbus clouds unless they are embedded in clouds, haze, or dust.

The vertical extent of cumulonimbus layer is specified by top and base heights. Bases that extend below FL250 (the lowest altitude limit of the chart) are encoded **XXX**.

Cumulonimbus clouds (CBs) are depicted by an enclosed (red) scalloped lines (Figure 8-31). The identification and characterization of each cumulonimbus area will appear within or adjacent to the outlined area. If the identification and characterization is adjacent to an outlined area, an arrow will point to the associated cumulonimbus area.

On significant weather charts, the inclusion of **CB** or the thunderstorm symbol should be understood to include all weather phenomena normally associated with cumulonimbus or thunderstorm, namely, moderate or severe icing, moderate or severe turbulence, and hail.

Figure 8-31. High-Level SIGWX Chart Thunderstorm and Cumulonimbus Cloud Examples

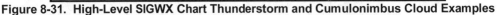

8.4.1.2 Moderate or Severe Turbulence

Forecast areas of moderate or severe turbulence (Figure 8-32) associated with wind shear zones and/or mountain waves are enclosed by bold yellow dashed lines. Intensities are identified by standard symbols (Appendix J).

The vertical extent of turbulence layers is specified by top and base heights, separated by a horizontal line. Turbulence bases which extend below the layer of the chart are identified with **XXX**.

Thunderstorm turbulence is not identified.

DEPICTION	MEANING
1. 380 / 270	MODERATE TURBULENCE FROM FL380 TO FL270.
2. 400 / XXX	MODERATE TO SEVERE TURBULENCE FROM FL400 TO BELOW LOWER LIMIT OF THE PROG (FL250). REFER TO LOW-LEVEL PROG FOR TURBULENCE FORECASTS FOR FL240 AND BELOW.

Figure 8-32. High-Level SIGWX Chart Turbulence Examples

8.4.1.3 Moderate or Severe Icing

Moderate and severe icing (outside of thunderstorms) above FL240 is rare and is not generally forecasted on High-Level Significant Weather Prog charts.

8.4.1.4 Jet Streams

A jet stream axis with a wind speed of more than 80 knots is identified by a bold green line. An arrowhead is used to indicate wind direction. Wind change bars (double-hatched, light green lines) positioned along a jet stream axis identifies 20 knot wind speed changes (Figure 8-33).

Symbols and altitudes are used to further characterize a jet stream axis. A standard wind symbol (light green) is placed at each pertinent position to identify wind velocity. The flight level **FL** in hundreds of feet MSL is placed adjacent to each wind symbol to identify the altitude of the jet stream axis.

Jet stream vertical depth (jet depth) forecasts are included when the maximum speed is 120 knots or more. Jet depth is defined as the vertical depths to the 80 knot wind field above and below the jet stream axis using flight levels. Jet depth information is placed at the maximum speed point only, normally at one point on each jet stream. When the jet stream is very long and there are several wind maxima, then each maximum should include forecasts of the vertical depth.

Figure 8-33. High-Level SIGWX Chart Jet stream Example
Forecast maximum speeds of 100 knots at FL310 at one location and 120 knots at FL290 at another location. At the latter location, the base of the 80 knot wind field it FL210, and the top of the 80 knot wind field is FL340.

8.4.1.5 Tropopause Heights

Tropopause heights are plotted at selected locations on the chart. They are enclosed by rectangles and plotted in hundreds of feet MSL (Figure 8-35). Centers of high (**H**) and low (**L**) tropopause heights are enclosed by polygons and plotted in hundreds of feet MSL.

Figure 8-35. High-Level SIGWX Chart Tropopause Height Examples

8.4.1.6 Tropical Cyclones

Tropical cyclones are depicted by the appropriate symbol (Figure 8-36) with the storm's name positioned adjacent to the symbol. Cumulonimbus clouds meeting chart criteria are identified and characterized relative to each storm.

Figure 8-36. High Level SIGWX Chart Tropical Cyclone Examples

8.4.1.7 Severe Squall Lines

Severe squall lines are lines of CBs with 5/8 coverage or greater. They are identified by long dashed (white) lines with each dash separated by a **V** (Figure 8-37).Cumulonimbus clouds meeting chart criteria are identified and characterized with each squall line.

Figure 8-37. High-Level SIGWX Chart Severe Squall Line Example

8.4.1.8 Volcanic Eruption Sites

Volcanic eruption sites are identified by a trapezoidal symbol (Figure 8-38). The dot on the base of the trapezoid identifies the location of the volcano. The name of the volcano, its latitude, and its longitude are noted adjacent to the symbol.

Figure 8-38. High-Level SIGWX Chart Volcanic Eruption Site Example

8.4.1.9 Widespread Sandstorms and Dust storms

Widespread sandstorms and dust storms are labeled with the appropriate symbol (Appendix I). The vertical extent of sand or dust is specified by top and base heights, separated by a horizontal line. Sand or dust which extends below the lower limit of the chart (FL240) is identified with **XXX** (Figure 8-39).

Figure 8-39. High-Level SIGWX Chart Widespread Sandstorm and Dust Storm Example

8.4.2 Issuance

In accordance with the World Meteorological Organization (WMO) and the World Area Forecast System (WAFS) of the International Civil Aviation Organization (ICAO), High-Level significant weather (SIGWX) forecasts are provided for the en-route portion of international flights. The National Weather Service (NWS) Aviation Weather Center (AWC) in Kansas City, MO provides a suite of SIGWX forecast products for the World Area Forecast Center (WAFC) in Washington, D.C. The charts are available for different ICAO areas around the world as defined in Table 8-7. The charts are not amended.

Table 8-7. High-Level SIGWX Chart Issuance Schedule – WAFC Washington

ICAO Area	Chart Type	Chart Area	Valid Times (UTC)			
			Issued 0800	Issued 1400	Issued 2000	Issued 0200
A Americas	Mercator		0000	0600	1200	1800
B1 Americas/ Africa	Mercator		0000	0600	1200	1800
F Pacific	Mercator		0000	0600	1200	1800
H N America/ Europe	Polar Stereographic		0000	0600	1200	1800
I N Pacific	Polar Stereographic		0000	0600	1200	1800
J S Pacific	Polar Stereographic		0000	0600	1200	1800
M Pacific	Mercator		0000	0600	1200	1800

The WAFC in London, England also issues High-Level Significant Weather (SIGWX) Charts for other geographical areas of the world. Both Washington and London WAFC charts are available online at: http://aviationweather.gov/iffdp/sgwx.shtml

8.4.3 Use

High-Level Significant Weather (SIGWX) Charts are provided for the en route portion of international flights. These products are used directly by airline dispatchers for flight planning and weather briefings before departure and by flight crew members during flight.

Figure 8-40. High-Level SIGWX Chart - ICAO Area A Example

Figure 8-41. High-Level SIGWX Chart - ICAO Area B1 Example

Figure 8-42. High-Level SIGWX Chart - ICAO Area F Example

Figure 8-43. High-Level SIGWX Chart - ICAO Area H Example

Figure 8-44. High-Level SIGWX Chart - ICAO Area I Example

Figure 8-45. High-Level SIGWX Chart - ICAO Area J Example

Figure 8-46. High-Level SIGWX Chart - ICAO Area M Example

9 NEW GENERATION WEATHER PRODUCTS

9.1 Collaborative Convective Forecast Product (CCFP)

The CCFP is a graphical representation of forecast convective occurrence at 4-, 6-, and 8-hours after issuance time (Figure 9-1). Convection, for the purposes of the CCFP forecast, is defined as a polygon of at least 3,000 square miles containing all of the following threshold criteria:

- A coverage of at least 25 percent of echoes with at least 40 dBZ composite reflectivity,
- A coverage of at least 25 percent of echoes with echo top of FL250 or greater, and
- A forecaster confidence of at least 25 percent.

All three threshold criteria must be met for any area of convection 3,000 square miles or greater to be included in a CCFP forecast. This is defined as the minimum CCFP criteria. Any area of convection, which is forecasted to *not* meet all three of these criteria, is *not* included in a CCFP forecast.

The CCFP is intended to be used as a strategic planning tool for air traffic flow management. It aids in the reduction of air traffic delays, reroutes, and cancellations due to significant convection. It is *not* intended to be used for tactical air traffic flow decisions, in the airport terminal environment, or for pilot weather briefing purposes. The graphical representation is subject to annual revision.

Figure 9-1. CCFP Example

9.1.1 Issuance

The CCFP is issued by the Aviation Weather Center (AWC) from March through October for the 48-contiguous states. Canadian forecasts are included on the product and are available for southern Ontario and Quebec between April through September. This area is roughly from north of Wisconsin extending eastward to north of Maine.

The CCFP is issued every 2 hours, eleven times per day. Issuance times are from 08Z to 04Z during standard time and from 07Z to 03Z during daylight savings time. The product can be found on the AWC web page at http://aviationweather.gov/products/ccfp/.

9.1.2 Collaboration

The CCFP is produced from a collaborative effort between public and private meteorologists. The collaboration occurs between meteorologists from the AWC, Center Weather Service Units (CWSU), Meteorological Services of Canada (MSC), commercial airlines offices, and other private weather companies.

9.1.3 Content

Data graphically displayed on the CCFP consist of coverage of convection within a defined polygon, forecaster confidence of convective occurrence, and forecast movement of the convective areas. A data block also displays text information about coverage and confidence as well as forecast echo top and convective growth information.

9.1.3.1 Coverage

The convective coverage within the forecast polygon is represented by the amount of fill within the polygon (Figure 9-2).

- Solid coverage, depicted by solid fill, means 75 to 100 percent of the polygon is forecast to contain convection.

- Medium coverage, defined by medium fill, indicates 40-74 percent of the polygon is forecast to contain convection.

- Sparse coverage, represented by sparse fill, means 25-39 percent of the polygon is forecast to contain convection.

A line of forecast convection, either within a forecast area or alone, is depicted by a solid purple line for solid (75 to 100 percent) or a dashed purple line for medium (40-74 percent) coverage. For a line of convection to be forecast, it must meet the flowing criteria:

- Its length must be at least 100 miles long,

- The width of the line must be 40 nautical miles (NM) wide, and

- For a solid line, greater than 75 percent of the line must be expected to contain convection. For a medium line, 40 to 74 percent of the line must be expected to contain convection.

LINE

Figure 9-2. CCFP Forecast Convective Coverage

9.1.3.2 Confidence

Confidence represents the subjective opinion of the forecasters that the polygon will meet the minimum CCFP threshold criteria. The forecaster's confidence is represented by the color used to depict the polygon (Figure 9-2).

- A blue color represents high forecaster confidence (50-100 percent) the forecast convection will meet the minimum criteria.

- A gray color indicates low forecaster confidence (25-49 percent) the forecast convection will meet the minimum criteria.

Confidence is not to be associated with probability of occurrence.

9.1.3.3 Movement

Forecast movement for each polygon or line is indicated with a gray or blue arrow (Figure 9-3). The arrow points in the direction of forecast movement. A number at the tip of the arrow represents the speed in knots.

Figure 9-3. CCFP Forecast Convective Movement

9.1.3.4 Data Block

A data block is located adjacent to every polygon forecast (Figure 9-4 and Figure 9-5). A thin line connects the data block to the associated forecast area. Each data block contains information about forecast maximum echo tops (TOPS) and convective growth rates (GWTH).

Figure 9-4. CCFP Data Block

Figure 9-5. CCFP Data Block Example

9.1.3.4.1   TOPS

The word, TOPS, is used to depict the forecast maximum echo tops, in thousands of feet MSL, specified by four selected layers listed in Table 9-1. The heights of the forecast echo tops must cover at least 25 percent of the polygon. The exact location of the highest echo top within the polygon cannot be determined.

Table 9-1. CCFP Tops

HEIGHT
TOPS: 100's OF FEET MSL

25000 - 29000	= 290
30000 - 34000	= 340
35000 - 39000	= 390
40000 +	= > 400

9.1.3.4.2   Growth
The contraction, GWTH, is used to depict the forecast average growth rate of the convection. The growth rate applies to both the height and coverage of the echoes (Table 9-2).

Table 9-2. CCFP Growth

GROWTH RATES:

⬆ = POSITIVE
= NO CHANGE
⬇ = NEGATIVE

9.1.3.4.3   Confidence
Confidence depicted on the chart is the confidence the depicted polygon will meet the minimum CCFP criteria (Table 9-3).

Table 9-3. CCFP Confidence

CONFIDENCE:

HIGH 50 - 100%   LOW 25 - 49%

9.1.3.4.4   Coverage
Coverage is used to depict the forecast convective coverage within the polygon (Table 9-4). The coverage represents the percentage of the area forecast to be covered by convection.

Table 9-4. CCFP Coverage

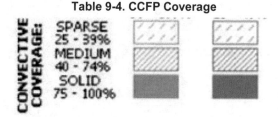

CONVECTIVE COVERAGE:
SPARSE 25 - 39%
MEDIUM 40 - 74%
SOLID 75 - 100%

9.1.4 Strengths and Limitations
The primary strength of the CCFP is it relies on the vital collaborative efforts between several meteorological units in the private and public sector. The process helps produce the best possible convective forecast to assist in strategic air traffic decision-making.

The limitation of the CCFP is it does not include a forecast for all convection. If the convection does not meet the threshold criteria, it is not included in the CCFP. It is not intended to be used as a tactical short-term decision tool.

9.1.5 Use

The CCFP is a strategic planning tool for air traffic flow management in the 4- to 8-hour forecast period.

The product is not intended to be used as a pilot weather briefing tool; however CCFP is available to pilots and aircraft dispatchers as an additional tool for strategic planning.

9.2 Extended Convective Forecast Product (ECFP)

The ECFP Planning Tool (Figure 9-2) is a graphical representation of the forecast probability of thunderstorms. The product identifies graphically where in the United States thunderstorms are likely over the next 72 hours. It is intended to enhance the CCFP. The CCFP is only valid out to 8 hours. This graphical product will use CCFP-style graphics, to facilitate ease of interpretation and use by those already familiar with the CCFP. The product is not a CCFP forecast (it is not forecasting the exact CCFP criteria), but intended to support the long range planning for CCFP type of constraints in the National Airspace System (NAS).

9.2.1 Issuance
The development of the ECFP planning tool was a response to Federal Aviation Administration (FAA) and Industry needs in planning for weather hazards, specifically convection, 1 to 2 days in advance. To meet these planning needs, and to support CCFP planning beyond 8 hours, the ECFP intends to provide traffic planners and collaborators a quick-look forecast of the greatest probability of convection/thunderstorms. By utilizing CCFP-style graphics, users familiar with CCFP can easily determine where traffic constraints are most likely to occur over the next 3 days.

Figure 9-6. ECFP Example

9.2.2 Content
This automated graphical forecast is created from the Short Range Ensemble Forecast (SREF) Calibrated Thunderstorm guidance. Probability of Thunderstorm contours are depicted at 40, 60, and 80 percent probabilities, using CCFP-like shading. Hashed areas represent 40–59 percent probability, solid lined areas represent 60–79 percent probability, and solid blue filled areas represent greater than 80 percent probability.

9.2.3 Use

The ECFP is intended for FAA Traffic Managers at Air Route Traffic Control Centers (ARTCC), FAA Air Traffic Control System Command Center (ATCSCC), airline and aviation industry dispatch and flight planners, as well as commercial weather information providers supporting airline/FAA.

9.2.4 Frequency

The ECFP is available 24/7 with updates issued at 01:00, 07:00, 13:00, and 19:00 UTC each day.

9.3 National Convective Weather Forecast (NCWF)

The National Convective Weather Forecast (NCWF) is a near real-time, high resolution display of current and 1-hour extrapolated forecasts of selected hazardous convective conditions for the conterminous United States. The NCWF may be used in conjunction with the report and forecast information contained within Convective SIGMETs. The NCWF is available for use by General Aviation, aircraft dispatchers, and Traffic Management Units (TMU).

9.3.1 Issuance

The NCWF is issued by the Aviation Weather Center (AWC) and is updated every 5 minutes. The product is available on the Aviation Digital Data Service (ADDS) web page at: http://aviationweather.gov/products/ncwf/.

9.3.2 Content

The NCWF displays current convective hazard fields, 1-hour extrapolated forecast polygons, forecast speed and directions, and echo tops. Previous performance polygons can also be selected for display (Figure 9-7).

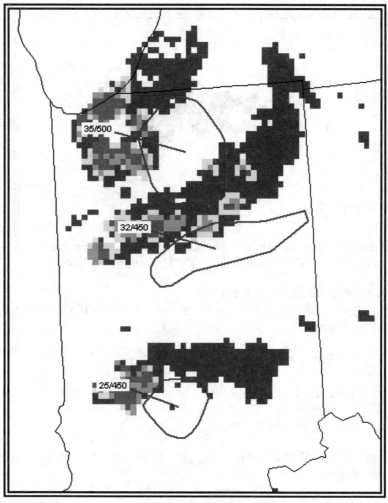

Figure 9-7. NCWF Example

9.3.2.1 Current Convective Hazard Fields

The current convective hazard field is a high-resolution display that identifies selected hazards associated with convective precipitation. The field is created from WSR-88D national reflectivity and echo-top mosaics and cloud-to-ground lightning data.

WSR-88D radar reflectivity data are filtered to identify locations having significant convective precipitation. Reflectivity data with echo tops of less than 17,000 feet MSL are eliminated from the data. This process removes ground clutter and anomalous propagation as well as significantly reduces the amount of stratiform (non-convective) precipitation from the data. Most stratiform precipitation tops are below 17,000 feet. The filter also removes shallow convection with tops below 17,000 feet. Shallow convection is often short-lived but can contain conditions hazardous to aviation and may be embedded in stratiform convection.

Frequencies of cloud-to-ground lightning are added to the filtered radar data to provide a more accurate picture of current hazardous convective conditions.

Current convective hazard fields are color coded according to the convective hazard scale for display on the NCWF (Figure 9-8).

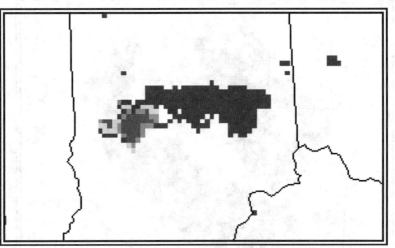

Figure 9-8. NCWF Current Convective Hazard Fields Example

9.3.2.1.1 Convective Hazard Field Scale

The convective hazard field scale uses six hazard levels (Figure 9-10) to characterize hazardous convection conditions.

The six hazard levels are determined by two factors:

- Intensities and maximum tops of WSR-88D reflectivity data, and

- Frequencies of cloud-to-ground lightning.

Higher hazard levels are associated with higher radar reflectivity intensities and higher frequencies of lightning strikes.

The six hazard levels are reduced to four-color codes for display on the NCWF. The relationships between the six hazard levels and four-color codes are summarized in Figure 9-9.

NCWF Hazard Scale		
Level	Color	Effect
6	RED	Thunderstorms may contain any or all
5	RED	of the following: severe turbulence, severe icing,
4	Orange	hail, frequent lightning, tornadoes, and low-level wind shear.
3	Yellow	The risk of hazardous weather generally increases
2	Green	with levels on the NCWF hazard scale
1	Green	

Figure 9-9. NCWF Hazard Scale

9.3.2.2 One-Hour Extrapolated Forecast Polygons

One-hour extrapolated forecast polygons are high-resolution polygons outlining areas expected to be filled by selected convective hazard fields in 1 hour. Extrapolated forecasts depict new locations for the convective hazard fields based on their past movements. Extrapolation forecasts do *not* forecast the development of new convective hazard conditions or the dissipation of existing conditions. Forecasts are provided *only* for convective hazard scale levels 3 or higher. The forecast polygons do not depict specific forecast hazard levels. On Figure 9-10, the light blue polygon denotes the location of the 1-hour forecast convective hazard field.

9.3.2.3 Forecast Speed and Direction

Forecast speed and direction are assigned to current convective hazard fields having a 1-hour extrapolated forecast. A line (or arrow on the AWC JavaScript product) is used to depict the direction of movement (Figure 9-10). The speed in knots is depicted by the first group of two numbers located near the current convective hazard field. The second group of three numbers identifies echo tops.

Forecast speed and direction is only updated every 10 minutes. The larger update time-interval (compared to 5-minute updates for the NCWF) smooths erratic forecast velocities. On Figure 9-10, the forecast direction (depicted by an arrow) is pointing to the southeast and the speed is 25 knots.

9.3.2.4 Echo Tops

Echo tops are assigned to current convective hazard fields having a 1-hour extrapolated forecast. Echo tops are depicted by a group of three numbers located near the current convective hazard field and is plotted in hundreds of feet MSL (Figure 9-10). The first number of the group identifies forecast speed of movement. On Figure 9-10, the echo tops are 45,000 feet MSL.

Figure 9-10. NCWF One-Hour Extrapolated Forecast Polygon, Forecast Movement Velocity, and Echo Tops Example

9.3.2.5 Previous Performance Polygons

Previous performance polygons are magenta polygons displaying the previous hour's extrapolated forecast polygons *with* the current convective hazard fields. A perfect forecast would have the polygons filled with convective hazard scale levels 3 or higher data. Levels 1 and 2 would be outside the polygons. The display of previous performance polygons allows the user to review the accuracy of the previous hour's forecast.

Figure 9-11 depicts current convective hazard fields and previous performance polygons (magenta) valid at 1500Z. The previous performance polygons are the 1-hour extrapolated forecasts made at 1400Z. Although the polygons do not perfectly match the current level 3 and higher hazard fields, the forecasts are still fairly accurate.

Newly developed convective hazard levels 3 and higher do not have previous performance polygons. Extrapolated forecasts do not forecast developing hazardous convective.

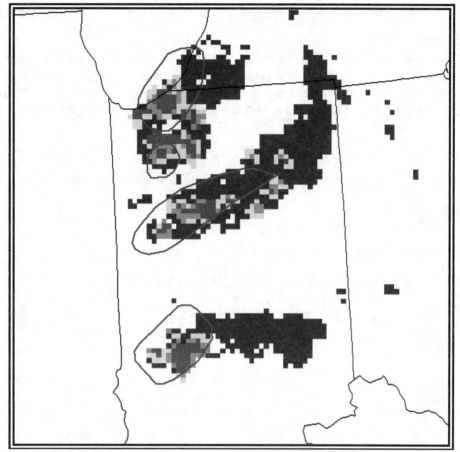

Figure 9-11. NCWF Previous Performance Polygons Example

9.3.3 Strengths and Limitations

9.3.3.1 Strengths
Strengths of the NCWF include:

- Convective hazard fields that agree very well with radar and lightning data,

- Updated every five minutes,

- High-resolution forecasts of convective hazards, and

- Long-lived convective precipitation is well forecast.

9.3.3.2 Limitations
Limitations of the NCWF include:

- Initiation, growth, and decay of convective precipitation are not forecast,

- Short-lived or embedded convection may not be accurately displayed or forecast,

- Low-topped convection that contains little or no lightning may not be depicted,

- Erroneous motion vectors are occasionally assigned to storms, and

- Convective hazard field scales are not identified within the forecast polygons.

9.3.4 Uses of the NCWF

The purpose of the National Convective Weather Forecast (NCWF) is to produce a convective hazard field diagnostic and forecast product based on radar data, echo top mosaics, and lightning data. The target audience includes the FAA and other government agencies, pilots, aircraft dispatchers, aviation meteorologists, and other interested aviation users in the general public.

9.4 Current and Forecast Icing Products (CIP/FIP)

The Current Icing Product (CIP) combines sensor and numerical weather prediction (NWP) model data to provide an hourly three-dimensional diagnosis of the icing environment. This information is displayed on a suite of graphics available for the 48 contiguous United States, much of Canada and Mexico, and their respective coastal waters. The Forecast Icing Product (FIP) provides the same suite of products describing the icing environment in the future and is solely NWP model-based.

The CIP/FIP product suites are automatically produced with no human modifications. Information on the graphics is determined from NWP model output, observational data including WSR-88D radar, satellite, pilot weather reports, surface weather reports, and lightning network data.

9.4.1 Issuance

The CIP and FIP product suites are issued hourly ~15 minutes after the hour by the Aviation Weather Center (AWC). The products are available through the Aviation Digital Data Service (ADDS) web site at: http://www.aviationweather.gov/adds/icing/.

9.4.2 Content

The CIP/FIP product suite consists of 10 graphics including:

- Icing Probability,

- Icing Probability Maximum (Max),

- Icing Severity,

- Icing Severity Max,

- Icing Severity – Probability > 25 percent,

- Icing Severity – Probability > 25 percent Max,

- Icing Severity – Probability > 50 percent,

- Icing Severity – Probability > 50 percent Max,

- Icing Severity plus Supercooled Large Drop (SLD), and

- Icing Severity plus Supercooled Large Drop (SLD) Max.

The CIP/FIP products are generated for individual altitudes from 1,000 feet MSL to Flight Level (FL) 300 at intervals of 1,000 feet. Horizontal resolution is 20 km. FIP products are available at 1, 2, 3, 6, 9, and 12- h forecast lead times. With near-term NWP enhancements, these are planned to change to 500 ft. MSL horizontal and 13 km vertical resolution, and forecasts will be extended to 18 h with 1-h granularity.

The CIP/FIP Max products are a composite product which displays information about icing at all altitudes from 1,000 feet MSL to FL300. Single altitudes are referenced to MSL from 1,000 to

17,000 feet and Flight Levels above 17,000 feet. The ADDS web site allows for access to every other altitude (1,000 FT, 3,000 FT, 5,000 FT, etc...). However, all altitudes can be accessed by use of the Flight Path Tool on the ADDS site.

Icing PIREPs are plotted on a single altitude graphic if the PIREP is within 1,000 feet of the selected altitude and has been observed within 75 minutes of the chart's valid time. On the CIP/FIP Max graphics, PIREPs for all altitudes (i.e. 1,000 feet MSL to FL300) are displayed. However, negative reports of icing are not plotted on the CIP Max products in an effort to reduce clutter. The PIREP legend is located on the bottom of each graphic.

9.4.2.1 Icing Probability

The Icing Probability product (Figure 9-12) displays, at a single altitude, the probability of icing. Probabilities range from 0 percent (no icing expected) to 85 percent or greater (nearly certain icing).

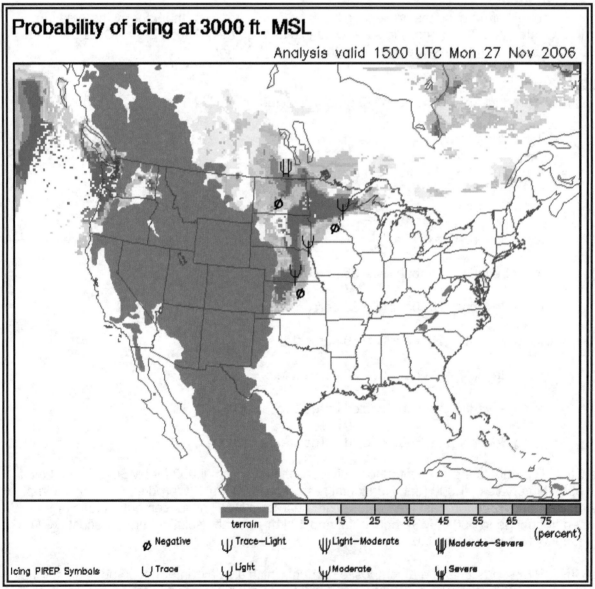

Figure 9-12. CIP/FIP Icing Probability (3,000 feet MSL) Example

"Cool" colors represent low probabilities and "warm" colors represent higher probabilities. Probabilities do not reach 100 percent because the data used to determine the probability of icing cannot diagnose, with absolute certainty, the presence of icing conditions at any location and altitude. White regions indicate that the probability of icing is zero. Brown regions indicate where higher-elevation terrain extends above the altitude of the particular graphic.

9.4.2.2 Icing Probability—Maximum

The Icing Probability - Maximum graphic (Figure 9-13) displays the probability of icing at *all* altitudes from 1,000 feet MSL to FL300. Probabilities range from 0 percent (no icing expected) to 85 percent or greater (nearly certain icing).

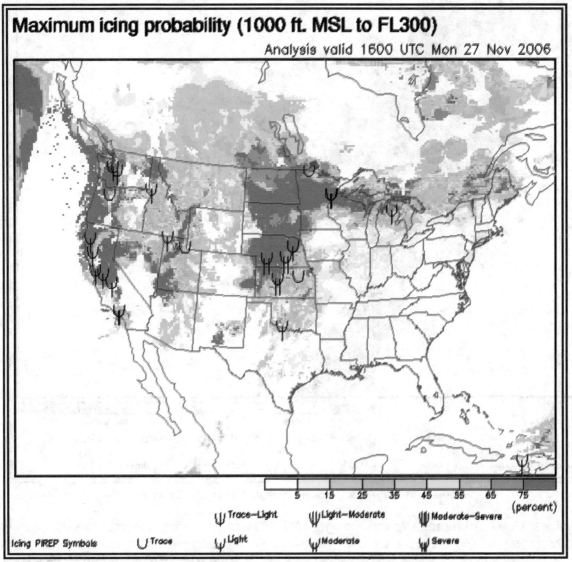

Figure 9-13. CIP/FIP Icing Probability – Max Example

"Cool" colors represent low probabilities and "warm" colors represent higher probabilities. Probabilities do not reach 100 percent because the data used to determine the probability of icing cannot diagnose, with absolute certainty, the presence of icing conditions at any location and altitude. White regions indicate the probability of icing is zero.

9.4.2.3 Icing Severity

The Icing Severity product (Figure 9-14) depicts, at a single altitude, the intensity of icing expected at locations where the Icing Probability product depicts possible icing. Icing intensity is displayed using icing intensity categories: trace, light, moderate, and heavy.

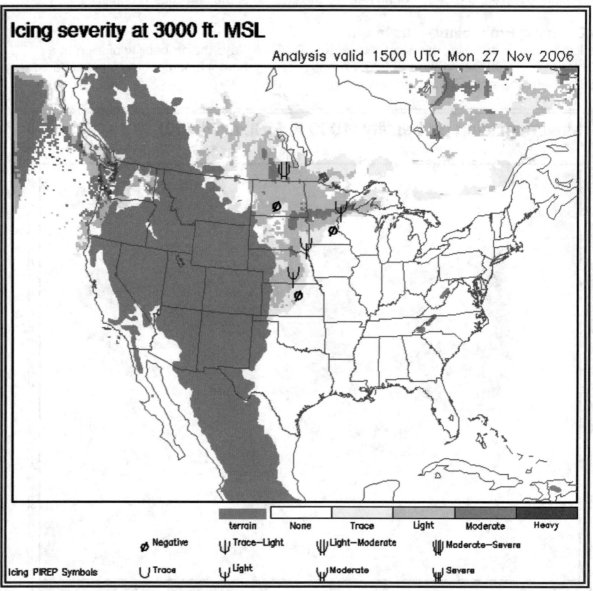

Figure 9-14. CIP/FIP Icing Severity (3,000 feet MSL) Example

The lightest blue color represents trace icing. As the blue-color shades become darker, the icing intensity increases. The darkest blue color represents heavy icing. White regions indicate where no probability of icing exists and, therefore, no intensity is necessary. Brown regions indicate where higher-elevation terrain extends above the altitude of the particular graphic.

9.4.2.4 Icing Severity - Maximum

The Icing Severity - Maximum product (Figure 9-15) displays the intensity of icing at all altitudes from 1,000 feet MSL to FL300. Icing intensity is displayed using icing intensity categories: trace, light, moderate, and heavy.

Figure 9-15. CIP/FIP Icing Severity – Max Example

The lightest blue color represents trace icing. As the blue color shades become darker, the icing intensity increases. The darkest blue color represents heavy icing. White regions indicate where no probability of icing exists and, therefore, no intensity is necessary.

9.4.2.5 Icing Severity – Probability > 25 percent

The Icing Severity – Probability > 25 percent product (Figure 9-16) depicts, at a single altitude, where a 26 to 100 percent probability exists for the indicated icing intensity. Icing intensity is displayed using icing intensity categories: trace, light, moderate, and heavy.

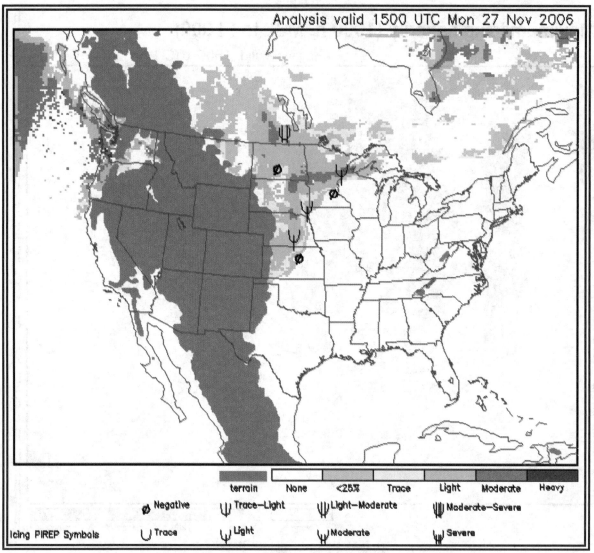

Figure 9-16. CIP/FIP Icing Severity Probability >25 percent Example

The lightest blue color represents trace icing. As the blue color shades become darker, the icing intensity increases. The darkest blue color represents heavy icing. White regions indicate where no probability of icing exists and, therefore, no intensity is necessary. Brown regions indicate higher-elevation terrain extending above the altitude of the particular graphic. A gray color is used to mask the intensity pixels where the probability of icing is 25 percent or less.

9.4.2.6 Icing Severity – Probability > 25 percent - Maximum

The Icing Severity – Probability > 25 percent - Maximum product (Figure 9-17) depicts, at all altitudes from 1,000 feet MSL to FL300, where the probability of the indicated icing intensity is 26 to 100 percent. Icing intensity is displayed using icing intensity categories: trace, light, moderate, heavy.

Figure 9-17. CIP/FIP Icing Severity Probability >25 percent Example

The lightest blue color represents trace icing. As the blue color shades become darker, the icing intensity increases. The darkest blue color represents heavy icing. White regions indicate where no probability of icing exists and, therefore, no intensity is necessary. A gray color is used to mask the intensity pixels where the probability of icing is 25 percent or less.

9.4.2.7 Icing Severity – Probability > 50 percent
The Icing Severity – Probability > 50 percent product (Figure 9-18) depicts, at a single altitude, where the probability of the indicated icing intensity 51 to 100 percent. Icing intensity is displayed using icing intensity categories: trace, light, moderate, and heavy.

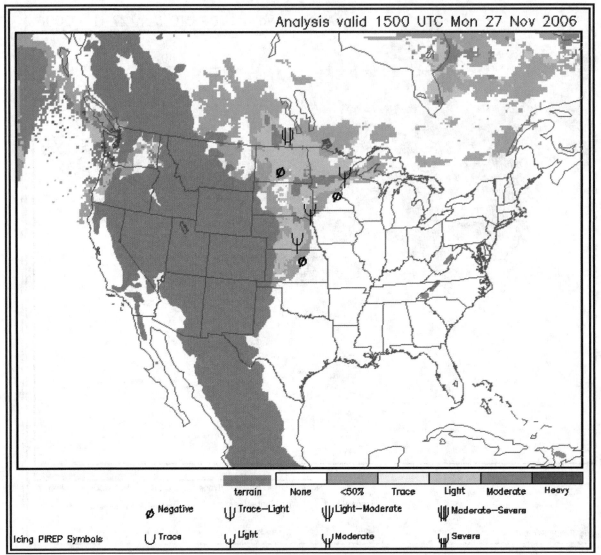

Figure 9-18. CIP/FIP Icing Severity Probability > 50 percent Example

The lightest blue color represents trace icing. As the blue color shades become darker, the icing intensity increases. The darkest blue color represents heavy icing. White regions indicate where no probability of icing exists and, therefore, no intensity is necessary. Brown regions indicate where higher-elevation terrain extends above the altitude of the particular graphic. A gray color is used to mask the intensity pixels where the probability of icing is 50 percent or less.

9.4.2.8 Icing Severity – Probability > 50 percent - Maximum

The Icing Severity – Probability > 50 percent - Maximum product (Figure 9-19) depicts, at all altitudes from 1,000 feet MSL to FL300, where the probability of the indicated icing intensity is 51 to 100 percent. Icing intensity is displayed using icing intensity categories: trace, light, moderate, and heavy.

Figure 9-19. CIP/FIP Icing Severity Probability > 50 percent - Max Example

The lightest blue color represents trace icing. As the blue color shades become darker, the icing intensity increases. The darkest blue color represents heavy icing. White regions indicate where no probability of icing exists and, therefore, no intensity is necessary. A gray color is used to mask the intensity pixels where the probability of icing is 50 percent or less.

9.4.2.9 Icing Severity plus Supercooled Large Drops (SLD)

The Icing Severity plus Supercooled Large Drops (SLD) product (Figure 9-20) depicts, at a single altitude, the intensity of icing expected as well as locations where a threat for SLD exists.

SLD is defined as supercooled water droplets larger than 50 micrometers in diameter. These size droplets include freezing drizzle and/or freezing rain aloft. SLD, which are outside the icing certification envelopes (14 CFR part 25 Appendix C), can be particularly hazardous to some aircraft.

Icing intensity is displayed using icing intensity categories: trace, light, moderate, and heavy.

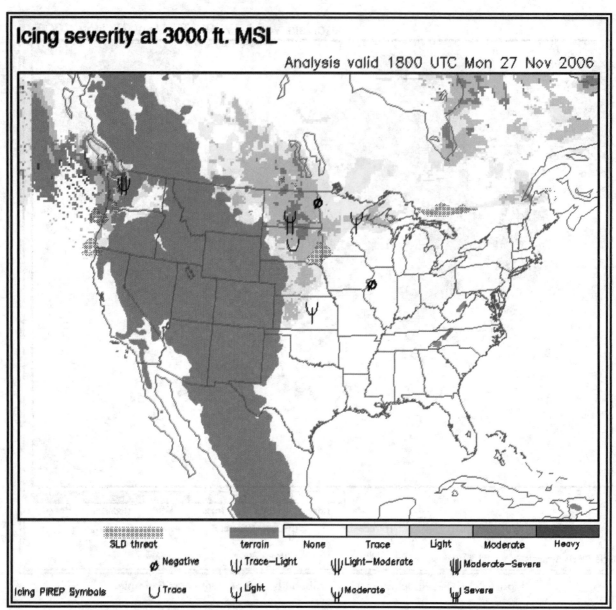

Figure 9-20. CIP/FIP Icing Severity plus Supercooled Large Drops (SLD) Example

The lightest blue color represents trace icing. As the blue color shades become darker, the icing intensity increases. The darkest blue color represents heavy icing. White regions indicate where no probability of icing exists and, therefore, no intensity is necessary. Brown regions indicate where higher-elevation terrain extends above the altitude of the particular graphic. Locations where a threat for SLD exists are depicted with red hatching.

9.4.2.10   Icing Severity plus Supercooled Large Drops (SLD) - Maximum

The SLD-Maximum product (Figure 9-21) depicts at all altitudes, between 1,000 feet MSL and FL300, the intensity of icing expected as well as locations where a threat for SLD exists.

SLD is defined as supercooled water drops larger than 50 micrometers in diameter. These size drops include freezing drizzle and/or freezing rain aloft. SLD, which are outside the icing certification envelopes (14 CFR part 25 Appendix C), can be particularly hazardous to some aircraft.

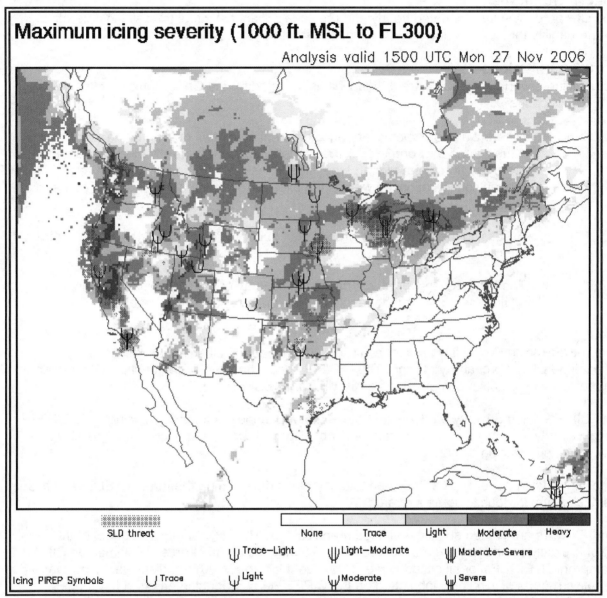

Figure 9-21. CIP/FIP Icing Severity plus Supercooled Large Droplets (SLD) – Max Example

The lightest blue color represents trace icing. As the blue color shades become darker, the icing intensity increases. The darkest blue color represents heavy icing. White regions indicate where no probability of icing exists and, therefore, no intensity is necessary. Locations where a threat for SLD exists are depicted with red hatching.

9.4.3 Strengths and Limitations

9.4.3.1 Strengths
The CIP product suite is updated hourly and provides a diagnostic tool to assist in determining the probability for icing, the intensity of icing, and the threat for SLD.

9.4.3.2 Limitations
Actual icing severity may be different than what is depicted on the CIP graphics and plotted PIREPS because:

- Different aircraft types experience different severities of icing in the same atmospheric environments. Severity definitions are currently pilot-based and thus are a function of the aircraft type, flight phase (takeoff/landing, cruise, etc.), aircraft configuration, as well as the pilot's experience and perception of the icing hazard.

- Assessing the amount and drop size of supercooled liquid water (SLW) in the atmosphere is difficult.

- The Icing Severity products depict the severity of the meteorological icing environment and *not* the resultant icing that may occur on the aircraft.

9.4.4 Uses
The CIP/FIP Icing Probability product can be used to identify the current and forecast three-dimensional probability of icing. The CIP/FIP should be used in conjunction with the report and forecast information contained in an AIRMET and SIGMET.

The CIP/FIP Icing Severity product can be used to determine the intensity of icing. The CIP/FIP Icing Severity – Probability > 25 percent or Probability > 50 percent depicts the probability of a given intensity of icing occurring.

Finally, the Icing Severity plus SLD product can help in determining the threat of SLD, which is particularly hazardous to some aircraft.

Icing PIREPs are plotted on single altitude graphics if the PIREP is within 1,000 feet of the graphic's altitude and has been observed within 75 minutes of the chart's valid time. On CIP/FIP Max product, PIREPs for all altitudes (i.e. 1,000 feet MSL to FL300) are displayed. However, negative reports of icing are not plotted on the CIP/FIP Max product in an effort to reduce clutter. The PIREP legend is located on the bottom of each graphic.

9.5 Graphical Turbulence Guidance (GTG2)

The Graphical Turbulence Guidance (GTG) product suite provides a three-dimensional diagnosis and forecast of Clear Air Turbulence (CAT) potential. The GTG is created using a combination of computer model output and turbulence observations. The GTG product suite, which consists of the GTG analysis and forecast and Composite analysis and forecast, is automatically generated with no human modifications. It should be used in conjunction with the report and forecast information contained in an AIRMET and SIGMET. The GTG is available for the 48 contiguous states, much of Canada and Mexico and their respective coastal waters.

9.5.1 Issuance

The GTG analysis is issued hourly. The 3-, 6-, 9-, and 12-hour forecasts are issued every three hours beginning at 00Z. For example, a forecast suite issued at 0600Z would have valid times at 0900Z, 1200Z, 1500Z, and 1800Z respectively. The GTG Analysis and Forecasts, along with the Composite products, are issued by the Aviation Weather Center (AWC) and are available through the Aviation Digital Data Service (ADDS) Web site at: http://aviationweather.gov/adds/turbulence/.

9.5.2 Content

9.5.2.1 GTG Analysis and Forecast

The GTG Analysis and Forecast graphics depict the location and intensity of potential Clear Air Turbulence (CAT) (Figure 9-22). Standard intensity terminology is used. The GTG output is available for 1,000-foot vertical intervals between 10,000 feet MSL and FL450. ADDS turbulence page displays every second level starting at 10,000 feet MSL, while the ADDS Flight Path Tool provides access to all levels.

GTG2 - Turbulence forecast at FL250

Valid 1300 UTC Fri 18 Oct 2013   00-hr forecast from 1300 UTC 18 Oct

None   Light   Moderate or greater

Figure 9-22. GTG Example

9.5.2.2 GTG Composite Analysis and Forecast

The GTG Composite products display the *maximum* intensity of potential turbulence between 10,000 feet MSL and FL450 (Figure 9-23). In other words, at any given location, the displayed value represents the maximum potential turbulence between 10,000 feet MSL and FL450. Single altitude graphics must be examined to determine the altitude of the potential turbulence.

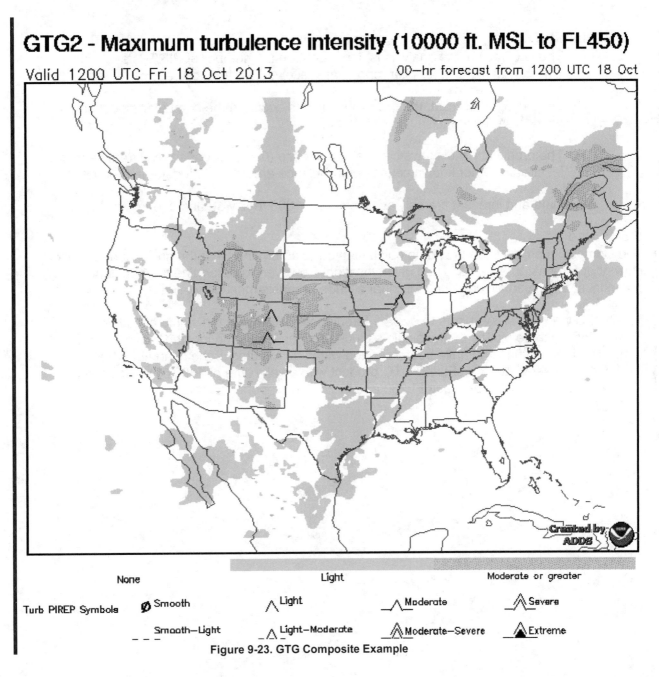

Figure 9-23. GTG Composite Example

9.5.3 Strengths and Limitations

The GTG provides an hourly, high resolution analysis and forecast of clear-air eddy dissipation rate (EDR) at and above 10,000 feet MSL. However, the product is only for turbulence associated with upper level fronts and jet streams while other known causes of turbulence are not forecasted.

9.5.3.1 Strengths

- The product is issued hourly

- Turbulence is plotted to a high resolution.

9.5.3.2 Limitations

- The accuracy of the analysis is dependent on the number of PIREPs available. Typically at night fewer pilot reports are received, so the accuracy decreases.

- For the GTG forecast, the product is only as accurate the computer model output used to create them.

- The product only displays clear-air turbulence (CAT) for upper-level fronts and the jet stream. Other known causes of turbulence are not included in the product.

- Data and forecast are only available for 11,000 feet MSL and above.

9.5.4 Use

The Composite product can provide a quick method to determine what the greatest potential of current or forecast turbulence is at a given location. However, to determine the turbulence potential at any given altitude, the individual altitude products must be viewed.

The ADDS web site allows users to overlay turbulence PIREPS on the single altitude graphics. For the PIREP to be plotted on the single altitude product, it must be located within 1,000 feet vertically of the altitude and have been reported within 90 minutes of the chart time. For example, if a user viewed the FL240 GTG product with a valid time of 1400Z the displayed PIREPS could be located between FL230 and FL250 and reported between 1230Z and 1400Z.

9.6 Meteorological Impact Statement (MIS)

An MIS is an unscheduled flow control and flight operations planning forecast issued by Center Weather Service Units (CWSUs) (Figures 9-24 and 9-25 and Table 9-5). It is a forecast and briefing product for personnel at Air Route Traffic Control Centers (ARTCCs), Air Traffic Control System Command Center (ATCSCC), Terminal Radar Approach Control Facilities (TRACONS) and Airport Traffic Control Towers (ATCTs) responsible for making flow control-type decisions.

An MIS may be tailored to meet the unique requirements of the host ARTCC. These special requirements will be coordinated between the host ARTCC and the CWSU.

MISs are available on the Aviation Weather Center (AWC) Web site at: http://aviationweather.gov/products/cwsu/.

9.6.1 Valid Period
An MIS is valid up to 12 hours after issuance time and details weather conditions expected to adversely impact air traffic flow in the CWSU area of responsibility. The MIS can be immediately effective for existing conditions when CWSU operations begin or for rapidly deteriorating conditions or be effective up to 2 hours in advance of expected conditions.

9.6.2 MIS Criteria
An MIS enables Air Traffic Control (ATC) facility personnel to include the impact of specific weather conditions in their flow control decision-making. At a minimum, an MIS should be issued when:

- Any of the following conditions occur, are forecast to occur, and, if previously forecast, are no longer expected:

    - Conditions meeting convective SIGMET criteria (Section 5.1.8)

    - Icing - moderate or greater

    - Turbulence - moderate or greater

    - Heavy precipitation

    - Freezing precipitation

    - Conditions at or approaching Low Instrument Flight Rules (IFR)

    - Surface winds/gusts >30 knots

    - Low Level Wind Shear (surface - 2,000 feet)

    - Volcanic ash, dust storms, or sandstorms; and

    - In the forecaster's judgment, the conditions listed above, or any others, will adversely impact the flow of air traffic within the ARTCC area of responsibility.

9.6.3 MIS Issuance

MIS phenomena forecasts use the location reference point identifiers depicted on the In-Flight Advisory Plotting Chart (Appendix F), and include the height, extent, and movement of the conditions. MIS product issuances are numbered sequentially beginning at Midnight local time each day. The MIS is disseminated and stored as a "replaceable" product. Therefore, each issuance will contain the details of all pertinent known conditions meeting MIS issuance criteria, including ongoing conditions described in previously issued MISs.

The MIS is for internal use by ARTCC personnel, including Traffic Management Unit (TMU) and TRACON as needed. The MIS is not intended for use by pilots or dispatchers.

9.6.4 Format

Figure 9-24. Meteorological Impact Statement (MIS) Decoding Example

Table 9-5. Meteorological Impact Statement (MIS) – Decoding

LINE	CONTENT	DESCRIPTION
1	ZFW	ARTCC Identification
	MIS	Product type
	01	Issuance number
	VALID 190200-191200	Valid period UTC date/time
2	...FOR ATC PLANNING PURPOSES ONLY...	Product use statement
3	FROM OKC TO CDS TO GAG TO END TO OKC	Phenomenon location
4	LLWS BLO 020 AGL DUE TO LLJ. CONDS GRDLY IPVG AFT 10Z	Phenomenon description

Any remarks such as "SEE CONVECTIVE SIGMET 8W"; "NO UPDATES AVBL AFT 0230Z"; and forecaster initials and/or facility identifier may be placed at the end of the MIS.

If the phenomenon described in an MIS is no longer expected, a cancellation MIS message may be issued. The FAA header does not contain an issuance number. If the phenomenon described in the MIS is expected to continue beyond the operating hours of the CWSU, then the remark "NO UPDATES AFT ttttZ" (where "ttttZ" is the UTC closing time of the CWSU) is added at the text end.

9.6.5 Examples

```
ZOA MIS 01 VALID 041415-041900
...FOR ATC PLANNING PURPOSES ONLY...
FOR SFO BAY AREA
BR/FG WITH CEILING BLW 005 AND VIS OCNL BLW 1SM.
ZOA CWSU
```

Meteorological Impact Statement issued by the Freemont, California CWSU. First MIS issuance of the day, valid from the 4th day of the month at 1415 UTC, to the 4th day of the month at 1900 UTC. For air traffic control planning purposes only. For the San Francisco Bay Area...mist and fog with ceilings below 500 feet MSL and visibility occasionally below 1 statute mile.

```
ZOA MIS 02 VALID 041650
...FOR ATC PLANNING PURPOSES ONLY...
FOR SFO BAY AREA
CNL ZOA MIS 01. CONDS HAVE IMPRD.
ZOA CWSU
```

Meteorological Impact Statement issued by the Freemont, California CWSU. The second MIS issuance of the day, valid the 4th day of the month at 1650 UTC. For air traffic control planning purposes only. For the San Francisco Bay Area. Cancel Freemont, California Meteorological Impact Statement number 1. Conditions have improved.

```
ZID MIS 03 VALID 041200-042330
...FOR ATC PLANNING PURPOSES ONLY...
FROM IND TO 17WSW APE TO LOZ TO 13NE PXV TO IND
TIL 21Z MOD TURB FL310-390 DUE TO JTST WS.
ZID W OF A LINE FM FWA TO BWG
AFT 18Z OCNL SEV TSGR TOPS TO FL450. MOV FM 24035KT. MAX SFC WINDS
60KT.
ZID E OF A LINE FM FWA TO 35SE BKW
MOD MXD ICE IN CLDS/PRECIPITATION 020-120. CONDS ENDING W OF
A 40S CLE TO 20NE BKW LINE BY 19Z.
ZID CWSU
```

Meteorological Impact Statement issued by the Indianapolis, Indiana CWSU. The third MIS issuance of the day, valid from the 4th day of the month at 1200 UTC to the 4th day of the month at 2330 UTC. For air traffic control planning purposes only. From Indianapolis, Indiana to 17 nautical miles west-southwest of Appleton, Ohio to London, Kentucky to 13 nautical miles northeast of Pocket City, Indiana to Indianapolis, Indiana. Until 21Z, moderate turbulence between flight level 310 and flight level 390 due to jet stream wind shear.

For the Indianapolis ARTCC airspace west of a line from Fort Wayne, Indiana to Bowling Green, Kentucky. After 18Z, occasional severe thunderstorms, hail, tops to flight level 450. Moving from 240 degrees at 35 knots. Maximum surface winds 60 knots.

For the Indianapolis, Indiana ARTCC airspace east of a line from Fort Wayne, Indiana to 35 nautical miles southeast of Beckley, West Virginia. Moderate mixed icing in clouds and precipitation between 2,000 feet to 12,000 feet MSL. Conditions ending west of a line from 40 nautical miles south of Cleveland, Ohio to 20 nautical miles northeast of Beckley, West Virginia by 1900Z.

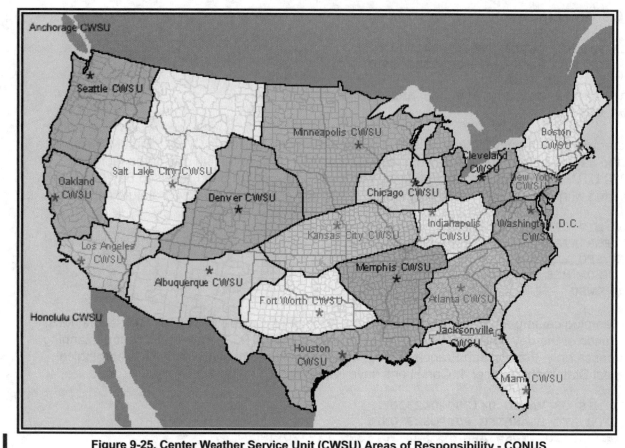

Figure 9-25. Center Weather Service Unit (CWSU) Areas of Responsibility - CONUS

Figure 9-26. CWSU Anchorage, AK (PAZA) Area of Responsibility

9.7 Ceiling and Visibility Analysis (CVA)

The Ceiling and Visibility Analysis (CVA) product provides a real-time analysis of current observed and estimated C&V (ceiling and visibility) conditions across the continental United States. The product is primarily intended to help the general aviation pilot (particularly the Visual Flight Rules (VFR)-only pilot) avoid IFR conditions. However, CVA's overview of ceiling and visibility conditions can be useful to others involved in flight planning or weather briefing.

9.7.1 Issuance
CVA is issued every five minutes and is available through the Aviation Weather Center's (AWC) Aviation Digital Data Service (ADDS) Web site at: http://aviationweather.gov/add/cv.

9.7.2 Content
CVA presents information via a full-CONUS graphic and 18 regional graphics. Each graphic is rendered on a horizontal grid of 5 km resolution and shows viewer-selectable representations of ceiling height above ground level (AGL), surface visibility in statute miles (sm) and FAA flight category designation.

Each regional display includes an overlay of station plots showing the current ceiling and visibility observations reported at selected METAR stations. To avoid overcrowding, the overlay shows only a subset of the total number of stations available.

9.7.2.1 CVA Ceiling Analysis
The CVA Ceiling Analysis uses observed and estimated ceiling heights as follows:

At display points corresponding to METAR locations, CVA uses the ceiling values observed by the nearest METAR.

At display points between METAR locations (where there are no direct observations), CVA uses estimated ceiling values derived by adjusting the ceiling observation from the nearest METAR to take into account intervening changes in terrain height. When corresponding **Geostationary Operational Environmental Satellite (**GOES) satellite observations yield an unambiguous indication that no cloud is present, adjusted ceiling observations are reset to indicate clear conditions.

At display points where observed or estimated ceiling height is less than 200 ft. AGL, CVA reports "Possible Terrain Obstruction."

The CVA Ceiling Analysis graphic is rendered as follows:

- Ceiling less than 1000 ft. AGL – pale yellow.

- Ceiling greater than or equal to 1000 ft. AGL – pale blue.

- Ceiling less than 200 ft. AGL and Possible Terrain Obstruction – orange.

Figure 9-27 shows a CONUS-scale CVA Ceiling Analysis. Figure 9-28 shows a regional-scale Ceiling Analysis.

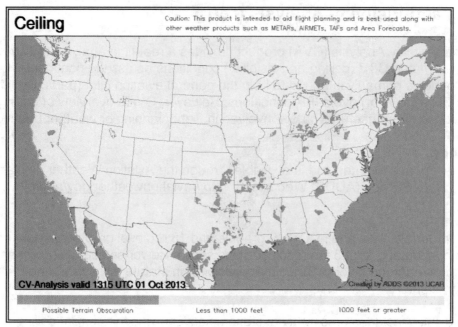

Figure 9-27. CONUS display of CVA Ceiling Analysis.

Figure 9-28. Regional display of CVA Ceiling Analysis.

9.7.2.2 CVA Visibility Analysis

The CVA Visibility Analysis (shown as a regional view in Figure 9-29) reports the observed visibility at the nearest METAR. The graphic is rendered as follows:

- Surface visibility less than 3 sm – pale yellow

- Surface visibility greater than or equal to 3 sm – pale blue

Figure 9-29. Regional display of CVA Visibility Analysis.

9.7.2.3 CVA Flight Category Analysis

The CVA Flight Category Analysis (shown as a regional view in Figure 9-30) uses observed and estimated ceiling and visibility values to report the FAA flight category at each display point. The graphic is rendered as follows:

- VFR – pale blue: Ceiling greater than or equal to 1000 ft. AGL and visibility greater than or equal to 3 sm.

- IFR – pale yellow: Ceiling less than 1000 ft. AGL and/or visibility less than 3 sm.

- Ceiling less than 200 ft. AGL and Possible Terrain Obstruction – orange.

Figure 9-30. Regional display of CVA Flight Category Analysis. Areas of possible terrain obscuration (indicated by estimated ceiling less than 200 ft. AGL) are also shown.

9.7.3 Strengths and Limitations

9.7.3.1 CVA Strengths

- CVA's area-wide graphics highlight observed and estimated IFR, VFR, and possible ground obscuration conditions, enabling a user's quick recognition of ceiling and visibility hazards, as represented by existing observational tools.

- CVA is issued every 5 minutes using the most current METAR and GOES satellite observations available. These rapid updates enhance recognition of trends when conditions are changing. CVA incorporates "special" METAR observations as they are issued.

- CVA fills a gap in existing presentation of C&V information. No other NWS product provides analyzed C&V guidance with comparable spatial and temporal resolution.

9.7.3.2 CVA Limitations

- CVA is an analysis of estimated real-time conditions only. It is not a forecast and cannot be used in place of a forecast.

- CVA must only be used with products such as METARs, TAFs, AIRMETs, and Area Forecasts.

- CVA's representation of ceiling and visibility conditions in regions between METARS (where direct observations are unavailable) can be significantly in error. As distance from the nearest METAR increases, the uncertainty in represented conditions increases.

- Impacted ceiling and visibility conditions can be highly localized and smaller in scale than the 5 km grid used to convey CVA information. Thus, small-scale variations in C&V conditions may not be represented by CVA, even in regions close to observing stations.

9.7.4 Use

General aviation pilots, weather briefers and others involved in flight planning can use CVA as a companion to METARS, TAFs, AIRMETs, and Area Forecasts to help them recognize and avoid IFR conditions. Along with the foregoing weather information sources, CVA can aid IFR avoidance and escape for the en route pilot who inadvertently encounters IFR conditions.

Airmen and flight planners must exercise judgment when using CVA information, as it is based in recent weather information and calculated estimations. Degrading conditions are more likely as the distance and time increase from the station's reported weather.

10 APPENDIX A: DEFINITION OF COMMON TERMS USED IN EN ROUTE FORECASTS AND ADVISORIES

Table A-1. Definition of Common Terms Used in En route Forecasts and Advisories (FA, SIGMET, AIRMET, TCA, VAA, ROFOR)

Contraction	Translation	Definition
EMBD	Embedded thunderstorms or cumulonimbus	Thunderstorms or cumulonimbus (CB) clouds that are embedded in cloud layers or concealed by haze.
EXTREME TURB	Extreme Turbulence	Turbulence in which aircraft is violently tossed about and is practically impossible to control. It may cause structural damage.
FIR	Flight Information Region	An airspace of defined dimensions within which flight information service and alerting service are provided.
FL	Flight Level	A surface of constant atmospheric pressure which is related to a specific pressure datum, 1013.2 hectopascals (hPa), and is separated from other such surfaces by specific pressure intervals.
FRQ	Frequent thunderstorms or cumulonimbus	Consisting of elements with little or no separation between adjacent thunderstorms with a maximum spatial coverage greater than 75 percent of the area affected by the phenomena at a fixed time or during the period of validity.
IMC	Instrument Meteorological Conditions	Ceiling greater than or equal to 500 feet to less than 1,000 feet and/or visibility greater than or equal to 1 to less than 3 miles. LIMC is a sub-category of IMC, thus, IMC conditions are ceiling less than 1,000 feet and /or visibility less than 3 miles.
ISOL	Isolated thunderstorms or cumulonimbus	Consisting of individual features affecting an area with a maximum spatial coverage less than 50 percent of the area affected by the phenomena at a fixed time or during the period of validity.
LINE TS	Line (of thunderstorms)	A line of thunderstorms being at least 60 miles long with thunderstorms affecting at least 40 percent of its length
LIMC	Low Instrument Meteorological Conditions	Ceiling less than 500 feet and/or visibility less than 1 SM. LIMC is a sub-category of Instrument Meteorological Conditions.
MVMC	Marginal Visual Meteorological Conditions	Ceiling greater than or equal to 1,000 feet to less than or equal to 3,000 feet and/or visibility greater than or equal to 3 to less than or equal to 5 miles.
MOD ICE	Moderate Icing	The rate of accumulation is such that even short encounters become potentially hazardous and use of deicing/anti-icing equipment or diversion is necessary.
MOD TURB	Moderate Turbulence	Turbulence that causes changes in attitude (pitch, roll, yaw) and/or altitude, but the aircraft remains in positive control at all times. It usually causes variations in indicated airspeed.

Contraction	Translation	Definition
MT OBSC	Mountain Obscuration	Conditions over significant portions of mountainous geographical areas are such that pilots in flight should not expect to maintain visual meteorological conditions or visual contact with mountains or mountain ridges near their route of flight.
OBSC	Obscured thunderstorm or cumulonimbus	Obscured by haze, smoke or cloud or cannot be readily seen due to darkness.
OCNL	Occasional thunderstorms or cumulonimbus	An area with a maximum spatial coverage between 50 and 75 percent of the area affected by the phenomena at a fixed time of during the period of validity.
SCT	Scattered	25 to 50 percent of area affected.
SEV ICE	Severe Icing	The rate of accumulation is such that normal deicing/anti-icing equipment fails to reduce or control the hazard. Immediate diversion is necessary.
SEV TURB	Severe Turbulence	Turbulence that causes large, abrupt changes in altitude and/or attitude. It usually causes large variations in indicated airspeed. Aircraft may be momentarily out of control.
VMC	Visual Meteorological Conditions	Ceiling greater than 3,000 feet and visibility greater than 5 miles.
VOLCANIC ERUPTION	Volcanic Eruption	A volcano eruption has occurred when an eruption report is received from a volcano observatory. A volcanic eruption is also considered to have occurred regardless of volcano observatory notification if reported by PIREP, or ground observer, or if remote sensing data indicates that an eruption has occurred based on satellite imagery or WSR-88D radar data or any other reliable sources are identified.
VOLCANIC ASH	Volcanic Ash	Any ash that can be seen by any one or more of the following: satellite imagery (visible, IR, multi channel or TOMS), PIREPs, ground observations, radar and VAFTAD (In the event volcanic ash is entrained in clouds, the volcanic ash will be treated as visible using the VAFTAD as guidance).
WDLY SCT	Widely Scattered	Less than 25 percent of area affected
WDSPR	Widespread	50 percent or greater of the area affected

Appendix A: Definition of Common Terms

11 APPENDIX B: CONTRACTIONS AND ACRONYMS

A

AAA	(or AAB, AAC…etc., in sequence) Amended meteorological message (message type designator)
AAWU	Alaskan Aviation Weather Unit
ABNDT	Abundant
ABNML	Abnormal
ABT	About
ABV	Above
AC	Altocumulus or Convective Outlook
ACARS	Aircraft communication and addressing system
ACC	Altocumulus Castellanus
ACCID	Notification of an aircraft accident
ACCUM	Accumulate
ACFT	Aircraft
ACPY	Accompany
ACRS	Across
ACSL	Altocumulus Standing Lenticular
ACT	Active or activated or activity
ACYC	Anticyclone
ADA	Advisory area
ADDN	Addition or additional
ADJ	Adjacent
ADQT	Adequate
ADQTLY	Adequately
ADRNDCK	Adirondack
ADVCT	Advect
ADVCTD	Advected
ADVCTG	Advecting
ADVCTN	Advection
ADVCTS	Advects
ADVN	Advance
ADVNG	Advancing
ADVY	Advisory
ADVYS	Advisories
AFCT	Affect
AFCTD	Affected
AFCTG	Affecting

AFT	After…(time or place)
AFTN	Afternoon
AFSS	Automated Flight Service Station
AGL	Above ground level
AGN	Again
AGRD	Agreed
AGRS	Agrees
AGRMT	Agreement
AHD	Ahead
AIREP	Air-report
AIRMET	Airman's Meteorological Information (Information concerning en-route weather phenomena which may affect the safety of low-level aircraft operations)
AK	Alaska
AL	Alabama
ALF	Aloft
ALG	Along
ALGHNY	Allegheny
ALQDS	All quadrants
ALSTG	Altimeter setting
ALT	Altitude
ALTA	Alberta
ALTHO	Although
ALTM	Altimeter
ALUTN	Aleutian
AMD	Amend or amended (used to indicate amended meteorological message; message type designator)
AMDG	Amending
AMDT	Amendment
AMP	Amplify
AMPG	Amplifying
AMPLTD	Amplitude
AMS	
AMSL	Above mean sea level
AMT	Amount
ANLYS	Analysis
ANS	Answer
AOA	At or above
AOB	At or below

AP	Airport or anomalous propagation
APCH	Approach
APCHG	Approaching
APCHS	Approaches
APLCN	Appalachian
APLCNS	Appalachians
APPR	Appear
APPRG	Appearing
APPRS	Appears
APR	April
APRNT	Apparent
APRX	Approximate or approximately
AR	Arkansas
ARFOR	Area Forecast (in aeronautical meteorological code)
ARND	Around
AS	Altostratus
ASC	Ascend to or ascending to
ASSOCD	Associated
ASSOCN	Association
AT...	At (followed by time at which weather change is forecast to occur)
ATLC	Atlantic
ATP	At...(time or place)
ATTM	At this time
ATTN	Attention
AUG	August
AVBL	Available or availability
AVG	Average
AWC	Aviation Weather Center
AWT	Awaiting
AZ	Arizona
AZM	Azimuth

B

BACLIN	Baroclinic
BAJA	Baja, California
BASE	Cloud base
BATROP	Barotropic
BC	British Columbia
BCFG	Fog patches
BCH	Beach
BCKG	Backing

BDA	Bermuda
BDRY	Boundary
BECMG	Becoming
BFR	Before
BGN	Begin
BGNG	Beginning
BGN	Begins
BHND	Behind
BINOVC	Breaks in overcast
BKN	Broken
BL...	Blowing (followed by DU = dust, SA = sand or SN = snow)
BLD	Build
BLDG	Building
BLDUP	Buildup
BLKHLS	Black Hills
BLKT	Blanket
BLKTG	Blanketing
BLKTS	Blankets
BLO	Below clouds
BLW	Below...
BLZD	Blizzard
BND	Bound
BNTH	Beneath
BR	Mist
BRF	Brief
BRK	Break
BRKG	Breaking
BRKHIC	Breaks in higher clouds
BRKS	Breaks
BRKSHR	Berkshire
BRM	Barometer
BLDU	Blowing Dust
BLSA	Blowing Sand
BLSN	Blowing Snow
BTL	Between layers
BTN	Between
BYD	Beyond

C

C	Degrees Celsius (Centigrade) or centre (runway identification)
CA	California
CAA	Cold air advection
CAPE	Convective Available

	Potential Energy
CARIB	Caribbean
CASCDS	Cascades
CAT	Category or Clear air turbulence
CAVO	Visibility, cloud and present weather better than prescribed values or conditions
CB	Cumulonimbus
CC	Cirrocumulus
CCA	(or CCB, CCC...etc., in sequence) Corrected meteorological message
CCLDS	Clear of clouds
CC	Counterclockwise
CCSL	Cirrocumulus Standing Lenticular
CDFNT	Cold front
CDN	Coordination
CFP	Cold front passage
CHC	Chance
CHCS	Chances
CHG	Modification (message type designator)
CHGD	Changed
CHGG	Changing
CHGS	Changes
CHSPK	Chesapeake
CI	Cirrus
CIG	Ceiling
CIGS	Ceilings
CIT	Near or over large towns
CLA	Clear type of ice formation
CLD	Cloud
CLDNS	Cloudiness
CLDS	Clouds
CLKWS	Clockwise
CLR	Clear(s) or cleared to...or clearance
CLRG	Clearing
CLRS	Clears
CLSD	Close or closed or closing
CM	Centimeter
CMPLX	Complex
CNL	Cancel or cancelled
CNDN	Canadian
CNTR	Center
CNTRD	Centered
CNTRL	Central

CNTY	County
CNTYS	Counties
CNVG	Converge
CNVGG	Converging
CNVGNC	Convergence
CNVTN	Convection
CNVTV	Convective
CNVTVLY	Convectively
CONFDC	Confidence
CO	Colorado
COMPR	Compare
COMPRG	Comparing
COMPRD	Compared
COMPRS	Compares
COND	Condition
CONS	Continuous
CONT	Continue(s) or continued
CONTLY	Continually
CONTG	Continuing
CONTRAILS	Condensation trails
CONTDVD	Continental Divide
CONUS	Continental U.S.
COORD	Coordinates
COR	Correct or correction or corrected (used to indicate corrected meteorological message; message type designator
COT	At the coast
COV	Cover or covered or covering
CPBL	Capable
CPC	Climate Prediction Center
CRLC	Circulate
CRLN	Circulation
CRNR	Corner
CRNRS	Corners
CRS	Course
CS	Cirrostratus
CSDR	Consider
CSDRBL	Considerable
CST	Coast
CSTL	Coastal
CT	Connecticut
CTSKLS	Catskills
CU	Cumulus
CUFRA	Cumulus Fractus
COV	Cover or covered or covering
CWSU	Center Weather Service Unit

CYC	Cyclonic		DMG	Damage
CYCLGN	Cyclogenesis		DMGD	Damaged
			DMGG	Damaging
			DMNT	Dominant
D			DMSH	Diminish
			DMSHD	Diminished
D	Downward (tendency in RVR during previous 10 minutes)		DMSHG	Diminishing
			DMSHS	Diminishes
			DNG	Danger or dangerous
DABRK	Daybreak		DNS	Dense
DALGT	Daylight		DNSLP	Downslope
DBL	Double		DNSTRM	Downstream
DC	District of Columbia		DNWND	Downwind
DCR	Decrease		DOM	Domestic
DCRD	Decreased		DP	Dew point temperature
DCRG	Decreasing		DPND	Deepened
DCRGLY	Decreasingly		DPNG	Deepening
DCRS	Decreases		DPNS	Deepens
DE	Delaware or from (used to precede the call sign of the calling station) (to be used in AFS as a procedure signal)		DPR	Deeper
			DPT	Depth
			DR…	Low drifting (followed by DU =dust, SA = sand or SN = snow)
DEC	December		DRFT	Drift
DEG	Degrees		DRFTD	Drifted
DELMARVA	Delaware-Maryland-Virginia		DRFTG	Drifting
DFCLT	Difficult		DRFTS	Drift
DFCLTY	Difficulty		DRG	During
DFNT	Definite		DS	Duststorm
DFNTLY	Definitely		DSCNT	Descent
DFRS	Differs		DSIPT	Dissipate
DGNL	Diagonal		DSIPTD	Dissipated
DGNLLY	Diagonally		DSIPTG	Dissipating
DIF	Diffuse		DSIPTN	Dissipation
DIGG	Digging		DSIPTS	Dissipates
DIR	Direction		DSND	Descend
DISC	Discontinue		DSNDG	Descending
DISCD	Discontinued		DSNDS	Descends
DISCG	Discontinuing		DSNT	Distant
DISRE	Disregard		DSTBLZ	Destabilize
DISRED	Disregarded		DSTBLZD	Destabilized
DISREG	Disregarding		DSTBLZG	Destabilizing
DIST	Distance		DSTBLZS	Destabilizes
DKTS	Dakotas		DSTBLZN	Destabilization
DLA	Delay or delayed or delay (message type designator)		DTG	Date-time group
			DTRT	Deteriorate or deteriorating
DLT	Delete		DU	Dust
DLTD	Deleted		DUC	Dense upper cloud
DLTG	Deleting		DUR	Duration
DLY	Daily		DURC	During climb

DURD	During descent
DVLP	Develop
DVLPD	Developed
DVLPG	Developing
DVLPMT	Development
DVLPS	Develops
DVRG	Diverge
DVRGG	Diverging
DVRGNC	Divergence
DVRGS	Diverges
DVV	Downward vertical velocity
DWNDFTS	Downdrafts
DZ	Drizzle

E

E	East or eastern longitude
EB	Eastbound
EFCT	Effect
ELEV	Elevation
ELNGT	Elongate
ELNGTD	Elongated
ELSW	Elsewhere
EMBD	Embedded in a layer (to indicate cumulonimbus embedded in layers of clouds)
EMC	Environmental Modeling Center
EMERG	Emergency
ENCTR	Encounter
ENDG	Ending
ENE	East-northeast
ENELY	East-northeasterly
ENERN	East-northeastern
ENEWD	East-northeastward
ENHNC	Enhance
ENHNCD	Enhanced
ENHNCG	Enhancing
ENHNCS	Enhances
ENHNCMNT	Enhancement
ENR	En route
ENTR	Entire
EQPT	Equipment
ERN	Eastern
ERY	Early
ERYR	Earlier
ESE	East-southeast
ESELY	East-southeasterly

ESERN	East-southeastern
ESEWD	East-southeastward
ESNTL	Essential
ESTAB	Establish
EST	Estimate or estimated or estimate (message type designator)
ETA	Estimated time of arrival or estimating arrival
ETC	Et cetera
ETD	Estimated time of departure or estimating departure
ETIM	Elapsed time
EV	Every
EVE	Evening
EWD	Eastward
EXCLV	Exclusive
EXCLVLY	Exclusively
EXC	Except
EXP	Expect or expected or expecting
EXTD	Extend or extending
EXTRAP	Extrapolate
EXTRAPD	Extrapolated
EXTRM	Extreme
EXTRMLY	Extremely
EXTSV	Extensive

F

F	Degrees Fahrenheit or fixed
FA	Area Forecast (U.S. domestic)
FAA	Federal Aviation Administration
FAM	Familiar
FAX	Facsimile transmission
FBL	Light (used to indicate the intensity of weather phenomena, interference or static reports, e.g. FBL RA = light rains)
FC	Funnel cloud (tornado or waterspout)
FCST	Forecast
FEB	February
FEW	Few
FG	Fog
FIG	Figure

FILG	Filling	G	Gust or green
FIR	Flight information region	GA	Georgia
FIRAV	First available	GAMET	Area forecast for low level flights
FL	Florida or Flight Level		
FLD	Field	GEN	General
FLRY	Flurry	GENLY	Generally
FLRYS	Flurries	GEO	Geographic or true
FLT	Flight	GEOREF	Geographical reference
FLUC	Fluctuating or fluctuation or fluctuated	GFS	Global Forecast System (model)
FLW	Follow(s) or following	GLFALSK	Gulf of Alaska
FLY	Fly or flying	GLFCAL	Gulf of California
FM	From	GLFMEX	Gulf of Mexico
FM...	From (followed by time weather change is forecast to begin)	GLFSTLAWR	Gulf of St. Lawrence
		GND	Ground
FMT	Format	GR	Hail
FNCTN	Function	GRAD	Gradient
FNTGNS	Frontogenesis	GRDL	Gradual
FNTLYS	Frontolysis	GRDLY	Gradually
FORNN	Forenoon	GRIB	Processed meteorological data in the form of grid point values expressed in binary form (aeronautical meteorological code)
FPM	Feet per minute		
FQTLY	Frequently		
FRI	Friday		
FRM	Form		
FRMG	Forming	GRT	Great
FRMN	Formation	GRTLY	Greatly
FRNG	Firing	GRTLKS	Great Lakes
FRONT	Front (relating to weather)	GS	Small hail and/or snow pellets
FROPA	Frontal passage		
FROSFC	Frontal surface	GSTS	Gusts
FRQ	Frequent	GSTY	Gusty
FRST	Frost	GTS	Global Telecommunication System
FRWF	Forecast wind factor		
FSS	Flight Service Station		
FST	First		
FT	Feet (dimensional unit)	**H**	
FTHR	Further		
FU	Smoke	HAZ	Hazard
FVRBL	Favorable	HDFRZ	Hard freeze
FWD	Forward	HDSVLY	Hudson Valley
FYI	For your information	HDWND	Head wind
FZ	Freezing	HGT	Height
FZ LVL	Freezing level	HI	Hawaii or high
FZDZ	Freezing drizzle	HIFOR	High level forecast
FZFG	Freezing fog	HJ	Sunrise to sunset
FZRA	Freezing rain	HLDG	Holding
		HLF	Half
		HLTP	Hilltop
G		HN	Sunset to sunrise

HND	Hundred		IMT	Immediate or immediately
HOL	Holiday		IMPT	Important
HPA	Hectopascal		INC	In cloud
HPC	Hydrometeorological Prediction Center		INCL	Include
			INCLD	Included
HR	Hours		INCLG	Including
HRZN	Horizon		INCLS	Includes
HTG	Heating		INCR	Increase
HURCN	Hurricane		INCRD	Increased
HUREP	Hurricane report		INCRG	Increasing
HVY	Heavy or heavy (used to indicate the intensity of weather phenomena, e.g. heavy rain = HVY RA)		INCRGLY	Increasingly
			INCRS	Increases
			INDC	Indicate
			INDCD	Indicated
HVYR	Heavier		INDCG	Indicating
HVYST	Heaviest		INDCS	Indicates
HWVR	However		INDEF	Indefinite
HWY	Highway		INFO	Information
HYR	Higher		INOP	Inoperative
HZ	Haze		INPR	In progress
			INSTR	Instrument
			INSTBY	Instability
			INTCNTL	Intercontinental
I			INTL	International
			INTMD	Intermediate
IA	Iowa		INTMT	Intermittent
IAO	In and out of clouds		INTMTLY	Intermittently
IC	Icing (PIREPs only) or ice crystals (very small ice crystals in suspension, also known as diamond dust)		INTR	Interior
			INTRP	Interrupt or interruption or interrupted
			INTRMTRGN	Intermountain region
ICAO	International Civil Aviation Organization		INT	Intersection
			INTS	Intense
ICE	Icing		INTSFCN	Intensification
ICGIC	Icing in clouds		INTSF	Intensify or intensifying
ICGICIP	Icing in clouds and in precipitation		INTST	Intensity
			INTVL	Interval
ICGIP	Icing in precipitation		INVRN	Inversion
ID	Idaho or identifier or identity		IOVC	In overcast
IDENT	Identification		INVOF	In vicinity of
IFR	Instrument flight rules		IPV	Improve
IGA	International general aviation		IPVG	Improving
			ISA	International standard atmosphere
IL	Illinois			
ILS	Instrument landing system		ISOL	Isolated
IMC	Instrument meteorological conditions			
IMD	Immediate or immediately		**J**	
IMPL	Impulse			
IMPLS	Impulses		JAN	January
IMPR	Improve or improving			

JCTN	Junction
JTST	Jet stream
JUL	July
JUN	June

K

KFRST	Killing frost
KG	Kilograms
KLYR	Smoke layer aloft
KM	Kilometers
KMH	Kilometers per hour
KOCTY	Smoke over city
KPA	Kilopascals
KS	Kansas
KT	Knots
KY	Kentucky

L

L	Left (runway identification)
LA	Louisiana
LABRDR	Labrador
LAN	Inland
LAT	Latitude
LAWRS	Limited aviation weather reporting station
LCTMP	Little change in temperature
LFTG	Lifting
LGT	Light or lighting
LGWV	Long wave
LI	Lifted Index
LIS	Lifted indices
LK	Lake
LKS	Lakes
LKLY	Likely
LLJ	Low level jet
LLWAS	Low-level wind shear alert system
LLWS	Low-level wind shear
LN	Line
LOC	Local or locally or location or located
LONG	Longitude
LONGL	Longitudinal
LRG	Long range
LRGLY	Largely
LRGR	Larger

LRGST	Largest
LST	Local standard time
LTD	Limited
LTG	Lightning
LTGCC	Lightning cloud-to-cloud
LTGCG	Lightning cloud-to-ground
LTGCCCG	Lightning cloud-to-cloud, cloud-to-ground
LTGCW	Lightning cloud-to-water
LTGIC	Lightning in cloud
LTL	Little
LTLCG	Little change
LTR	Later
LTST	Latest
LV	Light and variable (relating to wind)
LVE	Leave or Leaving
LVL	Level
LWR	Lower
LWRD	Lowered
LWRG	Lowering
LRY	Layer or layered

M

M	Meters (preceded by figures) or Mach number (followed by figures)
MA	Massachusetts
MAG	Magnetic
MAINT	Maintenance
MAN	Manitoba
MAR	March
MAX	Maximum
MAY	May
MB	Millibar
MBST	Microburst
MCD	Mesoscale discussion
MD	Maryland
MDFY	Modify
MDFYD	Modified
MDFYG	Modifying
MDL	Model
MDLS	Models
MDTLY	Moderately
ME	Maine
MED	Medium
MEGG	Merging
MESO	Mesoscale

MET	Meteorological or meteorology
METAR	Aviation routine weather report (in aeronautical meteorological code)
METRO	Metropolitan
MEX	Mexico
MHKVLY	Mohawk Valley
MI	Michigan
MID	Mid-point (related to RVR)
MIDN	Midnight
MIFG	Shallow fog
MIL	Military
MIN	Minutes
MISG	Missing
MLTLVL	Melting level
MN	Minnesota
MNLD	Mainland
MNM	Minimum
MNLY	Mainly
MNT	Monitor or monitoring or monitored
MNTN	Maintain
MO	Missouri
MOD	Moderate (used to indicate the intensity of weather phenomena, interference or static reports, e.g. moderate rain = MOD RA)
MOGR	Moderate or greater
MON	Monday or above mountains
MOPS	Minimum operational performance standards
MOV	Move or moving or movement
MPH	Miles per hour
MPS	Meters per second
MRG	Medium range
MRGL	Marginal
MRGLLY	Marginally
MRNG	Morning
MRTM	Maritime
MS	Mississippi or minus
MSG	Message
MSL	Mean sea level
MST	Most
MSTLY	Mostly
MSTR	Moisture
MT	Montana or mountain

MTW	Mountain waves
MULT	Multiple
MULTILVL	Multilevel
MWO	Meteorological watch office
MX	Mixed type of ice formation (white and clear)

N

N	North or northern latitude or no distinct tendency (in RVR during previous 10 minutes)
NAB	Not above
NAM	North American Mesoscale (model)
NAT	North Atlantic
NAV	Navigation
NB	New Brunswick or northbound
NBFR	Not before
NBRHD	Neighborhood
NC	North Carolina or no change
NCEP	National Center of Environmental Prediction
NCO	NCEP Central Operations
NCWX	No change in weather
ND	North Dakota
NE	Nebraska or northeast
NEB	Northeast bound
NEC	Necessary
NEG	No or negative or permission not granted or that is not correct
NEGLY	Negatively
NELY	Northeasterly
NERN	Northeastern
NEWD	Northeastward
NEW ENG	New England
NFLD	Newfoundland
NGT	Night
NH	New Hampshire
NHC	National Hurricane Center
NIL	None or I have nothing to send to you
NJ	New Jersey
NL	No layers
NLT	Not later than

NLY	Northerly		observation
NM	New Mexico or nautical miles	OBSC	Obscure or obscured or obscuring
NMBRS	Numbers	OCFNT	Occluded front
NML	Normal	OCLD	Occlude
NMRS	Numerous	OCLDS	Occludes
NNE	North-northeast	OCLDD	Occluded
NNELY	North-northeasterly	OCLDG	Occluding
NNERN	North-northeastern	OCLN	Occlusion
NNEWD	North-northeastward	OCNL	Occasional or occasionally
NNW	North-northwest	OCR	Occur
NNWLY	North-northwesterly	OCRD	Occurred
NNWRN	North-northwestern	OCRG	Occurring
NNWWD	North-northwestward	OCRS	Occurs
NNNN	End of message	OCT	October
NOAA	National Oceanic and Atmospheric Administration	OFC	Office
		OFP	Occluded frontal passage
NOPAC	Northern Pacific	OFSHR	Offshore
NOSIG	No significant change (used in trend-type landing forecasts)	OH	Ohio
		OHD	Overhead
		OK	Oklahoma or we agree or it is correct
NOV	November	OMTNS	Over mountains
NPRS	Non-persistent	ONSHR	On shore
NR	Number	OPA	Opaque, white type of ice formation
NRLY	Nearly		
NRN	Northern	OPC	Ocean Prediction Center
NRW	Narrow	OPN	Open or opening or opened
NS	Nova Scotia or nimbostratus	OPR	Operator or operate or operative or operating or operational
NSC	Nil significant cloud		
NSW	Nil significant weather	OR	Oregon
NTFY	Notify	ORGPHC	Orographic
NTFYD	Notified	ORIG	Original
NTL	National	OSV	Ocean station vessel
NV	Nevada	OTLK	Outlook (used in SIGMET messages for volcanic ash and tropical cyclones)
NVA	Negative vorticity advection		
NW	Northwest		
NWB	Northwest bound		
NWD	Northward	OTP	On top
NWLY	Northwesterly	OTR	Other
NWRN	Northwestern	OTRW	Otherwise
NWS	National Weather Service	OUBD	Outbound
NY	New York	OUTFLO	Outflow
NXT	Next	OVC	Overcast
		OVNGT	Overnight
		OVR	Over
O		OVRN	Overrun
		OVRNG	Overrunning
OAT	Outside air temperature	OVTK	Overtake
OBS	Observe or observed or	OVTKG	Overtaking

OVTKS	Overtakes

P

PA	Pennsylvania
PAC	Pacific
PATWAS	Pilot's automatic telephone weather answering service
PBL	Planetary boundary layer
PCPN	Precipitation
PD	Period
PDMT	Predominant
PEN	Peninsula
PERM	Permanent
PGTSND	Puget Sound
PHYS	Physical
PIBAL	Pilot balloon observation
PIREP	Pilot weather report
PL	Ice pellets
PLNS	Plains
PLS	Please
PLTO	Plateau
PLVL	Present level
PM	Postmeridian
PNHDL	Panhandle
PO	Dust/sand whirls (dust devils)
POS	Positive
POSLY	Positively
POSS	Possible
PPI	Plan position indicator
PPINA	Plan position indicator not available (U.S. Weather Radar Report)
PPINE	Plan position indicator no echoes (U.S. Weather Radar Report)
PPSN	Present position
PRBL	Probable
PRBLY	Probably
PRBLTY	Probability
PRECD	Precede
PRECDD	Preceded
PRECDG	Preceding
PRECDS	Precedes
PRES	Pressure
PRESFR	Pressure falling rapidly
PRESRR	Pressure rising rapidly
PRFG	Aerodrome partially

	covered by fog
PRI	Primary
PRIN	Principal
PRIND	Present indications are
PRJMP	Pressure jump
PROB	Probability
PROC	Procedure
PROD	Produce
PRODG	Producing
PROG	Forecast
PROGD	Forecasted
PROGS	Forecasts
PRSNT	Present
PRSNTLY	Presently
PRST	Persist
PRSTS	Persists
PRSTNC	Persistence
PRSTNT	Persistent
PRVD	Provide
PRVDD	Provided
PRVDG	Providing
PRVDS	Provides
PS	Plus
PSG	Passing
PSN	Position
PSND	Positioned
PSR	Primary surveillance radar
PTCHY	Patchy
PTLY	Partly
PTNL	Potential
PTNLY	Potentially
PTNS	Portions
PUGET	Puget Sound
PVA	Positive vorticity advection
PVL	Prevail
PVLD	Prevailed
PVLG	Prevailing
PVLS	Prevails
PVLT	Prevalent
PWB	Pilot weather briefing
PWR	Power

Q

QFE	Atmospheric pressure at aerodrome elevation
QN	Question

QNH	Altimeter sub-scale setting to obtain elevation when on the ground
QSTNRY	Quasistationary
QTR	Quarter
QUAD	Quadrant
QUE	Quebec

R

R	Right (runway identification) or rain (U.S. Weather Radar Reports)
RA	Rain
RADAT	Radiosonde additional data
RAFC	Regional area forecast centre
RAG	Ragged
RAOB	Radiosonde observation
RCH	Reach or reaching
RCKY	Rocky
RCKYS	Rockies
RCMD	Recommend
RCMDD	Recommended
RCMDG	Recommending
RCMDS	Recommends
RCRD	Record
RCRDS	Records
RDC	Reduce
RDGG	Ridging
RDL	Radial
RDVLP	Redevelop
RDVLPG	Redeveloping
RDVLPMT	Redevelopment
RE...	Recent (used to qualify weather phenomena, e.g. RERA = recent rain)
REC	Receive or receiver
RECON	Reconnaissance
REF	Reference to...or refer to...
REP	Report or reporting or reporting point
RES	Reserve
REQ	Request or requested
RESP	Response
RESTR	Restrict
RGLR	Regular
RGN	Region
RGNS	Regions

RH	Relative humidity
RI	Rhode Island
RITE	Right (direction of turn)
RIOGD	Rio Grande
RLBL	Reliable
RLTV	Relative
RLTVLY	Relatively
RMK	Remark
RMN	Remain
RMND	Remained
RMNDR	Remainder
RMNG	Remaining
RMNS	Remains
RNFL	Rainfall
ROFOR	Route forecast (in aeronautical meteorological code)
ROT	Rotate
ROTD	Rotated
ROTG	Rotating
ROTS	Rotates
RPD	Rapid
RPDLY	Rapidly
RPLC	Replace or replaced
RPT	Repeat or I repeat (to be used in AFS as a procedure signal)
RPTG	Repeating
RPTS	Repeats
RQMNTS	Requirements
RQR	Require
RQRD	Required
RQRG	Requiring
RQRS	Requires
RRA	(or RRB, RRC...etc., in sequence) Delayed meteorological message (message type designator)
RSG	Rising
RSN	Reason
RSNG	Reasoning
RSNS	Reasons
RSTR	Restrict
RSTRD	Restricted
RSTRG	Restricting
RSTRS	Restricts
RTD	Delayed (used to indicate delayed meteorological message; message type designator)

RTE	Route
RTN	Return or returned or returning
RTS	Return to service
RUC	Rapid Update Cycle (model)
RUF	Rough
RUFLY	Roughly
RVR	Runway visual range
RVS	Revise
RVSD	Revised
RVSG	Revising
RVSS	Revises
RWY	Runway

S

S	South or southern latitude
SA	Sand
SAP	As soon as possible
SARPS	Standards and Recommended Practices (ICAO)
SASK	Saskatchewan
SAT	Saturday
SATFY	Satisfactory
SB	Southbound
SBSD	Subside
SBSDD	Subsided
SBSDNC	Subsidence
SBSDS	Subsides
SC	South Carolina or stratocumulus
SCND	Second
SCSL	Stratocumulus Standing Lenticular
SCT	Scattered
SD	South Dakota
SE	Southeast
SEB	Southeast bound
SEC	Seconds
SECT	Sector
SELY	Southeasterly
SEP	September
SEPN	Separation
SEQ	Sequence
SER	Service or servicing or served
SERN	Southeastern

SEV	Severe (used to qualify icing and turbulence reports)
SEWD	Southeastward
SFC	Surface
SG	Snow grains
SGFNT	Significant
SGFNTLY	Significantly
SH...	Showers (followed by RA = rain, SN = snow, PL = ice pellets, GR = hail, GS = small hail and/or snow pellets or combinations thereof, e.g. SHRASN = showers of rain and snow)
SHFT	Shift
SHFTD	Shifted
SHFTG	Shifting
SHFTS	Shifts
SHLD	Shield
SHLW	Shallow
SHRT	Short
SHRTLY	Shortly
SHRTWV	Shortwave
SHUD	Should
SIERNEV	Sierra Nevada
SIG	Signature
SIGMET	Significant Meteorological Information (Information concerning en-route weather phenomena which may affect the safety of aircraft operations)
SIGWX	Significant weather
SIMUL	Simultaneous or simultaneously
SKC	Sky clear
SKED	Schedule or scheduled
SLD	Solid
SLGT	Slight
SLGTLY	Slightly
SLP	Slope
SLPG	Sloping
SLW	Slow
SLY	Southerly
SM	Statute mile
SML	Small
SMLR	Smaller
SMRY	Summary
SMTH	Smooth

SMTHR	Smoother		STBLTY	Stability
SMTHST	Smoothest		STD	Standard
SMTM	Sometime		STDY	Steady
SMWHT	Somewhat		STFR	Stratus Fractus
SN	Snow		STF	Stratiform
SNBNK	Snow bank		STG	Strong
SNFLK	Snowflake		STGLY	Strongly
SNGL	Single		STGR	Stronger
SNOINCR	Snow increase		STGST	Strongest
SNOINCRG	Snow increasing		STM	Storm
SOP	Standard operating procedure		STMS	Storms
			STN	Station
SPC	Storm Prediction Center		STNR	Stationary
SPCLY	Especially		STS	Status
SPD	Speed		SUB	Substitute
SPECI	Aviation selected special weather Report (in aeronautical meteorological code)		SUBTRPCL	Subtropical
			SUF	Sufficient
			SUFLY	Sufficiently
			SUG	Suggest
SPECIAL	Special meteorological report (in abbreviated plain language)		SUGG	Suggesting
			SUGS	Suggests
			SUN	Sunday
SPKL	Sprinkle		SUPG	Supplying
SPLNS	Southern Plains		SUPR	Superior
SPRD	Spread		SUPSD	Supersede
SPRDG	Spreading		SUPSDG	Superseding
SPRDS	Spreads		SUPSDS	Supersedes
SPRL	Spiral		SVC	Service message
SQ	Squall		SVRL	Several
SQL	Squall line		SW	Southwest
SR	Sunrise		SWB	Southwest bound
SRG	Short range		SWD	Southward
SRN	Southern		SWWD	Southwestward
SRND	Surround		SWLY	Southwesterly
SRNDD	Surrounded		SWRN	Southwestern
SRNDG	Surrounding		SX	Stability index
SRNDS	Surrounds		SXN	Section
SRY	Secondary		SYNOP	Synoptic
SS	Sunset or sandstorm		SYNS	Synopsis
SSE	South-southeast		SYS	System
SSELY	South-southeasterly			
SSERN	South-southeastern			
SSEWD	South-southeastward			
SSW	South-southwest		**T**	
SSWLY	South-southwesterly			
SSWRN	South-southwestern		T	Temperature
SSWWD	South-southwestward		TAF	Terminal aerodrome forecast
ST	Stratus			
STAGN	Stagnation		TAIL	Tail wind
STBL	Stable		TB	Turbulence (PIREPs only)
			TC	Tropical Cyclone

TCNTL	Transcontinental
TCU	Towering cumulus
TDA	Today
TDO	Tornado
TEMPO	Temporary or temporarily
TEND	Trend forecast
THK	Thick
THKNG	Thickening
THKNS	Thickness
THKR	Thicker
THKST	Thickest
THN	Thin
THNG	Thinning
THNR	Thinner
THNST	Thinnest
THR	Threshold
THRFTR	Thereafter
THRU	Through
THRUT	Throughout
THSD	Thousand
THTN	Threaten
THTND	Threatened
THTNG	Threatening
THTNS	Threatens
THU	Thursday
TIL	Until
TL...	Till (followed by time by which weather change is forecast to end)
TMW	Tomorrow
TN	Tennessee
TNDCY	Tendency
TNDCYS	Tendencies
TNGT	Tonight
TNTV	Tentative
TNTVLY	Tentatively
TO	To...(place)
TOC	Top of climb
TOP	Cloud top
TOPS	Tops
TOVC	Top of overcast
TPC	Tropical Prediction Center
TPG	Topping
TR	Track
TRBL	Trouble
TRIB	Tributary
TRKG	Tracking
TRML	Terminal
TRMT	Terminate
TRMTD	Terminated
TRMTG	Terminating

TRMTS	Terminates
TRNSP	Transport
TRNSPG	Transporting
TROF	Trough
TROFS	Troughs
TROP	Tropopause
TRPCD	Tropical continental air mass
TRPCL	Tropical
TRRN	Terrain
TRSN	Transition
TS	Thunderstorm (in aerodrome reports and forecasts, TS used alone means thunder heard but no precipitation at the aerodrome)
TS...	Thunderstorm (followed by RA = rain, SN = snow, PL = ice pellets, GR = hail, GS = small hail and/or snow pellets or combinations thereof, e.g. TSRASN = thunderstorm with rain and snow)
TSFR	Transfer
TSFRD	Transferred
TSFRG	Transferring
TSFRS	Transfers
TSNT	Transient
TUE	Tuesday
TURB	Turbulence
TURBT	Turbulent
TWD	Toward
TWDS	Towards
TWI	Twilight
TWR	Aerodrome control tower or aerodrome control
TWRG	Towering
TX	Texas
TYP	Type of aircraft
TYPH	Typhoon

U

U	Upward (tendency in RVR during previous 10 minutes)
UA	Pilot weather report (U.S.)
UDDF	Up- and downdrafts

UFN	Until further notice
UNA	Unable
UNAVBL	Unavailable
UNEC	Unnecessary
UNKN	Unknown
UNL	Unlimited
UNREL	Unreliable
UNRSTD	Unrestricted
UNSATFY	Unsatisfactory
UNSBL	Unseasonable
UNSTBL	Unstable
UNSTDY	Unsteady
UNSTL	Unsettle
UNSTLD	Unsettled
UNUSBL	Unusable
UPDFTS	Updrafts
UPR	Upper
UPSLP	Upslope
UPSTRM	Upstream
URG	Urgent
USBL	Usable
UT	Utah
UTC	Coordinated Universal Time
UVV	Upward vertical velocity
UWNDS	Upper winds

V

VA	Virginia or volcanic ash
VAAC	Volcanic Ash Advisory Center
VAAS	Volcanic Ash Advisory Statement
VAL	In valleys
VARN	Variation
VC	Vicinity of the aerodrome (followed by FG = fog, FC = funnel cloud, SH = showers, PO = dust/sand whirls, BLDU = blowing dust, BLSA = blowing sand or BLSN = blowing snow, e.g. VC FG = vicinity fog)
VCOT	VFR conditions on top
VCTR	Vector
VCY	Vicinity
VER	Vertical
VFR	Visual flight rules
VFY	Verify

VFYD	Verified
VFYG	Verifying
VFYS	Verifies
VIS	Visibility
VLCTY	Velocity
VLCTYS	Velocities
VLNT	Violent
VLNTLY	Violently
VLY	Valley
VMC	Visual meteorological conditions
VOL	Volume
VOLMT	Meteorological information for aircraft in flight
VORT	Vorticity
VR	Veer
VRB	Variable
VRG	Veering
VRISL	Vancouver Island, BC
VRS	Veers
VRT	Vertical motion
VRY	Very
VT	Vermont
VV	Vertical velocity

W

W	West or western longitude
WA	Washington
WAA	Warm air advection
WAFC	World area forecast centre
WAFS	Word area forecast system
WB	Westbound
WDI	Wind direction indicator
WDLY	Widely
WDSPR	Widespread
WED	Wednesday
WEF	With effect from or effective from
WFO	Weather Forecast Office
WFP	Warm front passage
WI	Wisconsin or within
WIBIS	Will be issued
WID	Width
WIE	With immediate effect or effective immediately
WINT	Winter
WINTEM	Forecast upper wind and temperature for aviation

WK	Weak		WY	Wyoming
WKDAY	Weekday			
WKEND	Weekend		**X**	
WKN	Weaken or weakening			
WL	Will		X	Cross
WLY	Westerly		XCP	Except
WND	Wind		XNG	Crossing
WNDS	Winds		XPC	Expect
WNW	West-northwest		XPCD	Expected
WNWLY	West-northwesterly		XPCG	Expecting
WNWRN	West-northwestern		XPCS	Expects
WNWWD	West-northwestward		XPLOS	Explosive
WO	Without		XS	Atmospherics
WPLTO	Western Plateau		XTND	Extend
WRM	Warm		XTNDD	Extended
WRMG	Warming		XTNDG	Extending
WRN	Western		XTRM	Extreme
WRMR	Warmer		XTRMLY	Extremely
WRMST	Warmest			
WRMFNT	Warm front			
WRMFNTL	Warm frontal			
WRNG	Warning		**Y**	
WRS	Worse			
WS	Wind shear		YDA	Yesterday
WSPD	Wind speed		YKN	Yukon
WSHFT	Wind shift		YLSTN	Yellowstone
WSTCH	Wasatch Range			
WSW	West-southwest			
WSWLY	West-southwesterly			
WSWRN	West-southwestern		**Z**	
WSWWD	West-southwestward			
WTR	Water		Z	Coordinated Universal Time (in meteorological messages)
WTSPT	Waterspout			
WUD	Would			
WV	West Virginia		ZN	Zone
WVS	Waves		ZNS	Zones
WW	Watch notification message			
WWD	Westward			
WWW	World wide web			
WX	Weather			

12 APPENDIX C: STANDARD CONVERSION CHART

Figure C-1. Standard Conversion Chart

13 APPENDIX D: DENSITY ALTITUDE CALCULATION

To determine density altitude:

1. Set the aircraft's <u>altimeter</u> to 29.92 <u>inches of Mercury</u>. The <u>altimeter</u> will indicate pressure altitude.

2. Read the outside air temperature.

3. Mark the intersection of pressure altitude (horizontal) and temperature (vertical) lines on the chart.

4. Read the density altitude from the diagonal lines.

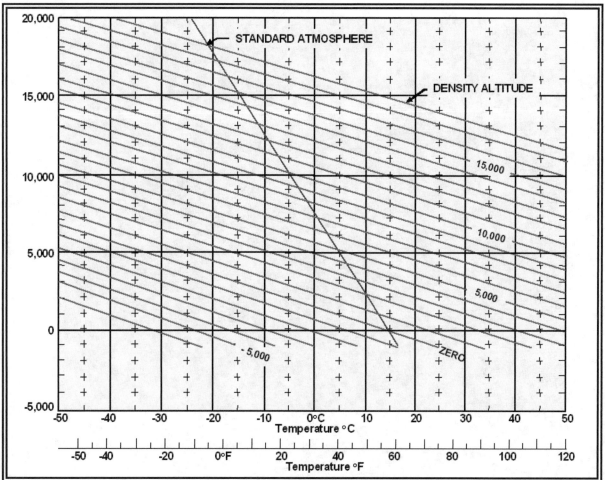

Figure D-1. Density Altitude Computation Chart

14 APPENDIX E: INTERNET LINKS

Table E-1. Selected National Weather Service (NWS) Links

SITE	WEB ADDRESS
National Weather Service (NWS)	http://weather.gov/
Aviation Digital Data Service (ADDS)	http://adds.aviationweather.noaa.gov/
Aviation Weather Center (AWC)	http://aviationweather.gov
Hydrometeorological Prediction Center (HPC)	http://www.hpc.ncep.noaa.gov/
Storm Prediction Center (SPC)	http://www.spc.noaa.gov/
Tropical Prediction Center (TPC)	http://www.nhc.noaa.gov/
Alaska Aviation Weather Unit (AAWU)	http://aawu.arh.noaa.gov/
Center Weather Service Units (CWSU)	http://aviationweather.gov/products/cwsu/
Weather Forecast Offices (WFO)	http://www.srh.noaa.gov/
Weather Forecast Office (WFO) Honolulu, HI – Aviation Products	http://www.prh.noaa.gov/hnl/pages/aviation.php
Telecommunication Operations Center - NWS Fax Charts	http://weather.noaa.gov/fax/nwsfax.html
NWS Office at the FAA Academy	http://www.srh.noaa.gov/faa/

Table E-2. Selected Federal Aviation Administration (FAA) Links

SITE	WEB ADDRESS
Federal Aviation Administration (FAA)	http://www.faa.gov/
Air Traffic Control System Command Center (ATCSCC)	http://www.fly.faa.gov/flyfaa/usmap.jsp
Automated Flight Service Station (AFSS)	http://fsfeedback.gosysops.info

Table E-3. Selected Links to Aviation Weather Products

PRODUCT	WEB ADDRESS
Average Surface to 500 MB Relative Humidity Chart	http://weather.noaa.gov/pub/fax/QRUA00.TIF
Collaborative Convective Weather Forecast (CFP)	http://aviationweather.gov/products/ccfp/
Constant Pressure Charts	http://weather.noaa.gov/fax/barotrop.shtml
Convective Outlooks	http://www.spc.noaa.gov/products/outlook/
Current Icing Product (CIP)	http://adds.aviationweather.noaa.gov/icing/icing_nav.php
Center Weather Advisory (CWA)	http://aviationweather.gov/products/cwsu/
Area Forecast (FA)	http://aviationweather.gov/products/fa/
Significant Meteorological Advisory (SIGMET) – US (CONUS)	http://adds.aviationweather.noaa.gov/airmets/
Significant Meteorological Advisory (SIGMET) – International	http://aviationweather.gov/products/sigmets/intl/
Airmen's Meteorological Advisory (AIRMET)	http://adds.aviationweather.noaa.gov/airmets/
Forecast Icing Potential (FIP)	http://adds.aviationweather.noaa.gov/icing/icing_nav.php
Freezing Level Graphics	http://adds.aviationweather.noaa.gov/icing/frzg_nav.php
High Level SIGWX Charts	http://aviationweather.gov/products/swh/
Lifted Index (LI) Analysis Chart	http://weather.noaa.gov/pub/fax/QXUA00.TIF
Low Level SIGWX Charts	http://aviationweather.gov/products/swl/
Mid Level SIGWX Chart	http://aviationweather.gov/products/swm/
Meteorological Impact Statement (MIS)	http://aviationweather.gov/products/cwsu/
National Convective Weather Forecast (NCWF)	http://adds.aviationweather.noaa.gov/convection/java/ http://adds.aviationweather.noaa.gov/convection/java/?appletsize=large http://aviationweather.gov/products/ncwf/

PRODUCT	WEB ADDRESS
Pilot Weather Report	http://adds.aviationweather.noaa.gov/pireps/
Radar Summary Chart	http://weather.noaa.gov/pub/fax/QAUA00.TIF
Aviation Routine Weather Report (METAR) / Aviation Selected Special Weather Report (SPECI)	http://adds.aviationweather.noaa.gov/metars/
Surface Analysis Charts	http://www.hpc.ncep.noaa.gov/html/sfc2.shtml http://www.hpc.ncep.noaa.gov/html/avnsfc.shtml http://www.opc.ncep.noaa.gov/ http://www.nhc.noaa.gov/marine_forecasts.shtml http://www.opc.ncep.noaa.gov/UA.shtml
Short Range Surface Prog Charts	http://adds.aviationweather.noaa.gov/progs/
Strike Probabilities of Tropical Cyclone Conditions (SPF)	http://www.nhc.noaa.gov/
Terminal Aerodrome Forecast (TAF)	http://adds.aviationweather.gov/tafs/
Aviation Tropical Cyclone Advisory (TCA)	http://www.nhc.noaa.gov/
Tropical Cyclone Public Advisory (TCP)	http://www.nhc.noaa.gov/
Volcanic Ash Advisory Statement (VAAS)	http://aviationweather.gov/iffdp/volt.shtml
Volcanic Ash Forecast Transport and Dispersion (VAFTAD) Chart	http://aviationweather.gov/iffdp/volc.shtml
Watch Notification Messages	http://www.spc.noaa.gov/products/watch/
Weather Depiction Chart	http://weather.noaa.gov/pub/fax/QGUA00.TIF
Wind and Temperature Aloft Forecast Graphics	http://adds.aviationweather.noaa.gov/winds/
Wind and Temperature Aloft Forecasts (FB) Text	http://aviationweather.gov/products/nws/winds/

15 APPENDIX F: AWC ADVISORY PLOTTING CHART

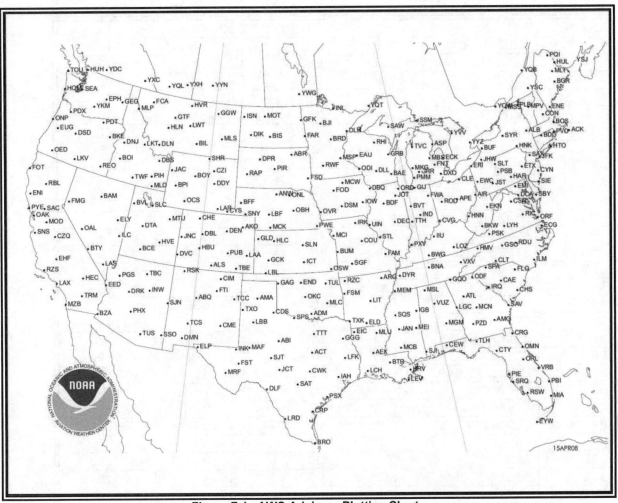

Figure F-1. AWC Advisory Plotting Chart

Table F-1. AWC Advisory Plotting Chart Reference Points

STATION ID	NAME	STATE	COUNTRY	LATITUDE (degrees)	LONGITUDE (degrees)
ABI	ABILENE	TX	US	32.48	-99.86
ABQ	ALBUQUERQUE	NM	US	35.04	-10.682
ABR	ABERDEEN	SD	US	45.42	-98.37
ACK	NANTUCKET	MA	US	41.28	-70.03
ACT	WACO	TX	US	31.66	-97.27
ADM	ARDMORE	OK	US	34.21	-97.17
AEX	ALEXANDRIA	LA	US	31.26	-92.50
AIR	BELLAIRE	OH	US	40.02	-80.82
AKO	AKRON	CO	US	40.16	-103.18
ALB	ALBANY	NY	US	42.75	-73.80
ALS	ALAMOSA	CO	US	37.35	-105.82
AMA	AMARILLO	TX	US	35.29	-101.64
AMG	ALMA	GA	US	31.54	-82.51
ANW	AINSWORTH	NE	US	42.57	-99.99
APE	APPLETON	OH	US	40.15	-82.59
ARG	WALNUT RIDGE	AR	US	36.11	-90.95
ASP	OSCODA	MI	US	44.45	-83.39
ATL	ATLANTA	GA	US	33.63	-84.44
BAE	MILWAUKEE	WI	US	43.12	-88.28
BAM	BATTLE MNTN	NV	US	40.57	-116.92
BCE	BRYCE_CANYON	UT	US	37.69	-112.30
BDF	BRADFORD	IL	US	41.16	-89.59
BDL	WINSOR LOCKS	CT	US	41.94	-72.69
BFF	SCOTTSBLUFF	NE	US	41.89	-103.48
BGR	BANGOR	ME	US	44.84	-68.87
BIL	BILLINGS	MT	US	45.81	-108.63
BIS	BISMARK	ND	US	46.77	-100.67
BJI	BEMIDJI	MN	US	47.58	-95.02
BKE	BAKER	OR	US	44.84	-117.81
BKW	BECKLEY	WV	US	37.78	-81.12
BNA	NASHVILLE	TN	US	36.14	-86.68
BOI	BOISE	ID	US	43.55	-116.19
BOS	BOSTON	MA	US	42.36	-70.99
BOY	BOYSEN RESV.	WY	US	43.46	-108.30
BPI	BIG PINEY	WY	US	42.58	-110.11
BRD	BRAINERD	MN	US	46.35	-94.03
BRO	BROWNSVILLE	TX	US	25.92	-97.38
BTR	BATON ROUGE	LA	US	30.48	-91.30
BTY	BEATTY	NV	US	36.80	-116.75
BUF	BUFFALO	NY	US	42.93	-78.65
BUM	BUTLER	MO	US	38.27	-94.49
BVL	BONNEVILLE	UT	US	40.73	-113.76
BVT	LAFAYETTE	IN	US	40.56	-87.07
BWG	BOWLING GREEN	KY	US	36.93	-86.44
BZA	YUMA	AZ	US	32.77	-114.60

STATION ID	NAME	STATE	COUNTRY	LATITUDE (degrees)	LONGITUDE (degrees)
CAE	COLUMBIA	SC	US	33.86	-81.05
CDS	CHILDRESS	TX	US	34.37	-100.28
CEW	CRESTVIEW	FL	US	30.83	-86.68
CHE	HAYDEN	CO	US	40.52	-107.31
CHS	CHARLESTON	SC	US	32.89	-80.04
CIM	CIMARRON	NM	US	36.49	-104.87
CLE	CLEVELAND	OH	US	41.42	-81.85
CLT	CHARLOTTE	NC	US	35.22	-80.93
CME	CHISUM	NM	US	33.34	-104.62
CON	CONCORD	NH	US	43.22	-71.58
COU	COLUMBIA	MO	US	38.82	-92.22
CRG	JACKSONVILLE	FL	US	30.34	-81.51
CRP	CORPUS CHRISTI	TX	US	27.90	-97.45
CSN	CASSANOVA	VA	US	38.64	-77.87
CTY	CROSS_CITY	FL	US	29.60	-83.05
CVG	COVINGTON	KY	US	39.02	-84.70
CWK	CENTEX	TX	US	30.38	-97.53
CYN	COYLE	NJ	US	39.82	-74.43
CYS	CHEYENNE	WY	US	41.21	-104.77
CZI	CRAZY WOMAN	WY	US	44.00	-106.44
CZQ	FRESNO	CA	US	36.88	-119.82
DBL	EAGLE	CO	US	39.44	-106.90
DBQ	DUBUQUE	IA	US	42.40	-90.71
DBS	DUBOIS	ID	US	44.09	-112.21
DCA	WASHINGTON	DC	US	38.86	-77.04
DDY	CASPER	WY	US	43.09	-106.28
DEC	DECATUR	IL	US	39.74	-88.86
DEN	DENVER	CO	US	39.81	-104.66
DIK	DICKINSIN	ND	US	46.86	-102.77
DLF	LAUGHLIN AFB	TX	US	29.36	-100.77
DLH	DULUTH	MN	US	46.80	-92.20
DLL	DELLS	WI	US	43.55	-89.76
DLN	DILLON	MT	US	45.25	-112.55
DMN	DEMING	NM	US	32.28	-107.60
DNJ	MC CALL	ID	US	44.77	-116.21
DPR	DUPREE	SD	US	45.08	-101.72
DRK	PRESCOTT	AZ	US	34.70	-112.48
DSD	REDMOND	OR	US	44.25	-121.30
DSM	DES MOINES	IA	US	41.44	-93.65
DTA	DELTA	UT	US	39.30	-112.51
DVC	DOVE CREEK	CO	US	37.81	-108.93
DXO	DETROIT	MI	US	42.21	-83.37
DYR	DYERSBURG	TN	US	36.02	-89.32
EAU	EAU CLAIRE	WI	US	44.90	-91.48
ECG	ELIZABETH CITY	NC	US	36.25	-76.18
ECK	PECK	MI	US	43.26	-82.72
EED	NEEDLES	CA	US	34.77	-114.47

STATION ID	NAME	STATE	COUNTRY	LATITUDE (degrees)	LONGITUDE (degrees)
EHF	BAKERSFIELD	CA	US	35.48	-119.10
EIC	SHREVEPORT	LA	US	32.77	-93.81
EKN	ELKINS	WV	US	38.92	-80.10
ELD	EL DORADO	AR	US	33.26	-92.74
ELP	EL PASO	TX	US	31.82	-106.28
ELY	ELY	NV	US	39.30	-114.85
EMI	WESTMINSTER	MD	US	39.50	-76.98
END	VANCE AFB	OK	US	36.35	-97.92
ENE	KENNEBUNK	ME	US	43.43	-70.61
ENI	UKIAH	CA	US	39.05	-123.27
EPH	EPHRATA	WA	US	47.38	-119.42
ERI	ERIE	PA	US	42.02	-80.30
ETX	EAST TEXAS	PA	US	40.58	-75.68
EUG	EUGENE	OR	US	44.12	-123.22
EWC	ELLWOOD CITY	PA	US	40.83	-80.21
EYW	KEY WEST	FL	US	24.59	-81.80
FAM	FARMINGTON	MO	US	37.67	-90.23
FAR	FARGO	ND	US	46.75	-96.85
FCA	KALISPELL	MT	US	48.21	-114.18
FLO	FLORENCE	SC	US	34.23	-79.66
FMG	RENO	NV	US	39.53	-119.66
FNT	FLINT	MI	US	42.97	-83.74
FOD	FT DODGE	IA	US	42.61	-94.29
FOT	FORTUNA	CA	US	40.67	-124.23
FSD	SIOUX FALLS	SD	US	43.65	-96.78
FSM	FT SMITH	AR	US	35.38	-94.27
FST	FT STOCKTON	TX	US	30.95	-102.98
FTI	FT UNION	NM	US	35.66	-105.14
FWA	FT WAYNE	IN	US	40.98	-85.19
GAG	GAGE	OK	US	36.34	-99.88
GCK	GARDEN CITY	KS	US	37.92	-100.73
GEG	SPOKANE	WA	US	47.56	-117.63
GFK	GRAND FORKS	ND	US	47.95	-97.19
GGG	LONGVIEW	TX	US	32.42	-94.75
GGW	GLASGOW	MT	US	48.22	-106.63
GIJ	NILES	MI	US	41.77	-86.32
GLD	GOODLAND	KS	US	39.39	-101.69
GQO	CHATTANOOGA	TN	US	34.96	-85.15
GRB	GREEN BAY	WI	US	44.56	-88.19
GRR	GRAND RAPIDS	MI	US	42.79	-85.50
GSO	GREENSBORO	NC	US	36.05	-79.98
GTF	GREAT FALLS	MT	US	47.45	-111.41
HAR	HARRISBURG	PA	US	40.23	-77.02
HBU	GUNNISON	CO	US	38.45	-107.04
HEC	HECTOR	CA	US	34.80	-116.46
HLC	HILL CITY	KS	US	39.26	-100.23
HLN	HELENA	MT	US	46.61	-111.95

STATION ID	NAME	STATE	COUNTRY	LATITUDE (degrees)	LONGITUDE (degrees)
HMV	HOLSTON MNTN	TN	US	36.44	-82.13
HNK	HANCOCK	NY	US	42.06	-75.32
HNN	HENDERSON	WV	US	38.75	-82.03
HQM	HOQUIAM	WA	US	46.95	-124.15
HRV	HARVEY	LA	US	29.85	-90.00
HTO	EAST HAMPTON	NY	US	40.92	-72.32
HUH	WHATCOM	WA	US	48.95	-122.58
HUL	HOULTON	ME	US	46.04	-67.83
HVE	HANKSVILLE	UT	US	38.42	-110.70
HVR	HAVRE	MT	US	48.54	-109.77
IAH	HOUSTON INTL	TX	US	29.96	-95.35
ICT	WICHITA	KS	US	37.75	-97.58
IGB	BIGBEE	MS	US	33.48	-88.52
IIU	LOUISVILLE	KY	US	38.10	-85.58
ILC	WILSON CREEK	NV	US	38.25	-114.39
ILM	WILMINGTON	NC	US	34.35	-77.87
IND	INDIANAPOLIS	IN	US	39.81	-86.37
INK	WINK	TX	US	31.87	-103.24
INL	INTL FALLS	MN	US	48.57	-93.40
INW	WINSLOW	AZ	US	35.06	-110.80
IOW	IOWA CITY	IA	US	41.52	-91.61
IRK	KIRKSVILLE	MO	US	40.14	-92.59
IRQ	COLLIERS	SC	US	33.71	-82.16
ISN	WILLISTON	ND	US	48.18	-103.63
JAC	JACKSON	WY	US	43.62	-110.73
JAN	JACKSON	MS	US	32.51	-90.17
JCT	JUNCTION	TX	US	30.60	-99.82
JFK	NEW YORK/JFK	NY	US	40.63	-73.77
JHW	JAMESTOWN	NY	US	42.19	-79.12
JNC	GRAND JUNCTION	CO	US	39.06	-108.79
JOT	JOLIET	IL	US	41.55	-88.32
JST	JOHNSTOWN	PA	US	40.32	-78.83
LAA	LAMAR	CO	US	38.20	-102.69
LAR	LARAMIE	WY	US	41.33	-105.72
LAS	LAS VEGAS	NV	US	36.08	-115.16
LAX	LOS ANGELES	CA	US	33.93	-118.43
LBB	LUBBOCK INTL	TX	US	33.70	-101.92
LBF	NORTH PLATTE	NE	US	41.13	-100.72
LBL	LIBERAL	KS	US	37.04	-100.97
LCH	LAKE CHARLES	LA	US	30.14	-93.11
LEV	GRAND ISLE	LA	US	29.18	-90.10
LFK	LUFKIN	TX	US	31.16	-94.72
LGC	LA GRANGE	GA	US	33.05	-85.21
LIT	LITTLE ROCK	AR	US	34.68	-92.18
LKT	SALMON	ID	US	45.02	-114.08
LKV	LAKEVIEW	OR	US	42.49	-120.51
LOZ	LONDON	KY	US	37.03	-84.12

STATION ID	NAME	STATE	COUNTRY	LATITUDE (degrees)	LONGITUDE (degrees)
LRD	LAREDO	TX	US	27.48	-99.42
LWT	LEWISTOWN	MT	US	47.05	-109.61
LYH	LYNCHBURG	VA	US	37.25	-79.23
MAF	MIDLAND	TX	US	32.02	-102.18
MBS	SAGINAW	MI	US	43.53	-84.08
MCB	MC COMB	MS	US	31.30	-90.26
MCI	KANSAS CITY	MO	US	39.29	-94.74
MCK	MC COOK	NE	US	40.20	-100.59
MCN	MACON	GA	US	32.69	-83.65
MCW	MASON CITY	IA	US	43.09	-93.33
MEI	MERIDIAN	MS	US	32.38	-88.80
MEM	MEMPHIS	TN	US	35.06	-89.98
MGM	MONTGOMERY	AL	US	32.22	-86.32
MIA	MIAMI	FL	US	25.80	-80.30
MKG	MUSKEGON	MI	US	43.17	-86.04
MLC	MC CALESTER	OK	US	34.85	-95.78
MLD	MALAD CITY	ID	US	42.20	-112.45
MLP	MULLAN PASS	ID	US	47.46	-115.65
MLS	MILES CITY	MT	US	46.38	-105.95
MLT	MILLINOCKET	ME	US	45.58	-68.52
MLU	MONROE	LA	US	32.52	-92.03
MOD	MODESTO	CA	US	37.63	-120.96
MOT	MINOT	ND	US	48.26	-101.29
MPV	MONTPELIER	VT	US	44.22	-72.57
MRF	MARFA	TX	US	30.30	-103.95
MSL	MUSCLE SHOALS	AL	US	34.70	-87.48
MSP	MINNEAPOLIS	MN	US	44.88	-93.23
MSS	MASSENA	NY	US	44.91	-74.72
MTU	MYTON	UT	US	40.15	-110.13
MZB	MISSION BAY	CA	US	32.78	-117.23
OAK	OAKLAND	CA	US	37.73	-122.22
OAL	COALDALE	NV	US	38.00	-117.77
OBH	WOLBACH	NE	US	41.38	-98.35
OCS	ROCK SPRINGS	WY	US	41.59	-109.02
ODF	TOCCOA	GA	US	34.70	-83.30
ODI	NODINE	MN	US	43.91	-91.47
OED	MEDFORD	OR	US	42.48	-122.91
OKC	OKLAHOMA CITY	OK	US	35.36	-97.61
OMN	ORMOND BCH	FL	US	29.30	-81.11
ONL	ONEILL	NE	US	42.47	-98.69
ONP	NEWPORT	OR	US	44.58	-124.06
ORD	O'HARE INTL	IL	US	41.98	-87.90
ORF	NORFOLK	VA	US	36.89	-76.20
ORL	ORLANDO	FL	US	28.54	-81.34
OSW	OSWEGO	KS	US	37.15	-95.20
OVR	OMAHA	NE	US	41.17	-95.74
PBI	WEST PALM BCH	FL	US	26.68	-80.09

STATION ID	NAME	STATE	COUNTRY	LATITUDE (degrees)	LONGITUDE (degrees)
PDT	PENDLETON	OR	US	45.70	−118.94
PDX	PORTLAND	OR	US	45.58	−122.60
PGS	PEACH SPRINGS	AZ	US	35.62	−113.54
PHX	PHOENIX	AZ	US	33.43	−112.02
PIE	ST PETERSBURG	FL	US	27.91	−82.68
PIH	POCATELLO	ID	US	42.87	−112.65
PIR	PIERRE	SD	US	44.40	−100.17
PLB	PLATTSBURGH	NY	US	44.69	−73.52
PMM	PULLMAN	MI	US	42.47	−86.11
PQI	PRESQUE ISLE	ME	US	46.77	−68.09
PSB	PHILLIPSBURG	PA	US	40.92	−77.99
PSK	DUBLIN	VA	US	37.09	−80.71
PSX	PALACIOS	TX	US	28.76	−96.31
PUB	PUEBLO	CO	US	38.29	−104.43
PVD	PROVIDENCE	RI	US	41.72	−71.43
PWE	PAWNEE CITY	NE	US	40.20	−96.21
PXV	POCKET CITY	IN	US	37.93	−87.76
PYE	POINT REYES	CA	US	38.08	−122.87
PZD	PECAN	GA	US	31.66	−84.29
RAP	RAPID CITY	SD	US	43.98	−103.01
RBL	RED BLUFF	CA	US	40.10	−122.24
RDU	RALEIGH-DURHAM	NC	US	35.87	−78.78
REO	ROME	OR	US	42.59	−117.87
RHI	RHINELANDER	WI	US	45.63	−89.45
RIC	RICHMOND	VA	US	37.50	−77.32
ROD	ROSEWOOD	OH	US	40.29	−84.04
RSK	RATTLESNAKE	NM	US	36.75	−108.10
RSW	LEE COUNTY	FL	US	26.53	−81.78
RWF	REDWWOD FALLS	MN	US	44.47	−95.13
RZC	RAZORBACK	AR	US	36.25	−94.12
RZS	SANTA BARBARA	CA	US	34.51	−119.77
SAC	SACRAMENTO	CA	US	38.44	−121.55
SAT	SAN ANTONIO	TX	US	29.64	−98.46
SAV	SAVANNAH	GA	US	32.16	−81.11
SAW	SAWYER	MI	US	46.36	−87.40
SAX	SPARTA	NJ	US	41.07	−74.54
SBY	SALISBURY	MD	US	38.35	−75.52
SEA	SEATTLE	WA	US	47.44	−122.31
SGF	SPRINGFIELD	MO	US	37.36	−93.33
SHR	SHERIDAN	WY	US	44.84	−107.06
SIE	SEA ISLE	NJ	US	39.10	−74.80
SJI	SEMMNES	AL	US	30.73	−88.36
SJN	ST JOHNS	AZ	US	34.42	−109.14
SJT	SAN ANGELO	TX	US	31.38	−100.46
SLC	SALT LAKE CITY	UT	US	40.85	−111.98
SLN	SALINA	KS	US	38.93	−97.62
SLT	SLATE RUN	PA	US	41.51	−77.97

STATION ID	NAME	STATE	COUNTRY	LATITUDE (degrees)	LONGITUDE (degrees)
SNS	SALINAS	CA	US	36.66	-121.60
SNY	SIDNEY	NE	US	41.10	-102.98
SPA	SPARTANBURG	SC	US	35.03	-81.93
SPS	WICHITA FALLS	TX	US	33.99	-98.59
SQS	SIDON	MS	US	33.46	-90.28
SRQ	SARASOTA	FL	US	27.40	-82.55
SSM	SAULT STE MARIE	MI	US	46.41	-84.31
SSO	SAN SIMON	AZ	US	32.27	-109.26
STL	ST LOUIS	MO	US	38.86	-90.48
SYR	SYRACUSE	NY	US	43.16	-76.20
TBC	TUBA CITY	AZ	US	36.12	-111.27
TBE	TOBE	CO	US	37.27	-103.60
TCC	TUCUMCARI	NM	US	35.18	-103.60
TCS	TRUTH OR CONS	NM	US	33.28	-107.28
TLH	TALLAHASSEE	FL	US	30.56	-84.37
TOU	NEAH BAY	WA	US	48.30	-124.63
TRM	THERMAL	CA	US	33.63	-116.16
TTH	TERRE HAUTE	IN	US	39.49	-87.25
TTT	MAVERICK	TX	US	32.87	-97.04
TUL	TULSA	OK	US	36.20	-95.79
TUS	TUCSON	AZ	US	32.10	-110.92
TVC	TRAVERSE CITY	MI	US	44.67	-85.55
TWF	TWIN FALLS	ID	US	42.48	-114.49
TXK	TEXARKANA	AR	US	33.51	-94.07
TXO	TEXICO	TX	US	34.50	-102.84
UIN	QUINCY	IL	US	39.85	-91.28
VRB	VERO BEACH	FL	US	27.68	-80.49
VUZ	VULCAN	AL	US	33.67	-86.90
VXV	KNOXVILLE	TN	US	35.90	-83.89
YDC	PRINCETON	BC	CANADA	49.47	-120.52
YKM	YAKIMA	WA	US	46.57	-120.45
YOW	OTTAWA	ON	CANADA	45.32	-75.67
YQB	QUEBEC	QB	CANADA	46.80	-71.38
YQL	LETHBRIDGE	AB	CANADA	49.63	-112.80
YQT	THUNDER BAY	ON	CANADA	48.37	-89.32
YQV	YORKTON	SA	CANADA	51.27	-102.47
YSC	SHERBROOKE	QB	CANADA	45.43	-71.68
YSJ	ST JOHN	NB	CANADA	45.32	-65.88
YVV	WIARTON	ON	CANADA	44.75	-81.10
YWG	WINNIPEG	MB	CANADA	49.90	-97.23
YXC	CRANBROOK	BC	CANADA	49.60	-115.78
YXH	MEDICINE HAT	AB	CANADA	50.02	-110.72
YYN	SWIFT CURRENT	SA	CANADA	50.28	-107.68
YYZ	TORONTO	ON	CANADA	43.67	-79.63

16 APPENDIX G: WSR-88D WEATHER RADAR NETWORK

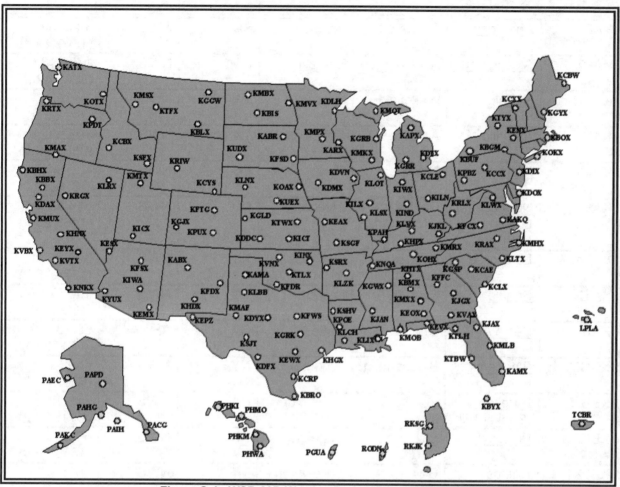

Figure G-1. WSR-88D Weather Radar Network Sites

Table G-1. WSR-88D Weather Radar Network

ICAO	NEXRAD SITENAME	CITY	COUNTY	STATE	AGENCY	ELEVATION
KABR	Aberdeen	Aberdeen	Brown	SD	NWS	396.85 m (1302.49 ft)
KABX	Albuquerque	Albuquerque	Bernalillo	NM	NWS	1789.18 m (5869.42 ft)
KAKQ	Norfolk	Wakefield	Sussex	VA	NWS	34.14 m (111.55 ft)
KAMA	Amarillo	Amarillo	Potter	TX	NWS	1093.32 m (3585.96 ft)
KAMX	Miami	Miami	Dade	FL	NWS	4.27 m (13.12 ft)
KAPX	Northcentral Lower Michigan	Gaylord	Alpena	MI	NWS	446.23 m (1463.25 ft)
KARX	La Crosse	La Crosse	La Crosse	WI	NWS	388.92 m (1276.25 ft)
KATX	Seattle	Everett	Island	WA	NWS	150.57 m (495.41 ft)
KBBX	Beale AFB	Oroville	Butte	CA	AFWA	52.73 m (173.88 ft)
KBGM	Binghamton	Binghamton	Broome	NY	NWS	489.51 m (1607.61 ft)
KBHX	Eureka (Bunker Hill)	Eureka	Humboldt	CA	NWS	732.13 m (2401.57 ft)
KBIS	Bismarck	Bismarck	Burleigh	ND	NWS	505.36 m (1656.82 ft)
KBLX	Billings	Billings	Yellowstone	MT	NWS	1096.67 m (3599.08 ft)
KBMX	Birmingham	Alabaster	Shelby	AL	NWS	196.6 m (646.33 ft)
KBOX	Boston	Taunton	Bristol	MA	NWS	35.97 m (118.11 ft)
KBRO	Brownsville	Brownsville	Cameron	TX	NWS	7.01m (22.97 ft)
KBUF	Buffalo	Buffalo	Erie	NY	NWS	211.23 m (692.26 ft)
KBYX	Key West	Boca Chica Key	Monroe	FL	NWS	2.44 m (6.56 ft)
KCAE	Columbia	West Columbia	Lexington	SC	NWS	70.41 m (229.66 ft)
KCBW	Caribou	Houlton	Aroostook	ME	NWS	227.38 m (744.75 ft)
KCBX	Boise	Boise	Ada	ID	NWS	932.99 m (3061.02 ft)

ICAO	NEXRAD SITENAME	CITY	COUNTY	STATE	AGENCY	ELEVATION
KCCX	State College	State College	Centre	PA	NWS	733.04 m (2404.86 ft)
KCLE	Cleveland	Cleveland	Cuyahoga	OH	NWS	232.56 m (764.44 ft)
KCLX	Charleston, SC	Grays	Beaufort	SC	NWS	29.57 m (98.43 ft)
KCRP	Corpus Christi	Corpus Christi	Nueces	TX	NWS	13.72 m (45.93 ft)
KCXX	Burlington	Colchester	Chittenden	VT	NWS	96.62 m (318.24 ft)
KCYS	Cheyenne	Cheyenne	Laramie	WY	NWS	1867.81 m (6128.61 ft)
KDAX	Sacramento	Davis	Yolo	CA	NWS	9.14 m (29.53 ft)
KDDC	Dodge City	Dodge City	Ford	KS	NWS	789.43 m (2588.58 ft)
KDFX	Laughlin AFB	Bracketville	Kinney	TX	AFWA	344.73 m (1131.89 ft)
KDGX	Jackson/ Brandon, MS	Brandon	Rankin	MS	NWS	150.92 m (495.41 ft)
KDIX	Philadelphia	Fort Dix	Burlington	NJ	NWS	45.42 m (147.64 ft)
KDLH	Duluth	Duluth	St Louis	MN	NWS	435.25 m (1427.17 ft)
KDMX	Des Moines	Johnston	Polk	IA	NWS	299.01 m (980.97 ft)
KDOX	Dover AFB	Ellendale State Forest	Sussex	DE	AFWA	15.24 m (49.21 ft)
KDTX	Detroit	White Lake	Oakland	MI	NWS	326.75 m (1072.83 ft)
KDVN	Quad Cities	Davenport	Scott	IA	NWS	229.82 m (754.59 ft)
KDYX	Dyess AFB	Moran	Shackelford	TX	AFWA	462.38 m (1515.75 ft)
KEAX	Pleasant Hill	Pleasant Hill	Cass	MO	NWS	303.28 m (994.09 ft)
KEMX	Tucson	Tucson	Pima	AZ	NWS	1586.48 m (5203.41 ft)
KENX	Albany	East Berne	Albany	NY	NWS	556.56 m (1827.43 ft)
KEOX	Ft Rucker	Echo	Dale	AL	AFWA	132.28 m (433.07 ft)
KEPZ	El Paso	Santa Teresa	Dona Ana	NM	NWS	1250.9 m (4104.33 ft)

ICAO	NEXRAD SITENAME	CITY	COUNTY	STATE	AGENCY	ELEVATION
KESX	Las Vegas	Las Vegas	Clark	NV	NWS	1483.46 m (4865.49 ft)
KEVX	Eglin AFB	Red Bay	Walton	FL	AFWA	42.67 m (141.08 ft)
KEWX	Austin/San Antonio	New Braunfels	Comal	TX	NWS	192.94 m (633.2 ft)
KEYX	Edwards AFB	Boron	San Bernadino	CA	AFWA	840.33 m (2755.91 ft)
KFCX	Roanoke	Roanoke	Floyd	VA	NWS	874.17 m (2867.45 ft)
KFDR	Altus AFB	Frederick	Tillman	OK	AFWA	386.18 m (1266.4 ft)
KFDX	Cannon AFB	Field	Curry	NM	AFWA	1417.32 m (4648.95 ft)
KFFC	Atlanta	Peachtree City	Fayette	GA	NWS	261.52 m (859.58 ft)
KFSD	Sioux Falls	Sioux Falls	Minnehaha	SD	NWS	435.86 m (1430.45 ft)
KFSX	Flagstaff	Flagstaff	Coconino	AZ	NWS	2260.7 m (7417.98 ft)
KFTG	Denver	Front Range	Arapahoe	CO	NWS	1675.49 m (5495.41 ft)
KFWS	Dallas/Ft Worth	Fort Worth	Tarrant	TX	NWS	208.18 m (682.41 ft)
KGGW	Glasgow	Glasgow	Valley	MT	NWS	693.72 m (2276.9 ft)
KGJX	Grand Junction	Grand Junction	Mesa	CO	NWS	3045.26 m (9990.16 ft)
KGLD	Goodland	Goodland	Sherman	KS	NWS	1112.82 m (3651.57 ft)
KGRB	Green Bay	Green Bay	Brown	WI	NWS	207.87 m (682.41 ft)
KGRK	Ft Hood	Granger	Bell	TX	AFWA	163.98 m (538.06 ft)
KGRR	Grand Rapids	Grand Rapids	Kent	MI	NWS	237.13 m (777.56 ft)
KGSP	Greer	Greer	Spartanburg	SC	NWS	286.51 m (941.6 ft)
KGWX	Columbus AFB	Greenwood Springs	Monroe	MS	AFWA	145.08 m (475.72 ft)
KGYX	Portland, Me	Gray	Cumberland	ME	NWS	124.66 m (410.1 ft)
KHDX	Holloman AFB	Ruidoso	Dona Ana	NM	AFWA	1286.87 m (4222.44 ft)
KHGX	Houston	Dickinson	Galveston	TX	NWS	5.49 m (16.4 ft)

ICAO	NEXRAD SITENAME	CITY	COUNTY	STATE	AGENCY	ELEVATION
KHNX	San Joaquin Valley	Hanford	Kings	CA	NWS	74.07 m (242.78 ft)
KHPX	Ft Campbell	Trenton	Todd	KY	AFWA	175.56 m (577.43 ft)
KHTX	Northeast Alabama	Hytop	Jackson	AL	NWS	537.06 m (1761.81 ft)
KICT	Wichita	Wichita	Sedgwick	KS	NWS	406.91 m (1335.3 ft)
KICX	Cedar City	Cedar City	Iron	UT	NWS	3230.88 m (10600.39 ft)
KILN	Cincinnati	Wilmington	Clinton	OH	NWS	321.87 m (1056.43 ft)
KILX	Lincoln	Lincoln	Logan	IL	NWS	177.39 m (580.71 ft)
KIND	Indianapolis	Indianapolis	Marion	IN	NWS	240.79 m (790.68 ft)
KINX	Tulsa	Inola	Rogers	OK	NWS	203.61 m (669.29 ft)
KIWA	Phoenix	Phoenix	Maricopa	AZ	NWS	412.39 m (1351.71 ft)
KIWX	Northern Indiana	North Webster	Kosciusko	IN	NWS	292.3 m (958.01 ft)
KJAX	Jacksonville	Jacksonville	Duval	FL	NWS	10.06 m (32.81 ft)
KJGX	Robins AFB	Jefferson-ville	Twiggs	GA	AFWA	158.8 m (521.65 ft)
KJKL	Jackson, KY	Jackson	Breathitt	KY	NWS	415.75 m (1364.83 ft)
KLBB	Lubbock	Lubbock	Lubbock	TX	NWS	993.34 m (3257.87 ft)
KLCH	Lake Charles	Lake Charles	Calcasieu	LA	NWS	3.96 m (13.12 ft)
KLIX	Slidell	Slidell	St Tammany	LA	NWS	7.32 m (22.97 ft)
KLNX	North Platte	North Platte	Logan	NE	NWS	905.26 m (2969.16 ft)
KLOT	Chicago	Romeoville	Will	IL	NWS	202.08 m (662.73 ft)
KLRX	Elko	Elko	Lander	NV	NWS	2055.57 m (6745.41 ft)
KLSX	St Louis	Weldon Spring	St Charles	MO	NWS	185.32 m (606.96 ft)
KLTX	Wilmington	Shallotte	Brunswick	NC	NWS	19.51 m (65.62 ft)
KLVX	Louisville	Fort Knox	Hardin	KY	NWS	219.15 m (718.5 ft)

ICAO	NEXRAD SITENAME	CITY	COUNTY	STATE	AGENCY	ELEVATION
KLWX	Sterling	Sterling	Loudoun	VA	NWS	82.91 m (272.31 ft)
KLZK	Little Rock	North Little Rock	Pulaski	AR	NWS	173.13 m (567.59 ft)
KMAF	Midland/ Odessa	Midland	Midland	TX	NWS	874.17 m (2867.45 ft)
KMAX	Medford	Medford	Jackson	OR	NWS	2289.96 m (7513.12 ft)
KMBX	Minot AFB	Deering	Mchenry	ND	AFWA	455.07 m (1492.78 ft)
KMHX	Morehead City	Newport	Carteret	NC	NWS	9.45 m (29.53 ft)
KMKX	Milwaukee	Dousman	Waukesha	WI	NWS	292 m (958.01 ft)
KMLB	Melbourne	Melbourne	Brevard	FL	NWS	10.67 m (36.09 ft)
KMOB	Mobile	Mobile	Mobile	AL	NWS	63.4 m (206.69 ft)
KMPX	Minneapolis	Chanhassen	Carver	MN	NWS	288.34 m (944.88 ft)
KMQT	Marquette	Negaunee	Marquette	MI	NWS	430.07 m (1410.76 ft)
KMRX	Knoxville	Morristown	Hamblen	TN	NWS	407.52 m (1338.58 ft)
KMSX	Missoula	Missoula	Missoula	MT	NWS	2394.2 m (7854.33 ft)
KMTX	Salt Lake City	Salt Lake City	Salt Lake	UT	NWS	1969.01 m (6459.97 ft)
KMUX	San Francisco	Los Gatos	Santa Clara	CA	NWS	1057.35 m (3467.85 ft)
KMVX	Fargo/Grand Forks	Grand Forks	Traill	ND	NWS	300.53 m (987.53 ft)
KMXX	Maxwell AFB	Carrville	Tallapoosa	AL	AFWA	121.92 m (400.26 ft)
KNKX	San Diego	San Diego	San Diego	CA	NWS	291.08 m (954.72 ft)
KNQA	Memphis	Millington	Shelby	TN	NWS	85.95 m (282.15 ft)
KOAX	Omaha	Valley	Douglas	NE	NWS	349.91 m (1148.29 ft)
KOHX	Nashville	Old Hickory	Wilson	TN	NWS	176.48 m (577.43 ft)
KOKX	Brookhaven	Upton	Suffolk	NY	NWS	25.91 m (85.3 ft)
KOTX	Spokane	Spokane	Spokane	WA	NWS	726.64 m (2385.17 ft)

ICAO	NEXRAD SITENAME	CITY	COUNTY	STATE	AGENCY	ELEVATION
KPAH	Paducah	Paducah	Mccracken	KY	NWS	119.48 m (390.42 ft)
KPBZ	Pittsburgh	Coraopolis	Allegheny	PA	NWS	361.19 m (1184.38 ft)
KPDT	Pendleton	Pendleton	Umatilla	OR	NWS	461.77 m (1515.75 ft)
KPOE	Ft Polk	Ft Polk	Vernon	LA	AFWA	124.36 m (406.82 ft)
KPUX	Pueblo	Pueblo	Pueblo	CO	NWS	1599.9 m (5249.34 ft)
KRAX	Raleigh/ Durham	Clayton	Wake	NC	NWS	106.07 m (347.77 ft)
KRGX	Reno	Nixon	Washoe	NV	NWS	2529.54 m (8300.52 ft)
KRIW	Riverton/ Lander	Riverton	Fremont	WY	NWS	1697.13 m (5567.59 ft)
KRLX	Charleston, WV	Charleston	Kanawha	WV	NWS	329.18 m (1079.4 ft)
KRTX	Portland, OR	Portland	Washington	OR	NWS	479.15 m (1571.52 ft)
KSFX	Pocatello	Springfield	Bingham	ID	NWS	1363.68 m (4475.07 ft)
KSGF	Springfield	Springfield	Greene	MO	NWS	389.53 m (1279.53 ft)
KSHV	Shreveport	Shreveport	Caddo	LA	NWS	83.21 m (272.31 ft)
KSJT	San Angelo	San Angelo	Tom Green	TX	NWS	576.07 m (1889.76 ft)
KSOX	Santa Ana Mountains	Santa Ana Mountains	Orange	CA	NWS	927 m (3041.34 ft)
KSRX	Western Arkansas	Chaffee Ridge	Sebastian	AR	NWS	195.07 m (639.76 ft)
KTBW	Tampa	Ruskin	Hillsborough	FL	NWS	12.5 m (39.37 ft)
KTFX	Great Falls	Great Falls	Cascade	MT	NWS	1132.03 m (3713.91 ft)
KTLH	Tallahassee	Tallahassee	Leon	FL	NWS	19.2 m (62.34 ft)
KTLX	Norman	Midwest City	Oklahoma	OK	NWS	369.72 m (1213.91 ft)
KTWX	Topeka	Topeka	Wabaunsee	KS	NWS	416.66 m (1368.11 ft)
KTYX	Ft Drum	Montague	Lewis	NY	AFWA	562.66 m (1847.11 ft)
KUDX	Rapid City	New Underwood	Pennington	SD	NWS	919.28 m (3015.09 ft)

ICAO	NEXRAD SITENAME	CITY	COUNTY	STATE	AGENCY	ELEVATION
KUEX	Grand Island	Blue Hill	Webster	NE	NWS	602.28 m (1975.07 ft)
KVAX	Moody AFB	South Stockton	Lanier	GA	AFWA	54.25 m (177.17 ft)
KVBX	Vandenberg AFB	Orcutt	Santa Barbara	CA	AFWA	372.77 m (1223.75 ft)
KVNX	Vance AFB	Cherokee	Alfalfa	OK	AFWA	368.81 m (1210.63 ft)
KVTX	Los Angeles	Los Angeles	Ventura	CA	NWS	830.88 m (2726.38 ft)
KVWX	Evansville, IN (Non-NEXRAD)	Owensville	Gibson	IN	NWS	155.75 m (511.81 ft)
KYUX	Yuma	Yuma	Pima	AZ	NWS	53.04 m (173.88 ft)
LPLA	Lajes AB	Santa Barbara	N/A	AZO RES	AFWA	1016.2 m (3333.33 ft)
PABC	Bethel FAA	Bethel	N/A	AK	FAA	49.07 m (160.76 ft)
PACG	Sitka FAA	Biorka Island	N/A	AK	FAA	63.09 m (206.69 ft)
PAEC	Nome FAA	Nome	N/A	AK	FAA	17.68 m (59.06 ft)
PAHG	Anchorage FAA	Kenai	N/A	AK	FAA	73.76 m (242.78 ft)
PAIH	Middleton Island	Middleton Island	N/A	AK	FAA	20.42 m (65.62 ft)
PAKC	King Salmon FAA	King Salmon	N/A	AK	FAA	19.2 m (62.34 ft)
PAPD	Fairbanks FAA	Fairbanks	N/A	AK	FAA	790.35 m (2591.86 ft)
PGUA	Andersen AFB	Andersen AFB	N/A	GUAM	AFWA	80.47 m (262.47 ft)
PHKI	South Kauai FAA	South Kauai	Kauai	HI	FAA	54.56 m (180.45 ft)
PHKM	Kamuela/ Kohala Apt	Kamuela	Hawaii	HI	FAA	1161.9 m (3812.34 ft)
PHMO	Molokai FAA	Molokai	Molokai	HI	FAA	415.44 m (1361.55 ft)
PHWA	South Shore FAA	Naalehu	Hawaii	HI	FAA	420.62 m (1381.23 ft)
RKJK	Kunsan AB	Kunsan Ab	N/A	KOREA	AFWA	23.77 m (78.74 ft)
RKSG	Camp Humphreys	Camp Humphreys	N/A	KOREA	AFWA	15.85 m (52.49 ft)

ICAO	NEXRAD SITENAME	CITY	COUNTY	STATE	AGENCY	ELEVATION
RODN	Kadena AB	Kadena Ab	N/A	JAPAN	AFWA	66.45 m (216.54 ft)
TJUA	San Juan FAA	San Juan	N/A	PR	FAA	851.61 m (2795.28 ft)

17 APPENDIX H: AWC Geographical Area Designator Map

Figure H-1: AWC Geographical Area Designator Map

18 APPENDIX I: Present Weather Symbols

	0	1	2	3	4	5	6	7	8	9
00	Cloud development not observed or not observable during past hour	Clouds generally dissolving or becoming less developed during past hour	State of sky on the whole unchanged during past hour	Clouds generally forming or developing during past hour	Visibility reduced by smoke	Haze	Widespread dust in suspension in the air, not raised by wind, at time of obs	Dust or sand raised by wind, at time of obs	Well developed dust devil(s) within past hour	Duststorm or sandstorm within sight of station or at station during past hour
10	Light fog	Patches of shallow fog at station not deeper than 6 feet on land	More or less continuous shallow fog at station not deeper than 6 feet on land	Lightning visible, no thunder heard	Precipitation within sight, but not reaching the ground	Precipitation within sight, reaching ground, but distant from station	Precipitation within sight, reaching the ground, near to but not at station	Thunder heard but no precipitation at the station	Squall(s) within sight during past hour	Funnel cloud(s) within sight during past hour
20	Drizzle (not freezing, not showers) during past hour, not at time of obs	Rain (not freezing, not showers) during past hour, not at time of obs	Snow (not falling as showers) during past hour, not at time of obs	Rain and snow (not falling as showers) during past hour, not at time of obs	Freezing drizzle or rain (not showers) during past hour, not at time of obs	Showers of rain during past hour, but not at time of obs	Showers of snow, or of rain and snow during past hour, but not at time of obs	Showers of hail, or of hail and rain during past hour, but not at time of obs	Fog during past hour, but not at time of obs	Thunderstorm (with or without precip) during past hour, but not at time of obs
30	Slight or moderate duststorm or sandstorm, has decreased during past hour	Slight or moderate duststorm or sandstorm, has no appreciable change during past hour	Slight or moderate duststorm or sandstorm, has increased during past hour	Severe duststorm or sandstorm, has decreased during past hour	Severe duststorm or sandstorm, no appreciable change during past hour	Severe duststorm or sandstorm, has increased during past hour	Slight or moderate drifting snow, generally low	Heavy drifting snow, generally low	Slight or moderate drifting snow, generally high	Heavy drifting snow, generally high
40	Fog at distance at time of obs but not at station during past hour	Fog in patches	Fog, sky discernable, has become thinner during past hour	Fog, sky not discernable, has become thinner during past hour	Fog, sky discernable, no appreciable change during past hour	Fog, sky not discernable, no appreciable change during past hour	Fog, sky discernable, has begun or become thicker during past hour	Fog, sky not discernable, has begun or become thicker during past hour	Fog, depositing rime, sky discernable	Fog, depositing rime, sky not discernable
50	Intermittent drizzle (not freezing), slight at time of obs	Continuous drizzle (not freezing), slight at time of obs	Intermittent drizzle (not freezing), moderate at time of obs	Continuous drizzle (not freezing), moderate at time of obs	Intermittent drizzle (not freezing), thick at time of obs	Continuous drizzle (not freezing), thick at time of obs	Slight freezing drizzle	Moderate or thick freezing drizzle	Drizzle and rain, slight	Drizzle and rain, moderate or heavy
60	Intermittent rain (not freezing), slight at time of obs	Continuous rain (not freezing), slight at time of obs	Intermittent rain (not freezing), moderate at time of obs	Continuous rain (not freezing), moderate at time of obs	Intermittent rain (not freezing), heavy at time of obs	Continuous rain (not freezing), heavy at time of obs	Slight freezing rain	Moderate or heavy freezing rain	Rain or drizzle and snow, slight	Rain or drizzle and snow, moderate or heavy
70	Intermittent fall of snowflakes, slight at time of obs	Continuous fall of snowflakes, slight at time of obs	Intermittent fall of snowflakes, moderate at time of obs	Continuous fall of snowflakes, moderate at time of obs	Intermittent fall of snowflakes, heavy at time of obs	Continuous fall of snowflakes, heavy at time of obs	Ice needles (with or without fog)	Granular snow (with or without fog)	Isolated starlike snow crystals (with or without fog)	Ice pellets (sleet, U.S. definition)
80	Slight rain shower(s)	Moderate or heavy rain shower(s)	Violent rain shower(s)	Slight shower(s) of rain and snow mixed	Moderate or heavy shower(s) of rain and snow mixed	Slight snow shower(s)	Moderate or heavy snow shower(s)	Slight shower(s) of soft or small hail, with or without rain, and/or snow	Moderate or heavy shower(s) of soft or small hail, with or without rain and/or snow	Slight shower(s) of hail, with or without rain and/or snow, not assoc with thunder
90	Moderate of heavy shower(s) of hail and/or rain/snow, not associated with thunder	Slight rain at time of obs; thunderstorm during past hour not at time of obs	Moderate or heavy rain at time of obs; TS during past hour not at time of obs	Slight snow and/or rain/hail at time of obs; TS during past hour not at time of obs	Moderate or heavy snow and/or rain/ hail at time of obs; TS past hour not at obs time	Slight or moderate thunderstorm without hail but with rain and/or snow at obs time	Slight or moderate thunderstorm with hail at time of obs	Heavy thunderstorm without hail but with rain and/or snow at time of obs	Thunderstorm combined with duststorm or sandstorm at time of obs	Heavy thunderstorm with hail at time of obs

Figure I-1. Present Weather Symbols with Text Explanation

Matching of METAR present weather text to symbol in table below is not necessarily endorsed by the National Weather Service or the World Meteorological Organization. Blue numbers in upper-left corner of white boxes indicate the priority for plotting in event more than one symbol is possible (symbols in gray boxes have no corresponding METAR present weather text). Graphical representation of METARs using this table found at http://adds.aviationweather.gov

	0	1	2	3	4	5	6	7	8	9
00	○	○	○	○	3 FU VA	59 HZ	14 DU	13 SA BLSA VCBLSA BLDU VCBLDU BLPY	9 PO VCPO	12 VCSS VCDS
10	58 BR		56 MIFG	50 VCTS	57 VIRGA		51 VCSH	33 TS	2 SQ	1 FC +FC
20										
30		11 SS DS DRSA DRDU			10 +SS +DS		48 BLSN VCBLSN		47 DRSN	
40	55 VCFG	54 BCFG			53 PRFG	52 FG				49 FZFG
50		46 -DZ		42 DZ		39 +DZ	22 -FZDZ	21 FZDZ +FZDZ	35 DZ -RA -DZ RA -DZ -RA	34 DZ RA +DZ RA DZ +RA +DZ +RA
60		44 -RA		41 RA		37 +RA	24 -FZRA	23 FZRA +FZRA	26 -RA -SN -RA SN -DZ -SN -DZ SN	25 RA SN +RA SN RA +SN +RA +SN DZ SN +DZ SN DZ +SN +DZ +SN
70		43 -SN		40 SN		36 +SN	32 UP	19 SG	31 IC	20 PL PE SHPL SHPE
80	45 -SH -SHRA	38 SH +SH SHRA +SHRA		28 -SHRA SN -SHSN RA -SHRA -SN -SHSN -RA	27 SHRA SN SHSN RA +SHRA SN +SHSN RA	30 -SHSN	29 SHSN +SHSN	18 -GS -SHGS	16 GS SHGS +GS +SHGS	17 -GR -SHGR
90	15 GR SHGR +GR +SHGR					8 TSRA TSSN TSPL	7 TSGR TSGS	6 +TSRA +TSSN +TSPL	4 any TS and any SA or DU	5 +TSGS +TSGR

Figure I-2. Present Weather Symbols with Corresponding METAR/SPECI Present Weather Code

19 APPENDIX J: Turbulence and Icing Intensity Depictions

Table J-1. Turbulence Intensity

Intensity	Aircraft Reaction	Symbol
Light	Loose objects in aircraft remain at rest.	∧
Moderate	Unsecured objects are dislodged. Occupants feel definite strains against seat belts and shoulder straps.	⋀
Severe	Occupants thrown violently against seat belts. Momentary loss of aircraft control. Unsecured objects tossed about.	⋀
Extreme	Aircraft is tossed violently about, impossible to control. May cause structural damage.	⋀

Table J-2. Icing Intensity

Intensity	Aircraft Reaction	Symbol
Trace	Ice becomes perceptible. Rate of accumulation slightly greater than sublimation. Deicing/anti-icing equipment is not used unless encountered for an extended period of time (over 1 hour).	U
Light	The rate of accumulation may create a problem if flight is prolonged in this environment (over 1 hour). Occasional use of deicing/anti-icing equipment removes or prevents accumulation. It does not present a problem if this equipment is used.	ψ
Moderate	The rate of accumulation is such that even short encounters become potentially hazardous, and use of deicing/anti-icing equipment or diversion is necessary.	ᵈ
Severe	The rate of accumulation is such that deicing/anti-icing equipment fails to reduce or control the hazard. Immediate diversion is necessary.	₩